CITIES OF ALEXANDER THE GREAT

Cities of Alexander the Great

P. M. FRASER

CLARENDON PRESS · OXFORD
1996

Oxford University Press, Walton Street, Oxford OX2 6DP

Oxford   New York
Athens   Auckland   Bangkok   Bombay
Calcutta   Cape Town   Dar es Salaam   Delhi
Florence   Hong Kong   Istanbul   Karachi
Kuala Lumpur   Madras   Madrid   Melbourne
Mexico City   Nairobi   Paris   Singapore
Taipei   Tokyo   Toronto
and associated companies in
Berlin   Ibadan

Oxford is a trade mark of Oxford University Press

Published in the United States
by Oxford University Press Inc., New York

© P. M. Fraser 1996

British Library Cataloguing in Publication Data
Data available

Library of Congress Cataloging in Publication Data
Cities of Alexander the Great / P. M. Fraser.
Includes bibliographical references and index.
1. Alexander, the Great, 356–323 B.C.—Contributions in city
planning.   2. Cities and towns, Ancient.   3. Greece—History—
Macedonian Expansion, 359–323 B.C.   I. Title.
DF234.2.F73   1996   938'.07—dc20   95-19063
ISBN 0-19-815006-7

1 3 5 7 9 10 8 6 4 2

Typeset by Regent Typesetting, London
Printed in Great Britain on acid-free paper by
Bookcraft (Bath) Ltd.

D. M.
H. M. L.

PREFACE

My aim in this book has been to collect and analyse the traditions relating to the foundations of cities by Alexander the Great. They pose a different problem from that which arises with regard to the cities founded or refounded by the Hellenistic kings, the historical evidence for which is largely determined by reliable literary, epigraphical, and numismatic evidence. In the case of Alexander the problem is essentially to determine what cities he did indeed found, how many out of the large number attributed to him by our various sources are actually historical, and in what sense. That is the prime object of this enquiry, but I have added some more general considerations (Chs. VI–VII). In Chapters I–II I have tried to establish categories of evidence based to a large extent on the different types of sources, mainly Greek, some Persian and Arabic, which throw considerable light on the Greek and Latin material. Much of the evidence consists of lists of cities named Alexandria or Iskandarīya, and the enquiry is fundamentally concerned with their value, in other words with their origin. The problem, as analysed in those chapters is one of textual analysis, particularly, in Chapter I, as it concerns the development of local chronicles and of annalistic traditions, and of the early history, more precisely the pre-history, of the *Alexander-Romance*. This enquiry forms the focus of the book. In it I have tried to establish that the record of many of the foundations is fictitious, and not the product of a historically valid tradition. I hope that study of this section will be simplified by reference to the Table of the Alexander-foundations recorded in all sources, which I have added at the back of the book, and by my discussion of the evolution of the *a*- tradition and of the *A*-version of the *Romance* both in the body of the text and in Appendix (2) which some readers may find it a help to read at the outset. While, however, I regard only the cities recorded by the Alexander-historians and the geographers, and their trustworthy derivatives, as authentic foundations, problems inseparable from the nature of the geographical tradition (and not specifically associated with the problem here under investigation) make the geographers of limited use to our enquiry. I discuss the geographical evidence in the light of these general problems (largely resulting from the inexplicit nature of the evidence relating to the measurement of distances) in a separate chapter (IV), which forms a link with the enquiry into the identification of the cities regarded as historical, the subject of Chapter V, in which I have reconsidered the possible location of these cities. It will be clear that I cannot claim to have made any significant contribution to this aspect of the subject, which has been so thoroughly, if for the most part inconclusively, investigated by preceding generations of historians. Consequently, not wishing to turn this part of the book, which I regard as subordinate to the investigation of sources in Chs. I–II, into yet one more discussion of unverifiable ancient evidence and modern opinion, I have kept references to modern historical writing on the topics covered to a minimum, though I have considered some of the geographical problems in some detail.

The book, then, is essentially a study of sources. The form of analysis that I have adopted represents for the most part a different approach from that travelled by Droysen in his pioneer study of the foundations of Alexander and his Successors, in which he treated each recorded foundation as equally entitled to consideration as a historical reality, and perhaps did not always sufficiently consider the evidence in terms of the sources providing the information. Understandably in view of his pre-eminent authority, his route has remained the accepted approach of subsequent historians, notably of Tscherikower and Tarn, though the scintillating contributions of the latter cover a vast, previously unexplored field. The reader may feel that Alexander himself does not figure as largely as he might in this book, and that the drama lacks a Hamlet. To that I can only reply that it has not been my prime intention to investigate Hamlet.

By its lack of cohesion the book reveals the marks, I am aware, of a long period of gestation resulting, in part at least, from other preoccupations. Aspects of the theme, and explanations of particular problems, have been the subject of my thought, and occasionally of lectures and papers, over the years, but it has been only too often put on one side at the call of more urgent tasks. The work inevitably owes much to the labours of others in fields outside the normal scope of Alexander-studies, and I hope the footnotes make this abundantly clear. It would, however, be an act of ingratitude not to acknowledge the particular debt which I owe to the late Sir William Tarn, who first stimulated my interest in the Hellenistic Age. I remember very clearly how, more than fifty years ago, he explained to a young undergraduate over tea in the basement of the premises of the Hellenic Society in Bedford Square, that writing *The Greeks in Bactria and India* was like fiddling with a jigsaw-puzzle, the pieces of which would not fit; and I also remember sitting in spare hours on a gun-site early in the last war reading *Antigonos Gonatas*, and thus, amid much noise and clamour, having my eyes opened to the fascination of the age of which Tarn had at that time taught us almost all there was to know. I do not think that he would have liked this book, which, if its arguments prove acceptable, relegates to the world of fiction a considerable number of the Alexandrias which he laboured with unsurpassed skill and ingenuity to identify, but I hope that he would at least have welcomed it as one more attempt to solve a jigsaw puzzle. The critical reader may, I anticipate, conclude that my own very different conclusion has only been reached by the use of as much unverifiable argument as that of Droysen and Tarn, and will react accordingly. My justification is to be found in the words of an author much quoted in the pages of this book: *Εἰ δὲ πολλῶν προειπόντων ἐπιχειροῦμεν καὶ αὐτοὶ λέγειν περὶ τῶν αὐτῶν, οὔπω μεμπτέον, ἂν μὴ καὶ τὸν αὐτὸν τρόπον διελεχθῶμεν ἐκείνοις ἅπαντα λέγοντες.* The aphorism 'Experiment helps and error can clarify' has also sustained me.

I wish to thank Simon Hornblower for reading much of the manuscript and Alexander Fraser for rescuing me from numerous computer-crises.

P.M.F.

Oxford

CONTENTS

ABBREVIATIONS

Since I have given the full titles and other details of publication of most works cited as they appear in the notes I have not felt it necessary to burden the book with a detailed bibliography. However, the following list of expanded abbreviations, which are not fully described in the notes, may help the reader.

BEFEO
Bulletin de l'École française d'Extrème Orient (Hanoi, Paris, 1901-)

*BGA
Bibliotheca Geographorum Arabicorum (8 vols. Leiden, 1870–94; repr. 1967)

BSOAS
Bulletin of the School of Oriental and African Studies (London, 1937-)

IsMEO
Istituto Italiano per il medio ed estremo oriente, Reports and Memoirs (Rome, 1951-) (separate publications)

JASB
Journal of the Asiatic Society of Bengal (1832–1915)

JWCI
Journal of the Warburg [and Courtauld] Institute (London, 1937/8-)

Le Strange, LEC
G. Le Strange, *The Lands of the Eastern Caliphate* (Cambridge, 1905)

Masson, *Narrative*
C. Masson, *Narrative of various journeys in Balochistan, Afghanistan and the Punjab, in three volumes* (vols. i–iii, London, 1842, repr. OUP Karachi etc., 1974; vol. iv (*sic*) 1844, repr. OUP Karachi etc., 1977)

Mém. DAFA
Mémoires de Délégation Archéologique Française en Afghanistan (separate publications)

Ptol. Alex.
P. M. Fraser, *Ptolemaic Alexandria* (3 vols. Oxford, 1972)

RSO
Rivista degli studi orientali (Rome, 1907-)

Tarn, GBI[2]
W. W. Tarn, *The Greeks in Bactria and India* (2nd edn. CUP, 1951) [A 3rd edn., ed. F. H.

Holt (Ares Press, Chicago, 1980) has an introductory essay and a large bibliography on Central Asian archaeology, but the text is unaltered.]

ZDMG   *Zeitschrift der Deutschen Morgenländischen Gesellschaft* (1847-   )

* I have given references to the French translations of the Arabic geographers (which are mostly within the same volume as the text). A full translation into German of all the Arabic texts in *BGA* relating to Iran will be found in P. Schwarz's monumental *Iran in Mittelalter nach den arabischen Geographen*. I have not added references to this work, which was originally produced in nine parts (1896-1935), published largely as Volumes 1-6 of *Quellen und Forschungen zur Erd- und Kulturkunde* (subsequently(?) called *Quellen und Forschungen zur Kultur und Religionsgeschichte*), and photographically reprinted in one volume by Olm in 1969. Part 7 (1929) is a typescript index to the whole work (ninety-four pages long), followed by Part 8, a handwritten account of Aderbaigan (a continuation of the earlier pagination, pp. 959-1340). Part 9 contains 'Beweisstellen und Erlaüterungen zu Aderbaigan', also handwritten (pp. 1341-98, ending in the middle of a sentence).

CHAPTER I
The Alexandrian Lists

WE shall be concerned in this opening chapter, not with the cities attested by the Alexander-historians as having been founded by Alexander in the course of his campaigns but with the lists of cities named as Alexandrias in (a) the *Epitome* of Stephanus of Byzantium's Ἐθνικά, (b) the earliest surviving Greek and associated versions (henceforth called the α-tradition) of the *Alexander-Romance*, properly called the *Life of Alexander of Macedon*, and (c) the lists found in Alexandrian *World-Chronicles* and *Annals* of the Imperial period. These lists agree at several points, and the type of information they provide enables us to consider them collectively, but nevertheless each group presents different problems. It seems probable that, except for Stephanus, in the form and substance in which they survive they have a common origin in the same type of popular Alexandrian literature, and, specifically, in the lost original version of the Greek *Alexander-Romance*; although the text of Stephanus is associated with the same milieu, it only occasionally draws on the same sources. It is, in any case, essential that the traditions which they represent should in the first place be studied individually. We may begin with Stephanus.

Under the entry Ἀλεξάνδρεια Stephanus or his Epitomator(s) (whom we shall only distinguish from the original author when necessary) records a list of eighteen Alexandrias, which he lists seriatim, with ordinal numeration, with occasional 'cultural' comments, and his usual grammatical data regarding the forms of derived ethnics and ktetics (see below, p. 202, for the full text). These Alexandrias are:

1. *Αἰγυπτία ἤτοι Λίβυσσα, ὡς οἱ πολλοί*
2. *δευτέρα ἐστὶ πόλις Τροίας*
3. *τρίτη Θράικης, πρὸς τῆι Μακεδονίαι*

2　　　　　　　　*The Alexandrian Lists*

4. τετάρτη πόλις Ὠριτῶν
5. πέμπτη ἐν τῆι Ὠπιανῆι, κατὰ τὴν Ἰνδικήν
6. ἕκτη πάλιν Ἰνδικῆς
7. ἑβδόμη ἐν Ἀρίοις, ἔθνει Παρθυαίων κατὰ τὴν Ἰνδικήν
8. ὀγδόη τῆς Κιλικίας
9. ἐνάτη ἐν Κύπρωι
10. δεκάτη πρὸς τῶι Λάτμωι τῆς Καρίας
11. ἑνδεκάτη κατὰ Βάκτρα
12. δωδεκάτη ἐν Ἀραχώτοις
13. τρισκαιδεκάτη ἐν Μακαρηνῆι
14. τεσσαρεσκαιδεκάτη παρὰ Σωριανοῖς
15. πεντεκαιδεκάτη παρὰ Ἀραχώτοις, ὁμοροῦσα τῆι Ἰνδικῆι
16. ἑκκαιδεκάτη κατὰ τὸν Μέλανα κόλπον
17. ἑπτακαιδεκάτη ἐν τῆι Σογδιανῆι παρὰ Παροπαμισάδαις
18. ὀκτωκαιδεκάτη ἐπὶ τοῦ Ταναΐδος αὐτοῦ κτίσμα

Stephanus also adds

19. s.v. Βοὸς Κεφαλαί
20. s.v. Βουκεφάλεια

that Alexander founded Bucephala and Nikaia.

In addition, s.v. *Δῖον* we read, ζ', Κοίλης Συρίας, κτίσμα Ἀλεξάνδρου, καὶ Πέλλα, and s.v. Εὐπορία, πόλις Μακεδονίας, ἣν Ἀλέξανδρος ταχέως νικήσας ἔκτισε καὶ ὠνόμασε διὰ τὸ εὔπορον. Whatever their explanation, neither of these is historical. For the name Euporia see further below, p. 129 n. 49.

Before comparing this list with those in the other Alexandrian sources we must consider first whether it is a unique type of entry in Stephanus, or whether that work, in its present epitomised form, provides similar lists for other homonymous cities; and secondly, in the event of the list proving to be different from the great run of entries, what its probable source or sources are.

As to the first point, the situation is clear. The material in the Ἐθνικά is arranged in a straight alphabetical sequence. Reading through the entries we find, at the very beginning of the work, at the simplest level, Ἄβδηρα, πόλεις δύο. For the first, in Thrace, Stephanus quotes Hellanicus, 'and others'; for the second, in Iberia, Artemidorus, book ii. Again, s.v. Ἄβυδος, τρεῖς πόλεις, for the first of which (the Hellespontine) he quotes Dionysius the Periegete, for the second, 'the Egyptian', no source, for the third, in Iapygia, or S. Italy, Phileas. Again, s.v. Ἀθῆναι, a longer list, κατὰ τὸν μὲν

Ὧρον πέντε, κατὰ δὲ Φίλωνα ἕξ . . . Athens of Attica first, then δευτέρα πόλις Λακωνική, τρίτη Καρική, τετάρτη Λιγυστίων, πέμπτη Ἰταλίας, ἕκτη Εὐβοίας, with various sources for these vanished or mythical cities.

To come to the Hellenistic eponymous foundations. s.v. Ἀντιόχεια, we read Ἀντιόχεια, δέκα πόλεις ἀναγράφονται, εἰσὶ δὲ πλείους, followed by fourteen cities so named. For only one of these a source is given, the twelfth, Antiocheia ἐν Μαργιανῆι, for which Strabo is given as authority. For one of them, Ἀντιόχεια ἐν Μυγδονίαι, in Mesopotamia, Nisibis, three 'notable sons' are named—an unmistakable indication, as we shall see, of the ultimate source employed. On the other hand, surprisingly, by contrast, s.v. Σελεύκεια, only one city is recorded, namely Σελεύκεια ἐν Κιλικίαι, though many others are mentioned under the names that they bore before being changed to Seleukeia or Antiocheia. Many examples of metonomasies are given with Seleucus I as their subject, ἐκάλεσε, μετωνόμασεν.

But the two lists, of Antiochs and of Alexandrias, have this in common, that they are both (excepting Alexandria in Egypt, Alexandria Troas, and Antioch in Mygdonia) bare lists of names with no references either to famous sons or to their own metono-masies; and there is very little metonomastic material in these entries of Stephanus comparable to that given under cities, such as Babylon and Hyria, which became Seleukeias; with Alexander as subject virtually none, except under Bucephala, which was not, in any case, correctly called Alexandria.[1] However, though the lists of Antiochs and of Alexandrias have in common the absence of famous sons and of metonomasies, there are significant differences between them.

Thanks to the extensive quotations in the *Epitome*, the ultimate sources of Stephanus are not in much doubt.[2] He quotes, above all,

---

[1] See below, p. 162 n. 111.

[2] See in general P. A. Atenstädt, (*Quellenstudien zu Stephanos von Byzanz* (Progr. Schwarzenberg, no. 755, 1910); and the very full analysis by Honigmann, *RE* (12), cols. 2369 ff. (esp. cols. 2379 ff.), and Gudeman's article, ibid. on Herennius Philon, s.v. Herennius (2). These three works provide the raw material necessary for an understanding of the use made by Stephanus of earlier sources, though a final analysis will have to wait for a new critical edition of Stephanus (see meanwhile, A. Diller, *TAPA* 69, 1938, pp. 333 ff., with specimen revision of the main MSS). His use of a MS tradition of Strabo independent of the Byzantine tradition was recognized by Kramer in his edition, i, p. lxxxiii, and elaborated by W. Aly in his edition of the Vatican palimpsest of Strabo (Studi e Testi, 188, 1956), 253 ff., and

not for historical attestations (as with the Classical authors), but as
authorities for city-names and metonomasies on the one hand, and
for noteworthy citizens of the cities, the ἔνδοξοι, on the other, two
authors: first, Herennius Philo of Byblos (better known for his work
on Phoenician religion), the most important single source for many
of Stephanus' entries,[3] and, second, probably through him, the
'geographical' catena leads back to Alexander Polyhistor. In
addition, the grammatical writer Oros, of the fourth century AD,
whose work, Ὅπως τὰ Ἐθνικὰ λεκτέον, is embodied more particularly in late Etymologika, provided detailed information about
ethnics and their orthography, and played an important role as
intermediary, though the *Epitome* quotes him by name only
occasionally. As an author quoted by Stephanus, and himself an
Alexandrian, who later migrated to Constantinople, he may have
been a significant source for at least the grammatical section of the
entry on Alexandria.[4]

taken up in various contexts in his unfinished edition of Strabo: see esp. *Strabonis
Geographica,* i (Antiquitas, Reihe I. 9, Bonn, 1968), 104-6. See also the cogent
criticisms by J. M. Cook, JHS 79 (1959), 19-26, and A. Diller, *The Textual Tradition
of Strabo's Geography* (Amsterdam, 1975), 7-8, with references to earlier literature.
Diller's study of the few ancient citations of Strabo before Stephanus is fundamental.
His summary is (p. 18): 'For five centuries Strabo's *Geography* [unlike his *History*]
was almost unknown. Then in the sixth century we find seven authors citing it.'
Diller pointed out in *Tradition of the Minor Greek Geographers* (Amer. Philol. Soc.,
Philol. Monogr. 14, 1952), 45-6, that Marcianus of Heracleia (GGM i. 515 ff.;
trans. only by W. H. Schoff, *Periplus of the Outer Sea by Marcian of Heraclea*
(Philadelphia, Commercial Museum, 1919) should probably be regarded as a direct,
and perhaps contemporary, source of Stephanus, who quotes his three known
works on some forty occasions. The quotations from the *periploi* concern both the
eastern and the western seas.

  [3] For the demonstration that Stephanus took his homonymous cities largely from
Herennius Philon see Atenstädt, op. cit. 18-9; cf. also Gudeman, cols. 654-9;
Hönigmann, loc. cit. Gudeman points out, col. 654, that even though we have only
one *Epitome* of Stephanus there are over thirty quotations from Herennius in the
text.
  [4] Atenstädt, 9-11, gives grounds for supposing that the role of Oros' Ὅπως
τὰ Ἐθνικὰ λεκτέον was in general exaggerated by Reitzenstein, *Geschichte der
Griechischen Etymologika* (Leipzig, 1897), 287-350, esp. p. 325, who maintained
that all the material in Stephanus deriving from poetical scholia (Homer, Apollonius,
Lykophron, Callimachus) was drawn from Oros. Nevertheless, the peculiar nature
of Stephanus' entry s.v. Ἀλεξάνδρεια, and the fact that Oros was himself an
Alexandrian (see Suda, Ω 201 Ὦρος, Ἀλεξανδρεύς, γραμματικός, παιδεύσας ἐν
Κωνσταντίνου πόλει. ἔγραψε Περὶ διχρόνων, Ὅπως τὰ Ἐθνικὰ λεκτέον, Λύσεις προτάσεων
τῶν Ἡρωδιανοῦ, Πίνακα τῶν ἑαυτοῦ (?), Περὶ ἐγκλιτικῶν μορίων, Ὀρθογραφίαν κατὰ
στοιχεῖον, Περὶ τῆς ει διφθόγγου, Ὀρθογραφίαν περὶ τῆς αι διφθόγγου κατὰ Φρύνιχον
κατὰ στοιχεῖον, Ἀνθολόγιον (?), Περὶ γνωμῶν) raise the possibility of a particular role
for him in this context. Reitzenstein's complex chapter on Oros (loc. cit.) remains

Philon, to whom we owe so much of our knowledge of the earlier material in Stephanus, wrote in the second half of the first century or the first half of the second century AD a pinacographical work in thirty books entitled Περὶ πόλεων καὶ οὓς ἑκάστη αὐτῶν ἤνεγκε, later, on account of its size, epitomized by one Serenus.[5] (The title looks across the centuries and cultures to Yākūt's secondary geographical work, the *Mushtarik*, which is precisely such a list of homonymous cities and their distinguished sons).[6] As the title shows, Philon's work belongs to that mainstream of pinacography which was developed, if not initiated, by Callimachus. It centred on the compilation of catalogues of objects, natural features, homonymous places and peoples, distinguished persons in the arts and sciences, and so on, produced in the form of πίνακες and ἀναγραφαί.[7] The best surviving example of pinacography, perhaps reduced from its original form, is the so-called *Laterculi Alexandrini*, of the later Ptolemaic period.[8] That such

the fundamental study of his work and its *Nachleben*.; cf. also Wendel, *RE*, Oros (4), a convenient summary. For the enigmatic ὁ Μελήσιος or abbreviations of it, applied to Oros in the MSS of the *Etym. Gen.* see Reitzenstein, 10; Wendel, loc. cit.

[5] The fragments of Philon's Περὶ πόλεων καὶ οὓς ἑκάστη αὐτῶν ἤνεγκε in Stephanus are *FGrH* 790, F 15-21. The Suda-Life (T1) gives his dates as οὗτος γέγονεν ἐπὶ τῶν χρόνων τῶν ἐγγὺς Νέρωνος καὶ παρέτεινεν εἰς μακρόν, and assigns him a Περὶ τῆς βασιλείας Ἀδριανοῦ ἐφ' οὗ καὶ ἦν ὁ Φίλων (no fragments). Gudeman's article in *RE*, loc. cit. cols. 650-1, makes no further attempt to determine his dates. It is noteworthy, in view of the close links between paradoxography and pinacography, that Herennius also wrote a Παράδοξος Ἱστορία (F 12-B). For Serenus see *FGrH* 790 T4: Σερῆνος· ὁ καὶ Ἀθηναῖος (Ἀθηναῖος ?) χρηματίσας· γραμματικός· Ἐπιτομὴν τῆς Φίλωνος πραγματείας περὶ πόλεων καὶ τίνες ἐφ' ἑκάστης ἔνδοξοι, βιβλία γ̄. The *Epitome* is quoted twice in *Et. Gen.* (ibid. F 17-18); cf. also *RE*, s.v. Aelius (137). To approximately the same period must belong Diogenianus (*RE* (4)), author of Συναγωγὴ καὶ πίναξ τῶν ἐν πάσηι τῆι γῆι πόλεων. A more limited production of the same class is represented by e.g. Menippos' (? of Perinthos, *FGrH* 82) Τῶν κατὰ τὴν Σάμον ἐνδόξων περιγραφή, *FGrH* 541). [6] See below, pp. 53 ff.

[7] See Call. frs. 403 ff., and the Suda-Life, Test. 1 (Pf. ii. p. xcv). For the chief characteristics of these works see *Ptol. Alex.* i. 452 ff.; Regenbogen, *RE*, Suppbd. v, cols. 1409 ff., and the further bibliography in *Ptol. Alex.* ii. 654 ff., nn. 42 ff. Atenstädt, op. cit. 11, points out that the use of ἀναγράφει in Stephanus is an indication of Herennius as a source: cf. also Gudeman, col. 653 (cf. id. ibid. s.v. Satyros (16), cols. 233-4), who quotes Stephanus, s.v. Δυρράχιον (F2) . . . καὶ Ἐρέννιος Φίλων ἐν τοῖς Ἰατρικοῖς (cf. Gudeman, § 9) Δυρραχηνὸν ἀναγράφει Φιλωνίδην οὕτως . . .: and also s.v. Ἄβδηρα· πλεῖστοι δ' Ἀβδηρῖται ὑπὸ τῶν πινακογράφων ἀναγράφονται, s.v. Αἶνος· τὸ ἐθνικὸν Αἴνιος, ὡς Τήνιος· οὕτω γὰρ ἀναγράφεται ἐν τοῖς πίναξιν; and s.v. Ἀντιόχεια, quoted above, in the text.

[8] *Laterculi Alexandrini*, ed. H. Diels (Berl. Abh. 1904 (Pack, *Greek Lit. Pap.*² 2068); see *Ptol. Alex.* i. 777 ff. for this list of νομοθέται, ζωγράφοι, ἀγαλματοποιοί, μηχανικοί, τὰ ἑπτὰ θεάματα et al. For similar, later lists see O. Kroehnert, *Canones Poetarum* (Ratisbon, 1893), pp. 5 ff.

literature survived the Hellenistic Age in Alexandria and elsewhere, and continued in vogue into the late Imperial period, is evident from such works as the Καινὴ Ἱστορία of Ptolemy Chennos,[9] and the later Κτίσεις and Πάτρια, as also from the lists of metonomasies, that continued into the period of vernacular Greek.[10] In the biographical field it may be seen most clearly in the lists of homonyms at the end of the individual Lives of philosophers by Diogenes Laertius; the formula, for example, γεγόνασι δὲ Δημόκριτοι ἕξ, followed by a description of the field of activity of each homonym, or by his ethnic, reflects a similar tradition, different though the subject-matter is.[11]

Philon and Alexander are, however, like Strabo, Polybius, and others, general sources of Stephanus, who recur repeatedly, and it is evident that the entry s.v. Ἀλεξάνδρεια is of a different type from the entries derived from these two sources, neither of which is quoted in that entry. Instead, he quotes writers who were particularly concerned with Alexandrian antiquities and with details relating to Alexandrian philology—ethnic and ktetic forms and so on; and in between the historical first part of the entry and the philological second part, he has inserted his list of eighteen Alexandrias. We may therefore suppose that the entry contains a large amount of local Alexandrian material, and though this may have been drawn at second hand from the sources Stephanus used in general, if that is so it is surprising that we are given—at least in the Epitome—no hint of it. From the discussion of ethnics and so on we may perhaps conjecture the especial use of Oros, even though he is not quoted by name. In the entry s.v. Ἀθῆναι (above, pp. 2–3) Philon and Oros both gave the number of cities named Athens known to them: five according to Oros, six according to

⁹ For this work see Phot. Bibl. Cod. 190, and RE (77; cf. 69).

¹⁰ For the Πάτρια and Κτίσεις see Ptol. Alex. i. 513 ff., with nn. 159 ff. For the πάτρια Κωνσταντινουπόλεως of Hesychius Illustris and others see Th. Preger, Script. Orig. Constant. i–ii (1901–07), and for further bibliography R. Janin, Constantinople Byzantine, 2 (1964), pp. xxviii–xxix. For late lists of metonomasies in the vernacular see those published by A. Diller, BZ 63 (1970), 27 ff.

¹¹ Maass, Philol. Unt. iii (1880), De Biographis graecis quaestiones selectae, passim, esp. pp. 23 ff., has a full collection of such lists in Diogenes and elsewhere, but no individual source or sources for them can be identified in spite of much conjecture; see Wilamowitz, ibid. in calce, pp. 142 ff., Epistula ad Maasium (cf. id. AvK, Einleitung); there has been little further investigation into the lists as a whole: see Schwartz, RE, s.v. Diogenes (40) col. 742 (= Gr. Geschichtschreiber, 458 ff.). See also my remarks in Second Colloquium, Copenhagen Polis-Centre (Copenhagen, 1995), pp. 85–6.

Philon. In view of the priority of Philon over Oros, the most natural explanation of this is that the latter was Stephanus' source for a 'corrected' version of the information provided by Philon. In the case of the Alexandrias it may well be that Oros was a prime authority in his own right, and that the enumeration is his own.

Examination of the Table of Alexandrias (at end) shows two features. (1) Stephanus' list of Alexandrias is longer than, and in most instances different from, that found in the *Romance* tradition (see below, pp. 205 ff. and text on pp. 203-4). This may be explained as the result of a reworking, at one of several stages, of the same material, arising from the use of different sources. The problem is not helped by the fact that the A-text of the *Romance* claims that Alexander founded thirteen Alexandrias, but only nine appear in the list itself. As we shall see at a later stage, some of the items missing from A's list can be restored with some degree of certainty from the lists in the translations and derivatives of the α-text within the *Romance*-tradition and from external texts. Therefore, whatever may be the explanation of the discrepancy between a text inside the *Romance*-tradition and one, like Stephanus, outside it, there can be no doubt of the internal coherence of the former as compared with Stephanus, whose sources are varied and chronologically stratified. (2) All versions of the α-tradition of the *Romance* basically agree; though, as we shall see, there are variations, they are not enough to indicate different ultimate sources; there are only additions and variations from the same original text, once it had found circulation in different contexts, and was translated and adapted—and corrupted.

Our next task is to attempt to determine the sources of the list of Alexandrias in the α-tradition of the *Romance*. This line of approach does not superficially appear very fruitful when applied to the *Romance* in other than general terms. There are numerous possible candidates, but none outshines the others. Jason of Nysa or Argos, whose Βίος τῆς Ἑλλάδος Stephanus quotes, is one, but the quotation does not indicate any particular affinity with the *Romance*. There is also a Heracleides, referred to by Plutarch[12], who says that the Alexandrians of his day claimed, on the authority of Heracleides, that when Alexander wished to found the city he had

---

[12] For Jason see *Ptol. Alex.* ii. 65 n. 151. For Heracleides see Plut. Alex. 26, quoted below, p. 223 n. 44.

a vision in which Homer appeared to him, and quoted the lines of the *Odyssey* regarding the island of Pharos, that is, the same line that Stephanus quotes from Jason, but which the *Romance* does not quote. Of these two writers, then, we may say that they themselves show no link with the *Romance*; that they possibly represent the type of writer in whom the author of the α-version might have found relevant information; but that there is nothing to suggest that they were interested in other foundations of Alexander. We can see what their genre of writing consisted of, at least at a later date.

Malalas, referring to various versions of the death of Cleopatra VII, speaks of 'the authors of Alexandrian Πάτρια', as being the source of his information; the authors of the Πάτρια correctly recorded that her body remained in Egypt, whereas 'the wise chronographer Theophilos' claimed that it was embalmed and taken to Rome, to satisfy the sister of Augustus.[13] Πάτρια are a well-attested genre of antiquarian writing in Imperial Egypt, not least relating to Alexandria. We encounter as authors of Alexandrian Πάτρια the prolific poet Christodoros of Koptos, the Neoplatonist Horapollon (who lived, however, at a later date than that at which the α-version of the *Romance* was composed), and Aelius Dius, author of a like-named work, alongside works of a more general nature, such as that of Jason to which Stephanus had access, direct or indirect.[14] A Πάτρια of Hermoupolis in verse by one Hermeias,

[13] Mal. p. 220, Bonn: μετὰ δὲ τὴν τελευτῆς αὐτῆς ἀπηνέχθη τὸ λείψανον αὐτῆς ἐν τῆι Ῥώμηι σμυρνιασθέντα πρὸς θεραπείαν τῆς ἀδελφῆς τοῦ αὐτοῦ Αὐγούστου Ὀκταβιανοῦ, καθὰ Θεόφιλος ὁ σοφὸς χρονογράφος συνεγράψατο. οἱ δὲ ἐκθέμενοι τὰ πάτρια Ἀλεξανδρείας τῆς μεγάλης τὴν Κλεοπάτραν ἐν Αἰγύπτωι εἶπαν λειφθεῖσαν, καὶ ἄλλα δέ τινα μὴ συμφωνοῦντα τοῖς Ῥωμαίων συγγραφεῦσι.

[14] For Christodoros see the list of his works in the Suda-Life, X 525: Χριστόδωρος, Πανίσκου, ἀπὸ Κόπτου πόλεως τῆς Αἰγύπτου, ἐποποιός. ἤκμασεν ἐπὶ τῶν Ἀναστασίου τοῦ βασιλέως χρόνων. ἔγραψεν Ἰσαυρικὰ ἐν βιβλίοις ἕξ. ἔχει δὲ τὴν Ἰσαυρίας ἅλωσιν τὴν ὑπὸ Ἀναστασίου τοῦ βασιλέως γενομένην· Πάτρια Κωνσταντινουπόλεως ἐπικῶς βιβλία ιβʹ, Πάτρια Θεσσαλονίκης ἐπικῶς βιβλία κεʹ, Πάτρια Νάκλης· ἔστι δὲ πόλις περὶ Ἡλιούπολιν, ἐν ἧι τὰ καλούμενα Ἄφακα· Πάτρια Μιλήτου τῆς Ἰωνίας, Πάτρια Τραλλέων, Πάτρια Ἀφροδισιάδος, Ἔκφρασιν τῶν ἐν τῶι Ζευξίππωι ἀγαλμάτων· καὶ ἄλλα πολλά. Perhaps the same man as ibid. 526, stated to be from Thebes. A more complex problem is presented by Kallinikos, FGrH 281 (cf. Jacoby, RE, Kallinikos (1), and Stern, *Hermes*, 58 (1923), 448 ff. (id. PIR² p. 45, no. 229)). The essential information is in the Suda-Life, K 231: Καλλίνικος, Γάιος· . . . ὁ καὶ Σουητώριος (?) κληθείς, σοφιστής· σοφιστεύσας ἐν Ἀθήναις. ἔγραψε πρὸς Λοῦπον, Περὶ κακοζηλίας ῥητορικῆς, Προσφωνητικὸν Γαλιηνῶι, Πρὸς Κλεοπάτραν Περὶ τῶν κατ' Ἀλεξάνδρειαν ἱστοριῶν βιβλία δέκα, Πρὸς τὰς φιλοσοφικὰς αἱρέσεις, Περὶ τῆς Ῥωμαίων ἀνανεώσεως, καὶ ἄλλα τινα ἐγκώμια καὶ λόγους. The bizarre reference to a work addressed to 'Kleopatra' at such a date was explained by Stern and Jacoby as referring to

and (surprisingly) a Πάτρια of the Great Oasis by Soterichos, described like Christodoros, as an epic poet, remind us of the substantial sections in the *Romance* composed in scazons.[15] These writers of the fourth and fifth centuries seem to belong to the same milieu as the α-text of the *Romance*, and (less clearly) as that of Stephanus' entry s.v Ἀλεξάνδρεια. The *Acta* of Antioch, of the time of Justinian, to which Malalas also refers, provided not dissimilar information from that to be found in the Alexandrian antiquarian sections of the *Romance* and of Stephanus.[16]

In Alexandria amidst this mass of largely fabulous antiquarian literature in prose and verse, where names survive but texts are almost entirely lost, we cannot hope to identify a single individual as having made a decisive contribution to the literature of the Founder and his city. Indeed, as Jacoby said of the evolution of the

Zenobia, ruler of Egypt through her son Vaballath, in the reign of Gallienus, with reference to SHA Trig. Tyr. 24, 30: *Zenobia quae se de Cleopatrarum Ptolemaeorumque gente iactaret*. In ibid. *Prob.*, 9, 5, she is simply called Cleopatra: *pugnavit etiam (sc. Probus) contra Palmyrenos Odenati et Cleopatrae partibus Aegyptum defendentes*. Jacoby accepted the suggestion and, for his part, removed the notional comma after Κλεοπάτραν, thus creating one work entitled Πρὸς Κλεοπάτραν περὶ τῶν κατ' Ἀλεξάνδρειαν ἱστοριῶν βιβλία δέκα. This 'History of events in the neighbourhood of Alexandria' (for such, rather than 'concerning' seems to be the force of κατά) is attested in Jacoby's F1, a short series of events which formed part of the Sixth Syrian War, headed Εἰς τὰ πάτρια Ῥώμης. If this is correct we have, then, another Alexandrian Πάτρια, of the 3rd cent. AD. Finally, the work Περὶ τῆς Ῥωμαίων ἀνανεώσεως clearly refers to the restoration of Roman prestige in the reign of Aurelian, and is most naturally associated *inter alia* with the extension of the walls of Rome, which is referred to by Julius Valerius, and forms an important element in the enquiry into the date of the α-version of the *Romance*: see below, p. 222. If the attribution of this group of texts to Zenobia is correct we might have to consider whether some other late references to Cleopatra (as below, n. 38) do not refer to Zenobia, but any such identification must have been ephemeral. For Horapollon, on whom much has been written, see the basic article of Maspero, BIFAO 11 (1914), 163-95.

[15] For Hermeias and Soterichos see Ptol. Alex. ii. 739 n. 159.

[16] p. 443 (Bonn): Ἐν αὐτῶι δὲ τῶι χρόνωι μετεκλήθη Ἀντιόχεια Θεούπολις κατὰ κέλευσιν τοῦ ἁγίου Συμεῶνος τοῦ Θαυματουργοῦ. εὑρέθη δὲ καὶ ἐν τῆι Ἀντιοχείαι χρησμὸς ἀναγεγραμμένος, περιέχων οὕτως· Καὶ σύ, τάλαινα πόλις, Ἀντιόχου οὐ κληθήσηι. ὁμοίως δὲ καὶ ἐν τοῖς χαρτίοις εὑρέθη τῶν τὰ ἄκτα γραφόντων τῆς πόλεως· ὅτι ἔκραζον κληδόνα διδόντες εἰς τὸ μετακληθῆναι τὴν πόλιν. On this metonomasy see the remarks of Honigmann, RE, s.v. Stephanos, cols. 2370-1. Antioch appears as Θεούπολις in the Conciliar list of Constantinople II (553) at just this time, and Stephanus, s.v. Θεούπολις gives the same information: Θεούπολις, ἡ μεγίστη τῆς ἕω πόλις, ἥτις ἐξ Ἀντιοχείας μετὰ τὸν σεισμὸν ὠνομάσθη ἀπὸ Ἰουστινιανοῦ; cf. Proc. De Aedif. ii. 10. 2, 5, etc. We are told by Sophronius, Mirac. 62, of the miraculous cure effected in Alexandria shortly before the Arab Conquest by SS. Cyrus and John of the sickness of Rhodope of Antioch: Ῥοδόπη γέννημα μὲν ἦν Θεουπόλεως, ἣ πάσης Ἑώιας προκάθηται, Ἀντιόχου κληθεῖσα τοῦ βασιλέως ἐπώνυμος.

earliest Atthides, 'The subject-matter is more important than the writers who hand it down.'[17] We may also imagine that the analogous, usually metrical literature about the foundations of cities, the so-called *Ktiseis*, that were popularized by Callimachus and others in the third century BC, when Apollonius of Rhodes wrote his Κτίσις Ἀλεξανδρείας,[18] of which unfortunately little more than the title survives, contributed to the general conglomeration of mutually adhesive material available at the end of the Imperial period. They too were, naturally, almost entirely fabulous. They remain for us largely unspecifiable, but unmistakable, elements in the literary output of the Imperial Age, part of which can be seen in Stephanus' entry.

A third category of material that preserves lists of Alexander-foundations is also directly relevant to our search for the background of such lists. This, which we may call 'the Alexandrian World-Chronicles', is represented by three works, all originally illustrated, of which one, the 'Golenischev World-Chronicle', is preserved on a papyrus of the fifth century.[19] The two others are the so-called *Excerpta Latina Barbari*,[20] (the 'barbaric' (i.e. late) Latin

[17] See F. Jacoby, *Atthis* (Oxford, 1952), 2.

[18] For Κτίσις-literature in general see *Ptol. Alex.* i. 775-6, with notes; cf. below, pp. 44-5 for Apollonius.

[19] For the Golenischev papyrus see *Eine Alexandrinische Weltchronik, Text u. Miniaturen* (Wien. Denkschr. 51(2), 1905), ed. A. Bauer and J. Strzygowski, i, *Der Text*, ed. A. Bauer. The text alone is reproduced in Bilabel's *Historikerfragmente auf Pap.* no. 13.

[20] For the *Excerpta*, discovered in a Paris MS of AD vii-viii by Scaliger (see now the account of this by A. Grafton, *Joseph Scaliger*, ii (Oxford, 1993), 560-8), the best text is that of A. Schoene at the end of vol. i of his *Eusebi Chronic.*, i (Berlin, 1875), 177 ff., reprinted below, p. 204. The two other editions, that of C. Frick, *Chronica Minora*, i (Teubner, 1890; all pub.) pp. lxxxiii-ccix, with (the text) pp. 185-371, and of Mommsen, *Chron. Min.* (*MGH*, AA ix. 1. 274 ff.) are valuable by reason of the wealth of parallel chronicles quoted, but only Schoene's edition preserves the actual form of the MS, which it is important to understand, since the original was, like the Golenischev papyrus, illustrated; the illustrations did not survive the rendering of the text into Latin, but spaces are left in the published text to indicate where they once stood. I cannot go further here into the iconography of these annalistic chronicles, of which a further fragment, covering the later 4th cent., was published by H. Lietzmann, *Quantulacumque* (*Studies Presented to Kirsopp Lake*, London, 1937), 339 ff. For a general analysis see Jacoby, *RE*, s.v. Excerpta Barbari (= *Gr. Hist.* 257 ff.). All the Christian World-Chronicles, and their probable pagan predecessors, have been studied within a wide historical compass in recent years by B. Croke, in a series of articles reprinted in *Christian Chronicles and Byzantine History, 5th-6th Centuries* (Variorum edn., Aldershot, 1992), esp. item no. IV, 'City Chronicles of late Antiquity', with an extensive bibliography. I agree with much of what he says, but he is more concerned to establish antecedents and parallels between the eastern and

translation of a Greek original), and the *Paschal Chronicle*.[21] The
first two end with the epochal date of early Alexandrian Christian
annals, the destruction of the Serapeum in AD 392, and were
themselves composed early in the fifth century, while the last,
which, though Constantinopolitan in origin, contains a great deal
of Alexandrian annalistic material, belongs to the beginning of the
seventh century.[22]

We may examine these works more closely to see how far they
justify the general title of 'Alexandrian World-Chronicles', before
considering the links between them and the original version of the
Romance. Broadly speaking, their contents are a combination of
illustrated Universal History and Alexandrian Annals, linked by a
chronological framework. The best example is the Golenischev
papyrus, containing a fragmentary Greek text, which originally
consisted of an illustrated history of the world from Adam to the
destruction of the Alexandrian Serapeum; the work itself was composed after AD 412, for the length of Theophilos' Patriarchate,
which ended in that year, is correctly given. There also survives a
small fragment of a Greek version of the *Excerpta*,[23] which shows
that it was in circulation before the Golenischev papyrus itself
(dated to the sixth century); it contains a selected version of the
Excerpta covering the years 251-306 and 335-8, and is dated to
the later part of the fourth or the early fifth century, and is thus
contemporary with the closing entries in the *Excerpta*. This is, of
course, considerably later than the date of composition of the α-text
of the *Romance*. Much of the early part of the Chronicles is

western Chronicles than with the analysis of individual city-traditions. As regards
Alexandria, my remarks may therefore lend some local colour to what he has
to say. There is also a summary account of these interdependent Chronicles in
R. Bagnall and A. Cameron, *Consular and Other Lists of the Later Roman Empire*
(Papers of the Amer. Philosoph. Soc. 36, 1987), 47 ff. See also the recently
published edition of the *Hydatian Chronicle* and the *Consularia Constantinopolitana* by
R. W. Burgess (Oxford, 1993).

[21] ed. Bonn. (1832); the relevant passage is reprinted below, p. 204. The analysis of the *Paschal Chronicle* by Schwartz, *RE* s.v., cols. 2460 ff. (= *Gr. Geschichtschr.*
291 ff.) remains useful, and Wachsmuth, *Einleitung*, 195-6, is, as always, very
lucid. Mommsen's text of the *Chronicle* in *Chron. Min.* i. 199 ff. (only as far as the
death of Theodosius I) contains additions from other texts: see Wachsmuth, op. cit.
196 n. 1. The recent translation by M. and M. Whitby, *Chronicon Paschale, 284-628
A.D.* (Liverpool Univ. Press, 1989) contains a valuable introduction and excellent
notes.

[22] See Schwartz, cols. 2473 ff. (= *Gr. Geschichtschr.* 311 ff.), Whitby, op. cit.
190-1, in favour of 630 rather than 628 as the terminal date of the *Chronicle*.

[23] Pack, *Greek Lit. Pap.*², 243.

concerned with the Διαμερισμὸς Γῆς, the 'Division of the Earth' between the three sons of Noah, Ham, Shem, and Japhet, which derives originally, as a literary tradition, from the apocryphal *Book of Jubilees*, building on the Septuagint text of Genesis 10.[24] The Διαμερισμός first appears for us in Hippolytus' Χρονικά, the full title of which was Συναγωγὴ χρόνων καὶ ἐτῶν ἀπὸ κτίσεως κόσμου ἕως τῆς ἐνεστώσης ἡμέρας.[25] Thereafter it became a standard feature of Christian chronography and chronicles, but we need not consider its numerous ramifications further. In the Golenischev papyrus it is followed by illustrated sayings of the prophets, which occur, also illustrated, in the *Christian Topography* of Cosmas Indicopleustes,[26] of about the same date, and in the *Paschal Chronicle*, which was also once illustrated, as may be seen from the repeated explanatory formulae, which stood as captions beneath the representations: οὗτος Ἡλίας, οὗτος Ὡσηὲ τῶν ιβ΄ προφητῶν ἀξιωθεὶς εἰπεῖν, κ.τ.λ.[27] The prophets are followed by a list of world-rulers, in which, as in the *Paschal Chronicle*, Roman kings from Romulus, Spartan, and Macedonian kings are given; once again, the illustrations form the main thread, and the narrative is subordinated to them as in the *Paschal Chronicle* and the *Excerpta*. In the Golenischev papyrus the portraits of the Latin kings are preserved, and they were once present in the two other texts also.[28] The tradition of illustration, whether or not it was a universal feature of such texts, may go back as far as Varro's *Imagines*, though an unbroken line of descent is most unlikely. It is certain that in due course some of the Alexander-stories were also pictorially illustrated, with spaces left

[24] There is a very full account of the Διαμερισμὸς Γῆς in vol. v of von Gutschmid's *Kl. Schr.* 585-717. The tradition occurs in Mas'ūdī, *Murūj* § 311 (cf. § 314), from Abū Zaïd aṣ Ṣīrāfī (for whom see below, pp. 63-4), and Ya'qūbī, and also in Eutychius, 17-18, Cheiko.

[25] For this work see the edition by R. Helm (GCS 46), *Hippolyts Chronik* (1955), replacing A. Bauer's edition of 1905, *Texte u. Untersuchungen* (29)) Cf. also the fragment of the *Chronicle* pub. Bernstein, *Getty Museum Journal*, 12 (1984), 153 ff. on the *verso* of the relief with part of a letter from the *Romance*-tradition below it (see p. 217 n. 28 below).

[26] See the detailed discussion of the text and illustrations in the vol. i of Wolska-Conus's edn. (*Sources Chrét.* 141, 1968), 51 ff., 124 ff., 157 ff. Although Cosmas' place of origin, as indeed his true name, remains uncertain, there is little doubt that he lived and worked in Alexandria: see Wolska-Conus, i. 15 ff.

[27] *Chron. Pasch.* 274-5. There are many instances of this formula, which extends also to pagan figures: e.g. p. 262 (οὗτος Δαρεῖος).

[28] See Bauer, *Golenischev Pap.* 39 ff., and pl. IV-V. For a corresponding passage in the *Paschal Chronicle* see e.g. p. 217: οὗτος Νουμμᾶς ὁ καὶ Πομπήλιος δεξάμενος πρεσβευτὰς ἐκ τῆς χώρας τῶν λεγομένων Πελασγῶν, κ.τ.λ.

for the illustrations, but though this points to a single Alexandrian artistic tradition, there is no direct link in this respect between texts so different in character as the Alexandrian Annals and the *Romance*. Whether from the outset the α-version itself, as a consolidated text, was decorated with illustrations, as were many of the later versions in East and West, is uncertain.[29] The frescoes which illustrated the thaumaturgic activities of saints such as St Spyridon of Trimithus (see below, pp. 218-20), for the benefit of those unable to read the written accounts of his life, belong to the same milieu, and indicate that the illustrations may well have served a humble need rather than a luxury-seeking public.

The Golenischev papyrus and the *Excerpta* reveal their Alexandrian origin, like parts of the *Paschal Chronicle*, by their dating by Augustals, which is also found in Athanasius' *Historia Acephala*;[30] we may compare the presence of the *Praefecti Urbis* alongside the consuls in the text of the Roman Chronographer of 354, and, in the analogous Ravenna Chronicle, the *Consularia Ravennatia*, the frequent reference, alongside the consular fasti and the Imperial *Res Gestae*, to events referring only to Ravenna; for example, in a recent addition to the latter—its illustration preserved, unlike in the main text—which, beneath the year 443, refers to the effect of the general earthquake of that year in the city of Ravenna itself.[31] (In form and concept the *Ravenna Chronicle* is

[29] For illustrations of medieval and oriental MSS of the *Romance* and associated texts see the excellent work of D. J. A. Ross, *Alexander Historiatus* (Warburg Institute Surveys i, 1963), with addenda in *JWCI* 30 (1967), 383 ff. Ross gives a full survey of the late antique picture-cycle found in Byzantine and later MSS of the *Romance* and linked texts, and argues that the 4th-cent. mosaics from al-Sueida (Baalbek), illustrating scenes from the cycle (see *Ptol. Alex.* ii. 946 n. 11), with titles (*IGLS* 2884-7), reflects the development of the cycle 'within a century of the appearance of the text'; cf. id. *JWCI* 26 (1963) = *Studies in the Alexander Romance* (London, 1985), no. xx, 339-65 esp. p. 354. The same argument is advanced by Ruggini on the basis of the representation of Olympias and the snake on a coin of Syrian Beroia of the 3rd cent. AD (see *Ptol. Alex.* ibid.), but in neither case is there any warranty that the representation reflects the same complete version of the *Romance*, rather than earlier stories which later became constituent parts of the α-tradition. The story of Olympias and the snake, Ammon (Nectanebos in the *Romance*), was already known to Eratosthenes at a time when no comprehensive text of the *Romance* existed (see *Ptol. Alex.* ii. 951 n. 25, for a discussion of the passage in Plut. *Alex.* 3 where Eratosthenes is cited).

[30] For Athanasius see the *Hist. Aceph.* in Libr. of Ante-Nicene Writers, *Athanasius*, 500 ff. The Augustals stand in the introductory date-headings.

[31] For the *Ravenna Chronicle* see Frick, op. cit. 373 ff., and for the addition to the text see Bischoff and Koehler in *Essays in Honor of A. Kingsley Porter* (Cambridge, Mass., 1939), 125 ff. The passage for the year 443 reads: *Maximo II et Paterio | His*

probably closer to the *Excerpta* than is any other of the western group of texts.)

At the same time these texts, and especially the nearly complete *Excerpta Barbari*, contain substantial passages largely identical with material in the *Romance*, namely the list of Alexandrias and the *Last Days and Will of Alexander*. The Golenischev papyrus does not help, since it is very lacunose in this respect, but the *Excerpta* and the *Paschal Chronicle* both contain identical lists of twelve or thirteen Alexandrias with only a few discrepancies from that in the *Romance*, and in one of the cases where they deviate from the *A*-tradition they are in agreement with the inferior Greek tradition, *B*, and with Stephanus, by the inclusion of an Alexandria in Cyprus (see below, pp. 27, 43–4). It is still more striking that the *Excerpta* contains almost the same text, in Latin dress, of the *Will of Alexander* (fo. 33: *testamentum alexandri conditoris*) as the *Romance*, including the role assigned in that context to the Rhodians. Another and most striking demonstration of the link between the *Romance* and the *Excerpta* is provided by the sentence with which the A-text begins its list of Alexandrias in its last chapter: ἔκτισε δὲ πόλεις ιγ̅ αἵτινες μέχρι τοῦ νῦν κατοικοῦνται καὶ εἰρηνεύονται. This sentence, or at least the relative clause, which seems curiously anachronistic and out of place (see below pp. 40 ff.), but which nevertheless found its way into the Iranian tradition (see below, pp. 57 ff.), is present also in the *Excerpta*, which (ibid.) has *condidit autem Alexander civitates xii* (sic) *qui usque nunc habitantur*, but the list of cities and the preceding rubric are absent from the *Will*, the original composition of which is of much earlier date. It is also to be noted, in view of the Alexandrian origin of the *Excerpta*, that the description of Alexander as *conditor*, which does not occur in the *Romance*, is itself, in the form κτίστης, a title used of Alexander in Greek texts from Egypt of Imperial date. Germanicus, in his speech to the Alexandrians, described the Founder as ἥρως καὶ κτίστης, and the same title occurs in an Oxyrhynchus list of Egyptian rulers dated to the third century AD, which no doubt derives from Ptolemy's *Canon*, where the same title

---

consulibus terrae motus factus | est xv kal.Mai.die Iovis | Ravennae hora noctis viii | followed by an illustration (p. 132, IV). See in general Croke, op. cit. (iv) 187 ff.

[32] For the *Canon* see the discussion in *Ptol. Alex.* ii. 360 n. 182, and for an example of its use from the Ptolemaic period see ibid. n. 184, with reference to *SEG* ii. 849 (*SB* 6670). For a much later example, of Alexandrian origin, see Syncellus,

is used.[32] The Alexandrian focus of the later stages of the *Excerpta* is strongly marked. We have seen that from about AD 375 the text provides an eponymous dating by Augustals (i.e. the previous prefects) alongside the consular date; this is certainly an Alexandrian system of dating, though not exclusively so, and occurs in Athanasius and in the *Paschal Chronicle*.[33] Within the framework of this consular–Augustal dating we have in the *Excerpta* a whole series of events of Alexandrian Christian history, which show that such chronicles covered, in outline, the same ground as the œcumenical Christian historians, notably Socrates and Sozomenos, in so far as their narratives related to Alexandria. Thus the *Barbarus* records the persecution by Diocletian and the martyrdom of Peter, which, according to that text and to other sources, occurred on 25 November 311; the blank space in the MS indicates that in the original text the event was illustrated. His martyrdom was one of the great Passions of the Alexandrian Christian year, and various Greek and Latin accounts of it survive.[34] The death of Bishop Alexander, the predecessor of Athanasius, in AD 315, is recorded with its Egyptian date, Pharmouthi 22,[35] whereas the martyrdom of Peter has only the Roman date, the Egyptian date no doubt having been lost in transmission. We may recall that the last sentence of the A-text of the *Romance* consists of a statement of the days of the birth and death of Alexander the

as quoted in Arrian, *FGrH* 156F31, speaking of the Parthian rebellion against Seleucid rule, ὑπ' αὐτοὺς τελοῦντες ἀπὸ Ἀλεξάνδρου τοῦ κτιστοῦ διὰ τοιαύτην αἰτίαν, where the phrase is Syncellus', not Arrian's. Ausfeld believed that the title of the original *Romance* may have contained a reference to Alexander as Ktistes: see below, p. 206 with n. 4.

[33] The Augustal dating begins on fo. 61a (p. 364 Frick): in the upper margin is written *initium augustaliorum qui et praesites*, and in the body of the text ibid. *eo anno introivit Tatianus in Alexandria primus Augustalius, vi. kl. Februarias*. For papyri which refer to the Augustal see e.g. *PStrass*. 255. 9 (397 or 403): τοῦ ἐπάρχου Αὐγουσταλίου; *PMert*. 43 (?), note on verso, 1 (5th cent.); *PAnt*. iii. 188, verso, 1 (6th–7th cent.). Cf. Rouillard, *L'Administration byzantine en Égypte*[2] (Paris, 1929), 30 ff., for later developments of the office.

[34] For the martyrdom of Peter see fo. 57a (p. 354 Frick): *Hisdem consulibus venit Diocletianus in Alexandria et ecclesias exterminavit. Et multi martyrizaverunt, in quibus et beatus Petrus episcopus Alexandrinus capite truncatus est. Martyrizavit vii kl.Decem.* For the other sources on the martyrdom of Peter see the bibliography in Cross, *ODCC* s.v. Peter of Alexandria; Quasten, *Patrology*, ii. 113-18; *RE*, Petros (1), cols. 1281-8.

[35] Fo. 59a (p. 358 Frick): *eodem anno in Alexandria episcopus Alexander obiit Farmuthii xxii, et successit ei in sacerdotio Athanasius annos xlvi.* For Alexander see the very full account in *DCB* i. 79(1); *ODCC* s.v.; Quasten, *Patrology*, iii. 13-19.

Great in terms of the Egyptian calendar.[36] Other examples of the
Alexandrian focus of the chronicle could be given, but these suffice
to demonstrate the similarity of background of the *Excerpta* and the
Romance.

The lists of Alexandrias in these three groups of material, the
Epitome of Stephanus, the *Romance* and the World-Chronicles,
stand then in this relation to each other: they differ fundamentally
in number and identity from the Alexandrias of the historians and
also of the geographers; all the lists show substantial Alexandrian
elements, in two cases exclusively so; but the many variations in
form and matter in Stephanus show that he did not follow the
Romance tradition, though his text may occasionally coincide with
it. We must now examine more closely two questions, the first
of which has, in a manner, been very largely answered on our
way: (1) the likely relation of these texts to the lost texts that are
known to have been sources for the α-tradition of the *Romance*,
and (2) the historical value of the lists of Alexandrias which they
provide.

On the first point certainty is not possible. There can, on the one
hand, be no serious doubt that the original author of the *Excerpta*
included in his illustrated Annals sections taken directly from the
α-text of the *Romance*; in spite of some differences the hypothesis of
a common source here is implausible. No text other than the
Romance is likely to have provided the *Excerpta* with the details
regarding the Will of Alexander, the same list of cities, and the
same statement as to their 'lasting prosperity', a phrase of which
we shall consider the interpretation shortly. Even the *Testamentum*,
which existed as a separate text, did not contain these two latter
elements. That the cities listed differ in one or two respects need
not surprise us: the list as found in the A-text of the *Romance* is not
likely to be precisely that of the α-text, since the actual number of
cities listed does not correspond to the given total, and there are at
least three items preserved in the *Excerpta* which are not to be
found in the list in A; and at the same time the *Excerpta*, and
through it the *Paschal Chronicle*, lack one or two items present in
the *A*-list. Details of this are considered below.

The relationship between the Alexandria-entry in Stephanus and

---

[36] iii. 35 fin.: ἐγεννήθη μὲν οὖν Τύβι τῆι νεομηνίαι ἀνατολῆς οὔσης, ἐτελεύτησε δὲ
Φαρμοῦθι τετράδι δύσεως. In the *B*-tradition the dates are given according to the
Roman calendar.

these exclusively Alexandrian lists is less clear. His material, too, is Alexandrian in essence, but it is evident that, in addition to some coincidence with the *Romance* (as shown in the passage quoted from Jason) there are other sources involved, also Alexandrian. The relationship between the various strands is shown schematically by the stemma (Fig. 1), the main purpose of which is to indicate the traditions that differentiate Stephanus and the *Romance*, notwithstanding obvious common elements. What sources lie behind such generic titles as Πάτρια and Κτίσεις we usually cannot say, nor can we determine the precise relationship between the Πάτρια-literature and the more strictly Annalistic form and substance of the World-Chronicles.

FIG. 1. Stemma showing likely relationship between Steph. Byz. s.v. Ἀλεξάνδρεια and *The Alexander Romance* (cf. Fig. 2, p. 207)

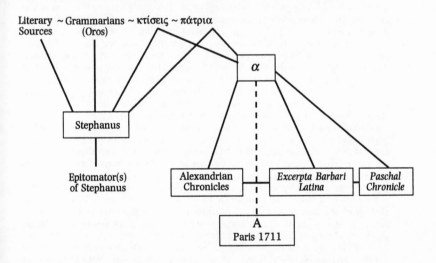

We must now consider whether such historical aberrations concerning Alexander and the cities he founded are represented in surviving sources other than those which form the main theme of this chapter. Here some chapters of Ammianus provide an excellent starting-point, the more so since there are indications that he himself had access to the *Romance* tradition in an early form.[37] In his description of Alexandria he presents to us a city the history of which was dominated, not so much by Alexander, who founded it, nor by those Ptolemies who embellished it, as by Cleopatra VII, to whom is given the credit for building much of the original city, especially the Pharos and the Heptastadion, and round whom is woven an entirely fabulous account of Rhodian control of the island of Pharos, as a result of which, we are told, the small island in the eastern harbour was called Antirrhodos—the name was known to Strabo, but it is not until the fourth century, in this passage, that we encounter any explanation of it. Nevertheless, in spite of the predominant role now played by Cleopatra, which extended even to the publication of an epic poem on her achievements,[38] Alexander was not forgotten in local tradi-

---

[37] xxii. 16. 7; *Alexandria enim vertex omnium est civitatum, quam multa nobilitant et magnifica, conditoris altissimi* . . . (9) *Hoc litus cum fallacibus et insidiosis accessibus affligeret antehac navigantes discriminibus plurimis, excogitavit in portu Cleopatra turrim excelsam, quae Pharos a loco ipso cognominatur* . . . (10) *Haec eadem regina heptastadium sicut vix credenda celeritate, ita magnitudine mira construxit, ob causam notam et necessariam. Insula Pharos, ubi Protea cum phocarum gregibus diversatum Homerus fabulatur inflatius, a civitatis litore mille passibus disparata, Rhodiorum erat obnoxia vectigali.* Ammianus goes on to describe the ruse by which the queen cheated the Rhodian tax-collectors of their tribute by adding causeways in the sea near the shore, so that Pharos could no longer be considered an island, and therefore subject to Rhodian tribute: § 11 ends with the words (emended) *equorumque cum vehiculo ingressa riserat Rhodios, insularum non continentis portorium flagitantes.* §§ 12–14 contain a highly coloured account of the wonders of the city, and § 15 the account of the partial destruction of the city in the time of Aurelian: *Sed Alexandria ipsa non sensim (ut aliae urbes), sed inter initia prima aucta per spatiosos ambitus internisque seditionibus diu aspere fatigata, ad ultimum multis post annis, Aureliano imperium agente, civilibus iurgiis ad certamina interneciva prolapsis, dirutisque moenibus, amisit regionum maximam partem, quae Bruchion appellabatur, diuturnum praestantium hominum domicilium.* This is followed by a flowery and frequently totally anachronistic cultural history of the city—from the time of Anaxagoras onwards (§ 22). On this passage see provisionally *Ptol. Alex.* ii. 24 n. 47; cf. also my remarks in *BSAA* 45 (1993) (*Alexandrian Studies in memoriam Daoud Abdu Daoud*) 98 ff. For the probable presence of an element of the early *Romance* in Ammianus, see xxiii. 6. 8: *Deinde cum Dareus posteaque Xerxes, Graeciam elementorum usu mutato aggressi, cunctis paene copiis terra marique consumptis, vix ipsi tutum invenere discessum, ut bella praetereamus Alexandri, ac testamento nationem omnem in successoris unius iura translatum.* The reference to the *Will* hangs very loosely to the preceding clause, and the words *Alexandri ac* are an emendation (though surely an inevitable one) by Heraeus for the MSS *Alexandrina et* (G) and *Alexandrinae testamento* (V). For Ammianus' description of the eastern cities named Alexandria, see below, p. 142.

[38] Suda Θ152: Θεόδωρος, ποιητὴς ὃς ἔγραψε διάφορα δι' ἐπῶν, καὶ εἰς Κλεοπάτραν δι' ἐπῶν. Theodoros is otherwise unknown (*RE* (18) is largely about somebody else). The second δι' ἐπῶν is omitted by the abbreviated MS T = Vat. 881 (see Adler, i, p. x). Whatever the precise form of the poem it can hardly have been other than adulatory. Cf. above, n. 14.

tions. He it was who, in Jewish and Christian Alexandrian sources, on the basis of a tradition reaching back to the Septuagint, transported to Alexandria the bones of the venerable Jeremiah, the prophet of the time of Nebuchadnessor, who supposedly died in the Delta, and set them in a peribolos (like Alexander himself in the Sema, which had disappeared by this time), near a tetrapylon itself not erected until some centuries after the death of the Founder, to act as a talisman to protect the city against venomous snakes.[39] This story was current in the city at least until the eve of the Arab conquest, and links the figure of the Founder with the Patriarchal tradition that forms a prominent element in the early parts of the Alexandrian World-Chronicles, following chronologically upon the story of the $\Delta\iota\alpha\mu\epsilon\rho\iota\sigma\mu\grave{o}s$ $\Gamma\hat{\eta}s$ mentioned above. The total unhistoricity of such stray stories that emerge from time to time over the centuries very clearly indicates the total ignorance of the people of Alexandria regarding their own past; an ignorance abetted to a

---

[39] The legend exists in more than one version. The germ of it lies in the account of the migration of Jeremiah from Jerusalem to Egypt with the disaffected Jews, including the prophet Baruch, at the time of Nebuchadnessor, for which see the LXX text of Jeremiah, probably the Hesychian recension (see Pfeiffer, *Introd. to the Old Test.*, 486-7). The 'Oracles' of Jeremiah come after 25: 13 of the Greek version whereas in the Hebrew they occur in ch. 46 (the LXX text of Jeremiah is very different from the Hebrew, being about one-eighth shorter, and the contents presented in a different order; ch. 43 of the Hebrew, which recounts the final phase of Jeremiah's life, linking him with Egypt, corresponds to chs. 50-1 of the LXX). The Jews arrive in the Delta at a site called $T\alpha\phi\nu\alpha s$ (Tahpantes, Heb.), the Daphnai of the Greek mercenaries of Amasis, who must have been there only a few years later. Jehovah tells Jeremiah that the Jews shall not return to Judah, and that he is to take $\lambda\acute{\iota}\theta o\iota$ $\mu\acute{\epsilon}\gamma\alpha\lambda o\iota$ and hide them in the gate of the palace of Pharaoh (Necho)— $\kappa\alpha\tau\acute{\alpha}\kappa\rho\upsilon\psi o\nu$ $\alpha\mathring{\upsilon}\tauo\mathring{\upsilon}s$ $\mathring{\epsilon}\nu$ $\pi\rho o\theta\acute{\upsilon}\rho o\iota s$ $\mathring{\epsilon}\nu$ $\pi\acute{\upsilon}\lambda\eta\iota$ $\tau\hat{\eta}s$ $o\mathring{\iota}\kappa\acute{\iota}\alpha s$ $\Phi\alpha\rho\alpha\grave{\omega}$ $\mathring{\epsilon}\nu$ $T\alpha\phi\nu\alpha s$, and he is to tell the Jews who are with him that Jehovah has ordained that Nebuchadnessor shall set his throne on these stones, and thus confirm his rule. The prophesied Assyrian domination did not occur, but there is nothing to suggest that the Jews returned to Judah, nor is there any indication in the biblical Book of Jeremiah of what befell Jeremiah; we may suppose that he died in Egypt. The subsequent embellishment of the story is to be found in the *Life of Jeremiah* in the two versions of the *Vitae prophetarum* that pass under the name of Epiphanius, where the story is entirely Egyptianized (see Schermann, *Propheten und Apostellegenden*, Texte u. Untersuch. 31(3), 1909). Jeremiah was stoned to death in 'Daphnai' by the people ($\mathring{\upsilon}\pi\grave{o}$ $\tauo\hat{\upsilon}$ $\lambda\alpha o\hat{\upsilon}$), and he lies in a part of the dwelling of Pharaoh, because the Egyptians venerated him: he saved them from a plague of crocodiles and snakes, and the faithful worship at his tomb today. 'And we', the author continues, 'were told this by Antigonos and Ptolemy in their old age, that Alexander came to the tomb of Jeremias, and recognized the miracle that he performed, and transported his bones to Alexandria and enclosed them in a peribolos, and Alexandria was thus preserved from snakes and crocodiles.' There are further ramifications to this story which I cannot pursue here.

very considerable degree by (or perhaps largely the result of) the physical disappearance of most of the Ptolemaic and early Imperial city, and the superimposition upon its crumbling ruins of the early Byzantine city that the Persians and Arabs eventually conquered.[40] It is against a background of such misinformation, trivial literary production and legend, that we must consider the value of the lists of Alexandrias as we have now extracted them from the *Romance*, the *Excerpta* and the other texts under discussion.

If we start with the unexpected doxology that describes the cities as 'surviving in peace' we shall not be prejudiced in favour of the lists. And if we compare them with the foundations recorded by the historians and the geographers our inclination might well be to dismiss them without more ado as idle fantasies. However, before reaching any conclusion about this, we may clear our way by considering those cities named as Alexandrias by Stephanus, and in some instances by other sources, but which (with one exception, that of Alexandria Troas, which was certainly not founded by Alexander,[41] but was evidently absorbed into the Alexandrian tradition as having been so) do not appear in the α-tradition of the *Romance* or in the *Excerpta*.

First to be noticed is Alexandria by Issos, or Alexandria of Cilicia. This city was known by name to Strabo (in a non-Eratosthenic passage), though he did not claim it as an Alexander-foundation, and it is referred to as an Alexander-foundation in the periegesis of 'pseudo-Scymnus', of the late second century BC.[42] There is, then, no reason to doubt that a city so called was built, or an existing city rebuilt or renamed, at some time in the Hellenistic Age to commemorate the great battle fought near the Cilician Gates—hence it is also called Alexandria of Cilicia by Stephanus—and it had a long

---

[40] For a study of some (but only a few) of the complicated problems connected with the topography of Byzantine and early Muslim Alexandria I must refer the reader provisionally to my article in *BSAA* 45 (above, n. 37).

[41] On Alexandria Troas, first founded as Antigoneia after 310 BC and refounded by Lysimachus after the Battle of Ipsos and given the name of Alexandria by him, see Tscherikower, p. 16 no. 1; J. M. Cook, *Troad* (Oxford, 1973), 198 ff. The history of the city does not fall within the scope of the present study.

[42] GGM i. 235 ll. 923 ff.: στενότατος αὐχήν ἐστιν εἰς τὸν Ἰσσικὸν | κόλπον διήκων τήν τ᾽ Ἀλεξάνδρου πόλιν | τῶι Μακεδόνι κτισθεῖσαν· ἡμερῶν δ᾽ ὁδὸν | εἰς τὴν Κιλικίαν ἑπτὰ τῶν πασῶν ἔχει. The city is referred to by Herod. iii. 4. 3; cf. Diller, *Minor Greek Geographers* p. 174 (ex Peripl. Eux., l.962): μένει δὲ ἔτι νῦν τρόπαιον καὶ δεῖγμα τῆς νίκης ἐκείνης, πόλις ἐπὶ τοῦ λόφου Ἀλεξάνδρεια καλουμένη, ἄγαλμά τε χαλκοῦν οὗ τὴν προσηγορίαν ὁ τόπος φέρει. Cf. below, n. 47, for the reference in the roughly contemporary *Res Gestae Divi Saporis*.

history as the Iskandarūn/Iskandariȳa of the Arabs. However, ps.-
Scymnus apart, there is no record of Alexander having founded it
after the battle, and few who read the ancient narratives of his
campaign can doubt that Alexandria in Egypt was his first foundation. That he ordered the Cilician city to be built on the site of the
battle at a later date, as has been supposed, is unsupported by any
evidence, and it does not seem very likely that he would have
reverted to this task in the course of his later campaigning: where
possible he looked at the present and the future, forwards, not
backwards. Strabo's silence as to the founder of the city is itself a
strong argument against a connection with Alexander.[43]

Nevertheless, although Ἀλεξάνδρεια κατ' Ἰσσόν does not occur
in the A-text or in the *Excerpta*, it occurs in the Armenian
version, which normally reflects a knowledge of the α-tradition, as
'Alexandria Kattisson', and in the Greek *B*-tradition and its derivatives (see Table (15)).[44] Moreover, the *Excerpta* has an 'Alexandria
qui(!) cabiosum, which reappears in the *Paschal Chronicle* as
Ἀλεξάνδρεια ἡ Καβίωσα,[45] in Malalas as Ἀλεξάνδρεια ἡ Καμβύσου,

[43] The view that the city was a later foundation of Alexander was put forward
by Droysen, GE iii (2). 200 = FT ii. 663 and this was accepted 'as a guess' by Tarn,
Alex. ii. 238. The same doubts exist regarding Nikopolis of Syria, on the east side
of the Amanus range, *RE* (7); this is most probably a foundation of Seleucus
Nicator; cf. Jones, CERP 243-4, Grainger, *The Seleukid Cities of Syria* (Oxford, 1990),
35-6. Rochette emended the Ἀλεξ. τὴν καὶ (!) Σκυθίαν of the *Pasch. Chron.* to τὴν
κατὰ Κιλικίαν, but Σκυθίαν is in Ps. Call. and the *Excerpta* (see p. 33).

[44] For the Armenian version of the *Romance* which stands in a very close
relationship to the A-text (see below, p. 210 and stemma, p. 207) see the
translation with notes by A. M. Wolohojian, *The Romance of Alexander the Great by
Pseudo-Callisthenes translated from the Armenian version* (Columbia Univ. Press,
1969), which supersedes the Grecized version of R. Raabe, Ἱστορία Ἀλεξάνδρου: *die
armenische Übersetzung der sagenhaften Alexander Biographie auf ihre mutmassliche
Grundlage zurückgefuhrt* (Leipzig, 1896). For the texts of the *B*-tradition see the
details given by me in *Ptol. Alex.* ii. 944 n. 8.

[45] p. 321, in the list of Alexandrias. The last of the Alexandrias in *Chron.*
Ἀλεξάνδρεια ἡ Κάσος occurs in no other list; in this position the *Excerpta* has
Alexandria fortissima, itself unexplained, and from this doublet it might be possible to
reconstruct an Ἀλεξάνδρεια κατ' Ἰσσόν, but both lists have Alexandria Cabiosa which,
I argue above, represents Ἀλεξάνδρεια κατ' Ἰσσόν. The solution could possibly lie in
the *Alexandria fortissima* of the *Excerpta*, which was rendered into Greek at some
point as κρατίστη, which could perhaps have been corrupted into Κάσος. Tarn
pointed out, (*Alex.*, ii, p. 246), that the Γ tradition has Ἀλεξάνδρειαν τὴν Κράτιστον
(see the texts as given in Parthe, *Der griechische Alexanderroman RezensionΓ, Buch III*,
pp. 458-9), but though this must also be linked to the *Excerpta* entry in some way,
just as the Ἀ. ἐπὶ Μεσέ(ά)γγιστα of R and C of that tradition reflects the *qui in mesas
gyges* of the *Excerpta* (i.e. Ἀ. πρὸς Μασσαγέτας, of α (Arm)), the introduction of the
entry into the *B* and Γ traditions belongs to a later stage than the formation of the

Cambyses' own Alexandria,[46] and in George of Cyprus in the rationalized form Κάβισσος, as a city of the eparchy of Κιλικίας β.[47] While, on the one hand, there is no good reason why a corruption of the familiar κατ' Ἰσσόν should occur in the text of George, whose sources are documentary and not popular, there can be no doubt that the corruption takes the form that occurs in the *Excerpta*. It is noteworthy that while Ἀλεξάνδρεια ἡ κατὰ Ἰσσόν occurs in Ptolemy,[48] the corrupted form occurs in the *Antonine Itinerary* and in at least one later western *Itinerary*.[49] Stephanus, for his part, is the victim of his sources (unfortunately anonymous), for while his eighth Alexandria is τῆς Κιλικίας, s.v. Ἰσσός he has πόλις μεταξὺ Συρίας καὶ Κιλικίας, ἐν ᾗ Ἀλέξανδρος Δαρεῖον ἐνίκησεν, ἥ ἐκλήθη διὰ τοῦτο Νικόπολις. It appears that the two forms of the name, κατ' Ἰσσόν and Κάβισσος or Καβίωσα existed contemporaneously, for a reason unknown to us: textual corruption hardly seems a sufficient explanation. If we suppose that the α-tradition contained either form, it is hardly possible to decide whether it was Ἀλεξάνδρεια κατ'

α-tradition to which the Κάσος of *Chron.* belongs. Whatever the explanation of this unique item may be, nobody will wish to accept Κάσον as an uncontaminated reference to the small island off the east coast of Crete.

[46] ii. 113: καὶ ἔφυγεν ὁ κόμης τῆς ἀνατολῆς εἰς Ἀλεξάνδρειαν τὴν Καμβύσου. The view of Krumbacher, *BLG*, i. 333, 338, and others, that the coincidences between Ps. Call. and the *Chron. Pasch.* derive from the (lost) complete text of Malalas is perhaps unnecessary now that we can see how much *Romance* material was in circulation in Egypt from the Hellenistic age onwards, though Malalas remains in general a main source of the *Chron. Pasch.*

[47] I. 824-5, Gelzer, with his note, which gives a summary of the other evidence for the name. It may be noted that the city still bears the name of Alexandria in the *Res Gestae Div. Sap.* (SEG xx. 324), i. 15-16: Ἀλεξάνδριαν πόλιν σὺν τῇ περιχώρῳ and ibid. I. 27, Ἀλεξάνδριαν τὴν κατ' Ἰσσόν πόλιν σὺν τῷ περιχώρῳ. Maricq rightly pointed out, in his study of the document in E. Honigmann and A. Maricq, *Recherches sur les Res Gestae divi Saporis* (Bull. Acad. belge, fac. des lettres, xlvii(4) (1953)), 143 n. 1, that the city is mentioned twice because in the first list it is counted as a city of Syria and in the second as a city of Cilicia; cf. Rostovtzeff, *Berytus*, viii (1943), 30 and 40 n. 54. Alexandria ad Issum seems to be the only Alexandria (other than the Egyptian) to occur in the Conciliar Lists (Chalcedon): see Jones, *CERP* 540, Tab. xxix, Cilicia, 5.

[48] v. 15. 2: Ἀλεξάνδρεια ἡ κατὰ Ἰσσόν.

[49] See *Itin. Ant.* (*Itin. Rom.* i (1929)), 141. 3 (between 'Bais' and 'Pagris') *Alexandria*; *Itin. Burdig.* 580, 8: mansio *Alexandria Scabiosa.*, between 'Baias' and 'Pictanus', on borders of Cilicia and Syria, i.e. Iskanderūn. There seems to be no reason to connect these Alexandrias or the Greek tradition with the Καβησ(σ)ός mentioned by Steph. s.v. Καβασσός, πόλις ἐν Καππαδοκίαι, who refers to Hecataeus and Hellanicus (*FGrH* 1 F 69, 4 F 147) for a Thracian and/or a Cappadocian city ὑπερβάντι τὸν Θράκιον Αἷμον, and quotes *Il.* 13. 363 for the topic form Καβησ(σ)όθεν. Cf. *Etym. Gud.* 80 (Reitz.): Κάβησος, πόλις Θραικική, ἀπὸ Καβησοῦ τινος, and Meineke, Steph. ad. loc.; cf. also *FGrH* 616 F 37.

Ἰσσόν, rather than Ἀλεξάνδρεια Κάβισσος, ἡ καὶ Κάβισσος, or Καβίωσα. The verdict should probably be given in favour of the latter, as being present in the *Excerpta*. A major complication, however, is created by the fact that the early Seleucid foundation of Laodicea ad Libanum (Λαοδίκεια πρὸς Λιβάνωι) appears in Ptolemy as Σκαβίωσα Λαοδίκεια, and this demands that we look at the problem from a different perspective. The Latin word *scabiosus*, 'rough', or, of animals, 'mangy', is itself uncommon, and is not elsewhere applied to a city, let alone two, one an Alexandria and the other an early Seleucid foundation. We may feel justified in concluding that, the addition of the initial consonant notwithstanding, the two names are the same, and that one of the two items is falsely so named, and in view of the more substantial evidence for Alexandria ad Issum being so called, it seems more likely that at some point the Roman nomenclature was added by error in the gazetteers available to Ptolemy, who, in any case, occasionally uses Latin terms masquerading in Greek dress. I do not regard this as an instance of the deliberate appropriation of a Seleucid city as an Alexandria, a procedure which I show below (pp. 34 ff.) to be the leading feature of one of the early sources of the α-version of the *Romance*, but simply as an error in transmission, the history of which cannot be traced, though it would certainly not be impossible to maintain that there has been contamination between the two traditions.[50]

We may turn now to another missing Alexandria not present in the A-text or the *Excerpta*, which might seem to be a fit partner (according to the logic of such lists) for Ἀλεξάνδρεια κατ' Ἰσσόν, namely Ἀλεξάνδρεια ἐν Γρανίκωι. It has no claim to historicity, but has itself an unusual history. It found its way into the translated versions at a very early date, for it occurs in Julius Valerius as *Alexandria apud Granicum*, and probably also in the Armenian, in

---

[50] Ptol. v. 15. 20: Λαοδικηνῆς πόλεις. Σκαβίωσα Λαοδίκεια . . . Παράδεισος . . . Ἰάβρουδα: cf. Honigmann, *RE* Laodikeia (2) for the history of the site (cf. Walbank on Polyb. v. 45. 7); Tscherikower, 64, notes without comment the analogy with Alexandria Scabiosa. The city is named Λαυδίκεια τῆς Κοιλῆς Συρίας in *PSI* 311 of m. AD IV., a text which shows very clearly the confusion caused among correspondents by urban homonymity. The writer (at Oxyrhynchus) states emphatically that his letter is intended for the Bishop of Laodicea ad Mare, ll. 21 ff.: οὕτως γὰρ ἔχει καὶ ἡ ἐπιγραφή· ἐπὶ δὲ δύο εἰσὶν Λαυδικί[α]ι, μία τῆς Φρυγίας καὶ μία ἡ κᾳ[τ]ὰ Συρίαν, with further details of location. The Peutinger Table has *Laudicia scabiosa*: cf. Gelzer, on George of Cyprus, l. 986. For Latinisms in Greek dress in Ptolemy see below, p. 130 n. 49.

which 'Alexandria of Undranikos', should, it has been suggested, be understood as representing 'of Granicus'.[51] However, the name is also found outside the *Romance* tradition in a passage of Appian, uniquely, and manifestly in error, for Alexandria Troas, in his account of the Roman negotiations with Antiochus III in 190 BC, which is otherwise an almost verbatim paraphrase of the words of Polybius. There is no doubt that Appian has written Ἀλεξάνδρεια ἡ ἐπὶ Γρανίκωι by error for Alexandria Troas, but the error is not easy to explain in spite of the likelihood that there is a link between the historian's error and the appearance of the name in Julius' list of cities.[52] Two possibilities seem to exist. First, it might be suggested that 'On the Granicus' was an alternative name for Alexandria Troas. However, not only does a glance at the map show that this is improbable, but the fact that Alexandria Troas itself appears (wrongly) in virtually all versions of the *Romance* and the associated Alexandrian texts argues very strongly against the identification of the two toponyms. The alternative is to suppose that one of the two traditions, or authors, borrowed the name from the other. If we make that assumption there can, I think, be little doubt that the name existed (wrongly) in an early version of the *Romance*-list and had dropped out, like others, before Julius translated the list. Appian, who was born and brought up in Alexandria, knew of it, and in a characteristically confused way inserted the name in his text of the negotiations of 190 instead of Alexandria Troas. If so, he joins Plutarch as a writer outside the *Romance* tradition who was influenced by it. At the same time the suppositious city fills one of the lacunae in the A-list (cf. above, pp. 15-16).

A more complex problem is provided by Ἀλεξάνδρεια ἡ πρὸς Ξάνθωι (*sic?*). This is absent from A and the *Excerpta*, but is found in the Armenian version and in the Presbyter Leo, who provides a Latin text closer to the *B*-tradition, and also probably in Julius Valerius' version of the α-text, which has *Alexandria apud Sanctum* naturally to be understood as referring to Xanthos, though

---

[51] For Julius see iii. 60, in his list of Alexandrias: see table at end. For the Armenian version see Wolohojian, § 285, with note ad loc.

[52] Appian, *Syr.* 29, reports of Heracleides of Byzantion's offer on behalf of Antiochus ἐπὶ διαλύσεσι τοῦ πολέμου, Σμύρναν τε καὶ Ἀλεξάνδρειαν αὐτοῖς διδοὺς τὴν ἐπὶ Γρανίκωι καὶ Λάμψακον, κ.τ.λ. The actual role of Alexandria Troas is well known: see Polyb. xxi, 13, and cf. v. 78. 6, with Walbank's note ad loc. Appian makes another blunder in connection with the episode, identifying Scipio Aemilianus as the son of Africanus.

whether *Xanthum* should be read in the text is another matter. Alexander received the submission of Xanthos in the early days of his campaign, but we can be virtually certain that the city was never an Alexandria. On the other hand the city, with its great shrine of Leto, was the main Ptolemaic base on the southern shore of Asia Minor in the third century BC, before passing into Seleucid hands at the beginning of the second century BC, and recent excavations have emphasized the Ptolemaic grip on the city.[53] It is possible that in the third century the city might have been included in a list of invented Alexandrias, in the same way as those invented for Crete and Cyrenaica, to be discussed below, and for that reason we should keep Xanthos-Alexandria in mind as having possibly figured in the original list of Alexandrias and as a possible candidate for one of the missing cities in the A-text and the *Excerpta*. It may perhaps also be suggested that the rather enigmatic dedication stated to have been made by Alexander at Xanthos, found in the French excavations there, which can hardly be the original text but is nevertheless of early Hellenistic date, may reflect the Alexandrian literary tradition under discussion.[54]

[53] Several documents of Xanthos are dated by the Ptolemaic regnal year, and the local eponymous priest of the Ptolemies. The earliest Ptolemaic text is *BMI* 262, of 256 BC, the prescript of which is dated by the 29th year of Philadelphus. A letter of Euergetes I to the city, *SEG* xxxvi. 1218, of 243 BC, is concerned with a visit to Alexandria of Xanthian theoroi in connection with the Ptolemaieia, and the long document published by Bousquet, *REG* 101 (1988), 10 ff. (*SEG* xxxviii. 1476), containing the remarkable story of the embassy of the Kytenians of Doris to Xanthos in pursuit of financial help in repairing their remote city (destroyed in 228 BC), is dated by the regnal year of Ptolemy IV and his son Epiphanes to 206 BC; cf. further below, n. 85. The dedication of Antiochus III, *OGIS* 746 + Herrmann, *Anadolu*, 9 (1965), 119-21, in which he claims the same συγγένεια as the Ptolemies had a few years earlier, dates to 197 BC.

[54] For this text see *SEG* xxx. 1533: Ἀλέξανδρος Βασιλεὺς ἀ[νέθηκε]. For the curious lettering and style of inscribing see Le Roy, *Actes du Coll. sur la Lycie antique* (Bibl. Inst. fr. Istambul, 27, 1980), 51 ff., and pl. xi. This does not appear to be a dedication of the type known for the Imperial period (e.g. from Bargylia, *I. Iasos* 620). It is perhaps noteworthy that Alexander does not figure in the omnium gatherum of Xanthian and Kytenian history in *SEG* xxxviii. 1476 (see previous n.). That would have been a splendid opportunity for stressing the link with the Conqueror, and even mentioning a metonomasy, had one occurred. In Julius *Xanthum* is now conjectured by Calderan ap. Rosellini (see below p. 210 n. 9). Leo calls the city *Alexandria, quae dicitur Iprosxanthon*, where the πρός suggests a reference to a region or a river, rather than to a city (cf. in text, above). It corresponds, in any case, to the formal style used of dynastic names of cities. The long text concerning relations between Nagidos and Arsinoe in Cilicia, the historical background of which, as recorded in the text, is the foundation of the latter by the Ptolemaic statesman Aetos in honour of Arsinoe Philadelphos, published in *ZPE*, 77, 1989,

A group of cities that occurs in Stephanus, but none of which appears in the *Romance* tradition (perhaps one of them survives in the *Excerpta*), presents separate and individual problems, for there is no means of control by reference to a parallel tradition, as in the items that we have just examined. First to be noticed are two Alexandrias in Europe.

1. Alexandria in Macedonia or Thrace, Stephanus' third, τρίτη Θράικης πρὸς τῆι Μακεδονίαι, ἣν ἔκτισε πρὸ τῆς μεγάλης Ἀλεξανδρείας, ἑπτακαίδεκα ὢν ἐτῶν. The circumstantiality of the date concerning this Macedonian Alexandria, founded when Alexander was 17 years old, does not conceal the similarity in pattern between this foundation and the refoundation of Krenides as Philippoi in 358 BC, two years before Alexander's birth. It is true that Philip was active in Greece in 342, the supposed year of the foundation, and it might be imagined that his son took advantage of his absence to assert his temporary authority, or to give expression to some plan that he had conceived; but there is no evidence to support the conjecture, and, unless it is a distorted reflection of the foundation of Philippoi, the name is likely to be a fabrication. As with almost all the other entries in this list, Stephanus quotes no source for his information. It is to be noted, however, that Plutarch speaks of a city named Alexandropolis in Thrace (see below, pp. 29-30), which Alexander is said to have founded at virtually the same age (16), and there may be some connection between the two. Alexandropolis itself, however, as we shall see (p. 29), is not above suspicion.

2. The second European city is Stephanus' sixteenth, ἑκκαιδεκάτη κατὰ τὸν Μέλανα κόλπον, sandwiched between an Alexandria among the Arachotoi and one 'in Sogdiana, by the Parapamisadai'; it is commonly regarded as 'European' because the only 'Black Gulf' known is that by the Thracian Chersonese. This led Meineke to suppose that the city was identical with the previous item, the Thraco-Macedonian city. That does not increase the plausibility of either entry, but, if correct, it reduces the number of redundant items by one. The same result can be achieved by identifying it with the city of Alexandropolis in Thrace,

pp. 55 ff. (*SEG* xxxix, 1426), emphasizes the close control exercised by Alexandria over her Cilician 'colonies' in the third century. See also the epigram preserved by Steph. s.v. Ἀγρίαι referring to Neoptolemos a third-century commander in the area, Page, *FGE* no. cxli, whose interpretation is corrected by L. Robert, *OMS* vii. 535 ff.

described by Plutarch. This identification is not impossible, though its Asiatic neighbours in Stephanus' list do not support it. The suggestion that it corresponds to Alexandria-Rambakia, in the Makrān, known to the historians but not listed by Stephanus or the *Romance*, cannot be right, for reasons explained in Chapter V.[55]

Three other Alexandrias, one located in Cyprus, one in Cyrenaica and one in Caria, may be considered next.

3. Alexandria in Cyprus, Stephanus' ninth, ἐνάτη ἐν Κύπρωι, has provoked considerable discussion. Droysen claimed to identify it with a Cypriot location known from medieval sources, but the problem has to be re-examined from a different standpoint. The final discussion of the context in which it is to be set is left to later, but it is to be stressed here that Alexandria in Cyprus belongs to the α-tradition of the *Romance*—though it does not occur in *A*, it occurs both in the *Excerpta* and in the *Paschal Chronicle*, thus deriving from the earliest stratum of the *Romance*,[56] as well as in Stephanus.

4. Stephanus also informs us, in an indirect manner, of the possible existence of an Alexandria in Cyrenaica, but he does not include it in his list, nor is it mentioned by the A-text of the *Romance*, though it occurs in the *Excerpta* which gives as its first Alexandria, *qui in Pentapolim*. Stephanus quotes Favorinus ἐν τῶι Περὶ Κυρηναϊκῆς πόλεως, which probably formed part of his Παντοδαπὴ Ἱστορία, for the otherwise unattested Alexandrian

---

[55] Bourguet, on *FD* iii(1). 497, suggested that the [*M*]ελανῖται mentioned in that geographical list (late 4th/early 3rd cent. BC), line 10, might be connected with the Black Gulf, but he pointed out that the ethnic stands in the text surrounded by the coastal islands Lesbos, Rhodes, Kos, *et al.* See further below, p. 166, with n. 116.

[56] Stephanus alone has the regular form ἐν Κύπρωι. The entry is present in the *Romance* only in the *B* and *Γ* traditions where it appears as τὴν ἐπὶ Κύπριδος (or, Κρήπιδος: see L. Bergson, *Der griechische Alexanderroman Rezension β*, p. 191); Pasch. Chron., p. 321, has Ἀ. ἡ περὶ Κύπριδος ποταμόν, while the *Excerpta* has *Alexandriam qui super Cypridum fluvium*, from which the former derives. I suggest below, pp. 43–4, that the fictitious Cypriot Alexandria must have a Ptolemaic origin, and is therefore one of the items missing from the list in the A-text. Tarn, *Alex.* ii. 241, is both dismissive and involved in his explanation of this item: '(9) is simple. The Romance list shows that it has nothing to do with Cyprus; it is the Alexandria ἐπὶ Κύπριδος ποταμοῦ of version *Γ*', which is merely Alexandria at the mouth of the Tigris, Τίγριδος having been corrupted into Κύπριδος'; cf. p. 243. Droysen, *GE* iii. 243 (FT ii. 693), maintained that he had found evidence (in T. Porcacchi, *Isole più famose del Mondo* (Venice, 1576), 145, with map; *non vidi*) of a medieval Alexandria located at the west end of the island, which he thought might be the survival of a city so named by Pasicrates of Soloi in honour of Alexander. He found support for this in the supposed metonomasy of Alinda by Ada in honour of Alexander: see below, p. 28.

ethnic form Ἀλεξανδρειώτης, and the city must have been mentioned along with the ethnic in Favorinus, whose work was in any
case known to the α-tradition of the *Romance*, since reference is
made to it both by Julius Valerius and by the Armenian version.[57]
The two false Alexandrias in Cyprus and Cyrenaica are, then,
associated both in the *Romance* tradition and in Stephanus. We
shall return to this point.

5. Alexandria in Caria on Mt. Latmos is treated more substan-
tially by Stephanus. He records that it contained a sanctuary of
Adonis, in which there was a statue of Aphrodite by Praxiteles:
δεκάτη πρὸς τῶι Λάτμωι τῆς Καρίας, ἐν ἧι Ἀδώνιον ἦν ἔχον
Πραξιτέλους Ἀφροδίτην. None of the Alexander-historians nor the
geographers refers to any foundation, or refoundation, by Alexander
during his campaign in Caria, and it was suggested by Droysen
that the city should be identified with Alinda, the capital which
Alexander bestowed on Ada, the last of the Hekatomnids, in place
of Halicarnassus; according to Droysen Ada called Alinda
Alexandria out of gratitude to Alexander. This explanation has
been accepted by Robert and others, and may be true, though
independent evidence for it is entirely lacking. Alinda and the
Alindeis were known by their common name throughout the
Hellenistic age, as were the inhabitants of nearby Heracleia, on
Latmos, an alternative candidate for the identification. We shall
have occasion in due course to suggest that in fact the city may be
Alabanda.[58]

---

[57] See Favorinus fr. 54 Barigazzi (Florence, 1966). Meineke saw that the
quotation probably came from the *Omnigena Historia*. Barigazzi emended τῶι περὶ
Κυρηναϊκῆς πόλεως to ⟨πρώ⟩τωι περὶ παντοδαπῆς ὕλης; cf. his discussion of earlier
emendations retaining Κυρηναϊκῆς (so also Jacoby, *FGrH*, IIIB, p. 427; cf. also
Mensching, *Favorin von Arelate*, i (Berlin, 1963), p. 34). Barigazzi's emendation is a
far cry from the text, which is not in need of emendation, at least as far as the reference to Cyrenaica is concerned.

[58] For Droysen's suggestion see *GE* iii p. 119 (FT ii. 662). He has been followed
by L. Robert in various passages of his writings on the area: see most recently
J. and L. Robert, *Amyzon*, i. 6, where other references are given; Hornblower,
Mausolus, 314 n. 156. Various aspects of the evidence need clarification. (1) The
coin which Droysen adduced in favour of the identification of Alinda with
Alexandria because it showed a figure of Venus Pudica, which would correspond to
the statue assigned to Praxiteles, is, as I had suspected, and as Dr C. Howgego has
kindly confirmed for me, a coin not of Alinda, but of Cnidus (*BMC, Caria*, 97, 100
(time of Caracalla and Plautilla)). The coin is not referred to by Robert. (2) The
identification with Heracleia on Latmos (on the south face of the mountain, while
Alinda is on the north side) is stronger, in my view, than Hornblower, loc. cit.,
allows. It is obvious that Alexander's close ancestral link with Heracles might

Before passing to the eastern Alexandrias we may note the traditions regarding the cities called Alexandro(u)polis, of which there are either three or four. They do not occur in the lists of Alexandrias, and indeed they are not known to the Alexandrian tradition as we have recreated it in this chapter. The first is the city mentioned by Plutarch as having been founded by Alexander in Thrace, and which Tarn suggested might lie behind Stephanus' third Alexandria, as discussed at (1) above.[59] Two others are recorded by Isidore of Charax as situated in Sakastane and Arachosia respectively, a fourth is given by Pliny as lying in the region of Nysa: *Arsace, regio Nisiaea, Parthyenes nobilis, ubi Alexandropolis a conditore*, and a fifth at Hekatompylos, described by him as *ipsius vero Parthiae caput*,[60] perhaps to be identified with the 'Alexandria oppidum' mentioned in the fourth century AD by Julius Honorius.[61] These oriental Alexandropolises raise insoluble problems. We shall see below (pp. 91–2) that the text of Isidore in the passage where he refers to the two cities is very confused and has to be emended, while the cities given by Pliny and Honorius seem quite unreal; there is no suggestion in any Greek source, geographical or historical, of a city founded by Alexander after his passage through the Caspian Gates, while the long and mono- tonous list of *oppida* in Honorius is so full of geographical non- sense that we may jettison it without qualms. Thus the only

prompt such a change of name of, or by, the city, but there is no evidence for any metonomasy, except briefly that into Pleistarcheia at the end of the 4th cent. (see Steph. s.v. Πλειστάρχεια, πόλις Καρίας ἥτις καὶ πρότερον καὶ ὕστερον Ἡράκλεια ὠνομάσθη). The entry in Stephanus gives Πλεισταρχείτης, but no documentary example of the ethnic survives. Tscherikower, 28–9, raised the possibility of Alexandria being a metonomasy of Heracleia, while Tarn, *Alex.* ii. 242, thought that Λάτμωι was probably a corruption of 'some word now irrecoverable'. (3) The ethnic of Alinda, Ἀλινδεύς, is not uncommon: see the decree of Amyzon, *Amyzon*, no. 14, of *c.*202 BC, in honour of the Seleucid governor of Alinda, Chionis, and the Rhodian tombstone, *NS* 144, probably of the 2nd cent. BC. There are numerous Ἀλινδεῖς at Iasos after 166: see *I.Iasos*, 174, 187–8, 192.

[59] See Tarn, *Alex.* ii. 248–9. This may be correct, for the reasons stated above, p. 26.

[60] *NH* vi. 113, and ibid. 44.

[61] A6 (p. 26, Riese): *Carrha oppidum, Alexandria oppidum, Nisibi oppidum*. For the *Cosmographia* of Julius Honorius see Riese, *Geogr. Lat. Minores* (Heilbronn, 1878; repr. Olms, 1964), pp. 21 ff., pp. xviii–xxvi, an excellent account of the various versions of the work; see also *RE* s.v. *Iulius* (277). His work seems to have been given to the world by a pupil, probably early in the 6th cent. Quite apart from the total ignorance it displays, its date deprives it of any independent value, since it is simply based on maps of an earlier date, the entries of which seem to have been copied out in a totally uncomprehending way.

Alexandropolis that carries some credibility remains that of Plutarch, which, as we have seen, may be the third Alexandria of Stephanus, 'in Thrace, towards Macedonia'.

To return to the Alexandrias, there remain those that occur for the most part in the α-version of the *Romance* and in the Alexandrian annals, represented by the *Excerpta* and also, in two cases, in the associated Iranian tradition. Almost all these cities are located east of the Euphrates, in Iranian, 'Scythian' or 'Indian' territory. Those in Indian territory contain confusions and duplications, but, these apart, comparison of the list with Stephanus' own list of Antiochs, indicates that they are probably politically motivated metonomasies of authentic early Seleucid foundations. That they are not derived from a current geographical tradition is demonstrated by the striking fact that virtually none of them is listed by Ptolemy, whose work, and that of Marinus, is undoubtedly earlier than the α-text of the *Romance*. Except for his own city in Egypt, Ptolemy knows only five Alexandrias and they coincide largely with those in the historical and geographical tradition: one, known only to him, Alexandria in Oxiana, which has been identified with the excavated site of Aï Khanūm, the Achaemenid and Hellenistic city at the junction of the Kokcha and Oxus rivers, on the south bank of the latter;[62] Alexandria in Arachosia;[63] Alexandria in Carmania (also attested by Pliny), which his co-ordinates place somewhere north-east of Hormµz;[64] Alexandria in Aria;[65] and Alexandria in Sogdiana or Alexandria Eschate.[66] On the other hand, by contrast with this only slight congruence with the Alexandrias of the *Romance*, Ptolemy knows of six Antiocheias and five Seleukeias. The contrast between the list in the *Romance* and the text of Ptolemy is a confirmation that current Imperial gazetteers knew only very few Alexandrias.

Let us now look more closely at the Alexandrias of the eastern world. They are solidly represented in the α-tradition of the *Romance*, including the oriental versions, and are all in the list in

[62] See below, pp. 154–6.

[63] See below, pp. 132–40.

[64] vi. 8. 13: πόλεις δὲ καὶ κῶμαι μεσόγειοι λέγονται τῆς Καρμανίας αἵδε· . . . §14, Ἀλεξάνδρεια . . .; cf. below, p. 167 n. 117.

[65] vi. 17. 6: Ἀλεξάνδρεια ἐν Ἀρείοις; cf. viii. 25. 5, computation of the longest day by comparison with Alexandria in Egypt. Cf. below, pp. 109–15.

[66] vi. 12. 6: μεταξὺ δὲ καὶ ἀνωτέρω τῶν ποταμῶν· Τρυβάκτρα . . . Ἀλεξάνδρεια Ὠξειανή . . . Ἰνδικομορδάνα . . . Δρέψα μητρόπολις . . . Ἀλεξάνδρεια Ἐσχάτη. Cf. below, pp. 151–6.

the *Excerpta*. Each of them corresponds to a known early Seleucid foundation, in regions where no historian or geographer attributes a foundation to Alexander. We may note, to begin with, one intruder, Ἀλεξάνδρεια ἐν Μαργιανῆι, which only occurs as an Alexander-foundation in the weakest part of the geographical tradition, Pliny, unsupported by other independent authority.[67] It was the Seleucid foundation (even though doubt surrounded its precise origin), Antiocheia in Margiane, the predecessor of Merv, the centre of Islamic culture before the Mongol destruction, which lies in the great oasis south of the Khorasmian desert. (The smaller Merv, nearer Herāt, on the Murghāb river, before its junction with the Hari-rūd, Merv-i-Rūd, though regularly mentioned by the early Arab Itineraries, is not recorded in classical sources.)

We may turn now to the Alexandrian lists (compare Table of Alexandrias at end), starting with (2) Ἀλεξάνδρεια πρὸς Πέρσας, which corresponds to Ἀντιόχεια τῆς Περσίδος, already in existence before the end of the third century BC; its location is unknown, but it has been placed at, or close to, Bushire.[68] (3) Ἀλεξάνδρεια ἐπὶ

[67] Plin. vi. 47: *et ipsa contra Parthiae tractum sita, in qua Alexander Alexandriam condiderat. qua diruta a barbaris Antiochus Seleuci filius eodem loco restituit Syrianam interfluente Margo qui conrivatur in Zothale; maluerat illam Antiochiam appellari.* I discuss this complex problem further below, pp. 116–7, as it concerns Alexander, but I may note one point that concerns the Seleucid foundation. Pliny's statement that the city was so named by Antiochus I is generally accepted, but it was rejected by Honigmann, *RE*, s.v. Seleukeia (10), col. 2560, in favour of the tradition preserved by Martianus Capella (vi. 691) and Solinus (48. 3), according to which the city was called Seleukeia. Capella, who otherwise follows Pliny vi. 28, at this point says: *regionis praedictae* [i.e. *Margiane*] *amoenitatem Alexander Magnus delegerat et ibi primo nominis sui condiderat civitatem. quae excisa est et ab Antiocho Seleuci filio reparata cum nomine patris eiusdem: circuitus habet stadia septuaginta quinque.* (692) *Inde Oxus amnis, qui circa Bactram cum eius nominis oppido fluvioque ultra Panda, oppidum Sogdianorum, ubi Alexander tertiam Alexandriam condidit ad contestandam itineris prolixitatem.* Solinus has *regionis huius amoenitatem Alexander Magnus usque adeo miratus est ut ibi primum Alexandriam condideret: quam mox barbaris excisam Antiochus Seleuci filius reformavit et de nuncupatione domus suae dixit Seleuciam: cuius urbis circuitus diffunditur in stadia septuaginta quinque. In hanc Orodes Romanos captos Crassiana clade deduxit.* The question whether the city should be called Antiocheia or Seleukeia cannot be resolved in the absence of independent attestation from non-literary sources: see below, p. 116, n. 24.

[68] For Antiocheia τῆς Περσίδος see *OGIS* 231 (Welles, *Roy. Corr.* 31; *I. von Magn.* 18): colonists from Magnesia, συμμείξαντες ἐν Ἀντιοχείαι τῆς Περσίδος (ll. 9–10); ib. 233 (*I. von Magn.* 61), [Π]αρὰ Ἀντιοχέων τῶν Π[ερσικῶι] (?τῶν ⟨τῆς⟩ Π[ερσίδος]); cf. Dittenberger's note 1 to no. 233; both inscriptions belong to the later 3rd cent. For the possible location at Bushire, or inland from there, see Bickerman in *La Persia e il mondo greco-romano* (*Accad. Linc.*, Quad. 76, 1966), 109; cf. S. M. Sherwin-White, *Chiron*, 15 (1985), 9 n. 18; J.-F. Salles in *Hellenism and the East* (ed. A. Kuhrt and

The Alexandrian Lists

τοῦ Τίγριδος ποταμοῦ, corresponds to Seleucus' eastern capital, Σελεύκεια τῆς Τίγριδος, the ruins of which were still standing at the time of the Arab conquest, and which, as a result of excavations carried out over many years, is the best-known of the eastern foundations of the Seleucids, rivalled only by the very different (and anonymous) Aï Khanūm on the Oxus;[69] (4) Ἀλεξάνδρεια ἐπὶ Βαβυλῶνος, is too vague to be identified, but there was at least one other Seleukeia in existence in Babylonia in the third century, in Elymaia, known from the same list of associated Seleucid cities that subscribed in 207 BC to the request of Magnesia on the Maeander for recognition of her great festival of Artemis Leukophryene. The city in Elymaia was called Σελεύκεια ἡ πρὸς τῶι Ἡδυφῶντι, after the tributary of the Tigris on which it lay, at a now unknown location.

S. Sherwin-White, London, 1987), 92 n. 24. P. Bernard, *JS* (1990), 46 ff. places Antioch in Persis on the Bushire peninsula, close to Rishahr, on the basis of the localization of the capital of the Kingdom of T'iao Che, mentioned in the *Han-Shu* (for this work see below, p. 126 n. 43), representing the Chinese form of Taoke, the Persian royal palace mentioned by Arr./Nearch., *Ind.* 39. 3: ἐκ Μεσαμβρίης δὲ ὁρμηθέντες καὶ διεκπλώσαντες σταδίους μάλιστα ἐς διακοσίους ἐς Τακόην ὁρμίζονται ἐπὶ ποταμῶι Γρανίδι. καὶ ἀπὸ τούτου ἐς τὸ ἄνω Περσῶν βασίλεια ἦν, ἀπέχοντα τοῦ ποταμοῦ τῶν ἐκβολέων σταδίους ἐς διακοσίους. Cf. Str. 728: ἦν δὲ καὶ ἄλλα βασίλεια τὰ ἐν Γάβαις ἐν τοῖς ἀνωτέρω που μέρεσι τῆς Περσίδος καὶ τὰ ἐν τῆι παραλίαι τὰ κατὰ τὴν Ταόκην λεγομένην; cf. Bernard, 46 n. 63; cf. Hulsewé and Loewe, (op. cit. below, p. 126, n. 43), n. 255. *OGIS* 233, the lengthy civic decree of Antiocheia, is taken by Dr Sherwin-White and Dr. Kuhrt in their new book, *From Samarkand to Sardis* (London, 1993), 162 ff., as an example of Seleucid policy of civic encouragement.

[69] The material relating to Seleukeia is extensive, and only a few items can be given here. Apart from the literary evidence, of which the description by Strabo 750 is the most valuable account, inhabitants of the city occur frequently in inscriptions from the Aegean and Asia Minor. See esp. *OGIS* 233, ll. 100–2, ὁμο[ί]ως δὲ ἔδοξε καὶ Σελευκεῦσιν τοῖς πρὸς Τίγρει; Klee, *Gymn. Agone*, p. 16, ΠΣ, 78 (182–178 BC), Λεωδάμας Ἀντιγόνου Σελευκ[εὺς ἀ]πὸ Τίγριο[ς], a κιθαριστάς, *ΑΔ*, 26 (1971), *Μελ.*, pp. 34–40, an agonistic inscription from Lebadea of the 2nd/1st cent. BC, in which the victors include two Σελευκεῖς ἀπὸ Τίγρεως. Several Seleukeians occur at Delos (see *EAD* xxx. 292 and *ID* 2429 and 2445), and from Rhodes we may note Θεμιστοκλῆς Σελευκεὺς ἀπὸ Τίγριος (*Suppl. rod.* 63. 18; 2nd cent. BC). For its survival in the 6th cent. AD see Procop. ii. 28. 4: οὗ (ἐν Ἀσσυρίοις) δὴ πολίσματα δύο Σελεύκειά τε καὶ Κτησιφῶν ἐστί, Μακεδόνων αὐτὰ δειμαμένων οἳ μετὰ τὸν Φιλίππου Ἀλέξανδρον Περσῶν τε ἦρξαν καὶ τῶν ταύτηι ἐθνῶν. For the University of Michigan's excavations, which were restricted in scope, see, apart from the specialized volumes on coins, terracottas, etc., C. Hopkins, *Topography and Architecture of Seleucia on Tigris* (Ann Arbor, 1972), comprising (pt. II, 149 ff.) McDowell's *History of Seleucia from Classical Sources* (which ends with the capture of the city in 198/9 by Septimius Severus). For later Italian work on the site see the bibliography by S. M. Sherwin-White in *ZPE* 47 (1982), 51 n. 4. For older studies see the characteristically thorough articles of Honigmann in *RE*, Seleukeia (1) and s.v. Ktesiphon. For Aï Khanūm, the identification of which has generated a bibliography of its own, see below, pp. 154–6.

Strabo describes it as a great city.[70] (5), Ἀλεξάνδρεια ἐν Σούσοις probably represents Σελεύκεια ἡ πρὸς Εὐλαίωι, Achaemenian Susa, one of the great centres of Seleucid power east of the Tigris, well documented from the third century BC to the Sassanian period.[71] In a different region (6) Ἀλεξάνδρεια ἐν Σκύθαις, common to the same traditions (see Table), corresponds to Stephanus' tenth Antioch, ἐν Σκυθίαι, a foundation which was perhaps the work of the Seleucid commander Demodamas, who was in the region beyond the Jaxartes between 290 and 280 BC.[72] (7) Ἀλεξάνδρεια τῆς Μεσοποταμίας, which is one of the items missing from A and the *Excerpta*, and which occurs only in the Armenian version of the α-tradition, corresponds to Stephanus' third Antioch, Μεσοποταμίας, Μυγδονία καλουμένη, ἥτις πρὸς τῶν ἐπιχωρίων Νάσιβις καλεῖται . . . ἥτις [καὶ] Νέσιβις λέγεται καὶ Νίσιβις.[73] Finally, to revert to an earlier item, (8), Ἀλεξάνδρεια ἡ πρὸς Λάτμωι, is probably Alabanda-Antiocheia, which Stephanus does not quote under Antiocheia, though he gives the metonomasy of Alabanda under its own entry:

[70] Strab. 744: ᾑρέθη δὲ καὶ πρὸς τῶι Ἡδυφῶντι ποταμῶι Σελεύκεια, μεγάλη πόλις· Σολόκη δὲ ἐκαλεῖτο πρότερον. For the subscription see again *I. von Magn.* 61. 105 (*OGIS* 233), with the reading in *SEG* iv. 504: Σελευκεῦσιν τοῖς πρὸς τῆι Ἐρυθρᾶι θαλάσσηι, Σελευκεῦσιν τοῖς πρὸς τῶι Εὐλαίωι, Σ[ε]λευκ[εῦσι]ν τ[οῖς] π[ρὸ]ς τῶ[ι Ἡδυφῶντι], due to Haussoullier.

[71] See in the first place *OGIS* 233, l. 106, quoted in the previous note. Greek inscriptions found on the site, published by Cumont, are reproduced in *SEG* vii. 1–34; none is earlier than Antiochus III and most belong to the Parthian period. Robert restored the ethnic in manumissions from Susa in *Gnomon*, 1963, 75–6. Out of the abundant material relating to the site I may mention especially G. Le Rider's excellent work, *Suse sous les Séleucides et Parthes* (Mém. Miss. franç. en Iran, 38, Paris, 1965), *passim*, and the brief but lively sketch by Tarn, *GBI* 27–31; cf. also Ghirshman, *Parthes et Sassanides* (Paris, 1962), 102 ff. Ps.-Sallust, *Epist. Mithr.* 19, says, *Tu [Arsace] vero, cui Seleucea, maxima urbium, regnumque Persidis inclutis divitiis est, quid ab illis nisi dolum in praesens et postea bellum expectas?*

[72] See Plin. vi. 49: *transcendit eum amnem* [sc. the Jaxartes] *Demodamas, Seleuci et Antiochi regum dux, quem maxime sequimur in his, arasque Apolloni Didymaeo statuit* (*FGrH* 428 T3). Cf. Tscherikower, 106; Tarn, *GBI* 83–4 (who suggests that 'conceivably it was only Alexandria-Eschate refounded': see below, pp. 151 ff.). Demodamas appears as the proposer of the Milesian decree, *I.Did.* 479 (*OGIS* 23) in honour of the future Antiochus I, for his σπουδή towards the Temple of Apollo Didymaeus; cf. Haussoullier, *Milet*, 34 ff., for the identification. Note that Pliny speaks only of *arae*.

[73] For Antiocheia Mygdoniae = Nisibis see Polyb. v. 51: (Ἀντίοχος) διανύσας εἰς Ἀντιόχειαν τὴν ἐν Μυγδονίαι περὶ τροπὰς χειμερινὰς ἐπέμεινε. It occurs in inscriptions of the Imperial period, e.g. *IG* xiv. 1374; *FD* iii(1), 199, in honour of M. Aelius Magnus, a native of Nisibis, known also from Eunap. *VP* 497. Amm. Marc. xxv. 81, describes it as the key to Mesopotamia: *constabat orbem Eoum in ditionem potuisse transire Persidis nisi haec civitas habili situ et magnitudine moenium restituisset.*

πόλις Καρίας, ἥ ποτε Ἀντιόχεια.[74] The relevance of the metonomasy Alabanda-Antiocheia in the present context is discussed further below.[75] Ἀντιόχεια Καρίας ἥ τις καὶ Πυθόπολις ἐκαλεῖτο, about which Stephanus quotes a confusing aetiological story to explain the existence of a Laodikeia, a Nysa and an Antiocheia in Caria, seems to have been intended to represent Nysa, which, however, though under Seleucid control, never bore an eponymous name; but the whole aetiology of the story is full of errors and no explanation is satisfactory: the city does not occur in Ptolemy's list of Carian cities in the province of Asia, in which Nysa, Tralles and Alabanda all occur, and Antiocheia of Caria (which cannot be Alabanda, which appears *proprio nomine* alongside it), occurs independently in the Conciliar list of Nikaia I, while Nysa itself appears at Ephesus and Chalcedon.[76]

We cannot expect to explain all the 'false' Alexandrias, if we may now so designate them, as, in some sense, deliberate metonomasies of Seleucid foundations, but nevertheless the coincidence of

[74] The rest of the long entry has no reference to the metonomasy, but the ποτε is worthy of note.

[75] p. 42, with n. 82.

[76] Ἀντιόχεια τῆς Καρίας is Stephanus' eleventh: ἑνδεκάτη Καρίας ἥτις καὶ Πυθόπολις ἐκαλεῖτο· Ἀντιόχωι γὰρ τῶι Σελεύκου τρεῖς γυναῖκες ἐπέστησαν ὄναρ, κτίσαι πόλιν ἐν Καρίαι ἑκάστη λέγουσα· ὁ δὲ ὑπολαβὼν τὴν μητέρα καὶ τὴν γυναῖκα καὶ τὴν ἀδελφήν, κτίζει [τρεῖς πόλεις,] ἀπὸ μὲν τῆς ἀδελφῆς Λαοδίκης Λαοδίκειαν, ἀπὸ δὲ τῆς γυναικὸς Νύσης Νύσαν, ἀπὸ δὲ τῆς μητρὸς Ἀντιοχίδος Ἀντιόχειαν. Ἀντιοχὶς οὖν ὄνομα καὶ τῆς μητρὸς καὶ ἐθνικὸν τῆς πόλεως καὶ φυλῆς ὄνομα. Meineke commented, 'Haec Arriani esse, videntur; leguntur item paucis mutatis apud Eustathium ad Dion. Per. 918', but that is not the case, for Eustathius, who quotes Arrian profusely in his commentary, in this particular item quotes οἱ παλαιοί as his source. If the metonomasy—or even the city—is historical, it probably resulted from a local Nysaean tradition, for s.v. Πυθόπολις Stephanus has Πυθόπολις, Καρίας πόλις, ἡ μετὰ ταῦτα κληθεῖσα Νύσα (though under Νύσα he does not mention Pythopolis), with no reference to another metonomasy. The tribe-names Ἀντιοχίς and Σελευκίς attested at the time of Augustus as part of a double titulature (Ἀγριππηῒς Ἀντιοχίς, Γερμανὶς Σελευκίς: see Ruge, RE, s.v. Nysa (10) col. 1637), probably gave rise to this. These, however, naturally do not necessarily indicate royal eponymity for the city; cf. Hiller von Gaertringen in W. von Diest, Nysa ad Maeandrum (JDAI, Ergheft, 10 (1913)), 66 ff. For Seleucid control, a different matter, see Welles, RC 64 (after Antiochus III). At the period when we might expect to find Nysa called Antiocheia, if it ever had been, it was in fact still called by its original name Athymbra: see IG xi (4) 1235 (3rd-2nd cent. BC), a dedication to Kore, Demeter, Hermes and Anubis by Ἰατροκλῆς Δημαγάθου Ἀθυνβριανός. For Ptolemy see v. 2. 18-19: Νύσσα (sic) . . . (19) . . . Τράλλεις . . . Ἀλάβανδα. A bishop Ἀντιοχείας Καρίας is a signatory at Nikaia I, where Alabanda is not present (though it is at Chalcedon: see Jones, 529, no. 11; cf. Ruge, col. 1639), but the bishoprics named in the Conciliar lists are frequently puzzling. The identity with Alabanda for this entry is more likely than that with Nysa, even though Nysa may have only adopted an unrecognised metonomasy.

seven Alexandrias mentioned only by the *Romance* and the *Excerpta* with four Antiochs and three Seleukeias, mostly historically authenticated, suggests that in the Alexandrian tradition represented by these lists (but not in Stephanus, who has none of these Alexandrias, and, as we have seen, presents a more varied Alexandrian tradition), the Alexandrias have usurped the identity of the Seleucid cities of the east. Suspicions about the reality of these Alexandrias are increased by the fact that, except for Alexandria Troas, which was not founded by Alexander, no ethnic of an Alexandria has survived that can be attributed to any Alexandria except that of Egypt.[77] Another aspect of this lacuna is discussed later; here it suffices to indicate that none of the 'false' Alexandrias is attested either epigraphically or in literary sources independent of the *Romance* (the historians and geographers) while the corresponding Antiocheias and Seleukeias are well attested from either epigraphical or geographical sources, or both.

It should be noted here that the coincidence cannot be explained on the assumption that the cities were named Alexandria by the Seleucids, whether as refoundations of destroyed cities or as new foundations. A Seleucid metonomasy of an Alexander-foundation, for which both eponymous names are independently attested, cannot be convincingly demonstrated. The two possible candidates for this role are Antiocheia in Margiane and Alexandria Eschate (the refoundation of Alexandria-Spasinou Charax belongs to a different context, and is also doubtful), and they are both, particularly the second, very uncertain. That apart, the preponderant weight of the evidence is that Seleucid foundations were the work of Seleucus Nicator and his immediate successors, possible in the relatively stable conditions of the first half-century of the dynasty. The assumption of such a change of name fails to account for the manifestly Alexandrian origin of the lists of the *Romance* and associated texts, stretching back to the years immediately after Alexander's death. There is, moreover, a marked contrast between

---

[77] Robert, *Hellenica*, 7, p. 20 n. 7, said of *I.von Magn.* 61 (*OGIS* 233), l. 107, where Kern had proposed *Ἀλ[εξανδρεῦσιν]*, 'Je n'ai pas de raison de supposer que O. Kern a lu, ligne 107B, *Ἀλ[εξανδρεῦσιν]*, au lieu de *Λα[οδικεῦσιν]*.' The temptation to believe that he did so is irresistible, but Dr K. Hallof, of *Inscriptiones Graecae*, who very kindly examined a squeeze in the collection on my behalf, tells me (letter of 16 January 1992) that he has been able to read nothing of the second column of the inscription (lines 100-11), and concludes that Kern's reading can only have come from the stone.

the Ptolemaic insistence on the dynastic links with Alexander, symbolized by the conspicuous gold statue of him carried in the Great Procession described by Kallixeinos (see below, pp. 42 f.), and the almost complete absence of surviving evidence for such a tendency in the Seleucid dynasty, whose deification of their πρόγονοι was confined in due course to their own ancestors back to Nicator. Alexander, on the other hand, was always included in the Ptolemaic royal cult and the eponymous dating which derived from it, right through the Ptolemaic period, and was also the subject of a cult of Alexander Κτίστης. The eponymous priest of Alexander is mentioned in the *Testament* itself, one further proof of its Alexandrian origin. The contrast is decisive, and not surprising: the Seleucids in the early third century were de facto masters of Asia, most of Alexander's empire, and did not need to bolster their claim, while the Ptolemies, for all their strength on the Inner Sea, could not claim that inheritance—save by tendentious propaganda.[78]

The possibility of a Seleucid response to this Ptolemaic provocation cannot be excluded, and in the circumstances here described such a response, to be effective, would not dwell on the link with the person of Alexander, but on the solid, historical achievement of the dynasty in a field where it far outstripped Alexander—as city-builders. Appian preserves, in chapters 52–70 of his *Syrian History* (esp. 56–61), a brief account of the early history of the dynasty that Pompey vanquished. It bears a generic resemblance to the Alexandrian *Romance* that may well be purely fortuitous. It begins with a story of the oracle of Didymaean Apollo, that foretold Seleucus' end, long before his greatness was apparent: as he set out for Persia with Alexander, he enquired, we are told, about the likelihood of his returning to Macedonia, and the prophet replied, 'Haste not to Europe, for Asia is better far for you.' This is followed by the story of the fire that was kindled of its own accord in his paternal hearth, and of the dream of his mother concerning the ring and the engraving of the anchor which he lost in the Euphrates, and the anchor that he found in the stone he stumbled against in Babylonia; then the story of his recovery of Alexander's

---

[78] The attempt by Rostovtzeff, *JHS* 55 (1935), 56 ff., esp. pp. 62 ff., to show that the Seleucids also claimed Alexander among their πρόγονοι is based on the dynastic ancestry claimed by Antiochus I of Commagene, and on a passage of Libanius. The link is most obscure, and indirect, if it exists at all, whereas that of the Ptolemies was manifest in every public document as well as in the lavish displays of cult.

diadem in the Euphrates, which he placed on his head while he swam to return it safely to Alexander (a version of that episode was also known to, but not accepted by, Arrian); then the list of the cities which he (and he alone) founded, to which we shall return; and then the two novelettes, of his sacrifice of his wife Stratonike to her stepson, Antiochus I, who was in love with her, and his dispatch of them both to the 'Upper Satrapies'; and finally the story of the trick played on him by the magi to delay the building of Seleukeia-on-Tigris, a city which they feared would last for ever.

The similarity of genre between this and the Alexander-*Romance* is clear. Sandwiched between the account of the earlier history of the dynasty, and especially of the conflict between Rome and Antiochus III, which, errors apart, bears a close resemblance to Polybius' narrative, followed by the final Roman conquest, and the narrative of the death of Seleucus in Europe (a propos of which Appian repeats the Didymaean oracle) it stands as an isolated Seleucus-*Romance*, of which one major feature is the list of cities founded, all, in this context, by Seleucus himself. As always with Appian, the precise, immediate sources of his narrative, and their dates, remain conjectural, but we can at least see here, not concealed by subsequent accretion, a romantic narrative of early date. To this we may, if we choose, add the fully developed mythology of the foundation of Antiocheia by Seleucus preserved by Malalas, which is a counterpart to the story of the foundation of Alexandria by Alexander in the A-text of the *Romance*.

However, most interest attaches for our purpose to the list of cities founded by Seleucus, not all of which are historical. The passage is of sufficient interest to quote at length: 'And he founded cities throughout the length of his Empire, sixteen Antiochs, after his father, five Laodikeias after his mother, nine named after himself, four after his wives, three Apameias and one Stratonikeia. And of these the most eminent at the present time are, of the Seleukeias that on the Sea and that on the Tigris, and Laodikeia in Phoenicia and Antiocheia below Lebanon, and Syrian Apameia. And he named the others either from cities in Greece or Macedonia, or after his own achievements or in honour of King Alexander. Wherefore there are in Syria and in the barbarian regions beyond it many names of Greek and Macedonian cities, Beroia, Edessa, Perinthos, Maroneia, Kallipolis, Achaia, Pella, Oropos (leg. Europos), Amphipolis, Arethousa, Astakos, Tegea, Chalkis, Larisa, Heraia,

Apollonia, while in Parthyene there are Soteira, Kalliope, Charis, Hekatompylos, Achaia, and in India Alexandropolis, and among the Scythians Alexandreschata. And founded to commemorate his own victories there are Nikephorion in Mesopotamia and Nikopolis in that part of Armenia that lies nearest to Cappadocia.'[79] The number of cities here attributed to Seleucus himself are considerably in excess of what can be substantiated independently, and some of cities named after Macedonian or Greek originals are not recorded independently. However, the historicity of some of these cities is a matter for the specialist of Seleucid history. The point that is relevant to our present theme is the very small part played in this ἀναγραφή by cities named after Alexander, in spite of Appian's express statement. While it has been maintained that Alexandreschata was indeed a Seleucid refoundation of Alexander's foundation on the Jaxartes it is more likely to be an unfounded claim, or an error. Equally little confidence can be placed in the nebulous 'Alexandropolis in India'. The conclusion may fairly be drawn from

[79] *Syr.* 57 (ed. K. Brodersen, 2 vols.; Munich, 1989–91): πόλεις δὲ ᾤκισεν ἐπὶ τὸ μῆκος τῆς ἀρχῆς ὅλης, ἑκκαίδεκα μὲν Ἀντιοχείας ἐπὶ τῶι πατρί, πέντε δὲ ἐπὶ τῆι μητρὶ Λαοδικείας, ἐννέα δ' ἐπωνύμους ἑαυτοῦ, τέσσαρας δ' ἐπὶ ταῖς γυναιξί, τρεῖς Ἀπαμείας καὶ Στρατονίκειαν μίαν. καὶ εἰσὶν αὐτῶν ἐπιφανέσταται καὶ νῦν Σελεύκειαι μὲν ἥ τε ἐπὶ τῆι θαλάσσηι καὶ ἡ ἐπὶ τοῦ Τίγρητος ποταμοῦ, Λαοδίκεια δὲ ἡ ἐν τῆι Φοινίκηι καὶ Ἀντιόχεια ἡ ὑπὸ τῶι Λιβανῶι ὄρει καὶ ἡ τῆς Συρίας Ἀπάμεια. τὰς δὲ ἄλλας ἐκ τῆς Ἑλλάδος ἢ Μακεδονίας ὠνόμαζεν, ἢ ἐπὶ ἔργοις ἑαυτοῦ τισιν, ἢ ἐς τιμὴν Ἀλεξάνδρου τοῦ βασιλέως. ὅθεν ἔστιν ἐν τῆι Συρίαι καὶ τοῖς ὑπὲρ αὐτὴν ἄνω βαρβάροις πολλὰ μὲν Ἑλληνικῶν πολλὰ δὲ Μακεδονικῶν πολισμάτων ὀνόματα, Βέρροια, Ἔδεσσα, Πέρινθος, Μαρώνεια, Καλλίπολις, Ἀχαία, Πέλλα, Ὠρωπός (*leg.* Εὐρωπός), Ἀμφίπολις, Ἀρέθουσα, Ἀστακός, Τεγέα, Χαλκίς, Λάρισα, Ἥραια, Ἀπολλωνία, ἐν δὲ τῆι Παρθυηνῆι Σώτειρα, Καλλιόπη, Χάρις, Ἑκατόμπυλος, Ἀχαία, ἐν δ' Ἰνδοῖς Ἀλεξανδρόπολις, ἐν δὲ Σκύθαις Ἀλεξανδρέσχατα. καὶ ἐπὶ ταῖς αὐτοῦ Σελεύκου νίκαις ἔστι Νικηφόριόν τε ἐν τῆι Μεσοποταμίαι καὶ Νικόπολις ἐν Ἀρμενίαι τῆι ἀγχοτάτω μάλιστα Καππαδοκίας. (58) φασὶ δὲ αὐτῶι τὰς Σελευκείας οἰκίζοντι, τὴν μὲν ἐπὶ τῆι θαλάσσηι, διοσημίαν ἡγήσασθαι κεραυνού, καὶ διὰ τοῦτο θεὸν αὐτοῖς κεραυνὸν ἔθετο, καὶ θρησκεύουσι καὶ ὑμνοῦσι καὶ νῦν κεραυνόν. That the list has been adapted to 'current' practice is clear from the repeated use of καὶ νῦν, whether the alteration is Appian's or that of a late Seleucid 'Vulgate' or some other intermediary. The only recorded Περὶ τῶν ἐν Συρίαι βασιλευσάντων is that of Athenaeus, (*FGrH* 166 = Ath. 211A) which may have been based on Polybius or Posidonius. Even if we take into account all the Seleucid cities—both of the early period and of later date—and also those which had a purely ephemeral metonomasy, we cannot reach Appian's total, let alone their assignment to Seleucus Nicator. The list has left historians at a loss: see Brodersen's commentary, *ad loc.*, pp. 168 ff. (also Grainger, *Cities of Seleucid Syria* (Oxford, 1992), pp. 38 ff.) Brodersen quotes E. Gabba's remark in the Addenda to the Teubner *Appian* that the list constitutes 'un lavoro di ricerca, o almeno di composito fra più fonti, per noi inidentificabili, dello stesso Appiano', and Tscherikower, *op. cit.*, p. 166: 'was seine Antiochien und Seleukien usw betrifft, so sind wir leider nicht imstande diese summarischen Angaben durch eine von bestimmten Städten zu ersetzen.'

this brief survey that the *Seleucus-Romance*, or early Seleucid chroniclers, call the tradition what we will, emphasized the Macedonian and dynastic derivation of the dynasty (thirty-four dynastic names, and twenty-five deriving from Greece and Macedonia), assigned them to Seleucus himself, and virtually ignored the role of Alexander. This cannot be explained as due to concentration of these early foundations in Syria itself, since the large number of Antiocheias and Seleukeias shows that cannot have been the case. We must therefore recognize that, by contrast with the Alexandrian court, which laid emphasis on its links with Alexander, the Seleucid dynasty emphasized the role of its founder and its πρόγονοι.

I do not wish to lay any particular emphasis on this parallelism of theme between this Seleucid list and one element of the α-text of the Alexander-*Romance*. In any case, the Ptolemaic thesis, to stand, has to be able to provide some answer to the obvious questions, When, why, and by whom, was this fabricated Alexandrian list compiled? The first two questions are linked, and the occasion at least can, within the widest limits, be determined. The list does not occur in the *Liber de Morte Alexandri*, the element in the *Romance* that contains, among items of later date, the earliest Hellenistic ingredients. We may therefore be fairly certain that if the list existed at that time it was still an independent work, like the *Liber*, but distinct from it, and probably containing more items than now appear in the *Romance*-tradition. Beyond this general chronological determination regarding the development of the tradition, two different interpretations must be considered.

The first is as follows. If the list of cities was not associated with the α-text of the *Romance* until the Imperial period, it may be argued that it was compiled by the author of the α-text himself in c. AD 300. It was directly relevant to his theme, and was a natural development of the known tradition that Alexander had built cities on his campaign; and there is no trace of such a list earlier than the derivatives of the α-text. Given the background of fantastic historical writing characteristic of Alexandrian antiquarian speculations, colourfully exemplified both by the *Romance* itself and by Ammianus' account of the city, it is possible to suppose that, without regard to any true historical tradition, and wishing to exaggerate the scale of Alexander's activity as a founder of cities, the author of the α-text, writing in the later third, or early fourth century after Christ, should seize on cities mostly in the remote east, still surviving in his day, Seleucid foundations bearing Seleucid names, and bestow them on his hero. That Alexander did not, *ex hypothesi*, in fact found cities at the places in question probably would not disturb him much, though he would have known their Seleucid names.

At this point the introductory phrase, ἔκτισε δὲ πόλεις ιγ', αἵτινες μέχρι τοῦ νῦν κατοικοῦνται καὶ εἰρηνεύονται, rendered by the *Excerpta* '*qui usque nunc inhabitantur*', needs consideration. It could be regarded as a simple heading, a cliché with a touch of colour about it, contemporary with the list that follows. As such it would not require a greater claim to historicity than the list itself. However, this does not adequately explain the comfortable generalization, 'which are still inhabited and at peace'. This would have had no especial point, would not have been worth the making, when the eastern, trans-Euphratic Greek cities were ruled either by Hellenistic monarchs or by Roman emperors: throughout such periods the cities were incorporated within the eastern satrapies or client kingdoms or provinces, and were part of the contemporary Hellenized Near East. Paradoxically, if the phrase had any significance at all it could only be as an affirmation made at a time when the 'continued peace and inhabitation' of such cities of the east, whether imaginary or real, was effectively unverifiable. Rubric and list could in that case have been written during one of the frequent phases of war either between Rome and Parthia, or between Rome and the Sassanids, around and across the Euphrates frontier, when the Greek cities of the Iranian world largely lost direct contact with the Mediterranean. If that was so, the statement would have been invented by the composer of the α-text, and inserted before the list of cities, also fabricated by him, regardless of the historical reality of the list that followed. Living in the twilight of historical knowledge, not in the living world of the Hellenistic states, the author of the *Romance* needed, on this hypothesis, to find or invent geographically remote cities that he could with plausibility include in his list of Alexander-foundations, and some of these were available in the once-Seleucid cities of the Iranian world now under Sassanian rule. He introduced the whole list by the bland formula under discussion. Such an invention is certainly not out of keeping with the general tenor of the α-text, and would be very modest compared with many others. In fact the statements of Curtius Rufus and Ammianus Marcellinus regarding

the impoverished and humble status of the Greek cities of the East
in the Sassanian period, if trustworthy, provide the necessary cor-
rective to the picture of peaceful prosperity provided by the rubric,
and indeed reinforce the conclusion that the phrase is simply
divorced from historical reality.[80]

This reconstruction, according to which both this introductory
phrase (more precisely, the relative clause attached to it) and the
list of Alexandrias which follows belong to the third century or
early fourth century AD, cannot be dismissed as wholly untenable.
In the world of the *Romance* nothing can be excluded. But it lacks
plausibility, even when full allowance is made for the intellectual
insouciance of Imperial Alexandria, and of the contributors to the
ongoing tradition of the *Romance*. Topicality and political relevance
for the list are provided by an alternative explanation, which provides a much earlier date for its fabrication, long before it entered
the α-text. We know that the α-text of the *Romance* contained many
quite independent constituent parts, the identity of which is discussed in Appendix II:[81] the Vulgate-tradition of the historians, to
accept a convenient term; a corpus of letters of Alexander, based
ultimately on, and developed from, the correspondence surviving in
the historians and elsewhere; a quantity of scazonic verse; the
pamphlet called *The Last Will and Testament of Alexander*, or, more
correctly, *Concerning the Illness and Will of Alexander the Great*.
These items in their present form, as embedded in the A-text, are
themselves all of late Hellenistic or early Imperial date, though
some were originally composed at an earlier date, and were
selected and welded into his narrative by the author of the α-text.
They, and in particular the *Last Will*, give overt expression to the
political aims of the rival power-groups of the period following the
death of Alexander which are wholly out of keeping with the non-
sensical narrative parts of the complete work. That being unmistakably so, we may perhaps see in this list of cities a reflection
of the rivalry that existed between the Ptolemaic dynasty and
that of the Seleucids throughout the third century BC. It may be
suggested that, just as there was a politically tendentious book on
the 'Last Days' of Alexander that was available for insertion in the
text, in which the roles of both Ptolemy Soter and Perdiccas were
in different ways exaggerated, and, at a somewhat later date, the
role of the Rhodians as heirs of Alexander was fabricated and

---

[80] See below, p. 188.   [81] See below, pp. 205-23.

inserted in the text of the *Will*, so there was also a *Liber de Urbibus Alexandri*, in which a writer in Ptolemaic Alexandria placed under the patronage of the Founder the cities founded, mostly in Mesopotamia and beyond, in the third century BC. It is noteworthy that the relevant Seleucid cities whose foundation can be dated belong to the early group of dynastic foundations, and not to the later foundations assigned to Antiochus III or even to Antiochus IV. Further, if we accept that Ἀλεξάνδρεια πρὸς τῶι Λάτμωι can be equated with the Seleucid metonomasy of Alabanda, that would provide independent evidence that the list was compiled while Alabanda was an Antiocheia, namely between c.260 and 190 BC.[82] The dates correspond very well to the most intense period of Ptolemaic–Seleucid rivalry, when the two dynasties were at constant, if not continuous, war with one another in Caria. In any case, if the existence of a fraudulent Ptolemaic *Liber de Urbibus Alexandri* be accepted, it seems to follow naturally that it should belong to the century between the Battle of Korupedion and the Peace of Apamea, and more particularly perhaps before the accession of Antiochus III and Ptolemy IV in c.221/0 BC. If that is so, the author may have been a witness of the famous Procession of Dionysus and the Other Gods held by Ptolemy Philadelphus in 275–4 BC, and later described in such vivid detail by the Rhodian historian Kallixeinos.[83] In that ostentatious pageant a prominent role was allotted to a tableau of those cities of Asia that had been enslaved by Persia and liberated by Alexander, represented by lavishly dressed ladies.[84] Then, or later, Alexander could be represented to the people of Alexandria in a double light; as the liberator of old cities and as the Κτίστης of new ones, as well as of their own capital city. In the belief that the existence of such a tendentious pamphlet best explains the list of Alexandrias in the

[82] For the precise period during which Alabanda bore its Seleucid name see L. Robert, in *Étud. Dél.* (*BCH* Suppl. iv (1973)), 448 ff.

[83] For this (*FGrH* 627) see the text and commentary by E. E. Rice, *The Great Procession of Ptolemy Philadelphus* (Oxford, 1982); cf. *Ptol. Alex.* i. 202–3 and the accompanying notes. The date is astronomically determined in an ingenious article by V. Fortmeyer, *Historia*, 37 (1988), 90–104, as having fallen between 31 Oct. 275 and 30 Oct. 274, that is, during the First Syrian War: for the phases of this obscure struggle see H. Heinen, *CAH²*, vii. 413 ff.

[84] See § ⟨33⟩ (Rice, ll. 205 ff.) τῆι δὲ τετρακύκλωι ταύτηι ἠκολούθουν γυναῖκες, ἔχουσαι ἱμάτια πολυτελῆ καὶ κόσμον ⟨χρυσοῦν ?Kaibel⟩. προσηγορεύοντο δὲ Πόλεις, αἵ τε ἀπ᾽ Ἰωνίας καὶ ⟨αἱ⟩ λοιπαὶ Ἑλληνίδες, ὅσαι τὴν Ἀσίαν καὶ τὰς νήσους κατοικοῦσαι ὑπὸ τοὺς Πέρσας ἐτάχθησαν· ἐφόρουν δὲ πᾶσαι στεφάνους χρυσοῦς.

A-text of the *Romance* and the other derivatives of the α-version, I have added a *Liber de Urbibus Alexandri* to the progenitors of that work in the stemma on p. 207.

It follows from this hypothesis that the linking phrase, discussed above, in which the cities are described as 'still inhabited and at peace', belongs to the author of the α-text himself, in the Imperial period, as suggested above, and not to the original author of the *De Urbibus*. The author of the α-version was indeed in a difficult position. He was faced with a list of cities of which he could make very little. The list could be added directly to the immediately preceding details dealing with Alexander's life, his years of warfare etc.: ἔκτισε δὲ πόλεις ιγ', followed simply by the list; or he could attempt to add some rhetorical link. He chose the latter course, to the greater glory of his hero, and thereby exposed once more his characteristic ignorance of the historical past and present. If that is the sum of the matter, we need not reconstruct a specific historical background to explain the phrase, which in itself provides one further clue to the evolution of the α-version. Here, as in his description of the topography of Alexandria, in the first book of the *Romance*, the author reveals himself as looking back to a much earlier original by his use of the phrase, μέχρι καὶ νῦν, 'even today'.[85]

Other considerations, one of which seems decisive, also indicate the Ptolemaic origin of the list of cities: the presence in Stephanus and in the *Excerpta* (and the *Paschal Chronicle*) of the Alexandrias of Cyrenaica and Cyprus,[86] and probably, Alexandria ἡ πρὸς Ξάνθωι, which are absent from A but present in other derivatives of the α-text. These extra Alexandrias, which form a sort of 'pool', cannot be attributed to a tendentious list aimed solely at increasing Ptolemaic prestige at the expense of their Seleucid rivals, for they lay within Ptolemaic territory. Their inclusion among the Alexandrias is none the less obviously of Ptolemaic origin, and any attempt to 'make sense of them', to 'identify them on the ground' is wasted effort. The occurrence of all three, two imaginary and one (Xanthos) real, as Alexandrias, points once more to the earlier Ptolemaic period, for whereas Cyrenaica and Cyprus were most intimately integrated into the central government in the

---

[85] See below, pp. 215-6 for an analogous retrospection in the account of Alexandrian topography. Note also the variation in the linking phrase, and in the number of Alexandrias given by the excerpts quoted on p. 208 n. 5.

[86] See above, pp. 27-8, and Table, nos. 18 and 31.

period down to approximately the latter part of the third century, after that time Cyrenaica at least began to drift away from the centre, as Cyprus did in the later Ptolemaic period, and Xanthos, which had been Ptolemaic during most of the third century, became Seleucid at the beginning of the second.[87] It is difficult not to connect their absence from the A-list with the discrepancy between the number of cities there said to have been founded by Alexander (thirteen) and the number actually preserved in the text (nine). These three, we may conjecture, are among the missing items: the presence of the first two in the *Excerpta* and the *Paschal Chronicle* guarantees that they were both in the original list, while their presence in Stephanus, in one instance on the authority of Favorinus, indicates that they also existed in a different tradition. But they could not be included in a list which was headed by the rubric that defined the cities as 'still at peace', which had a quite different significance, and were edited out at some stage between the composition of the original *Liber de Urbibus Alexandri* and the list in the A-text, most naturally by the author of the rubric himself. The case of Xanthos is less closely linked with the α-tradition, but it occurs in the Armenian text, Julius Valerius and the Presbyter Leo, and, given the situation envisaged for the composition of the original list, the case for accepting it as part of that list is very strong. It may indeed present us with the rationale of the whole complex of facts and fancies.

The *Liber de Urbibus Alexandri* does not stand alone; it seems rather to have formed part of a concatenated and systematic attempt by the Ptolemies in the third century to impose an image of their Empire both through literature and in the living world of political rivalries. Alongside this supposed work we may set, as a comparable attempt to rewrite what passed as history and thereby to influence public opinion, the appearance, particularly in the middle of the third century, and from the pen of Apollonius the so-called Rhodian, of a number of poems, all unfortunately subsequently consigned to oblivion, concerning the foundation of cities within the Ptolemaic Empire. The poet employed a traditional type of poetry which he refashioned for contemporary purposes. At the centre of the canvas stands his Κτίσις Ἀλεξανδρείας, which, we may suppose, extolled the role of the Founder against a background of mingled fact and fiction akin to the description of the foundation

[87] See above, p. 25 and n. 53.

and topography of Alexandria in the first book of the A-text of the *Romance*. Nor did Apollonius stop there: other foundations so treated were those of Kanopos and Naukratis in Egypt, of Kaunos, an important base in Ptolemaic Caria in the third century, and of Knidos, also Ptolemaic, lying on its twin-harboured promontory close to the independent island of Rhodes, itself the subject of a similar poem at a time when, we may suppose, Apollonius had, under pressure perhaps, transferred his affections and his residence from Alexandria to the republic. The little we know of these poems indicates the lavish use of recondite mythology, but we may at least wonder whether Apollonius chose his topics with encouragement from a higher authority.[88]

That the Empire at the level of Imperial policy projected its image of itself by means of the lavish use of the current concept of kinship (συγγένεια) as between different communities of the Greek world and the Ptolemaic dynasty is now brilliantly illuminated by the diplomatic exchange between the Xanthians and the Kytenians in 206 BC. In their response to the request of the ambassadors of Kytenion for assistance in rebuilding their city in the mountains of central Greece, which Antigonus Doson had destroyed a considerable time before, in 228 BC, the Xanthians accept that they have an obligation (which they fulfil in the issue in a very niggardly manner) to assist the Kytenians because of a number of mythological links, some at least manufactured *ad hoc* by the Kytenians, and also because of the Kytenian kinship, through the Argead house, with King Ptolemy, who being a descendant of Herakles traces back his kinship to the kings of Herakles' stock. The Kytenians for their part end their representations with the statement, 'Know that you will thus [by helping us] be deserving of gratitude from us, from the Aetolians [their political masters, who had patronized the whole operation], from all other Dorian peoples, and in particular from King Ptolemy, who is our kin through the line of (Heraclid) kings.' The Xanthians were within a very few years to experience the benevolent kinship of Antiochus III, on the basis of the same common descent.[89]

[88] For Apollonius' Κτίσεις see *Ptol. Alex.* i. 513-14 with notes. It does not seem likely to me that Callimachus' pinacographical work, Κτίσεις νήσων καὶ πόλεων καὶ μετονομασίαι, (sub fr. 412 Pf.) was of the same topical type.

[89] See n. 53. For the date of the destruction see Walbank in Hammond and Walbank, *Macedonia*, iii (1988), 339 and n. 4. Now that we can see, for the first time, the Aetolian League itself as part of, as recognizing, the Ptolemaic network

Finally there were the Ptolemaic metonomasies, largely, but not entirely, confined to the reigns of Philadelphus and Euergetes and to the Aegean and coastal Empire of the Ptolemies. The most significant feature of this aspect of Ptolemaic policy lies in the fact that the new Ptolemaises, Berenikes, and Arsinoes, were metonomasies of old Greek cities familiar to the inhabitants of the inner Greek world, whereas the majority of the Seleucid cities of the East, were not metonomasies, but new foundations, cities that the Seleucids had to build and embellish with new traditions—as indeed they did, and very effectively—just as Ptolemaic Alexandria itself. That the author of the *De Urbibus Alexandri* should have assigned these new Seleucid foundations to Alexander may be seen as an important element in the concerted and contorted propaganda of the Ptolemies against the Seleucids.

We must now revert to our central text. From the anonymous author of this original list or tract whom we may assign, I suggest, to the third century BC, via the equally anonymous author of the α-text itself in the third century AD or slightly later, the tradition of the Alexander-foundations passed in due course to the Greek A-text and to the parallel versions, the Latin of Julius Valerius, the Armenian and the Pehlevi, which all supply data for this early phase in the transmission that are sometimes lacking in A. From α also it passed to the Alexandrian annalists, represented for us by the Golenischev papyrus (in which the list is missing, owing to lacunae in the text), and to the Greek original of the *Excerpta*, composed in about AD 410, and eventually, through them, on the eve of the Sassanian and Arab conquests, to the *Paschal Chronicle*. Long before that, the Pehlevi text, also a product of the α-text, had started the oriental tradition on its long route, through Pehlevi originals and Syriac intermediaries to Arabic writers. To these we must now turn, leaving the miscellaneous cargo concealed in the entries of Stephanus, s.vv. Alexandreia, Antiocheia, and Seleukeia, to sail to Byzantium to start a new life.

of συγγένεια, it is worth considering whether the metonomasy of Konope to Arsinoe, which has hitherto been difficult to explain (see the references in *IG* ix (1)², Index, p. 106, s.v.), may not be connected with that recognition.

CHAPTER II

The Iranian Tradition

THE Iranian evidence for the foundation of cities by Alexander the Great supports, I believe, the interpretation offered of the Alexandrian lists in the previous chapter. It is not possible in the context of the present topic to provide a complete background for the Alexander-traditions of the Sassanian and early Islamic worlds, but a few observations may help the reader to follow my account of the Persian and Arabic evidence.

Although there are no known surviving Arabic translations of the Greek *Romance*[1] many isolated and loosely connected legends

[1] See especially the work of R. F. Weymann, *Die aethiopische und arabische Übersetzung des PseudoKallisthenes* (Kirchhain, 1901), which contains important observations regarding the possible contents of the presumed Arabic Ps.-Callisthenes, based on the frequent coincidences of substance between the Ethiopic version and Mubashshir b. Fātik's *'Akhbār Iskandar*, published by Meissner, *ZDMG* 49 (1895), 594 ff.: see Weymann's general conclusions, pp. 64 ff., and also the detailed study of M. Grignaschi, *Bull. d'Étud. d'Orient*, 19 (1965), 3–83, 'Les 'Rasā''il 'Arisṭāṭālisa 'ilā-l-Iskandar', in which he publishes parts of what he sees as a 'roman épistolaire grec remanié par un auteur arabe'. In his article in *Muséon*, 80 (1967), 211–64, Grignaschi discusses the whole Arabic tradition of the correspondence between Alexander and Aristotle, and claims that the supposed epistolary *Romance* derives from a Greek text of the *Γ*-tradition. The author of the letters in the first-mentioned article is identified by Grignaschi as Sālim Abū 'l-'Alā', the Wasīr of the Ummayid caliph, Hishām. There are links between this correspondence and passages in the *B*- and *Γ*-traditions of the *Romance*, which are quite remote from the α-tradition, but I am not convinced that all the material in the *Lamentations over Alexander* attested in Arabic gnomologia occurred in this supposed 'epistolary Romance', though D. Gutas, *Greek Wisdom Literature in Arabic Translation* (Amer. Or. Soc. New Haven, 1975), 444–5, accepts Grignaschi's thesis. The *Lamentations*, for which see below, p. 49 and n. 7, are in any case wholly absent from the Greek tradition. See also the classic study by Th. Nöldeke, *Wien. Denkschr.* 1890(5), 35 ff., 'Beiträge zur Geschichte des Alexanderromans'. Much new material, some of it relevant to the *Romance*, is discussed by N. Abbott, *Studies in Arabic Literary Papyri*, i (Chicago, 1957; Orient. Inst. Pub. 75), esp. pp. 50–6. G. Cary, *The Medieval Alexander* (Cambridge, 1956), 12 n. 19, wrote: 'Dr. S. Rice has recently found an Arabic Pseudo-Callisthenes in Constantinople which may prove to be the lost intermediary. This manuscript is MS Ayia Sofia 3003 and 3004 dated A. H. 871 = A.D. 1466. I have to thank Dr. Rice for this information.' This is repeated by A. M. H. Shboul, *Al-Mas'ūdī and his World* (London, 1979), 142 n. 181. I can find no indica-

and strands of tradition may ultimately derive from a lost work of this nature, which is known to have existed in the pre-Abbasid period. Equally, there can be no doubt that the Syriac version, which is of considerable importance for our purpose, derives not from an Arabic, but from a Pehlevi version.[2]

tion that this MS has been published, and have no information about it. In any case, it cannot be identical with 'Umārah b. Zaid's *Qiṣṣat al-Iskandar Dhū'l-Qarnein*, or one of his many sources (for which see Abbott, loc. cit.), since that work was largely concerned with the story of al-Khaḍr and the Fountain of Life, and proceeded for the most part along conventional lines. The fragments of 'Umārah are collected and translated in J. Friedländer's well-known book, *Die Chadirlegende und der Alexander-roman* (Berlin, 1913), 129 f. N. Abbott shows (against Friedländer) that 'Umārah was probably active in the late 8th/early 9th cent. AD, and used written sources for his *Qiṣṣat*. In a papyrus of the reign of al-Mu'izz (AH 341-65/AD 953-75) J. Karabaçek, *Führer Pap. Erzh. Rainer* (Vienna, 1892), p. 260, no. 1072, the addressee is requested by the sender to negotiate for him at Fusṭāṭ the purchase of a copy of what Karabaçek calls the *Alexander-Roman*, but he does not give the Arabic title. T. Nagel, *Alexander der Grosse in der frühislamischen Volksliteratur* (Beitr. z. Sprache- u. Kulturgeschichte des Orients, Bd. 28, Walldorf-Hessen, 1978) analyses only the Yemenite Alexander-story by Ibn Hishām, which does not concern us here. M. Brocker's very thorough Bonn dissertation, *Aristoteles als Alexanders Lehrer in der Legende* (Bonn, 1966), is especially concerned with the Arabic version of Ptolemaios, the Neoplatonist's (*RE* (69)) *Life of Aristotle*, by al-Qifṭī, given in Latin/Greek in Rose's *Arist. Fragm.* 18 ff., and in Ibn Abī 'Uṣaibi'a's *'Uyūn al-Anbā*, ed. Müller, 69. (A translation of all the Arabic texts relating to Aristotle's life, teaching, etc. (but not the correspondence and related fictional material, including the *Romance*) will be found in I. Düring, *Aristotle in the Biographical Tradition* (Göteborg, 1957) and F. E. Peters, *Aristotle and the Arabs: The Aristotelian Tradition in Islam* (New York and London, 1968)). There are useful summaries of the oriental *Romance* traditions in the lecture by J. A. Boyle, *JJRULB* 60 (1977-8), 13-27, 'The Alexander-Romance in the East and West', with especial reference to the 14th-cent. Mongolian fragment published by N. Poppe, *ZDMG* 107 (1957), 105-29, 'Eine Mongolische Fassung der Alexandersage' (Cf. Boyle, in *Zentralas. Stud.* ix (1975), 265-71), and in Appendix III to M. S. Southgate's abbreviated translation of the entertaining 12th-14th-cent. prose *Iskandernama*, (Columbia Univ. Press, Persian Heritage Series, 31; New York, 1978), 190-204.

[2] For the Syriac version see E. A. W. Budge, *The History of Alexander the Great* (Cambridge, 1889, text and trans.; repr. Amsterdam, 1976). Budge derived the version from an Arabic original, but Nöldeke, op. cit. 11 ff., showed on linguistic grounds that the text derived from a Pehlevi version. The Ethiopic version, for which see Budge, *The Life and Exploits of Alexander the Great etc.* (London, 2 vols. 1896, text and trans.; trans. only, Cambridge, *c.* 1906 (*non vidi*); reduced trans., London, 1933), has a list of Alexandrias markedly different from both the Alexandrian and the Iranian traditions: see further below, p. 58, with nn. 32-3; it is undoubtedly translated from an Arabic version which had much in common both with the Syriac version and with the *'Akhbār Iskandar* of Mubashshir b. Fātik: see Weymann, op. cit., *passim*, esp. pp. 4 ff., 28 ff., and, for supplementary bibliography on the Syriac life, Brock, (op. cit. below n. 7), 215 ff. Weymann showed (pp. 43 ff.) that the source of both Mubashshir and the Ethiopic version derived from the Syriac; but this is not true of the Ethiopic list of Alexandrias, which stands by itself

The close link between the list of Alexandrias in the Syriac version and the identifications given by the geographical encyclopaedist, Yākūt, and also the Alexandrias named in the Pehlevi *The Provincial Capitals of Eranshahr*,[3] underlines the Iranian origin of the Syriac text. This similarity does not, of course, necessarily indicate the existence at that time of an Arabic version of the *Romance*. In the present context it is no compensation for the absence of such a version that there exist numerous disconnected, frequently repeated legends about Alexander in Arabic, some of which also derive from Pehlevi originals, and reflect their Iranian origin; such surviving Pehlevi texts are *The Letter of Tansar*,[4] and the story of Alexander's destruction of the *Avesta* recorded in the *Denkard*,[5] and the later Alexander-stories in Firdawsī's *Shahnama* and Niẓāmī's *Iskandarnama*.[6] Others have a wide circulation in both Arabic and associated legends. As an example of the Arabic traditions we may mention the familiar story of the burial of Alexander in Alexandria (of Iskander in Iskandarīya), in the presence of Olympias, and the philosophical consolations offered her by Plato, Aristotle, Democritus, and other less distinguished representatives of Greek philosophy.[7] The second class is also represented by the connected

(see below, p. 58). It is noteworthy that the Ethiopic text contains a substantial insertion in the form of an exchange of letters between Darius and Alexander, from Eutychius (pp. 269–81, Pococke; pp. 77–8, Cheiko: see below, n. 8), which is not reproduced elsewhere: see Weymann, op. cit. 20 ff.

[3] See J. Markwart, *The Provincial Capitals of Erānshahr*, ed. G. Messina (Anal. Orient 3, 1931, Rome).

[4] ed. M. Boyce, *The Letter of Tansar* (London, 1968).

[5] See H. W. Bailey, *Ninth-Century Zoroastrian Books*[2] (Oxford, 1971), 151 ff. See also *The Provincial Capitals of Erānshahr*, which refers to the same episode in §§ 5, 12, 53.

[6] I need not describe these narratives, neither of which contains material directly relevant to our subject. See the summaries of their accounts of Alexander in Nöldeke, op. cit. 49 ff., Friedländer, 204 ff. For the prose *Iskandarnama* see the edition by Iraq Afshan (Persian Text Series, 17, Tehran, 1964), and the Eng. trans. by M. S. Southgate (op. cit. n. 1 above). For Niẓāmī's version the full discussion by A. Zarringkoob in *Colloquio sul Poeta Persiano Niẓāmī e la Leggenda Iranica di Alessandro Magno*, published by the Fondazione Leone Caetano (Accad. Linc. 1977), where the text is summarized (pp. 26 ff.): also the brief outline by Southgate, op. cit. 173 ff. [See Addenda]

[7] This tradition has been studied in detail a propos of a Syriac version by S. P. Brock, *Journ. Sem. Stud.* 15 (1970), 205 ff. The Laments are also trans. F. Rosenthal, *The Classical Heritage in Islam* (Univ. of California Press, 1975; rev. trans. of his *Das Fortleben der Antike in Islam* (Zurich, 1965)), 120 ff. Rosenthal also gives (pp. 124 ff.) a full translation of the Laments of the Philosophers in Mubashshir b. Fātik's *Mukhtār al-ḥikam*, with the parallel passages of the Greek gnomologia. It is from this longer work that Mubashshir's *Life of Alexander* (above n. 2) comes.

story, or stories, known in both East and West, of Alexander's search for the 'Fountain of Life' and the construction of the Wall (al-Sudd), and the penning-in of Gog and Magog.[8] But it is to be noted that the prototypes of most of these stories occur only in the B and Γ-traditions of the Greek *Romance*. They are to be considered as floating Alexander-material, current in the Pehlevi, Syriac, and Arab-speaking world, written, no doubt, rather than oral, mainly Iranian in origin, and later encapsulated in the Qu'rān, and subsequently recurring at many different points in the Syriac and Arabic literary traditions. (They are frequently designated in the stemmata of the oriental versions of the *Romance* by the letter δ.)

Of the Iranian, that is, Perso-Arabic Alexander-literature the most important for our study of Alexander's city-foundations consists of the almost contemporary Arabic chroniclers of Iranian origin, al-Ṭabārī and al-Dīnawārī, who record numerous Alexandrias (Iskandarīyas). It is noteworthy in this connection that while the Christian Egyptian physician, Saʿīd b. al-Batrīq, better known by his Greek name Eutychius,[9] later Melkite Patriarch of Alexandria, whose *Annals* are heavily dependent on unspecified Byzantine and oriental sources through Arabic translations, gives the fullest surviving account of the 'Lamentations over Alexander',

---

[8] For this see Friedländer, op. cit. *passim*, esp. pp. 4 ff. It is recorded in the Γ-tradition of the *Romance* in the Letter of Olympias (not in the A or B-traditions, and only fully in MS Par. Suppl. 113 (= C)). Friedländer translates the variant texts, with C (Bk. II, chs. 23-42) as base (Engelmann edn., *Rezenzion Γ, Buch II* (Beitr. z. Klass. Philol. 12, 1963) gives the text of C in the app. crit.; for further editions of Γ see below, pp. 205-6). For him the search forms the unifying link with the al-Khaḍr-legend. For the Wall of Gog and Magog see C. E. Wilson, *Asia Major*, Introd., *Hirth Anniversary Vol.* (London, 1923), 575-612 (discussion of the tradition of the Caliph al-Wāthiq's expedition in AD 842 to discover the Wall, recorded by Ibn Khordādhbeh, *BGA* vi. 124 ff., 162 ff.; Anderson, *Alexander's Gate, Gog and Magog* (Cambridge, Mass., 1932), *passim*, esp. pp. 91 ff. for the Arabic sources.

[9] For Eutychius see Graf, *GCAL* ii. 32 ff.; von Gutschmid, *Kl. Schr.* ii. 399-400 (chronology), 486; v. 688-92 (sources, esp. of the Διαμερισμὸς τῆς γῆς, the *quismat al-ʿarḍ*, pp. 15 ff. Cheiko); H. Gelzer, *Sextus Julius Africanus*, II, 1 (1885), 409-10 (summary of chronology); Brock, op. cit. For his life see Ibn Abī ʿUṣaibīʾaʾs *K. ʿUyūn al-Anbāʾ*, ii. 86-7. His *Annals* (*Naẓm al-Jawhar, The Necklace of Pearls*), pub. with Latin trans. by Pococke (Oxford, 1658-9, 2 vols.) was republished by L. Cheiko, *CSCO*, scr. arab. 6-7 (1906, repr. 1962). Later accounts add nothing to the scanty information regarding his life in Ibn Abī ʿUṣaibīʾa, and his sources, including those for the 'Lamentations for Alexander' studied by Brock, are incompletely known (for Thābit b. Sinān see Peters, op. cit. p. 289). For his Sassanian *Annals* see the analysis by Gabrieli, *RSO*, 13, 1932, pp. 209 ff. (parallels with al-Ṭabārī and Ibn Qutaība's *ʿUyūn al-Akhbār*, perhaps deriving from Ibn al-Moqaffaʾ's lost version of the *Hudaynāma*). For the interpolation from Eutychius in the Ethiopic Life see above, n. 2.

all that he has to say of Alexander as a city-builder is that 'he built thirteen [un-named] cities in the East and the West . . . and that he built Alexandria in Egypt and that he moved his capital thither from 'the city Macedonia', and built the Lighthouse.[10] But he records none of the Traditions, some local, or at least Egyptian, found in Ibn 'Abd al-Ḥakam's account of the origin of the city.[11]

One category of material relating to Alexander stands by itself in Arabic literature—that involving the identification of Alexander or Iskander with Dhū'l-Qarnein, 'He of the Two Horns', who is already referred to in the Qu'rān,[12] and who is there stated to have built the rampart that kept out Gog and Magog.[13] In the Qu'rān Dhū'l-Qarnein is not identified with any other figure, but the early Commentators on the Qu'rān and the writers of Traditions soon debated the merits of his identification with Iskander. It lay in the nature of Hadīth, the science of Traditions, that the debate, examples of which may be found in a wide variety of Traditions on different themes, had no finality. However, although it approaches our subject in one respect—in that the issue regarding the identity was debated among other contexts in that of the foundation (or, more precisely the early history) of Alexandria in Egypt[14]—it is not directly relevant to it, if only because Dhū'l-Qarnein is rarely represented as a founder of cities. Even more remote from our enquiry is the question, no less debated by the Traditionists, of the relation between the person of Iskander and the legendary servant of Moses (confused with Iskander himself), who figures anonymously in the Qu'rān, and is identified in Hadīth with

---

[10] See p. 81, ll. 7 ff. Cheiko (pp. 280-1, Pococke). Eutychius says *wa naqala al-mulk min madīna Makedunīya 'ilā madīnat al-Iskandarīya*; Pococke translated this *ad quam a Macedonia imperium transtulit*; but *madīna* perhaps has the usual sense of 'city' here, parallel to *al-Iskandarīya*. Μακεδονία is a city (identified with Alexandria) in a passage of Theodore's version of the Legend of St Spyridon (ed. Van de Ven (1953), 86, l. 3: the Patriarch of Alexandria appears to Spyridon and says "διαβὰς εἰς Μακεδονίαν βοήθησον ἡμῖν". Μακεδονίαν δὲ τὴν Ἀλεξάνδρου προσαγορεύουσιν πόλιν) which belongs to the time shortly after the Arab Conquest of Alexandria: see below, pp. 218 ff. for this work. The presence of this phrase in the text of Theodore suggests that it may have been current at the time, and weakens the force of Grignaschi's argument (op. cit. above, n. 1), p. 30, that the use of *madīna Makedunīya* in the Arabic letter he there publishes reflects the εἰς τὴν πόλιν of the *B*-tradition, erroneously transcribed from the εἰς (τὴν) Πέλλαν of A: for the reading of *B* see L. Bergson, *Der griech. Alexanderroman, Rezension β* (Acta Univ. Stockholm., Stud. Graec., Stockholm, iii (1965)), textual note on I, p. 4, l. 14.

[11] For these see Ibn 'Abd al-Ḥakam, 37 ff., ed. Torrey, *Futūḥ Miṣr* (Yale Oriental Series, Researches, III; New Haven, 1922).

[12] Sūr. 18, 83 ff.   [13] See above, n. 9.   [14] See al-Ḥakam 38-40.

Joshua b. Nūn, and with the servant of God al-Khaḍir or al-
Khiḍr. The exploits of the latter figure, whatever their origin,
and whether associated with Iskander or with Moses, belong
entirely to the world of fantasy.[15] It is to be noted only that,
unlike Dhū'l-Qarnein, he nowhere appears as the *Doppelgänger* of
Alexander–Iskander.

Early Arabic geographical literature, on the other hand, is an
essential element in our investigation. The classical Arab geographers, compilers of lists of postal routes, and cosmographers,
and the records of early travellers through the Islamic world,
describe the world of their own day, the world of the first two or
three Islamic centuries, through which they travelled, and which
they described in such vivid detail from Marrakesh to Ferghāna.
The works that most concern us describe the vast area of
Khorāsān, the Islamic term for the region between the north-
Persian desert and the Farghāna oasis, and including (with
northern Sijistān) all modern Afghanistān. Several of these
authors, whose accounts were based essentially either on the *barīd*
or postal-routes, or on personal knowledge filled in by the postal
records, were themselves natives of the great cultural centres of
Khorāsān, notably the greater Merv and Balkh. Various aspects of
their evidence on the condition of Khorāsān will be considered in
due course. These travellers in a region which, before the Islamic
conquest of Khorāsān in the seventh and eighth centuries of our
era, had been for centuries under Sassanian and fragmented
Hephthalite rule, record little or nothing of legend relating to
Alexander or his foundations; their importance for us lies in the
fact that they traversed much the same ground as Alexander, and
that they describe the country as it was before the destructive
advance of the Mongols that marks a watershed in the history of
all the cities of the Islamic world over which it passed.[16]

One geographer is in a different category, the great geographical
encyclopaedist, Yākūt, to whom we owe so much of our detailed

[15] See the exhaustive study of this question by Friedländer, op. cit. *passim*.
[16] I must acknowledge my great indebtedness to two classic works, G. Le
Strange's *The Lands of the Eastern Caliphate* (Cambridge, 1905), and V. Minorsky's
trans. and commentary of the anonymous *Ḥudūd al-'ālam* (Gibb Memorial Series,
NS xi, 1937); 2nd, considerably enlarged, edn., by C. E. Bosworth, with many
addenda by Minorsky, 1970), the notes of which, with the addenda, contain a
treasury of information on the geography of Central Asia. The text itself is largely
based on al-Balkhī-Iṣṭakhrī (see ibid. 15 ff. and *passim*).

and systematic knowledge of the Islamic world of the immediately pre-Mongol period. Yākūt b. Abdullah al-Rumī (i.e. 'the Byzantine', a reference to his alleged Greek origin) records a detailed list of Alexander-foundations, and we must examine it in detail. First, as to the author himself: he was born in *c.*575/1178 in Asia Minor, and was captured in infancy in an Arab raid. His life, written by Ibn Khallikān,[17] composed shortly after his death, states that he was enfranchised at Hama (whence his *nisba*, al-Hamawī), and resided in Baghdad (whence his other *nisba*, al-Baghdādī). The young Anatolian Greek (if such he was) was brought up by a Baghdad merchant, for whom in due course he travelled on business to the Persian Gulf and neighbouring regions. In 596/1199 he was manumitted, and became a copyist and bookseller. Having embraced the doctrines of the Kharājite sect, life became difficult in the main centres of Shi'ite teaching, and he fled to Mausil and Arbil, and then settled in Merv for a year or two, but he left that fair city, as did many others, when Ghenghis Khan's Tartars took it in 1221. After some harrowing experiences he finally returned to Mausil and Alep, where he died in 626/1229. It was at Alep that he wrote his numerous works including the great *Geographical Dictionary* (*Mu'jam al-Buldān*)[18] and the smaller and later *Dictionary of Geographical Homonyms* (*Mushtarik*)[19], as well as other books including a lengthy *Dictionary of Scholars*. Though supposedly Greek by birth, Yākūt, like many another fellow-countryman who found himself in a similar situation at that time, became a fully committed Muslim, and he shows no trace of Byzantine learning; it has been pointed out that some of the etymologies which he gives of place-names show quite clearly that he had no residual knowledge of Greek.[20] A letter that he wrote to the Wazīr of the

[17] Trans. de Slane, iv. 9 ff. On Yākūt's activity and milieu see also Wüstenfeld's two articles, *ZDMG* 18 (1864), 397-493, 'Jacut's Reisen, aus seinem geographischen Wörterbuch geschrieben', and *GGA* (1865) Nachr. (9), 233-43, 'Der Reisende Jacut als Schriftsteller und Gelehrter', and the very useful analysis of his sources by F. J. Heer, *Die historischen u. geographischen Quellen in Jacut's Geographischen Wörterbuch* (Strassb. 1898), and, for an excellent study of his cosmographical notions, W. Jwaideh, *The Introductory Chapters of Yāqūt's Mu'jam al-Buldān* (Brill, 1959), *passim*, with pp. x ff. for his sources.

[18] Ed. Wüstenfeld, (Göttingen, 5 vols. 1866-73), also ed. in 5 vols (Beyrouth, 1955-7). The list of Iskandarīyas in the *Mu'jam* is in vol. i (Wüst.) 255-6.

[19] Ed. id. *Jacut's Moschtarik* (Göttingen, 1846, repr. Baghdad with orig. title-page). The list of Iskandarīyas is on p. 23.

[20] See Wüstenfeld, *GGA* loc. cit. p. 237. Yākūt's ignorance of Greek tradition is well exemplified by the fact that in his article on Iskandarīya in the *Mu'jam* he

Emir of Alep, reproduced *in extenso* by Ibn Khallikān in his *Life*—a letter which contains, among much tedious complaint and fulsome praise, a highly poetical account of the natural beauties of the Greater Merv ('a copy of Paradise'),[21] and of its very considerable intellectual activity, which also occurs in the *Mu'jam*—shows that he devoted much intensive work to the compilation of this work,[22] but it is clear that his sources were in Arabic or Middle Persian. He thus belongs to the same cultural tradition as the much earlier Ṭabarī and Dīnawārī.[23]

It will be seen from the lists of Iskandarīyas in the *Mu'jam* and the *Mushtarik* (see also Table, at end) that they are virtually identical except for one displacement due to the intrusion of Bucephala in the *Mushtarik* list, and, although Yākūt's arithmetic is not quite correct, this and his misuse of his source, al-Faqīh, do not concern us directly.

As may be seen from the Table (at end), the lists in Yākūt up to the thirteenth entry agree closely with that in the Syriac *Romance*.

uniquely postulates the historical existence of two Alexanders, to explain his relationship with Dhū'l-Qarnein; the first built Alexandria in Egypt and was Dhū-l Qarnein, whose real name was Asak (= Arsak), the son of Seleucus, and the second was the son of Philip and the contemporary of Darius: see Friedländer, op. cit. 281 ff.

[21] The Praises of Merv are frequent from early Islamic times onwards (as are those of Herāt): see e.g. the lines of Fakhr al-Dīn Gurgānī (12th cent. AD), the Farsi poet, quoted by H. W. Bailey, *Afghan Studies*, i (1978), 7: 'Delightful Merv, the seat of Princes, delightful Merv, land of happy men, delightful Merv in summer and springtime, in autumn and winter, how could one who has been in heart-rejoicing Merv, live elsewhere?'

[22] For the libraries of Merv, and Yākūt's use of them, see Ibn Khallikān, loc. cit. p. 17.

[23] See Ṭabarī, I, 2, p. 702 l. 5 ff., who says that Alexander built twelve cities, all called Iskandarīya and lists Isbahān, Herāt, Merv, and Samarkand, one named after Darius' daughter, Rūshank, one in the land of the Greeks in the region of Hīlāqūs for the Persians, and some others. There is a full translation of Ṭabarī's account of Alexander in Nöldeke, op. cit. 42 ff. Nöldeke also translates Dīnawārī's narrative (ed. V. Guirgass-Kratchkovsky, 31 ff.), 35 ff.; see also Weymann, op. cit. (note 1, above), pp. 64 ff., who shows that those parts of Dīnawārī that belong to the *Romance* tradition probably derive from an Arabic translation of the Syriac *Romance*, and thus ultimately go back to a Pehlevi original. Dīnawārī also says that Alexander built twelve Iskandarīyas, but lists only seven (p. 41): see pp. 57–8, and Table at end. In listing these cities Ṭabarī and Dīnawārī do not call them Iskandarīyas individually; they are simply given their Arabic names. Yākūt, i. 255, seems to appreciate the historical metonomasy from Greek to Arabic: 'historians say that Alexander built thirteen cities and gave each of them his name; then their names were changed after his time, and each of them received a new name, etc.' I have not encountered this phrase in another text relating to Alexander.

Lists of Iskandarīyas in the Mu'jam *and the* Mushtarik

Alexandria designation	Mu'jam	Mushtarik
in Bāwarnaqūs (?) (Balwarnaqūs, *Musht.*)	1	1
'the Fortified'	2	2
in Hind	3	3
-Bucephala	–	4
in Jālīkūs (Jalīnafūs, *Musht.*)	4	5
in the land of Sakūyāsīs (Sakūbāsīs, *Musht.*)	5	6
on the shore of the Great River	6	7
in Babylon	7	8
in the land of Sugd called Samarkand	8	9
called Margablūs, that is, Merw	9	10
in the valleys of the rivers of Hind	10	11
called Kush, that is, Balkh	11	12
the Great, in the land of Miṣr	12	13

These are the thirteen Alexandrias . . .

between Hamā and Halab	13	14
on the Dijla, between Jamida and Wāsit	14	15
a small town between Mecca and Medina	15	16

This is emphasized by the presence in both lists of the great Islamic centres, Merv, Balkh, and Samarkand, and since interdependence (or rather, the dependence of Yākūt on the Syriac *Romance*) can be discounted, and since there can be no doubt that the Syriac *Romance* depends ultimately on a Pehlevi translation deriving from the original α-text, it may be assumed that the ultimate source for both is to be sought in a Pehlevi text, or, in general terms, in a Pehlevi tradition; and that it was a version of the *Romance* is obviously very probable. This impression of general indebtedness to a Pehlevi original is confirmed by the fact that the same identifications, along with the other cities (including Herāt, not given in Yākūt's list of Alexandrias, but recorded by him in the *Mu'jam* s.v. Herāt, and absent from the Syriac and Ethiopic versions of the *Romance*), reappear as Alexander-foundations in Ṭabārī and Dīnawārī, and in *The Provincial Capitals of Erānshahr*,[24] which dates in its present form from the reign of the Caliph Mansūr in the later eighth century AD, but utilizes sources of a much earlier date.[25]

[24] Op. cit., n. 1 above.
[25] See Markwart, op. cit. 5 ff. For the relevant identifications see §§ 11 (Merv and

Yākūt gives as his own major source the geographer Ibn al-Faqīh al-Hamadānī (d. 289/893), a Persian writer of vital importance in the transmission of the early geographical traditions.[26] It therefore seems reasonable to suppose that the lists in the Syriac *Romance* and in Yākūt, and, in a slightly different form, in Qodāma's *K.al-Kharāj*,[27] represent basically a Middle Persian, pre-Islamic tradition, perhaps originally transmitted to Ibn al-Faqīh through the translations of the shadowy but significant Ibn Moqaffa',[28] though the

Herāt), 53 (Isbahān, also claimed as an Alexander-foundation by Dīnawarī (see above n. 23) and Ibn Rosteh, *BGA* vii. 160, as well as by Ṭabārī (cf. also n. 23). The *Provincial Capitals* attributes the foundation of Samarkand (p. 8) to 'Kayos, the son of Kavat', who 'excavated the foundations of the capital of Samarkand, Siyavakhsh, the son of Kayos, finished it'. This seems to be an earlier tradition than that found in the Syriac *Romance* and in the Arabic authorities quoted, all of whom give the city as an Alexander-foundation: see Markwart, op. cit. 26-7. Jāḥiẓ indicates that the question of the founder of Samarkand was considerably debated, for among the unanswered questions in his *K.al-tarbī' wa al-tadwīr* (ed. Pellat, Damascus, 1955) (cf. id. *Life and Times of Jahiz* (London (1969), 127) is, 'And who built Kardabandad, and who built Samarkand?' The inclusion of Herāt in the Pehlevi text is, of course, explained by the fact that it was a provincial capital, but it is often included in the Arabic lists (see Table 1, no. 2), and its absence from the list in the Syriac and Ethiopic versions is surprising.

[26] Ibn al-Faqīh, in the present abbreviated state of his text (see *BGA* v. Introd.; Minorsky, p. 481, refers to a Mashshad MS of the complete text; cf. n. 29, below), gives only Alexandria in Egypt, Iskanderūn (Iskandarīya bil-Shām, *BGA* v. i. 111) and Merv (ib., p. 71; cf. al-Muqaddasī, *BGA* iii. 298), but Yākūt, who had his complete text (i. 255), says he found thirteen Alexandrias in it, though he himself, as noted above, p. 55, gives only twelve. The total given by Ibn al-Faqīh is repeated in the *Tāj al-'Arūs*, iii. 276, plus five more unnamed ones, to produce a total of sixteen (i.e. fifteen, since the *Tāj* repeats Yākūt's arithmetical error). It is to be noted that (a) in the *Mushtarik* Yākūt includes Bucephala (Table 1, no. 8), which was not properly an Alexandria, (b) in the *Mu'jam* s.v. Thagr, he lists Alexandretta-Iskanderūn as an Iskandarīya, though he does not attribute it to Alexander, as does the *Tāj* (a matter not relevant here), and (c) in the *Mu'jam* s.v. Herāt he makes Herāt an Alexander-foundation. These discrepancies are easily explained by Yākūt's method of compilation.

[27] For Qodāma's *K.al-Kharāj* see the excerpts in *BGA* vi, where his section on Dhū'l-Qarnein-Iskander begins on p. 263 (p. 204, French trans. ibid.). His material, unlike that of the other geographers in this context, is largely legendary narrative. He records (p. 265=F.T. p. 206) Alexander's dealings with the Kings of Tibet and China, where he builds Shūl or Shūk and Khumdān (see below, n. 38), then his return to Turkestan and Sugd, where he built Samarkand, Dabūsīya (mod. Ziaudin; cf. Minorsky, *Ḥudūd al-'ālam*, 352), and Iskandarīya al-Quṣwā, i.e. Eschate. He then went to Bukhārā and built that city, to Merv and built that, to Herāt and built that, and then to Zaranj. He next proceeded to Khargan and ordered the building of Ray, Isbahān, and Hamadān, and then returned to Babylon . . .

[28] On Ibn al-Moqaffa''s role as a transmitter of Persian traditions to the Arab world see the remarks of Nöldeke, *Tabari*, pp. xx-xxiii; cf. id. *Wien. Denkschr.*, loc. cit. 34; Inostranzov, *Iranian Influence in Muslim Literature* (trans. G. K. Nariman, Bombay, 1918), 57 ff.; Gabrieli, *RSO* 13 (1932), 197-247 (cf. P. Kraus, ibid. 14

absence of both an Arabic and a Pehlevi version of the *Romance* prevents our determining how much of this Iranian material may have been collected and pre-digested in these sources, and how much of it was derived from the Greek α-tradition.[29] To the same tradition belong the lists of Alexander-cities in Ṭabārī and Dīnawārī, though these are shorter (and expressly left incomplete by their authors). In all these sources which represent the Pehlevi tradition, the foundations of Alexander that are most prominent are the Iranian cities, Herāt, Merv, Isbahān, and Samarkand, of which only the first figures in the Greek historical and geographical tradition (but not in the *Romance*) if, as seems virtually certain, it is to be identified with Alexandria Ariana. It was all the more natural for the Pehlevi list to contain items that reflect the Sassanian tradition, since the Sassanian writers themselves (or, more precisely, the Arabs who represent their traditions) record the same founding-activity of several of their kings. Thus Ṭabārī and Dīnawārī record of Ardashīr, the founder of the kingdom, the 'foundation' of six cities. Here, as with the Alexander-lists, we are left in total uncertainty whether these cities are simply inventions (one or two are known to later writers under other names), or 'refoundations'—new walls, a new market-place, and so on—of Parthian or Roman Imperial origin.

There is one particular point that may be noted here, on which all the various traditions appear to agree within a very narrow compass: the number of cities founded by Alexander. In the Greek A-text the total is stated to be thirteen, though nine are actually listed, and so also in the Syriac version (thirteen in name and number) and in Eutychius (the number only, with no name except that of Alexandria in Egypt); whereas in the Greek *B* and *Γ* traditions,

(1934), 1–20). For references to him in the *Fihrist* see Dodge's index, esp. pp. 716–17; cf. also al-Qifṭī, *Tārīkh al-Hukamā'* (ed. Lippert, 1903), 220 ll. 1–10. For his possible role in the transmission of an Arabic *Romance* alongside 'Umārah b. Said see Abbott, *Arabic Lit. Pap.* i. 55–6; Grignaschi, op. cit. above, n. 1 (*Bull. d'Ét. d'Or.*), 18 ff. The link between the Iranian (i.e. Pehlevi-Syriac-Arabic) tradition of the *Romance* and the Greek α-tradition is indicated on my stemma below (p. 207) as D. The link within the oriental tradition seems assured, but since the sources of Ibn al-Faqīh, 'Umārah b. Said and Mohammad b. Moqaffa' remain so nebulous it is hardly possible to attach this Iranian tradition to that of the Greek *Romance*.

[29] In this connection our ignorance of the history and sources of Ibn al-Faqīh forms the major obstacle. Chronologically it is perfectly possible for him to have known the earliest Alexander-literature such as 'Umārah's *Qiṣṣat al-Iskandar* (see above, n. 1). For what is known of him see the bibliography in Minorsky's *Abū Dulaf Mis'ar ibn Muhalhil's Travels in Iran* (Cairo, 1955), 2 n. 3, and in *EI²* s.v. Abū Dulaf.

Julius Valerius, Leo the Presbyter, the Armenian and Ethiopic versions, as well in the *Paschal Chronicle* and the *Excerpta*, the figure is twelve, all numbered and listed. Finally, Ṭabārī and Dīnawārī say that he built twelve cities, but list only seven (the actual cities only agreeing in respect of Merv and Jay-Isbahān). It is clearly not a coincidence that Yākūt also gives thirteen cities in his list from Ibn al-Faqīh. The possibility of establishing a clear relationship between the figures and the sources is rendered more difficult by the fact that although the numbers virtually agree (Stephanus' total of nineteen is not relevant here), the cities listed show wide variations as between the Greek and its direct descendants on the one hand and the Iranian tradition on the other. It is clear from the tabular analysis of the data (Table 1) that the Iranian tradition centres on the cities that formed part of the Sassanian and then of the Islamic world, while the Alexandrian tradition was found ready-made, like the *Will of Alexander*, by the author of the α-version of the *Romance*.[30]

One list of Alexandrias, that in the Ethiopic version of the *Romance*, which is closely linked to the Syriac version through an Arabic translation,[31] does not conform to the Iranian pattern, or indeed to any other pattern. Though it consists of the now familiar total of twelve cities, it is in most cases the only testimony for those which it lists. Those not otherwise attested in any recognizable variants are: Alexandria of Sahil (i.e. of the Coast), Alexandria Barkas, Alexandria of Karnikas, Alexandria of Eutraos, Alexandria of Gebro, Alexandria of Babesdeyas (perhaps the same as Yākūt's 'Alexandria in the land of Sakuyasis'), Alexandria of Agmaweyan and Alexandria Bardas. It may be possible to offer rectified versions of these names on the assumption that they are known from other sources and deformed in the Ethiopic text,[32] but

---

[30] See above, pp. 42 ff. The second Iskandarīya in the Syriac and Arabic traditions is 'Iskandarīya the Fortified' (al-Muḥaṣṣana, Yākūt), with no location, and Tarn thought that this might be the (also unlocated) *Alexandria fortissima* of the *Excerpta* (see above p. 21 n. 45), which does not occur in any Greek text of the α-tradition, but occurs in the *B* and *Γ* traditions as ἡ κράτιστος (sic) and ἡ εἰς κράτιστον.

[31] See above, p. 48 with n. 2 for the text of the Ethiopic version, with translation, by Budge. The list is on p. 352 of the 1906 text of the translation, pp. 212–13 of the 1933 edn.

[32] Alexandria Barkas might be taken as representing Barqa of Ifrīqīya (though it would be hazardous to connect it with the Alexandria of Cyrenaica, discussed above) and Alexandria of Karnika might be a disorted version of 'Alexandria on the

even if that provides satisfactory results in itself (which seems very far from certain) it remains true that the list is very different from the Iranian lists, and that it is to that extent a foreign element in the general colour of the text itself. There is no obvious explanation of this marked divergence, which is clearly shown in the Table of Alexandrias.

The survival, outside the regions that belonged successively to the Parthian and Sassanian Empires, of the tradition that Alexander 'founded thirteen cities which are inhabited and dwell in peace until this day',[33] which does not occur in Julius Valerius or in the B and Γ and traditions, is found, slightly elaborated, in both the Armenian and the Syriac versions. The Armenian has 'he built twelve cities which remain to-day, rich and complete and populated by countless people.' The Syriac, closer to the truth has 'He built thirteen cities, some of which are flourishing to this day, but some are laid waste.'[34] I have suggested above that the first part of this phrase is an addition of the author of the α-version of the Romance, and it is of interest to see that the oriental versions have retained it, even invested it with some air of reality, while the later western tradition abandoned it. The final development of this historical, or semi-historical perspective may perhaps be seen in the remark of Yākūt, which derives from Ibn al-Faqīh, and has already been quoted: 'subsequently each of the Alexandrias was given a new name.' This seems to reflect an attempt to explain what happened to the historical cities that Alexander founded in the Iranian world. Alternatively, it is possible to regard it, like the Syriac reference to the destruction of some of the cities, as a

Granikos', found in some Romance lists (see pp. 23-4 nn. 50-1, and Table 1, no. 26). Of the others Budge (1906), 352 n. 1, says, 'It seems hopeless to attempt to emend these names.' Professor E. Ullendorff has, however, made the following suggestions to me: 'A. Barqas probably = Arabic Ba'urnaqus [i.e. no. 1 in Yākūt's list, above, p. 50]; A. of Karnika = A. ἐν Παροπαμισάδαις, i.e. Charikar [see below, pp. 140 ff.]; A. Entraos = A. ἡ Τρωάς; A. Gebro = ?Gedrosia; A. of Babesdayos, a possible corruption of Βουκέφαλα, easily explicable from a misreading of Arabic or Syriac by the Ethiopic; A. of Agamawyan, Merv, Mraw, probable misreading of Arabic r as w; A. of Bardas almost certainly derived from Porus, Portus.' A. of Persia is widely encountered in the various versions of the Romance (see Table 1, no. 22), mostly from the Alexandrian source (see above, p. 31), but A. of Arabia seems unparalleled, although Dīnawārī has a city Najrān allegedly founded by Alexander in ʿUmān (p. 41, l. 7).

[33] See above, pp. 40 ff.

[34] For the Armenian see § 285, ed. Wolohojian; for the Syriac passage, ch. xxiv, p. 142 (ET), Budge.

hypothesis made to accomodate the fact that thirteen cities called Iskandarīya could not be accounted for at the time of the ultimate source of Yākūt's list. Whatever may be the true explanation, there seems no doubt that this notion of the 'cities still at peace', was accorded a particular interpretation in the Iranian tradition.

The last echo of Alexander in the historical Sassanian world seems, appropriately enough, to derive from one of the stray Alexandrian traditions, but not from the *Romance*. It is found in a Byzantine writer of Alexandrian origin, who, on the eve of the Islamic invasion of the Sassanian Empire, reveals some knowledge of the legendary activity of Alexander in Central Asia: Theophylact Simocattes, to whose evidence Droysen long ago drew attention in this connection.[35] Theophylact, writing under Heraclius, and describing in his painfully elaborate style the events of the reign of the Emperor Maurice, and more precisely his Avar campaign of AD 596, devotes a brief description to the relations between two tribes of Chinese Turkestan, among the Avars of 'Sogdiana'. He calls one of these tribes the Taugast, a term which he also uses of their capital city,[36] and which seems to represent the whole region

[35] Theophylact, vii. 8–9, already noted by Droysen, *GE* iii. 224–8 = FT ii. 680–2, whose discussion of the topography and identification of the tribes mentioned by Theophylact, based on suggestions made to him by W. Schott in 1842, is naturally antiquated. The text of the whole of Theophylact's excursus on the Scythians, Avars etc. is the subject of a very detailed study by H. W. Haussig, *Byzantion*, 23 (1953), 275–462, with a critical edition of the text. I limit myself to quoting the immediately relevant passage.

[36] vii. 8. 16 (omitting the description of the customs of the people of Taugast: (p. 284, ll. 34 ff. Hauss.): κατ' αὐτὸν τὸν χρόνον οἱ Ταρνιὰχ καὶ οἱ Κοτζαγηροὶ (καὶ οὗτοι δὲ ἐκ τῶν Οὐὰρ καὶ Χουννὶ) ἀπὸ τῶν Τούρκων ἀποδιδράσκουσι, καὶ πρὸς τὴν Εὐρώπην γενόμενοι τοῖς περὶ τὸν Χαγάνον τῶν Ἀβάρων συνάπτονται. λέγεται δὲ καὶ τοὺς Ζαβενδὲρ ἐκ τοῦ γένους πεφυκέναι τῶν Οὐὰρ καὶ Χουννί. ἡ δὲ γεγονυῖα ἐπίθετος δύναμις τοῖς Ἀβάροις εἰς δέκα χιλιάδας ἠκρίβωτο. (9) ὁ μὲν οὖν τῶν Τούρκων Χαγάνος τὸν ἐμφύλιον καταλυσάμενος πόλεμον εὐδαιμόνως ἐχειραγώγει τὰ πράγματα, ποιεῖται δὲ καὶ συνθήκας πρὸς τοὺς Ταυγάστ, ὅπως βαθείαν πάντοθεν τὴν γαλήνην ἐμπορευόμενος ἀστασίαστον τὴν ἀρχὴν καταστήσεται. ὁ δὲ τῆς Ταυγὰστ κλιματάρχης Ταισὰν ὀνομάζεται, ὅπερ υἱὸς θεοῦ ταῖς Ἑλληνικαῖς φωναῖς ἐνσημαίνεται· ἡ δὲ ἀρχὴ τῆς Ταυγὰστ οὐ στασιάζεται· γένος γὰρ αὐτοῖς τὴν χειροτονίαν τοῦ ἡγεμόνος παρέχεται· τούτωι δὲ τῶι ἔθνει θρησκεία ἀγάλματα, νόμοι δὲ δίκαιοι, καὶ σωφροσύνης ἔμπλεως ὁ βίος αὐτοῖς . . . (p. 285, l. 22, Hauss. (9. 6)) ταύτην δὴ τὴν Ταυγὰστ οἱ βάρβαροι λέγουσι κτίσαι τὸν Μακεδόνα Ἀλέξανδρον, ὁπήνικα τούς τε Βακτριανοὺς καὶ τὴν Σογδιανὴν ἐδουλώσατο δέκα καὶ δύο καταφλέξας μυριάδας βαρβάρων . . . (ibid. l. 32 (9. 8)) λόγος δὲ καὶ ἑτέραν τὸν Ἀλέξανδρον δειμάσθαι πόλιν ἀπὸ σημείων ὀλίγων· Χουβδὰν ὀνομάζουσι ταύτην οἱ βάρβαροι . . . (ibid. p. 286, l. 10 (9. 12)) ἵνα δὲ μὴ ἔξω τῆς νύσσης τὴν ἱστορίαν παροδηγήσωμεν, μέχρι τούτων περὶ τῶν Σκυθῶν τῶν πρὸς τῆι Βακτριανῆι καὶ Σογδιανῆι καὶ τῶι Μέλανι ποταμῶι. For a translation of this see M. and M. Whitby, *The History of Theophylact Simocatta* (Oxford, 1986), 191–2.

The Iranian Tradition 61

of western China, as far west as the Oxus.[37] This 'city' he describes
as divided by a river which had originally separated two warring
sections of the population, but which had been united by the
victory of one side. According to Theophylact, local tradition maintained that the city had been founded by Alexander when he subdued the Bactrians and the Sogdians; and he adds that Alexander
was also said to have founded a second city named Chubdan a few
miles away, also traversed by two large rivers; this second city has
been identified with Hsi-an-fu, a town east of the Tarim basin.
Whatever the source of Theophylact's narrative here, the notice is
significant as indicating that a tradition of Alexander-foundations
on the route to China probably existed in the last days of Byzantine
Alexandria, independently of the *Romance*, before the Islamic
legends developed that took Alexander across the roof of the world
to Tibet and China, and that knowledge of these traditions passed
to the early Byzantine world.[38] The approximately contemporary
evidence of the Chinese pilgrims to the great Buddhist centres of

[37] The region in question, Chinistān, north of the Tarim basin, is covered by
various Arabic accounts of the overland route to China, and is also transmitted in
the *Hudūd al-'ālam*, § 9, from the earlier sources (esp. Jayhanī). It is noteworthy that
Qodāma (see above, n. 27), 264 (F.T. 205-6), in his account of Alexander's
campaign to China, mentions Khumdān, identified as Hsi-an-Fu (Singanfu); for its
possible location see Minorsky's map III (facing p. 230). Haussig, loc. cit. p. 391 ff.,
does not accept this identification, since Qodāma places Khumdān and Shūl
(= Taugast), which he gives as Alexander-foundations, in Shūl = Sogdiana.
Minorsky, loc. cit., suggested a Nestorian source, but Haussig, pp. 299 ff., 386 ff.,
regards a verbal report of the Turkish embassy to Maurice in 583, transmitted by
John of Epiphaneia (*FHG* iv. 272 ff.; cf. Krumbacher, *GBL* i. 244-5) as the ultimate
source for this part of the narrative, but adds (p. 398), 'ob das auch für den Bericht
über die von Alexander gegründeten, Städte Tabgac und Kubdan gilt, können wir
heute nicht mehr feststellen'; cf. also pp. 405-6, where Haussig prefers Menander
to John as a source for the Turkish embassy of 583; cf. T. Olajos, *Les Sources de
Théophylacte Simocatta historien* (Byzantina Neerlandica, 10, Leiden, 1988), 102 ff.
Whatever may be the immediate source or sources of Theophylact, there can be no
doubt that they were ultimately oriental.

[38] Theophylact also mentions (v. 7) a locality called Alexandriana (n. plur.)
near Arbela (AD 591): οἱ μὴν οὖν ἀμφὶ τὸν Χοσρόην Ῥωμαῖοί τε καὶ Πέρσαι
ἐν Ἀλεξανδριανοῖς οὕτω καλουμένωι χώρωι, τέσσαρσιν ἡμέραις ἀφίκοντο· τὴν δὲ
προσηγορίαν ὁ χῶρος ἀπὸ τῶν πράξεων τοῦ Μακεδόνος Ἀλεξάνδρου κατεκληρώσατο· ὁ
τοῦ Φιλίππου γὰρ ἐκεῖσε γενόμενος ἅμα τῆι Μακεδονικῆι δυνάμει τῆι τε Ἑλληνικῆι
ξυμμαχίαι ἐρυμνότατον κατεσκάψατο φρούριον, τούς τε ἐν αὐτῶι βαρβάρους διώλεσεν.
The same place is called Ἀλεξανδρινή, or Ἀλεξανδριανά, in Theoph. 266, De Boor,
p. 410 Bonn (cf. Rawlinson, *Seventh Oriental Monarchy*, p. 485). A locality (χωρίον),
as it is described, named in memory, if only local memory, of the decisive battle, or
some less notable military operation, is by no means unlikely, and there is no
suggestion that it was an Alexander-foundation. It is not recorded elsewhere.

Central Asia, surviving in the form of narratives of their journeys, provide no specific references to cities founded by Alexander.[39]

With this Greek tradition we may compare, on the Arab-Iranian side, a small and detached fragment of the large body (it can hardly be called a corpus) of Arabic literature containing letters that passed between Aristotle and his pupil, which records advice given by Aristotle to Alexander regarding the island of Suḳuṭrā, which lies in the Arabian Sea opposite Cape Guardafui, the Διοσκουρίδους νῆσος of the *Periplus of the Red Sea* and Ptolemy. This island, famous for its export of the aloe-plant, is not mentioned by Strabo, and has therefore been supposed to have remained unknown to Eratosthenes and other Hellenistic geographers. It seems, however, to have been known in the middle of the second century BC to Agatharchides who does not refer to the Island of Dioscourides by name, but calls the group 'The Fortunate Isles'.[40] In the fifth century AD Cosmas Indicopleustes says[41] that the

---

[39] For these sources see the brief summary of their main features in Appendix 3.

[40] GGM i. 190-1 (Phot. = Diod. iii. 47-8): νῆσοι δὲ εὐδαίμονες παρακεῖνται. Agatharchides also refers (ibid. 184 = Diod. iii. 45. 5) to the limited hospitality offered by the tribes in the neighbourhood of Jeddah (Δέβαι): οἱ δ' ἐγχώριοι τῆς μὲν ἐργασίας τῆς τοῦ χρυσοῦ παντελῶς εἰσὶν ἄπειροι, φιλόξενοι δ' ὑπάρχουσιν, οὐ πρὸς πάντας τοὺς ἀφικνουμένους, ἀλλὰ πρὸς μόνους τοὺς ἀπὸ Βοιωτίας καὶ Πελοποννήσου διά τινα παλαιὰν ἀφ' Ἡρακλέους οἰκειότητα πρὸς τὸ ἔθνος, ἣν μυθικῶς ἑαυτοὺς παρειληφέναι παρὰ τῶν προγόνων ἱστοροῦσιν. For the eponymous name see *Peripl.* 30: καὶ κατὰ τοῦτον [Σύαγρος] . . . καὶ κατὰ τοῦτον ἐν τῶι πελάγει νῆσος . . . ἡ Διοσκορίδου καλουμένη, μεγίστη μὲν ἔρημος δὲ καὶ κάθυγρος, κ.τ.λ. Ptol. viii. 22. 17: Ἡ δὲ Διοσκορίδους νῆσος τὴν μεγίστην ὥραν ἔχει ὡρῶν ιβ γο´ κ.τ.λ.; cf. ibid. vi. 7. 45: Διοσκορίδους πόλις in his list of islands in the Persian Gulf.

[41] iii. 65, ed. Wolska-Conus: Ἐν Ταπροβάνηι ἐν τῆι ἐσωτέραι Ἰνδίαι, ἔνθα τὸ Ἰνδικὸν πέλαγός ἐστι, καὶ Ἐκκλησία Χριστιανῶν ἐστιν ἐκεῖ καὶ κληρικοὶ καὶ πιστοί, οὐκ οἶδα δὲ εἰ καὶ περαιτέρω. Ὁμοίως καὶ εἰς τὴν λεγομένην Μαλέ, (the Malay Peninsula) ἔνθα τὸ πιπέρι γίνεται, καὶ ἐν τῆι Καλλιάναι δὲ τῆι καλουμένηι καὶ ἐπίσκοπός ἐστιν ἀπὸ Περσίδος χειροτονούμενος. Ὁμοίως καὶ ἐν τῆι νήσωι τῆι καλουμένηι Διοσκουρίδους κατὰ τὸ αὐτὸ Ἰνδικὸν πέλαγος, ἔνθα καὶ οἱ παροικοῦντες ἑλληνιστὶ λαλοῦσι, πάροικοι τῶν Πτολεμαίων τῶν μετὰ Ἀλέξανδρον τὸν Μακεδόνα ὑπάρχοντες, καὶ κληρικοί εἰσιν ἐκ Περσίδος χειροτονούμενοι καὶ πεμπόμενοι τοῖς αὐτόθι καὶ Χριστιανοὶ πλῆθος· ἣν νῆσον παρέπλευσα μέν, οὐ κατῆλθον δὲ ἐν αὐτῆι. The *Periplus Mar. Erythr.* regards the Greeks who formed part of the population as having gone there for trading purposes (§ 30): οἱ δὲ ἐνοικοῦντες αὐτὴν ὀλίγοι κατὰ μίαν πλευρὰν τῆς νήσου πρὸς ἀπαρκίαν οἰκοῦσι, καθ' ὃ μέρος ἀποβλέπει τὴν ἤπειρον· εἰσὶν δὲ ἐπίξενοι καὶ ἐπίμικτοι Ἀράβων τε καὶ Ἰνδῶν καί τινα μὲν Ἑλλήνων τῶν πρὸς ἐργασίαν ἐκπλεόντων. Both Cosmas and the *Periplus* may be correct, but the latter needs no special justification, whereas Cosmas can have known little of the affairs of Ptolemaic trade. I find it hard to accept the traditional view (most recently expressed by the late G. W. B. Huntingdon, *The Periplus of the Erythraean Sea* (Hakluyt Soc. London, 1980), 103, s.v. (cf. Müller, GGM i. 190, n. on § 103,; Tkatsch; EI¹ s.v. Soḳotrā cols. 476 ff.), that the Island of Dioscourides represents a Hellenization of the Sanskrit *dvipa sukhadhara*, 'island of bliss'; the

island was originally settled by colonists from Ptolemaic Egypt, a statement which, if true, would indicate a Ptolemaic interest not only on the east coast of Africa, where the elephant-stations lay, but also in securing a strategic point for trade to India via the south Arabian coast.[42] In the light of known Seleucid authority over the islands of the Gulf, the foundation, if Hellenistic, might more plausibly be claimed for the kings of Asia; both parties will have had Dioscourideses available for the task and the name of the settlement. Be that as it may, the fullest version of the story about Suḳuṭrā occurs in Yākūt's entry under Suḳuṭrā, but an earlier version, perhaps the first from an Arabic source, is preserved in the narrative of Abū Zayd al-Hasan, a merchant of Sīrāf, of the ninth century AD, whose short text provides a picture of early Islamic knowledge of India and China, forming a supplement to the slightly earlier narrative of the same regions with which it is linked in the one manuscript that contains it. Abū Zayd, and after him Yākūt, links the island with Alexander and Aristotle, and though the whole story is probably an Arab or, more precisely Sīrāfian, concoction (for it does not seem to occur outside the very small group of texts relating to Suḳuṭrā), it shows how Alexander might have developed his plan for trade in the south and east. Abū Zayd says:[43] 'And in the sea is an island known as Sukuṭra, and the aloe of Sukutra grows there, and its position is close to the land of

name, like that of many other Ptolemaic stations down to the Bab al-Mandeb, may well derive from a leader of an expedition, governor or colonizer. The suggestion reported by Huntingdon (p. 146) of the name Τρωγοδύται, that the word 'is akin to the Arabic ṭawāriq, sing. ṭāriqa' is equally unconvincing.

[42] See *Ptol. Alex.* i. 173 ff.

[43] This text was published by Reinaud in his *Relations des Voyages*, etc., ii. 133-4 (FT i. 139-40) (Paris, 1845), and subsequently by J. Sauvaget, *'Akhbar as-Sin wa' l-Hind* (Paris, 1948) (the text of the first part only); see also A. Miquel, *La Géographie humaine du monde musulman jusqu'au milieu de Xᵉ siècle* (Paris, 1967), i. 121 ff. There is a bibliography and a discussion of the use al-Masū'dī made in the *Murūj* of Abū Zayd in Sauvaget, op. cit. pp. xxiv-xxvi; a summary in Miquel, loc. cit., and also in A. M. H. Shboul, *Al-Mas'ūdī and his World* (London, 1979), 155 ff., with notes. Al-Hamdānī, (ed. D. H. Müller (1884), 53) attributes the Greek presence on Suḳuṭrā to Sassanian deportations of Greeks of Rūm to the island: 'and on it are members of all the tribes of Mahra, and there are about 10,000 warriors, who are Christians, and they record that people from the territories of Rūm, whom Kisra settled in it; and it was after that that tribes of the Mahra settled there and they became Christians alongside them . . .'; cf. Yākūt *Mu'jam* s.v. Suḳuṭrā , from Ibn Quṭā'. The Arabs, like their predecessors, were chiefly interested in the island as the source of aloe. The story does not seem to belong to the usual canon of correspondence between Alexander and Aristotle.

the Zenj [the head of the Persian Gulf, as far as Baṣra] and Arabia, and the majority of the inhabitants are Christians. The reason for this is that when Alexander overcame the King of Persia he wrote to his teacher Aristotle, and told him what had befallen him in the lands he had conquered. And Aristotle wrote to him and instructed him to find the island in the sea called Suḵuṭrā where grew the aloe, which is a most potent medicine, without which any collection of drugs would be incomplete; and told him that the proper course would be for him to deport the present inhabitants of the island and to establish there some Greeks to guard the aloe, so that it might be exported to Syria, Rūm and Miṣr. And Alexander proceeded to remove the population and settled the island with Greeks, and told the "minor kings", who, since he had defeated Darius, were under his dominion, that they too should protect the island. And the population remained in safety until Allah sent Jesus (the Peace of Allah be upon him), and the Greek inhabitants then heard his message and they all embraced Christianity, as did the whole of Rūm. The survivors of these Greeks remained on the island until the present time along with the rest of the inhabitants who were of different stock.' The text is a curiosity both in itself and for the link it establishes on the one hand with exploration in the Ptolemaic period, as transmitted by Cosmas, and on the other with the earliest recorded Arab trading records in the Gulf.

With the main strands of the various traditions thus separated, in so far as that is possible when dealing with so interwoven a mesh of material, we must now consider the possibility of identifying the authentic foundations on the ground. This is the main purpose of the remaining chapters of the book. I omit any further consideration of those sites that have been dismissed above as unhistorical.

CHAPTER III
Summary of the Eastern Campaigns

IT is not my purpose in this brief chapter to do more than indicate, on the basis of Arrian's narrative of Alexander's campaigns, where Alexander is recorded as having founded major settlements, or actual cities, with a brief note also of the circumstances in which this occurred. This introduction will, it is hoped, help the reader to follow the problems that arise in identifying the foundations thereafter.[1]

The first foundation recorded to have been made by Alexander in the narrative of his campaign is that of Alexandria in Egypt in spring 331.[2] We need not concern ourselves with the details of this foundation, the site and occasion of which are not in doubt, though we should keep it in mind as providing the fullest statement of motive and procedure in the construction of any of Alexander's foundations. Alexandria in Egypt apart, Alexander did not, as has frequently been observed, make any foundations—a term I use here and elsewhere to include both cities properly so called (πόλεις) and major settlements not specifically described as cities—until he had crossed the Tigris in autumn 331, won the Battle of Gaugamela and advanced into the Iranian regions later known as 'The Upper Satrapies', that is, east of Media. Effectively, it was not until the midsummer of the following year, with the conclusion of the very inadequately chronicled campaigns against the Hyrcanian tribes on the south shore of the Caspian Sea, that this activity

---

[1] Since this is only a skeleton narrative, without any attempt at analysis of sources, I have confined my quotations to Arrian, where he provides the necessary information. For a critical analysis of the text see A. B. Bosworth's commentary on Books 1-3 (Oxford, 1980); the second volume of this will have appeared before the present work (Oxford, 1995). P. A. Brunt's comprehensive Loeb edition of Arrian contains the details of the variant traditions.

[2] Arr. iii. 1, etc. For a full discussion see *Ptolemaic Alexandria*, ch. 1, *passim*.

began, with his entry into the Persian satrapy of Aria, the capital of which was Artacoana. As we shall see, it was somewhere in the neighbourhood of Artacoana that Alexandria 'of the Arians', or Alexandria Ariana, was founded; but our historical sources neither refer to the foundation nor name the city at all; on any count, a very striking omission. His route thereafter ran in general through the regions of Drangiana and Arachosia, until he reached the foot of Mt. Caucasus, the main range of the Hindu Kush (as opposed to the westward extension of it, the Koh-i-Bābā of today). Here, we are told, before crossing the mountain-range in the winter of 330/29, he founded at its foot a city called Alexandria.[3] This, the first of the eastern settlements recorded by Arrian, probably set the general pattern for the later foundations made in the campaign, in respect of the choice of location, settlement and demographic plan, but Arrian gives little information on these points.

Once across the mountains, by whichever pass he may have taken, Alexander was in the southern part of Bactria, the Iranian and Arab Tocharistān, the Turkestan of modern nomenclature, the province which lay on both sides of the Oxus. Snow, we are told, was still on the plains, and unless this is a rhetorical exaggeration we must suppose that he and his forces had climbed over one of the snow-bound passes,[4] by April 329, by which time, or shortly after, the snow would have melted in the northern plain of Turkestan.

Still in the same year, having crossed the Oxus and the northern part of Bactria and then Sogdiana and the region of the Islamic and modern Samarkand and Farghāna, Alexander reached the Tanais (Jaxartes; the Syr-Darya), where he undertook the foundation of a new city named after him;[5] this city, planned primarily for defensive purposes, on a large scale, was evidently close

---

[3] iii. 28. 1: ἐπῆλθε δὲ καὶ τῶν Ἰνδῶν τοὺς προσχώρους Ἀραχώταις. ξύμπαντα δὲ ταῦτα τὰ ἔθνη διὰ χιόνος τε πολλῆς καὶ ξὺν ἀπορίαι τῶν ἐπιτηδείων καὶ τῶν στρατιωτῶν ταλαιπορίαι ἐπῆλθε. For the possibly exaggerated experience of the Chinese pilgrim Hsüan-Tsang in crossing the Hindu Kush in winter see below, pp. 230–1.

[4] See pp. 157 ff., for the question of the most likely pass to have been used.

[5] iv. 1. 3–4; Αὐτὸς δὲ πρὸς τῶι Ταναΐδι ποταμῶι ἐπενόει πόλιν οἰκίσαι, καὶ ταύτην ἑαυτοῦ ἐπώνυμον. ὅ τε γὰρ χῶρος ἐπιτήδειος αὐτῶι ἐφαίνετο αὐξῆσαι ἐπὶ μέγα τὴν πόλιν καὶ ἐν καλῶι οἰκισθήσεσθαι τῆς ἐπὶ Σκύθας, εἴποτε ξυμβαίνοι, ἐλάσεως καὶ τῆς προφυλακῆς τῆς χώρας πρὸς τὰς καταδρομὰς τῶν πέραν τοῦ ποταμοῦ ἐποικούντων βαρβάρων. ἐδόκει δ' ἂν καὶ μεγάλη γενέσθαι ἡ πόλις πλήθει τε τῶν ἐς αὐτὴν ξυνοικιζομένων καὶ τοῦ ὀνόματος τῆι λαμπρότητι.

to the river; it is the Alexandreschata of Appian.[6] Its precise location will be discussed at a later stage, but we may note that Arrian emphasizes here that Alexander made a point of naming it after himself, and it is likely that he intended it to supersede the native or Iranian settlement which he calls Cyropolis, founded by Cyrus the Great, the sixth of the seven cities of the region which he took over.[7] The city appears to have been planned with the same care as Alexandria in Egypt, and, as in Egypt, Alexander is said to have taken an active part in supervising its construction: he spent twenty days devising the circuit of the walls, settled time-expired Greek mercenaries and local natives in it, and held a gymnastic and equestrian festival there, as he had done at Memphis in 331 and as he did later at Taxila.[8] The care and attention given to this foundation is worthy of note, but in general we know so little of what occurred when a foundation was made that we can hardly single it out as a special case.

The following winter, that of 329/8, Alexander spent at Bactra-Zariaspa,[9] enjoying the fruits of that land of grapes, but his excesses and serious errors of judgement—the murder of Kleitos, the substitution of Persian court-dress for Macedonian military accoutrement, the incarceration of Callisthenes—enacted the first stages of that process of deterioration that slowly unfolded in the grim years of fighting and hardship that lay ahead. At that time, too, if not in the previous season's campaign in Sogdiana, there seems to have formed in his mind the determination to press on down the great river-valleys that he had seen on his right hand as he marched towards the Hindu Kush, into Gandhara, the furthest satrapy of the Achaemenian Empire, and beyond.[10] In spring 328 he returned

---

[6] App. *Syr.* 57; see below, pp. 151 ff.

[7] Arr. iv. 2. 1–2: ταῦτα ὡς ἀπηγγέλθη Ἀλεξάνδρωι, παραγγείλας τοῖς πεζοῖς κατὰ λόχους κλίμακας ποιεῖσθαι ὅσαι ἑκάστωι λόχωι ἐπηγγέλθησαν, αὐτὸς μὲν ἐπὶ τὴν πρώτην ἀπὸ τοῦ στρατοπέδου ὁρμηθεὶς πόλιν προὐχώρει, ἧι ὄνομα ἦν Γάζα· ἐς γὰρ ἑπτὰ πόλεις ξυμπεφευγέναι ἐλέγοντο οἱ ἐκ τῆς χώρας βάρβαροι· Κράτερον δὲ ἐκπέμπει πρὸς τὴν καλουμένην Κυρούπολιν, ἥπερ μεγίστη πασῶν καὶ ἐς αὐτὴν οἱ πλεῖστοι ξυνειλεγμένοι ἦσαν τῶν βαρβάρων.

[8] See below, p. 160.

[9] Arr. iv. 7. 1: ταῦτα δὲ διαπραξάμενος ἐς Ζαρίασπα ἀφίκετο· καὶ αὐτοῦ κατέμενεν ἔστε παρελθεῖν τὸ ἀκμαῖον τοῦ χειμῶνος.

[10] Ibid. 15. 6: αὐτῶι δὲ τὰ Ἰνδῶν ἔφη ἐν τῶι τότε μέλειν. τούτους γὰρ καταστρεψάμενος πᾶσαν ἤδη ἔχειν τὴν Ἀσίαν· ἐχομένης δὲ τῆς Ἀσίας ἐπανιέναι ἂν ἐς τὴν Ἑλλάδα, ἐκεῖθεν δ' ἐφ' Ἑλλησπόντου τε καὶ τῆς Προποντίδος ξὺν τῆι δυνάμει πάσηι τῆι τε ναυτικῆι καὶ τῆι πεζικῆι ἐλάσειν εἴσω τοῦ Πόντου· καὶ ἐς τὸ τότε ἠξίου ἀποθέσθαι Φαρασμάνην ὅσα ἐν τῶι παραυτίκα ἐπηγγέλλετο.

to Sogdiana in a further attempt to subdue the country, and once more destroyed villages and townships of the oasis of Samarkand. He seems here to have concentrated scattered villages into larger units for ease of supervision, but it is not stated that he settled any of his own troops in the area. The task itself he entrusted to Hephaestion, and the operation can hardly be regarded as constituting a complete operation aimed at permanent settlement.[11] The winter of 328/7 he passed at Nautaka, one of the old cities of Sogdiana,[12] on one of the right hand affluents of the Oxus, and in the spring of that year made his famous assault on the Sogdian and Chorienes Rocks.[13] Then, in early summer 327, he finally left Sogdiana, and set out towards India. He passed back over the Hindu Kush, by a different route from that by which he had entered Bactria, and made his stay at his new city, Alexandria ad Caucasum, where he established more settlers, both natives and unusable military personnel, and appointed Nikanor, one of the Companions, to continue the development of the site.[14] In this context also we are told by Arrian that Alexander reached Nikaia, a settlement which he established somewhere on the south side of the range when travelling north, before reaching the latter site; it is a settlement of which we hear nothing more; its possible location is discussed in due course.

The army then turned eastward and followed the course of the upper valley of the Kophen river (the Kābul), and at some point the forces divided. Hephaestion probably followed that river to Peukelaotis on the western side of the Indus,[15] and established contact with the ruler, Taxiles, while Alexander made a lengthy detour

[11] Ibid. 16. 3: The cities were evidently already in existence: καὶ οἱ ἄλλοι ὡς ἑκάστοις προὐχώρει ἐπήιεσαν, τοὺς μέν τινας τῶν ἐς τὰ ἐρύματα ξυμπεφευγότων βίαι ἐξαιροῦντες. τοὺς δὲ καὶ ὁμολογίαι προσχωροῦντάς σφισιν ἀναλαμβάνοντες. ὡς δὲ ξύμπασα αὐτῶι ἡ δύναμις ἐπελθοῦσα τῶν Σογδιανῶν τῆς χώρας τὴν πολλὴν ἐς Μαράκανδα ἀφίκετο, Ἡφαιστίωνα μὲν ἐκπέμπει τὰς ἐν τῆι Σογδιανῆι πόλεις συνοικίζειν, κ.τ.λ.

[12] Ibid. 18. 2: Ἀλέξανδρος δὲ περὶ Ναύτακα ἀναπαύων τὴν στρατιὰν ὅ τι περ ἀκμαῖον τοῦ χειμῶνος, κ.τ.λ.

[13] Cf. ibid. in continuation of the passage quoted in the preceding note.

[14] Ibid. 22. 5: προσκατοικίσας δὲ καὶ ἄλλους τῶν περιοίκων τε καὶ ὅσοι τῶν στρατιωτῶν ἀπόμαχοι ἦσαν ἐς τὴν Ἀλεξάνδρειαν Νικάνορα μέν, ἕνα τῶν ἑταίρων, τὴν πόλιν αὐτὴν κοσμεῖν ἐκέλευσε, κ.τ.λ.

[15] Ibid. 22. 7: ἔνθα δὴ διελὼν τὴν στρατιὰν Ἡφαιστίωνα μὲν καὶ Περδίκκαν ἐκπέμπει ἐς τὴν Πευκελαῶτιν χώραν ὡς ἐπὶ τὸν Ἰνδὸν ποταμόν, ἔχοντας τήν τε Γοργίου τάξιν καὶ Κλείτου καὶ Μελεάγρου καὶ τῶν ἑταίρων ἱππέων τοὺς ἡμισέας καὶ τοὺς μισθοφόρους ἱππέας ξύμπαντας, προστάξας τά τε κατὰ τὴν ὁδὸν χωρία ἢ βίαι ἐξαιρεῖν ἢ ὁμολογίαι παρίστασθαι καὶ ἐπὶ τὸν Ἰνδὸν ποταμὸν ἀφικομένους παρασκευάζειν ὅσα ἐς τὴν διάβασιν τοῦ ποταμοῦ ξύμφορα.

by a route which cannot be determined with certainty, but which probably lay north along the Kunar river, and across the Lowarai pass (or south of it) into the tribal areas of southern Swat, the home of the Aspasii, the Gouraioi, and the Assaceni.[16] When he eventually reached the plain north of Charsadda, by way of the Malakand pass, at a place called Arigaion, he reconstructed the site which had been burnt and deserted by its inhabitants, and enlarged it. Regarding the position as advantageously situated, he instructed Krateros to fortify it and to synoecize and populate it with local volunteers and time-expired troops; but apparently he did not choose to give the city his name.[17] Similarly, he fortified Massaga and Ora, two other native towns which he captured, the first after overcoming considerable resistance,[18] and encircled Bazira with a wall,[19] while Hephaestion and Perdiccas with their forces fortified and garrisoned another settlement said to have been called Orobatis, the name of which sounds suspiciously Greek.[20] All these native forts and refortified settlements on the foothills that skirt the plain of Peshawar served a purely military purpose, and they do not appear to have had the mixed population assigned to the larger garrison-cities.

It was only after the victory over Poros on the Hydaspes (Jhelum) in the early summer of 326 that Alexander founded two new cities,[21]

---

[16] Arr. iv. 23-7.

[17] Ibid. 24. 6-7: ὑπερβαλὼν δὲ τὰ ὄρη Ἀλέξανδρος ἐς πόλιν κατῆλθεν, ἧι ὄνομα ἦν Ἀριγαῖον· καὶ ταύτην καταλαμβάνει ἐμπεπρησμένην ὑπὸ τῶν ἐνοικούντων καὶ τοὺς ἀνθρώπους πεφευγότας. ἐνταῦθα δὲ ἀφίκοντο αὐτῶι καὶ οἱ ἀμφὶ Κράτερον ξὺν τῆι στρατιᾶι πεπραγμένων σφίσι ξυμπάντων ὅσα ὑπὸ τοῦ βασιλέως ἐτέτακτο. ταύτην μὲν δὴ τὴν πόλιν, ὅτι ἐν ἐπικαίρωι χωρίωι ἐδόκει ὠικίσθαι, ἐκτειχίσαι τε προστάσσει Κρατέρωι καὶ ξυνοικίσαι ἐς αὐτὴν τούς τε προσχώρους ὅσοι ἐθελονταὶ καὶ εἰ δή τινες ἀπόμαχοι τῆς στρατιᾶς.

[18] The siege of Massaga, ἡ μεγίστη τῶν ταύτηι πόλεων, is described at length, ibid. 26-7. It is noteworthy that on this occasion the Indian chiefs or the Persian authorities were able to rely on a military organization which included what Arrian, no doubt from Ptolemy, calls mercenaries: 26. 1: θαρρήσαντες οἱ βάρβαροι τοῖς μισθοφόροις τοῖς ἐκ τῶν πρόσω Ἰνδῶν, ἦσαν γὰρ οὗτοι ἐς ἑπτακισχιλίους κ.τ.λ. The subsequent unwillingness of the Indian mercenaries to join forces with Alexander and fight other Indians is recorded (27. 3).

[19] Ibid. 27. 5-28. 1.

[20] Ibid. 28. 5: καὶ οἱ ἀμφὶ Ἡφαιστίωνά τε καὶ Περδίκκαν αὐτῶι ἄλλην πόλιν ἐκτειχίσαντες, Ὀροβάτις ὄνομα τῆι πόλει ἦν, καὶ φρουρὰν καταλιπόντες ὡς ἐπὶ τὸν Ἰνδὸν ποταμὸν ἤιεσαν.

[21] Arr. v. 19. 4 fin.: ἵνα δὲ ἡ μάχη ξυνέβη καὶ ἔνθεν ὁρμηθεὶς ἐπέρασε τὸν Ὑδάσπην ποταμὸν πόλεις ἔκτισεν Ἀλέξανδρος. καὶ τὴν μὲν Νίκαιαν τῆς νίκης τῆς κατ' Ἰνδῶν ἐπώνυμον ὠνόμασε, τὴν δὲ Βουκεφάλαν ἐς τοῦ ἵππου τοῦ Βουκεφάλα τὴν μνήμην, ὃς ἀπέθανεν αὐτοῦ, κ.τ.λ.

Nikaia on the left bank, Bucephala on the right, the former evidently on, or close to, the scene of the battle, east of the river. These cities (they are called πόλεις) were built and fortified again by Krateros, who must be regarded as the most active agent of Alexander's Indian foundations, and, once more, Alexander celebrated his victory and foundations with games.[22] It seems that their construction was not sufficiently substantial to provide protection against the coming rains, for both cities needed repairs after the monsoons, when Alexander returned a few months later.[23] In the meantime he had advanced across the eastern tributaries of the Indus until the mutiny at the Hyphasis forced him to retrace his steps, preventing him from advancing to the Sutlej, beyond which, across the Punjab, lay the first drainage of the Ganges water-system. The furthest point of the advance was marked at the Beas, according to Diodorus, by the construction of twelve altars as tall as, and wider than, towers, 'memorials of his labours', and a ditch with a rampart and an earth wall.[24] The journey back to the Indus was marked by no significant foundations, though Arrian tells us that on reaching the Akesines he found 'the city that he had ordered Hephaestion to build' completed, and that he settled as many of the native population as volunteered and some time-expired mercenaries (not said to be volunteers) in it.[25] This, the most eastern of Alexander's foundations, mentioned only casually, is left without a name.

The following year at the main junction of the Akesines with the Indus, above Mithankot, he ordered Philippos, whom he appointed satrap of the Indus valley region, to build a city, and we are

[22] Arr. v. 20. 1: ὁ δὲ τοῖς θεοῖς τὰ νομιζόμενα ἐπινίκια ἔθυε, καὶ ἀγὼν ἐποιεῖτο αὐτῶι γυμνικὸς καὶ ἱππικὸς αὐτοῦ ἐπὶ τῆι ὄχθηι τοῦ Ὑδάσπου, ἵνα τὸ πρῶτον διέβη ἅμα τῶι στρατῶι.
[23] Ibid. 29. 5 fin.: καὶ τὸν Ἀκεσίνην αὖ διαβὰς ἐπὶ τὸν Ὑδάσπην ἧκεν, ἵνα καὶ τῶν πόλεων τῆς τε Νικαίας καὶ τῶν Βουκεφάλων ὅσα πρὸς τῶν ὄμβρων πεπονηκότα ἦν ξὺν τῆι στρατιᾶι ἐπεσκεύασε καὶ τὰ ἄλλα τὰ κατὰ τὴν χώραν ἐκόσμει.
[24] Diod. xvii. 95. 1-2: κρίνας δ' ἐπὶ ταύτης τοὺς ὅρους θέσθαι τῆς στρατιᾶς πρῶτον μὲν τῶν δώδεκα θεῶν βωμοὺς πεντήκοντα πηχῶν ὠικοδόμησεν, ἔπειτα τριπλασίαν τῆς προϋπαρχούσης στρατοπεδείαν περιβαλόμενος ὤρυξε τάφρον τὸ μὲν πλάτος πεντήκοντα ποδῶν τὸ δὲ βάθος τεσσαράκοντα, τὴν δ' ἀναβολὴν ἐντὸς τῆς τάφρου σωρεύσας τεῖχος ἀξιόλογον ὠικοδόμησε κ.τ.λ.
[25] Arr. v. 29. 2-3: διαβὰς δὲ τὸν Ὑδραώτην, ἐπὶ τὸν Ἀκεσίνην αὖ ἐπανήιει ὀπίσω. καὶ ἐνταῦθα καταλαμβάνει τὴν πόλιν ἐξωικοδομημένην, ἥντινα Ἡφαιστίων αὐτῶι ἐκτειχίσαι ἐτάχθη· καὶ ἐς ταύτην ξυνοικίσας τῶν τε προσχώρων ὅσοι ἐθελονταὶ κατωικίζοντο καὶ τῶν μισθοφόρων ὅ τι περ ἀπόμαχον, αὐτὸς τὰ ἐπὶ τῶι καταπλῶι παρεσκευάζετο τῶι ἐς τὴν μεγάλην θάλασσαν.

told that he did so 'in the hope that it would become great and glorious among men'; he also ordered dockyards to be built.[26] Unfortunately Arrian does not name the city thus envisaged at this vitally important and dramatically situated point, but Diodorus and Curtius Rufus say that it was an Alexandria, and that he assigned to it a population of 10,000 inhabitants.[27] It is not clear that it was ever built, and some believe, perhaps with good reason, that it was not.

Still further south, at the capital of Musicanus, whom he left in overall charge of his domain, Alexander fortified the acropolis and installed a garrison to supervise the tribes of the area—once more a purely military measure, the wisdom of which was shown by the immediate revolt of Musicanus. Arrian is curiously emphatic that though the planning of the fortification was once more entrusted to Krateros, Alexander was present himself.[28] Peithon was taken over the Indus to do the same on the west side, and Hephaestion was instructed to supervise the completion of the fortification of the acropolis at Patala,[29] while Alexander began the construction of yet another harbour in the Indus delta.[30]

Alexander left Patala and began his march through Baluchistan in advance of Nearchos, and crossing the river Arabios, invaded the territory of the Oritai, reaching their capital, Rambakia, probably near the modern Las Bela, at the northern extremity of the Porali delta, which he rebuilt as Alexandria, 'for it seemed to him that the city settled there would become great and prosperous'.

[26] Arr. vi. 15. 2: Φιλίππωι μὲν δὴ τῆς σατραπείας ὅρους ἔταξε τὰς συμβολὰς τοῦ τε Ἀκεσίνου καὶ Ἰνδοῦ καὶ ἀπολείπει ξὺν αὐτῶι τούς τε Θρᾶικας πάντας καὶ ἐκ τῶν τάξεων ὅσοι ἐς φυλακὴν τῆς χώρας ἱκανοὶ ἐφαίνοντο, πόλιν τε ἐνταῦθα κτίσαι ἐκέλευσεν ἐπ᾽ αὐτῆι τῆι ξυμβολῆι τοῖν ποταμοῖν, ἐλπίσας μεγάλην τε ἔσεσθαι καὶ ἐπιφανῆ ἐς ἀνθρώπους, καὶ νεωσοίκους ποιηθῆναι.

[27] Diod. xvii. 102. 4: περὶ δὲ τούτους τοὺς τόπους ἔκτισε πόλιν Ἀλεξάνδρειαν κατὰ τὸν ποταμόν, μυρίους καταλέξας οἰκήτορας; cf. Curt. Ruf. ix. 8. 8: *itaque oppido ibi condito, quod Alexandream appellari iussit.* Diodorus' narrative here bears little resemblance to that of Arrian, and he gives no clear geographical indication of the location.

[28] Arr. vi. 15. 7: καὶ οὖν καὶ Μουσικανῶι ἐπὶ τοῖσδε ἄδεια ἐδόθη ἐξ Ἀλεξάνδρου, καὶ τὴν πόλιν ἐθαύμασεν Ἀλέξανδρος καὶ τὴν χώραν, καὶ ἄρχειν αὐτῆς Μουσικανῶι ἔδωκε. Κράτερος δὲ ἐν τῆι πόλει ἐτάχθη τὴν ἄκραν ἐκτειχίσαι· καὶ παρόντος ἔτι ἐτειχίσθη Ἀλεξάνδρου καὶ φυλακὴ κατεστάθη, ὅτι ἐπιτήδειον αὐτῶι ἐφάνη τὸ χωρίον ἐς τὸ κατέχεσθαι τὰ κύκλωι ἔθνη φυλαττόμενα.

[29] Ibid. 17. 4.

[30] Ibid. 18. 2. At 20. 1, Hephaestion is instructed to complete the work begun by Alexander on the harbour and dockyards of Patala. For the changes in the Indus delta see below: pp. 163-4.

Here he left Hephaestion in charge of building and settling the site.[31]

The remainder of Alexander's journey along the coast of the Persian Gulf did not, so far as we know, include the foundation of settlements,[32] but right at the end of his life, when occupied with the problem of the irrigation of the Lower Euphrates and the marshlands on the Arabian side at the head of the Persian Gulf— which had then a very different configuration from that of modern times—he probably made one final foundation, which was to survive for a long time, Alexandria, later (as the capital of a petty ruler of the area) called Spasinou Charax.[33]

The picture thus presented by the historians, and primarily by Arrian, is, then, as follows. A few foundations, or refoundations, were evidently conceived as permanent centres of habitation, like Alexandria in Egypt, which had been established in very different circumstances from the eastern foundations, before the pressure of the onward movement of the campaign forced Alexander to give exclusive attention to military operations, most frequently at very short notice. These eastern foundations are, as recorded by the historians, Alexandria ad Caucasum, Nikaia, Alexandria on the Jaxartes, the first two south of the Hindu Kush, the latter on or near the Amū Darya; and in Gandhara and beyond, on the Jhelum, a second Nikaia and Bucephala, and an unnamed city at the junction of the Akesines and the Indus. In addition to these are the major settlements recorded as begun, but not necessarily completed, on the water-system of the Lower Indus, from the junction of the two last-named rivers down to the then Indus delta. On the

---

[31] Ibid. 21. 5: ἀφικόμενος δὲ εἰς κώμην, ἥπερ ἦν μεγίστη τοῦ ἔθνους τοῦ Ὠρειτῶν, Ῥαμβακία ἐκαλεῖτο ἡ κώμη, τόν τε χῶρον ἐπήνεσε καὶ ἐδόκει ἂν αὐτῶι πόλις ξυνοικισθεῖσα μεγάλη καὶ εὐδαίμων γενέσθαι. Ἡφαιστίωνα μὲν δὴ ἐπὶ τούτοις ὑπελείπετο; cf. 22. 3 (role of Leonnatos). Arrian does not state that this city was renamed Alexandria. This is recorded by Diod. xvii. 104, 6. Curt. Ruf. ix. 10. 7, says that it was populated with Arachosians, but the synoecism was no doubt largely of local Oritai tribesmen. See below, pp. 164 ff.

[32] For the supposed renaming of the capital of the Gedrosians as Alexandria, not recorded in the historical sources or by Nearchus (Arr. vi. 24. 1; *Ind.* 34), see below, pp. 166, n. 116.

[33] vii. 21. 7: τούτων ἕνεκα ἐπί τε τὸν Πολλακόπαν ἔπλευσε καὶ κατ᾽ αὐτὸν καταπλεῖ ἐς τὰς λίμνας ὡς ἐπὶ τὴν Ἀράβων γῆν. ἔνθα χῶρόν τινα ἐν καλῶι ἰδὼν πόλιν ἐξωικοδόμησέ τε καὶ ἐτείχισε, καὶ ἐν ταύτηι κατώικισε τῶν Ἑλλήνων τινὰς τῶν μισθοφόρων, ὅσοι τε ἑκόντες καὶ ὅσοι ὑπὸ γήρως ἢ κατὰ πήρωσιν ἀπόλεμοι ἦσαν. The Alexander-name is from Juba: see below, pp. 168 ff. where the metonomasy and location of the site are discussed.

return journey by land through the territory of the Oritai we hear of a formal (re)foundation in that region, Alexandria-Rambakia, and, finally, in the last months, of the foundation of Alexandria in the lower Euphrates-Pallacopas canal area, the later Spasinou-Charax.

This survey leaves out of account the numerous purely defensive positions, sometimes in open country, but not infrequently on the hill-forts of native chieftains, which were fortified by Alexander for immediate defensive purposes; these are easily identifiable in the narrative, and there is no need to cumber the discussion with further reference to these minor military outposts. The campaign could not have been fought without the use of such positions.

A chronological table, with reference to the historians, is appended. The dates, it need hardly be said, are only approximate. I have not distinguished the instances in which Alexander is said to have delegated the construction to another person (Hephaestion, Krateros, etc.).

Spring 331: foundation of Alexandria in Egypt (Arr. iii. 1 ff.).

Winter/Spring 329: Alexandria ad Caucasum (Arr. iii. 28; cf. Diod. xvii. 83. 1, Curt. Ruf. vii. 3. 23), and Nikaia (Arr. iv. 22. 5; cf. Diod. xvii. 83. 2).[34]

Early Summer 326: Nikaia (and Alexandria-Bucephala): (Arr. v. 19. 4; cf. ibid. 29. 4, Diod. xvii. 89. 6; Curt. Ruf. ix. 1. 56); an unnamed city at the junction of the Akesines and Indus (Arr. v. 29. 3).

Spring 325: Alexandria at the junction of the Akesines and Indus (Arr. vi. 15. 2; cf. Diod. xvii. 102. 4. Curt. Ruf. ix. 8. 8).

Summer 325: synoecism of existing walled cities on the west bank of the lower Indus (Arr. vi. 15. 4).

Autumn 325: construction of harbours etc. at Patala (Arr. vi. 18. 1, 20. 1).

[34] Diod. xvii. 83. 3: ὁ δὲ Ἀλέξανδρος καὶ ἄλλας πόλεις ἔκτισεν ἡμέρας ὁδὸν ἀπεχούσας τῆς Ἀλεξανδρείας. κατώικισε δ᾽εἰς ταύτας τῶν μὲν βαρβάρων ἑπτακισχιλίους, τῶν δ᾽ἐκτὸς τάξεως συνακολουθούντων τρισχιλίους καὶ τῶν μισθοφόρων τοὺς βουλομένους. It is difficult to believe in the 'cities' founded a day's march from Alexandria, and it seems likely that, if the narrative is to be rationalized, the passage should be taken to refer to Nikaia, to which Diodorus does not otherwise refer. See further below, p. 146, n. 79.

Winter 325/4: foundation of Alexandria-Rambakia in territory of Oritai (Arr. vi. 21. 5 (?)= Diod. xvii.
104. 8, Curt. Ruf. ix. 10. 7).

Winter 324/3: foundation of Alexandria at the mouth of the
Euphrates (Arr. vii. 21. 7).

Against the background of this small total of historically authenticated foundations, we may now consider the evidence provided
by the geographers, Hellenistic and Roman, who, whatever the
difficulties of interpretation involved, may be regarded as referring
to cities which had once existed, and possibly still survived at the
time of the earliest authority quoted by them.

CHAPTER IV
The Geographers

THE evidence provided by the geographers of Hellenistic and Roman date is of two kinds, the one geographical in the wide sense of providing locations and measurements of regions, the other chorographical, recording the location of tribes, cities and other settlements within the regions described, and also their physical features. The evidence covers a long period of the Greco-Roman geographical tradition, from the bematists of Alexander's expedition—the primary source in this context—to the time of Ammianus and even beyond. The lists of Alexandrias in the *Romance* tradition and in Stephanus, do not belong to this tradition, and have already been separately treated in Chapter I.

Although Eratosthenes had expressed in clear terms the fillip given to geographical knowledge of the East by Alexander's campaigns, and by his Seleucid successors, his statements on this point do not survive, and for the most part other writers show little specific interest in Alexander's campaigns, and hardly link the cities they record with them.[1] At the same time the absence from the texts of the surviving Alexander-historians of measurements of time and space (except for long periods of time) prevent the

---

[1] Str. 14 refers to Eratosthenes as having indicated the effect of Alexander's campaign on geographical knowledge, and adds a fuller description of the consequences of Roman conquests. The quotation from Eratosthenes (IB 10-11 Berger), is unfortunately not wholly clear (see *Ptol. Alex.* ii. 750 n. 1). Strabo ends his statement about the effect of Roman conquests with the interesting observation, οἱ δὲ Παρθυαῖοι τὰ περὶ τὴν Ὑρκανίαν καὶ τὴν Βακτριανὴν καὶ τοὺς ὑπὲρ τούτων Σκύθας γνωριμωτέρους ἡμῖν ἐποίησαν, ἧττον γνωριζομένους ὑπὸ τῶν πρότερον. Plin. has of course a number of specific references to the experiences of Alexander and his 'comites' (see below, pp. 93 ff.), but he does not generalize about the importance of the campaigns as a whole; note, however, regarding knowledge of India (vi. 58): *etenim patefacta est non modo Alexandri Magni armis regumque qui successere ei, circumvectis etiam in Hyrcaniam mare et Caspium Seleuco et Antiocho praefectoque classis eorum Patrocle, verum et aliis auctoribus Graecis, qui cum regibus Indicis morati, sicut Megasthenes et Dionysius a Philadelpho missus ex ea causa, vires quoque gentium prodidere*, a passage perhaps ultimately deriving from Eratosthenes.

assimilation and combination of the two categories of evidence into a composite picture.

In addition to this general feature, any investigation is beset by uncertainty as to the reliability of the distance measurements recorded by the geographers. The difficulties begin in the very foundations of our enquiry, in the smallest unit of measurement, the stade, for we cannot be certain which of the various *schoinoi* and stades attested contemporaneously in Greek mensuration were used for particular measurements of distances, and though the differences between them were small in themselves, they would result in substantial variations over a continental measurement. Ancient writers were well aware of the differences in the length of these units, and of the consequent uncertainty of all measurements by land and sea.[2] It was this uncertainty, no doubt, which

---

[2] This problem cannot be examined in depth here, but a few salient problems may be noted (see the paper of Engels, *AJP* 106 (1985), 298–311). (1) Herod. ii. 6, tells us that the *schoinos* was of sixty stades, and thus was equivalent to two parasangs: δύναται δὲ ὁ μὲν παρασάγγης τριήκοντα στάδια, ὁ δὲ σχοῖνος ἕκαστος, μέτρον ἐὸν Αἰγύπτιον, ἑξήκοντα στάδια. οὕτως ἂν εἴησαν Αἰγύπτου στάδιοι ἑξακόσιοι καὶ τρισχίλιοι τὸ παρὰ θάλασσαν. (2) Str. 803/4 states that two different *schoinoi* were in use in Egypt both in his own time and in that of Artemidorus: ἀπὸ μὲν δὴ τῆς Ἀλεξανδρείας ἐπὶ τὴν τοῦ Δέλτα κορυφὴν αὕτη ἡ περιήγησις. φησὶ δ᾽ ὁ Ἀρτεμίδωρος σχοίνων ὀκτὼ καὶ εἴκοσι τὸν ἀνάπλουν, τοῦτο δ᾽ εἶναι σταδίους ὀκτακοσίους τετταράκοντα, λογιζόμενος τριακονταστάδιον τὴν σχοῖνον· ἡμῖν μέντοι πλέουσιν ἄλλοτ᾽ ἄλλωι μέτρωι χρώμενοι τῶν σχοίνων ἀπεδίδοσαν τὰ διαστήματα, ὥστε καὶ τετταρακονταστάδιους καὶ ἔτι μείζους κατὰ τόπους ὁμολογεῖσθαι παρ᾽ αὐτῶν. καὶ διότι παρὰ τοῖς Αἰγυπτίοις ἄστατόν ἐστι τὸ τῆς σχοίνου μέτρον, αὐτὸς ὁ Ἀρτεμίδωρος ἐν τοῖς ἑξῆς δηλοῖ. (3) The existence of such an ἄστατον μέτρον for the σχοῖνος in the 3rd cent. BC, is demonstrated by e.g. *PCZ* 59. 132. 7, concerning a plot of land. A certain Symbotes has measured his κλῆρος, ἀλλὰ ἀντιλέγει πρὸς τὸν βασιλικὸν γραμμα[τέα], οἰόμενος δεῖν τῶι ⟨μεγάλωι⟩ δικαίωι σχοινίωι μετρηθῆναι, οὗ ἐστιν τὸ δ[ιάφο]ρον παρὰ τὰς ἑκατὸν ἀρούρας ἄρουραι δέκα . . ., i.e. a 10% difference. This distinction therefore certainly existed in the time of Eratosthenes. (4) The *schoinos* of forty stades is attested for Eratosthenes by Plin. xii. 53: *silvarum longitudo est schoeni xx, latitudo dimidium eius. schoenus patet Eratosthenis ratione stadia xl, hoc est p.v̄, aliqui xxxii stadia singulis schoenis dedere*. (The anonymous Byzantine fragment of *Metr. Gr.* i. 201 § 9, wrongly ascribed to Julian of Askalon, which states that Eratosthenes also used the *schoinos* of thirty-two stades: τὸ μίλιον κατὰ μὲν Ἐρατοσθένην καὶ Στράβωνα τοὺς γεωγράφους ἔχει σταδίους η' καὶ γ'' . . . κατὰ δὲ τὸ νῦν κρατοῦν ἔθος στάδια μὲν ἔχει ζ'ς. seems to be valueless, and is not evidence for his use of an alternative stade: see Diller, *CP* 45 (1950), 22–5; Engels, *loc. cit.*). Apart from observations by Pliny as to variations in figures (see below, pp. 94 ff.), which may be due to other causes as well as to the existence of different *schoinoi*, the post-Ptolemaic geographer Protagoras (*RE* (6)) is quoted by Marcianus of Heracleia as having written a book 'On the measurement of the stade', because of the different figures arrived at for nautical distances in the texts of *periploi*: Marc. *GGM* i. 516, proem: τῶν [δὲ] ὠκεανῶν ἑκατέρων τοῦ τε ἑώιου καὶ τοῦ ἑσπερίου . . . ἐκ τῆς

contributed to the application of 'rounded off' figures.[3] Secondly, we have virtually no precisely fixed points on the modern map for the beginning and end of recorded distances. Again, we do not know the exact route, or routes, on which the calculations of distances were made on any particular stretch of journey. It is a further deficiency of the geographical evidence, in so far as it relates to the identification of sites, that very few calculations based on the time taken for a stretch between one stopping-place and another have survived, as they do in the early Arab Itineraries, though the term ἡμεροδρόμας used by Philonidas the bematist of himself (see below) indicates that originally this dimension was not lacking. As a glance at the Table of Alexandrias at the end of the book shows, the geographers and the historians mostly do not agree in the places which they record as Alexander-

γεωγραφίας τοῦ θειοτάτου καὶ σοφωτάτου Πτολομαίου ἔκ τε τῆς Πρωταγόρου τῶν σταδίων ἀναμετρήσεως, ἢν τοῖς οἰκείοις τῆς γεωγραφίας προσέθεικεν . . . (§ 2) Τούτου δὴ χάριν καὶ τὴν αἰτίαν τῆς γινομένης περὶ τὴν ἀναμέτρησιν τῶν σταδίων διαφωνίας ὠιήθην δεῖν παραστῆσαι τοῖς ἐντευξομένοις· τῆς γὰρ τοιαύτης ὑποθέσεως τὸ ἀκριβὲς οὐκ ἐν ταῖς θέσεσι τῶν τόπων μόνον καὶ πόλεων καὶ νήσων καὶ λιμένων ἐχούσης, ἀλλὰ πρό γε πάντων ἐν τοῖς σταδίοις καὶ ταῖς τῶν χωρίων διαμετρήσεσιν, ἀκόλουθον οἶμαι δεῖν λόγον ἐρεῖν, καὶ τοῖς βουλομένοις κατὰ φύσιν σκοπεῖν τὴν ἐν τῶι περίπλωι τῆς θαλάττης ἀναμέτρησιν ἀληθῆ φανησόμενον, καίτοιγε τῶν περὶ τούτων σπουδασάντων οὐδενὸς ἐπισημηναμένου τοῦτο, ἀλλ' ὥσπερ σχοινίωι διαμεμετρημένης τῆς θαλάττης, οὕτω τὸν ἀριθμὸν τῶν σταδίων ἀπαγγειλάντων. He then proceeds to describe the difficulties involved in measuring distances at sea. Whether Protagoras' work was especially concerned with reducing the stades attested in Greek authors of periploi of an earlier date (such as Timosthenes of Rhodes, the older contemporary of Eratosthenes) to a single module, or simply recorded the varying calculations, can hardly be decided from Marcianus' words, but it is more likely that he pursued the latter course. The difference between the stade of Eratosthenes, the great, perhaps royal, stade, and the shorter one is of 8 : 10, a difference that would lead to substantial variations over long distances if these were not recorded in schoinoi. The difference between direct measurements and measurements along a road was noted by Strab. 106 fin: οἱ γὰρ νῦν ὁμολογοῦσιν, εἴ τις τὰς τῶν ὁδῶν ἀνωμαλίας ὑποτέμνοιτο, μὴ μείζω τῶν ἑξακισχιλίων σταδίων εἶναι τὸ μῆκος τὴν σύμπασαν Ἰβηρίαν ἀπὸ Πυρήνης ἕως τῆς ἑσπερίου πλευρᾶς. Cf. also Ptol. Geogr. i. 4: ἡ μὲν τῶν σταδιασμῶν ἀναμέτρησις οὔτε βεβαίαν ἐμποιεῖ τοῦ ἀληθοῦς κατάληψιν, διὰ τὸ σπανίως ἰθυτενέσι περιπίπτειν πορείαις, ἐκτροπῶν πολλῶν συναποδιδομένων καὶ κατὰ τὰς ὁδοὺς καὶ κατὰ τοὺς πλοῦς, κ.τ.λ. The direct route, as described by the later metrologists, is εὐθυμετρικόν: Metr. Gr. i. 181. 3: εὐθυμετρικὸν μὲν οὖν ἐστι πᾶν τὸ κατὰ μῆκος μόνον μετρούμενον (ὥσπερ ἐν ταῖς σκουτλώσεσιν οἱ στροφίολοι καὶ ἐν τοῖς ξυλικοῖς τὰ κυμάτια καὶ ὅσα πρὸς μῆκος μόνον μετρεῖται).

[3] This 'rounding off' is well illustrated by Polyb. iii. 39, where for his final figure for the distance from Nova Carthago to Rome, which in stages totals 8,400 st. becomes 9,000 st.: see Walbank, ad loc. The extent and effect of this practice can hardly be estimated in dealing with measurements estimated by unknown routes, as is the case usually in the regions with which we are concerned.

foundations.[4] Moreover, in addition to these insoluble difficulties, the almost total lack of archaeologically identified sites effectively prevents a solution from fixed points on the ground. Nevertheless the geographical sources sometimes provide us with valuable information as to the existence of foundations within a general area, a satrapy or a province, in the Hellenistic period, and also considerably later. There is no doubt that Alexander's expedition was accompanied by a staff of bematists, land-surveyors, distance-measurers and day-runners, at least as far as the Indus and possibly beyond it, whose task it was to measure the routes taken and the distances covered by the armies.[5] Several of these technicians are known to us by name, notably Philonides of Chersonasos in Crete, who erected a dedication at Olympia, in which he described himself as ἡμεροδρόμας καὶ βηματιστὴς τῆς Ἀσίας, and who was honoured by a decree of the Achaean League, Diognetos

---

[4] It may be noted here that the geographers frequently refer to cities which no longer existed at the time of writing—or at the time of writing of their source(s)—but were believed to have existed at some previous date. K. G. Sallmann, *Die Geographie des älteren Plinius in ihrem Verhältnis zu Varro* (Berlin, 1971), 193, gives many examples of such expressions in Pliny, e.g. iii. 116, *in hoc tractu interierunt Boi quorum tribus cxii fuisse auctor est Cato.* They are frequently introduced by the formula *in hoc tractu interierunt.* The Index to bk. iii has *populi qui sunt aut fuerunt . . . qua intercidere oppida aut gentes.* Pliny is also specific about deserted cities: e.g. vi. 15, speaking of the region of Colchis, *reliqua litora fere nationes tenent Melanchlaeni, Coraxi, urbe Colchorum Dioscoriade iuxta fluvium Anthemunta nunc deserta, quondam adeo clara ut Timosthenes in eam ccc nationes dissimilibus linguis descendere prodiderit; et postea a nostris cxxx interpretibus negotia gesta ibi.*; ib. 18: *ora ipsa Bospori utrimque ex Asia atque Europa curvatur in Maeotim. Oppida in aditu* [*Bospori primo*] *Hermonasa, dein Cepoe Milesiorum, mox Stratoclia et Phanagoria ac paene desertum Apaturos ultimoque in ostio Cimmerium, quod antea Cerberion vocabatur.* The survival of cities listed as existing is a particular problem, particularly when dealing with tralaticial material such as cartographic projections: see below, pp. 96 ff. for the problem in relation to Marinus and Ptolemy. Whether Pliny's main immediate sources for his eastern geography had access to the texts of the bematists may be doubted: see in general Sallmann, op. cit. 60 ff. (Artemidorus). It may be noted here that later Arab geographers refer to several Alexandrias (Iskandarīya/Iskandarūn) in the Near East which had vanished by their time: see Le Strange, *Palestine under the Moslems* (Cambridge, 1903), 458, s.v. Iskandarūnah (see esp. the passage of Abū-'l Fīda quoted on pp. 458-9); cf. also above p. 59.

[5] Eratosthenes' fundamental measurements for India as far as the Indus come from the Ἀσιατικοὶ σταθμοί (Str. 723 (IIIB 20), which are probably Alexander's records (see below, n. 10): μῆκος δὲ ἀπὸ Κασπίων πυλῶν ὡς ἐν τοῖς Ἀσιατικοῖς Σταθμοῖς ἀναγέγραπται, διττὸν ... the description of the two routes follows (see below, p. 83 ... εἶτα πάλιν ἡ λοιπὴ μέχρι τῶν ὅρων τῆς Ἰνδικῆς καὶ τοῦ Ἰνδοῦ. Pliny's additional figures, as far as the Beas, vi. 62, *qui fuit Alexandri itinerum terminus ... epistulae quoque regis ipsius consentiunt his,* are from another source: see below, p. 84. For the Seleucid survey of India see below, n. 13.

and Baiton, and Amyntas and Archelaos (the two groups seem to
be paired off in Pliny's references to them), who all recorded in
published form the information about stages and other data which
they had accumulated.[6] These accounts, the ἀναγραφαὶ τῶν
σταθμῶν, certainly comprised an officially recognized list of the
stages, by distance if not by time, and they are the ultimate source
of our information regarding the distances covered in Alexander's
eastern conquests. This system of stage-measuring, which also
existed in Achaemenid Persia,[7] continued for centuries. It must be

[6] For Philonides (Berve 800; FGrH 121) see Syll.³ 303 (Tod, GHI 188; FGrH
ibid. T1): β[α]σιλέως Ἀλε[ξάνδ]ρου | ἡμεροδρόμας καὶ | βηματιστὴς τῶς Ἀσίας |
Φιλωνίδης Ζωίτου Κρὴς | Χερσονάσιος ἀνέθηκε | Διὶ Ὀλυμπίωι (an incomplete copy, I.
von Olymp. 277). Plin. NH ii. 181, describes the notable achievement of a Philonides
in running from Sikyon to Elis and back, and this is no doubt the same man. For
the decree of the Achaean league see SEG xiv. 375; only the name of the honorand
survives. For a general account of Philonides see H. Bengtson, Kl. Schr. 208 ff.,
Robert, OMS iii. 1446-8. His work is included by Pliny in his Index, i. 4. 5, along
with the other bematists, but no fragments survive. Baiton and Diognetos are
known from Plin. vi. 61 (FGrH 119 and 120): Diognetus et Baeton itinerum eius
mensores. There are several fragments of Baiton, ὁ Ἀλεξάνδρου βηματιστής, in both
Pliny and Strabo, but not all in the latter are named quotations. His work was
entitled Σταθμοὶ τῆς Ἀλεξάνδρου πορείας (F1). Amyntas' Ἀσίας σταθμοί (FGrH 121
F1) or Περσικοὶ σταθμοί (F4), in not less than three books, of which a fragment concerning the drinking of τὸ ἀερόμελι καλούμενον (F1), 'oak-manna', survives, clearly
contained descriptions of local customs and monuments, and was much more than
a tabular record of distances. Aelian (NH xvii. 17), in quoting the longest surviving
fragment of the Σταθμοί (F3), concerning the fauna of the Caspian region (a
passage with a markedly paradoxographical flavour) describes the work as ἐν τοῖς
ἐπιγραφομένοις ὑπ' αὐτοῦ Σταθμοῖς. Archelaos of Cappadocia (apparently Archelaos
II, King of Cappadocia), described (FGrH 123 T1) as ὁ χωρογράφος τῆς ὑπ'
Ἀλεξάνδρου πατηθείσης γῆς, was mainly, to judge by the fragments assigned to him
(F1-5), interested in precious stones, and it does not follow from the description of
him by DL ii. 17 (T1) that he wrote Σταθμοί. In any case, if correctly identified with
the king, his dates make him a source of dubious authority—he died in the reign
of Tiberius (see Ptol. Alex. ii. 1089 n. 451, Jacoby, Komm. to 123, for the problem
of the identity of the Archelaoi). Pliny does not quote either Amyntas or Archelaos
for geographical information, and therefore only Baiton and Diognetos are of
significance for our purpose; these are both described as Alexander's mensores, but
it does not seem possible to distinguish between them and the writers of Σταθμοί.
In general it is important to note that the Σταθμοί contained observations of a
general nature regarding flora and fauna of the regions traversed, and formed one
source of the new zoology and botany of which Theophrastus made abundant use.
L. L. Gunderson, in Ἀρχαία Μακεδονία, i (1970), 369 ff., rightly stresses the variety
of information provided by the bematists, though his view that Baiton's account lay
behind some of the natural information in the Epistola Alexandri of the Romance
tradition (cf. p. 217, n. 28), based on the occurrence of the word metator, corrected
from meator (a meatoribus to a metatoribus) in two early MSS of Ep. 9, 11, lacks substance: Pliny's word for them is mensores.

[7] For the Persian Royal Road see Herod. v. 52, σταθμοί τε πανταχῆι εἰσι βασιλήϊοι
καὶ καταλύσιες κάλλισται, διὰ οἰκεομένης τε ἡ ὁδὸς ἅπασα καὶ ἀσφαλέος, see the

borne in mind in this connection that the task of Alexander's surveyors was carried out in much more difficult circumstances than their Achaemenian predecessors faced, in hostile and difficult country and without a stable organization of local guides to provide the necessary aid. The difficulties experienced, and overcome, by the Greek forces during the Anabasis described by Xenophon bear testimony to this.[8]

Almost nothing of the original texts of the bematists survives, and it is hardly possible to determine through later quotations and references what information derives from them. Pliny's statement in his *Index, situus, gentes . . . ex . . . Isidoro, Philonide, Xenagora, Astynomo . . . Baetone, Timosthene*, is a rag-bag, in which true bematists and others are conflated.[9] He uses them, in narrative passages, only for distances, calling them collectively, as already mentioned, *itinerum eius mensores*.

There can be no reasonable doubt that when, in the second half of the third century BC. Eratosthenes, the earliest and the most reliable user of early Hellenistic material, planned his great work on world geography, accompanied by a map, the bematists' records were available to him in their original form; it would indeed be paradoxical that they should have been absent from the Alexandrian Library which was founded by Ptolemy Soter, who had himself seen 'their work in the field.[10] However, Eratosthenes'

---

commentary of How and Wells, who rightly stress that such road-plans with distance-surveys are probably much older than Achaemenid times, a subject developed by E. von Ivanka, *Die Aristotelische Politik u.d. Städtegründungen Alexanders des Grossen* (Budapest, 1938), 20 ff., esp. pp. 25 ff. For the use made of the Royal Road, as revealed by the Persepolis Fortification Tablets, see D. M. Lewis, *Sparta and Persia* (Leiden, 1977), *passim*, esp. ch. 1. [See Addenda]

[8] See e.g. Xen. *Anab.* iii. 2. 23, where he admits the difficulties of crossing rivers without local guides: εἰ δὲ μήθ' οἱ ποταμοὶ διήσουσιν ἡγεμών τε μηδεὶς ἡμῖν φανεῖται, οὐδ' ὡς ἡμῖν γε ἀθυμητέον. What might happen with a faithless guide is shown by what befell Antony in 36 BC in Parthia: Str. 524. Information about the general lie of the land in larger regions was provided by prisoners-of-war: see Xen. loc. cit. 5. 15-16.

[9] See FGrH. 119 T2; 121 T2; cf. 120 T2a. In 121 T2 Pliny repeats the three names *Philonide, Xenagora, Astynomo* in the same order, presumably by oversight.

[10] Jacoby, *FGrH* 119-23, *Komm.* 407, does not believe that Eratosthenes saw the original texts of these works. He says: 'Eratosthenes, der sie [the Bematists] für seine karte stark heranzog, sah nicht die originale oder eine massgebende ausgabe, die offenbar so wenig wie eine solche der Ephemeriden existiert hat, sondern arbeitet mit eine mehrheit von σταθμοί, die schon in seiner zeit gelegentliche diskrepanzen aufwiesen, besonders natürlich in den zahlen. das werden eben jene bücher sein, die als Baiton's Σταθμοὶ τῆς Ἀλεξάνδρου πορείας und Amyntas' Ἀσίας Σταθμοί zitiert

work does not survive in its original form, and we have to be content with the lengthy, apparently largely verbatim quotations from it by Strabo, which provide very little general geographical and chorographical material from those sources.

The *Geography* was a description of the whole earth conceived as a land mass surrounded by water.[11] His projection of this was based on a meridian passing through Alexandria, Syene, and Meroe, and on parallels based on a central latitude conceived (wrongly) as passing through the Pillars of Hercules, Athens, Rhodes, and the line of the Taurus, which was regarded as extending eastwards along one and the same parallel, south of the Caspian, and forming one range with the Indian Caucasus, that is, the Hindu Kush.

werden.' I see no grounds for this excessive caution. At one point in his attack on Eratosthenes Hipparchus evidently stressed the library resources available to Eratosthenes: Str. 69 (IIIA 8): ταῦτα γὰρ ὁ Ἐρατοσθένης λαμβάνει πάντα ὡς καὶ ἐκμαρτυρούμενα ὑπὸ τῶν ἐν τοῖς τόποις γενομένων, ἐντετυχηκὼς ὑπομνήμασι πολλοῖς, ὧν εὐπόρει, βιβλιοθήκην ἔχων τηλικαύτην, ἡλίκην αὐτὸς Ἵππαρχός φησι. A clear reference to the direct use of the ἀναγραφαί occurs in Str. 70: Ἐροῦμεν δ᾽ ὅτι οὐ ψιλὴν τὴν διαφωνίαν (between Patrocles and Megasthenes) ᾐτιάσατο (sc. ὁ Ἐρατοσθένης), ἀλλὰ συγκρίνων πρὸς τὴν ὁμολογίαν καὶ τὴν ἀξιοπιστίαν τῆς ἀναγραφῆς τῶν σταθμῶν. Eratosthenes admitted that when drawing the northern boundaries of the Third Seal, in regard to the less well-explored regions, notably the area of Armenia, the Caucasus and the Elburz range, and northern Mesopotamia, he had had to draw on various less specific compilers of σταθμοί, including some anonymous productions: Str. 79 (IIIB 25): καὶ γὰρ καὶ τὰ διαστήματά φησιν (ὁ Ἐρατοσθένης) ἐκ πολλῶν συναγαγεῖν τῶν τοὺς σταθμοὺς πραγματευσαμένων ὧν τινας καὶ ἀνεπιγράφους καλεῖ. It is unlikely that Alexander's bematists had operated in these areas, which are all north of Thapsacus, and which Eratosthenes calls more than once ἀμέτρητα (see Str. 77-83, *passim*.), i.e. by Alexander's bematists. In the same passage (Str. 79 (IIIB 25)) he refers explicitly to the distance between Thapsacus and the point at which Alexander crossed the Tigris, μέχρι μὲν δὴ τοῦ Τίγριδος, ὅπου Ἀλέξανδρος διέβη, which must be from either an Alexander-historian or a bematist. It looks likely that Eratosthenes had access not only to the accounts of Alexander's bematists but also to those of the Seleucids (see below, n. 13). It may be added that he also made use of the little-known Ptolemaic bematists in his measurement of the earth, when calculating the distance between Syene and Alexandria: see Mart. Cap. vi. 598 (IIB, 41B): *Eratosthenes vero a Syene ad Meroen per mensores regios Ptolemaei certus de stadiorum numero redditus*, and cf. *Proc. Brit. Acad.* (1970), 189 n. 3.

[11] I may refer here to the summary of Eratosthenes' geography given by me, *Ptol. Alex.* i. 525 ff., with notes (cf. also pp. 413-15), where the passages of Strabo are quoted. I need not repeat them here, nor need I add to the substantial modern bibliography of the topic. Berger's *Die geographische Fragmente des Eratosthenes* (Berlin, 1880, repr. Amsterdam, 1964) remains indispensible. It is important to bear in mind that Eratosthenes' account was of the whole earth, ἡ σύμπασα γῆ, as Strabo says (48, IB 11), not just of the οἰκουμένη, as Strabo maintains it should have been. For an analysis of the relationship of the sphragides to the route of the campaign see W. Thonke, *Die Karte des Eratosthenes u.d.Züge Alexanders* (Diss. Strassb. 1914), 39 ff.

This land mass Eratosthenes divided into four roughly (ὁλοσχερῶς) geometrical divisions, the famous Seals (σφραγῖδες), of which the first in the series was the easternmost, India, comprising all the known land east of the Indus river (conceived as running almost on a meridian line); the second Ariana, the eastern boundary of which was the Indus, and the western a line drawn from the head of the Persian Gulf to the Caspian Gates. On the north both these sphragides were bounded by the fictitious eastward extension of the Taurus range, and on the south by the Indian Ocean and the Persian Gulf respectively. It will be seen therefore that all the cities reputedly or actually founded by Alexander during his campaign, except that on the Jaxartes and Alexandria in Egypt, fell within the first two Seals. With the other two Seals we are not concerned.

We are fortunate to possess in Strabo's transcription a fairly full report, indeed quotations, of Eratosthenes' account of at least a part of this region, broadly speaking that of the second Seal, since for India itself Strabo made more use of Megasthenes than of Eratosthenes. From these passages, and from corroborative material in Pliny, it is clear that, as stated above, Eratosthenes used the bematists' (or a bematist's) measurements at first hand (whether or not in terms of σταθμοί). Strabo expressly quotes him as having used an Ἀσιατικοὶ Σταθμοί[12] and also, for the length of India, an Ἀναγραφὴ τῶν Σταθμῶν, probably a different work, perhaps the same as the Seleucid ἀναγραφή referred to by Pliny.[13]

[12] Str. 723 (IIIB 20), περὶ ὧν Ἐρατοσθένης οὕτως εἴρηκεν . . . μῆκος δὲ ἀπὸ Κασπίων, ὡς ἐν τοῖς Ἀσιατικοῖς Σταθμοῖς ἀναγέγραπται; cf above p. 78 n. 5. It does not seem certain to me that this work, described in so impersonal a way, is necessarily the same as the Ἀσίας Σταθμοί of Amyntas, the fragments of which lack any specific evidence relating to mensuration: see above, n. 6. It might be the same as the Seleucid ἀναγραφὴ τῶν σταθμῶν, for which see next note.

[13] NH vi. 62, after giving the distances to the Hyphasis-Beas from Alexander's bematists (see below, in the text), he adds (63): reliqua inde Seleuco Nicatori peragrata sunt . . . This statement probably comes, via intermediaries, from Megasthenes: see Schwanbeck, Megasthenis Indica, 16 ff.; Detlefsen, Anordnung des geograph. Bücher des Plinius (Quell. u. Untersuch. 18, 1909), 127 ff. Eratosthenes' relation to this Seleucid survey is not clear. Str. refers to his measurements for the distance to Palibothra from the Indian Caucasus (69 (IIC 21)) thus: ἀπὸ γάρ τινος ἀναγραφῆς σταθμῶν ὁρμηθέντα (sc. τὸν Ἐρατοσθένη) τοῖς μὲν ἀπιστεῖν διὰ τὴν διαφωνίαν, ἐκείνηι δὲ προσέχειν; cf. the continuation quoted above, n. 10. This region lay in his first Seal. In 689 (IIIB 6), the account of Patrocles' alleged use of the material supplied by Xenocles in Babylon, Str. says (689 (IIIB 6)): ἔσται δὲ τὸ πᾶν ἧι βραχύτατον μυρίων ἑξακισχιλίων, ὡς ἔκ τε τῆς ἀναγραφῆς τῶν σταθμῶν τῆς πεπιστευμένης μάλιστα λαβεῖν Ἐρατοσθένης φησι· καὶ ὁ Μεγασθένης οὕτω συναποφαίνεται. Πατροκλῆς δὲ χιλίοις ἔλαττόν φησι. Since Patrocles here disagrees with Megasthenes and Eratosthenes, and it was Patrocles who allegedly had access to the ἀναγραφὴ τῶν ἀναγραψάντων τὴν ὅλην

The extract from Strabo–Eratosthenes relating to the Ἀσιατικοὶ Σταθμοί and the passage in Pliny are closely parallel to each other, and the figures may be quoted here.

Strabo, after quoting Eratosthenes' mistaken, or erroneously attributed, view of the location of the Arachotoi and the Massagetai, namely that they lie next to the Bactrians on the west, along the Oxus, and that the Sakai and the Sogdians lie 'opposite India', with details of tribal locations, gives two lists of distances, the first (probably from Theophanes, the general of Pompey) giving the distances from Mt. Caspius (i.e. the true Caucasus) westwards to the Cyrus river (the Kur), which at that time flowed as a separate river into the west side of the Caspian, and the second, from Eratosthenes, from the Cyrus river eastward, in two directions.[14]

χώραν, it looks, as if Eratosthenes' ἀναγραφή was a different one, and we may conclude that for this part of his work (the first Seal) he did use the Seleucid survey, though we must allow for the possibility that the various ἀναγραφαί became confused between the 3rd-cent. writers and the time of Strabo (perhaps by Strabo himself). It is also to be borne in mind that the Seleucid surveyors and Megasthenes were able to use the milliaria established on the roads of North India by the Maurya kings (if not earlier): see Str. 708: ὁδοποιοῦσι (sc. οἱ ἄρχοντες in general) δὲ καὶ κατὰ δέκα στάδια στήλην τιθέασι, τὰς ἐκτροπὰς καὶ τὰ διαστήματα δηλοῦσαν (Megasth. fr. xxxiv, p. 125, Schwanb.; FGrH 715 F 31). Hirschfeld, *Kl. Schr.* 705, called attention long ago to the reference in one of Asoka's edicts (the 7th Pillar Edict) to the provision of watering-points at specified distances: see now Mookerji, *Asoka*, 188-9, trans. with notes; Thapar, *Asoka*, 265. It does not seem likely that mechanical hodometers were used for military or civil purposes, though they are described as operable machines by Heron in his *Dioptra* (*Heronis Op.* iii, (Teubn. chs. 34-5)). The passage is too long to quote here, and must be studied with the diagrams, but Heron is quite explicit that his own contraption—a ratchet and wheel in a κιβώτιον, attached to the rim of a chariot—was superior to those previously in use. His definition is (ch. 34, init.): τὸ καλούμενον ὁδόμετρον, τὰ ἐπὶ γῆς μετρεῖν διαστήματα, ὥστε μὴ δι᾽ ἀλύσεως μετροῦντα ἢ διὰ σχοινίου κακοπαθῶς καὶ βραδέως ἐκμετρεῖν, ἀλλ᾽ ἐπ᾽ ὀχήματος πορευόμενον, διὰ τῆς τῶν τρόχων ἐκκυλίσεως ἐπίστασθαι τὰ προειρημένα διαστήματα. The calculator had to be set at zero at the beginning of every day's march. There is a brief account of the instrument in *RE* Suppbd. VI, s.v. Hodometron.

[14] Jacoby, *Komm.* nos. 119-21, pp. 407-8, gives the two tables in parallel. Eratosthenes (IIIB 20), (b) in the text on p. 84, and Pliny vi. 62-4, *passim*, had both found variants in the MSS of their sources, ultimately the bematists, and Eratosthenes' figures for the second table are ninety stades short of his own total figure of 15,500 stades, itself emended by Kramer to 15,300, the total given by Strabo himself (in the immediately preceding passage); cf. Berger, 240 n. 1; Sallmann, op. cit. 173 ff. It is idle to correct the figures when (1) we have no precisely fixed points for distances, (2) we do not know how correct Eratosthenes' and Pliny's sources were, and (3) we do not know the precise routes on which the calculations were made. We must be content that the variations in distances, as transmitted in the two parallel sources are not grotesquely large, save that from the Caspian Gates to Hekatompylos is 1,960 st. in Erat. ap. Strab. 514 (= IIIB 20) (perhaps about 245 m.), 1,064 (133 m.) in Pliny, a difference which Engels,

(a) (Str. 513; IIIB 63) [Mt. Caspius to Cyrus river: 1,800 st.]
Cyrus river to Caspian Gates: 5,600 st.
Caspian Gates to Alexandria in Aria: 6,400 st.
Alexandria in Aria to Bactra–Zariaspa: 3,870 st.
Bactra to the Jaxartes: 5,000 st.

(b) (514 = IIIB 20) (to India):
Caspian Gates to Hekatompylos: 1,960 st.
Hekatompylos to Alexandria in Aria: 4,530 st.
Alexandria in Aria to Prophthasia: 1,600 st.
Prophthasia to Arachotoi: 4,120 st.
Arachotoi to Ortospana (the fork from Bactra): 2,000 st.
Ortospana to 'borders of India': 1,000 st.

Pliny's version of the first itinerary, which he gives in the context of the geography of Media and Parthia, is (vi. 44–5):

Caspian Gates to Hekatompylos: 133 m. [= 1,064 st.]
⟨Caspii to Cyrus river: 225 m. [= 1,800 st.]
Cyrus river to Caspian Gates: 700 m. = [3,700 st.]⟩
Caspian Gates(?) to Bactra: [700 m.] = 3,700 st.
Bactra to Jaxartes: 5,000 st.=[625 m.]
Caspian Gates to 'the beginning of India': 15,68(9)0 st. = [1,960 m.]

This version does not agree very closely with the measurements of Eratosthenes, but his second itinerary (ibid. 61–2), given as a prelude to his account of the geography of India, and introduced with the statement *verum ut terrena demonstratio intellegatur, Alexandri Magni vestigiis insistemus. Diognetus et Baeton itinerum eius mensores scripsere* is more in parallel, as regards both stations and magnitudes:

(b) Caspian Gates to Hekatompylos, 'quot diximus milia'
Hekatompylos to Alexandria in Aria: 575 m. = [4,600 st.]
Alexandria in Aria to Prophthasia: 199 m. = [1,592 st.]

Logistics, 83 n. 61, and table on p. 157, explains as arising from the fact that Eratosthenes' figure is based on measurement taken from the northern Caspian Gates (cf. Apollod. Artem. ap. Strab. ibid.); cf. below, p. 108 n. 9. It is an additional problem, as we have seen above (n. 2), that the stadion might have two different values, one in which it formed the fortieth part, and another, the normal, in which it constituted the thirty-second part of the schoinos. Eratosthenes' forty-stade schoinos was also used in Theophanes of Mytilene's description of Armenia (*FGrH* 188 F 6 = Strab. 530); cf. Berger, 263: τιθεὶς τὴν σχοῖνον τετταράκοντα σταδίων.

Prophthasia to Arachosia: 565 m. = [4,520 st.]
Arachosia to Ortospana: 175 m. = [1,400 st.]
Ortospana to 'Alexandri oppidum' 50 m. = [400 st.]

(Here Pliny says *in quibusdam exemplaribus diversi sunt numeri*)

Alexander's Town to Kophen river and Peucolaotis 237 m
= [1,896 st.]
Peucolaotis to Indus and the town of Taxila 60 m = [480 st.]

The figures provided by the second list of Eratosthenes ((b), above)
and the second list of Pliny, based ultimately on the bematists, at
least as far as the borders of India (where Eratosthenes' measurements ceased), are reasonably close, apart from a few variations,
though the actual distances in modern terms are subject to all the
limitations indicated at the beginning of this chapter.[15]

The figures recorded, which cannot in themselves provide
decisive identifications, need not be further scrutinized here. More
important for our present purpose is the overall fact that the bematists as quoted by Pliny agree with Eratosthenes in calculating from
Hekatompylos, the Parthian capital (and, before Alexander, the
capital of the Persian satrapy of Parthava), to Ortospana and the
borders of India (οἱ ὅροι τῆς Ἰνδικῆς), embracing an area approximately equivalent to Ariana, Drangiana, and Arachosia, and that
within that region they mention one Alexandria, Alexandria in
Aria or Ariana, clearly identified as being the major city east of the
Caspian and Hekatompylos. It is a characteristic difficulty that this
Alexandria, attested by the bematists (as quoted directly by Pliny)

[15] Sallmann, op. cit. 173 ff., pointed out that Urlichs, *Vindiciae Plinianae*, ii
(Erlangen, 1866 (acc. Sallmann: 'i, 1853', but the page reference is the same))
90-1, noted that the variant figures in his sources, to which Pliny draws attention,
are largely confined to this section, based on Baiton and Diognetos, and that he
regarded these references to variants as due to later insertions in the text of Pliny.
Sallmann objects to this on the grounds that (1) there was no reason why the
interpolations should be confined to this section, and (2) the interpolator might be
expected to have introduced the correct figures by having recourse to other, supposedly more reliable sources. Detlefsen, op. cit. 127-8, regards the variants as deriving ultimately from additions made to the text of Megasthenes, Pliny's main source
for Indian measurements beyond the range of the bematists and Eratosthenes.
(Whether in fact Megasthenes included the whole of Gandhara and Arachosia in his
survey is doubtful: see below, note 26.) Eratosthenes himself for that part of India
that he covered evidently followed the bematists as long as possible: Str. 688 (IIIB
6), τὰ ὑπὸ τοῦ Ἐρατοσθένους . . . ἐκτεθέντα κεφαλαιωδῶς περὶ τῆς τότε νομιζομένης
Ἰνδικῆς, ἥνικα Ἀλέξανδρος ἐπῆλθε. These various arguments show only the impossibility of correcting texts explicitly embodying unspecified variations or corrections.

and by Eratosthenes, is not mentioned specifically by any of the Alexander-historians, while Alexandria ad Caucasum, mentioned by all the Alexander-historians, is not mentioned specifically by the bematists or Eratosthenes; it probably appears in Pliny's second list as 'Alexandri oppidum', which Eratosthenes omits and moves straight to 'the borders of India'. There seems, however, to be little doubt that Alexandria in Aria was a major centre, used as a point of orientation in all records available to Eratosthenes and Pliny. As Herāt, the main city of the great oasis watered by the Hari-Rūd, it has remained such ever since. The other end of the distance-chart, as available to us, must be set at the elusive Ortospana, the last point at which Eratosthenes and Pliny coincide, for Eratosthenes from there moves east. Though, as we have seen, it is quite clear that Eratosthenes used both Alexander's bematists, as well as the ἀναγραφαί of the early Seleucid administration,[16] and maintained the trustworthiness of its figures, with which Megasthenes agreed, as opposed to the slightly variant ones of Patrocles, no further fragments of the bematists touch on the whole region with which we are concerned. Thus the only information that the surviving fragments of the bematists, our primary geographical source, provide regarding Alexander's city-foundations is the single reference to Alexandria in Ariana in Pliny.

The evidence of the later geographers has to be seen against a different background from that of writers of the third century. The Seleucid Empire had vanished into the past between the time of Megasthenes and the next geographical text that we must consider, the *Parthian Staging Posts*, Παρθικοὶ Σταθμοί, of Isidore of Charax early in the first century AD. Just as it lost its western influence after the Peace of Apamea, so in the later third, and still more in the second, century, the eastern territories, which in the third century had been the Seleucid homelands *par excellence*, had been eaten away by the Parthians, by the Bactrians and others, and Rome had completed the process of elimination. As if to correspond

---

[16] See above, p. 81 and n. 13. It may be added here that Tarn, *GBI*² 153, assumes that the Ἀσιατικοὶ Σταθμοί used by Eratosthenes *was* the Seleucid survey because 'when the Seleucid empire replaced the Persian, the word "Asia" was transferred to signify that empire . . . Seleucus was "King of Asia", and the term "Stations of Asia" applied to the Seleucid survey of their empire, and the title "Saviour of Asia" given to Antiochus IV, are sufficient proof'. However, the title Ἀσίας Σταθμοί is attested for Amyntas at an earlier date (see above, n. 6), alongside the alternative title (presumably of the same work) Σταθμοὶ Περσικοί.

to these changed conditions there seem henceforth to have been few fresh contributions to geographical knowledge of the East. The great fillip produced by Alexander's campaigns and by the consolidation of the Seleucid Empire over so much of the highlands of Asia had been replaced by interest focused on the western Mediterranean and the lands bordering on it. Of the most significant writers in this field in the time between Eratosthenes and Isidore, Agatharchides and Artemidorus of Ephesus, and Polybius (all approximately contemporary with each other), Agatharchides' limited talents were focused mainly on the African mainland, those of Polybius on the western Mediterranean, while Artemidorus, a source much used by Strabo, was also largely concerned with the west and with *periploi*: Strabo emphasizes that he was little interested in the internal geography of Europe and Asia.[17] The 'writers on Parthian matters, especially Apollodorus of Artemita', as Strabo says,[18] occupied the new ground, and saw it from a different angle. Alexander had ceased to be a revered ancestor (if only an unauthentic one), and his cities no doubt lost considerable prestige after the rise of Parthia.

There is a further consideration. Strabo tells us that the 'Macedonians' (i.e., the Seleucids) were in the habit of renaming cities, rivers, and other prominent features of their kingdom to suit their needs, whatever they may have been. Indeed, he goes beyond this, and says that they were also accustomed to 'misname' places, not only μετονομάζειν but also παρονομάζειν.[19] What the Seleucids

---

[17] Artemidorus' fragments, largely from Strabo and Stephanus, were collected and discussed by Stiehle in *Philol.* 11 (1856). There is an account of the fragments in Susemihl, i. 693-6 and an article in Pauly-Wissowa by Berger, Artemidorus (27); see also Bunbury, ii. 61-9. Strabo used him considerably, but criticized him severely (172): Ἀρτεμίδωρος δὲ ἀντειπὼν τούτωι (sc. τῶι Πολυβίωι) καὶ ἅμα παρ᾽ αὐτοῦ τινα θεὶς αἰτίαν, μνησθεὶς δὲ καὶ τῆς Σιλανοῦ δόξης τοῦ συγγραφέως οὔ μοι δοκεῖ μνήμης ἄξια εἰπεῖν, ὡς ἂν ἰδιώτης περὶ ταῦτα καὶ αὐτὸς καὶ Σιλανός. For Strabo's substantial reliance on Artemidorus for the West see O. Steinbrück, *Die Quellen des Strabo im fünften Buche seiner Erdbeschreibung* (diss. Hall. 1909). Artemidorus' date is given precisely by Marcianus of Heracleia in his *Epit. Peripl. Menippi* (*GGM* i. 566: Ἀ. ὁ Ἐφέσιος γεωγράφος κατὰ τὴν ἑκατοστὴν ἑξακοστὴν ἐνάτην Ὀλυμπιάδα γεγονώς, κ.τ.λ.).

[18] Str. 118: ἀπήγγελται δ᾽ ὑμῖν καὶ ὑπὸ τῶν τὰ Παρθικὰ συγγραψάντων, τῶν περὶ Ἀπολλόδωρον τὸν Ἀρτεμιτηνόν κ.τ.λ. Apollodorus has been considerably invoked in discussions of Seleucid and Parthian affairs by Tarn (*GBI*² 144-5, and Index, s.v.) and, still more, by Altheim in his *Weltgeschichte Asiens*, i. 2 ff. His fragments, virtually all from Strabo, are collected as *FGrH* 779, but he has no entry in *RE*, or in *Der Kleine Pauly*. He was clearly the main representative of οἱ τὰ Παρθικὰ συγγράψαντες.

[19] For general remarks on this practice see e.g. Str. 518: τῶν Μακεδόνων

began the Parthians no doubt continued, and we must therefore be on our guard against regarding as of authentic origin cities (or rivers, or whatever) that may have been renamed by the Seleucids or their successors without regard to the true historical origin of the communities concerned. This, of course, would not apply to the great cities of Syria, or to others west of the Euphrates, but it is obviously a possibility to be reckoned with after the third century in the trans-Euphratic region, in Media and in peripheral regions. Alexander's name grew no less in popular imagination with the passage of time, and a city might easily be named after him, either officially or unofficially. This is a possibility which we must bear in mind when we turn to unravel the tangle of the *Parthian Stations* of Isidore of Charax.

The *Parthian Stations* is probably only a fragment.[20] There are numerous quotations from Isidore in Pliny at the beginning of his description of Arabia, but a difficulty arises because in the passage in which Pliny describes the site of Charax, and refers to the most recent authority on the East, dispatched by Augustus *ad commentanda omnia* the manuscripts agree that Pliny names not Isidore but 'Dionysius'.[21] No such 'Dionysius of Charax' can be identified, though Pliny emphasizes his authority as a geographical source as being a native of Charax. It is therefore widely, but not universally, accepted that the name should be emended to that of

⟨ὀνόματα?⟩ θεμένων (καθάπερ καὶ ἄλλα πολλὰ τὰ μὲν καινὰ ἔθεσαν, τὰ δὲ παρωνόμασαν) (the text is corrupted). As Fergus Millar has recently pointed out, *Rome and the Near East* (Harvard, 1993), 8, Josephus' account, *AJ* i. 5. 5, (§ 121), gives one 'insider's' view of this process: καὶ τῶν ἐθνῶν ἔνια μὲν διασώζει τὰς ὑπὸ τῶν κτισάντων προσηγορίας, ἔνια δὲ καὶ μετέβαλεν, αἱ δὲ καὶ πρὸς τὸ σαφέστερον εἶναι δοκοῦν τοῖς παροικοῦσι τροπὴν ἔλαβον. Ἕλληνες δ' εἰσὶν οἱ τούτου καταστάντες αἴτιοι· ἰσχύσαντες γὰρ ἐν τοῖς ὕστερον ἰδίαν ἐποιήσαντο καὶ τὴν παρὰ δόξαν, καλλωπίσαντες τὰ ἔθνη τοῖς ὀνόμασι πρὸς τὸ συνετὸν αὐτοῖς καὶ κόσμον θέμενοι πολειτείας ὡς ἀφ' αὐτῶν γεγονόσιν.

[20] For Isidore's Παρθικοὶ Σταθμοί see *GGM* i. 244 ff., with the quotations from Pliny and with valuable notes; *FGrH* 781 contains the same material, with the Σταθμοί as F2. The excerpt is transmitted by two main Paris MSS, 443(A) and 571(B) (cf. Müller, ad init.). Jacoby's laconic textual notes are valuable. The text (Müller's) and translation, with notes, by W. H. Schoff (Philadelphia, 1914), quote a considerable amount of parallel material. For the problem of the identity of the author and of the substance of the original work see Müller, i, pp. lxx ff., and the full discussion of modern views by Sallmann, op. cit. 50 ff.; also below, n. 27.

[21] vi. 141 (T1): *hoc in loco genitum esse Dionysium terrarum orbis situs recentissimum auctorem quem ad commentanda omnia in orientem praemiserat divus Augustus ituro in Armeniam ad Parthicas Arabicas res maiore filio non me praeteriit . . . in hac tamen parte arma Romana sequi placet nobis Iubamque regem ad eundem Gaium Caesarem scriptis voluminibus de eadem expeditione Arabica.*

Isidore, though the cause of the error, if such it is, is not explicable.[22] A further difficulty arises from the fact that Pliny says in the
same passage that he has used Juba as his main source for the
general geography of the *oikoumene* (from Britain to the Tanais)[23]
and for overall geodesy,[24] but not as an authority for the trans-
Euphratic region covered in the *Parthian Stations*, which, in its
turn, does not seem to fall very easily into the general structure
that can be envisaged for the work used by Pliny; it has therefore
been suggested that Isidore also wrote a Περίπλους τῆς Οἰκουμένης,
or a similar work.[25] It is further to be borne in mind that Isidore's
date depends largely on the reference to Augustus already noted,
though there can be no doubt that he was contemporary with the
Parthian Empire, and enough circumstantial evidence exists to
place him in the first century AD, even if the crucial alteration to
the name in Pliny be rejected.[26] In view of these difficulties we

[22] The emendation, made by Bernhardy in his edition of Dionysius the Periegete
(1828), p. 497, was favoured by Müller, p. lxxxi, and was printed in the text of
Pliny as Jacoby's T1 (though in the same fragment, printed as Juba, ibid. 275, F1,
he has 'Dionysium' in the text and 'Isidorum' in the app. crit.). Editors of Pliny have
been unwilling to accept the alteration; Jan and Detlefsen did not notice it, even in
their app. crit., and Mayhoff and Rackham (Loeb) retain 'Dionysium' (the former
adding 'Isidorum rectius Bernhardy' in his app. crit.); cf. Sallmann, 51 n. 5. It is
perhaps not impossible, in view of the origins of Isidore, that Διονύσιος is a second
name of the type found in the East.
[23] See e.g. *FGrH* 781, F 6–8, 11.
[24] F6 (circumference of the earth), 9 (length of Africa), 10 (extent of Asia from
Egypt to Tanais).
[25] So Müller, p. lxxxv, and Jacoby, who assigns all the quotations in Pliny to
such a *Periplous*. The title is. of course, uncertain, but Isidore of Charax is credited
with a *Periplous* in Marcianus, *Epit. Peripl. Menippi* (*GGM* i. 565. 2; *FGrH* 781 T2),
among a list of writers of *periploi* (including Simmeas, ὁ τῆς οἰκουμένης ἐνθεὶς τὸν
περίπλουν, thus justifying the possibility of ascribing such an ambitious—unrealiz-
able—project to Isidore). Various other suggestions for titles and subjects have been
made to cover the themes indicated by Pliny; cf. Sallmann, 51 ff. To follow these
numerous possibilities further would take us far from the *Mansiones Parthicae*.
Weissbach, *RE*, s.v. Isidoros (20) cols. 2065 ff., considered the possibility of two
Isidores of Charax, but concluded, 'Meine Absicht ist nicht sie [the view of Dodwell,
that two Isidores should be distinguished] wieder aufzunehmen. Aber die Frage,
ob einer oder zwei Schriftsteller Namens I. gelebt haben, musste aufs neue gestellt
werden. Beantwortet ist sie noch nicht und meiner Überzeugung nach gegenwärtig
überhaupt nicht spruchreif.' That suggestion deserves consideration. Tarn, *GBI*[2]
53 ff., maintained that the surviving text consists essentially of a Parthian survey of
*c.*100 BC, to which Isidore 'added some instructive notes of his own . . . We shall
blunder sadly if we do not distinguish the survey he is commenting on [?] from his
own comments made the better part of a century later.' This possibility does not
affect the use of the work in the present context (see p. 115 n. 23)
[26] See the passages discussed by Müller, pp. lxxii ff., and in particular: (1) *Mans.
Parth.* p. 248, ll. 12 ff. (F2, § 1):ἔνθα νῆσος κατὰ τὸν Εὐφράτην, σχοῖνοι ϛ'. ἐνταῦθα γάζα

can only take Isidore's Σταθμοί as it stands, without concerning ourselves with the question of its relation to the other and wider quotations in Pliny. It is probable that the text we possess is itself only an epitome of a larger work.[27] In its present form it corresponds to the type of ἀναγραφή material reworked in Eratosthenes–Strabo and Pliny, and provides comparable information for his own day—for the Parthian Stations, based, presumably, to a considerable extent on the model of the Seleucid ἀναγραφή, if not on

ἣν Φράατου τοῦ ἀποσφάξαντος τὰς παλλακίδας ὅτε Τιριδάτης φυγὰς ὢν εἰσέβαλεν; this, as Müller and Jacoby agree, can only refer to the invasion of Tiridates in c.25/4 BC (cf. Tarn, Mélanges Glotz, ii. 832 ff.; id. GBI² 53-4; Debevoise, Pol. Hist. of Parthia, 135-6; Le Rider, Suse sous les Séleucides, 412-13); (2) the identification in § 19 of Ἀραχωσία with Ἰνδικὴ Λευκὴ (ἐντεῦθεν Ἀραχωσία σχοῖνοι λς'· ταύτην δὲ οἱ Πάρθοι Ἰνδικὴν Λευκὴν καλοῦσιν) must refer to a period when Arachosia was part of the Scytho-Parthian kingdom (Tarn, loc. cit.), i.e. at the time of the Azes dynasty, c.30 BC-AD 14. These dates are now set considerably earlier, c.70-50 BC (cf. Narain, Indo-Greeks, 163-4), but there is no doubt of the conquest of Arachosia, and Azes coins have been found in overwhelming numbers near Ghazna, in the Mir-Zaka hoard (Schlumberger, Trésors monétaires d' Afghanistan (Mem. DAFA 14) 1953, 67 ff.; Jenkins, Journ. Num. Soc. India, 17 (1955 (2)), 1-26; id. and Narain, Coin-Types of the Saka-Pahlava Kings of India (Num. Soc. India, Num. Notes and Monogr. 4 (1957); Macdowall in Archaeology in Afghanistan (1978), 204-5. Tarn rightly dismisses the quotation from Isidore in Ps. Luc. Macrob. 218-19 (Müller, fr. 34/5; Jacoby, F*3-4) referring to Ἀρτάβαζος ὁ μετὰ Τίραιον ἕβδομος [i.e. the tenth king of Charakene] βασιλεύσας Χάρακος ἓξ καὶ ὀγδοήκοντα ἐτῶν καταταχθεὶς ὑπὸ Παρθῶν ἐβασίλευσε—i.e. an (otherwise unknown) Artabazos, who reigned between AD 72 and 100 (when there is a gap in the roll of known rulers), as fathered on Isidore by a later source; similarly Jacoby prints all the sections (in which the other rulers mentioned are all of the 1st cent. BC) in small font.

[27] Müller, pp. lxxxv-lxxxvi, argues this strongly both from the descriptive passages of the Σταθμοί of Amyntas and Baiton, discussed above, n. 6, which, he claims, show that a work in this genre necessarily contained much descriptive material, which would, in any case, be of use to the Romans, and from the fact that the route traversed is almost exclusively through the northern provinces of the Parthian Empire. By comparison with the surviving text of the Σταθμοί the quotations in Lucian (F*3-4; cf. previous note) and Athenaeus (F1, the description of the pearl-divers of the Persian Gulf, quoted as from Τὸ τῆς Παρθικῆς Περιηγητικόν, no doubt Athenaeus' own alternative title) are far fuller in ethnographical and historical detail. That seems certainly to be the case, but on the other hand the transmitted version closely resembles the bematists' ἀναγραφή in Strabo and Pliny, and I am reluctant to assume much (lost) elaboration throughout Isidore's text. It has been argued at length by Daffinà, L'Immigrazione dei Saka nella Drangiana (see below, note 46), pp. 5 ff., that Isidore should be dissociated from Pliny's 'Dionysius', and dated on independent grounds (the chronology of the Armenian kings mentioned by him, for which see n. 26) to a considerably earlier period. That may be correct, but the difficulty inherent in a consideration of the Stations—that they do not match what else is known of Isidore—remains. At all events the question whether he wrote in the 2nd or 1st cent. BC is not central to our use of him; he is in any case writing in the Parthian period, and his topography is Parthian, not earlier.

that work itself, served a practical purpose, like the Arab barīd-texts, and would not refer to either fictitious or defunct cities. The paragraphs of the Σταθμοί which concern us are §§ 14-19. These are:

14: Ἐνταῦθα Μαργιανή, σχοῖνοι λ'. ἔνθα Ἀντιόχεια ἡ καλουμένη Ἔνυδρος· κῶμαι δὲ οὐκ εἰσίν.

15: Ἐντεῦθεν Ἄρεια σχοῖνοι λ'. Ἔνθα Κανδὰκ πόλις καὶ Ἀρτακαύαν πόλις καὶ Ἀλεξάνδρεια ἡ ἐν Ἀρείοις· κῶμαι δὲ δ'.

16: Ἐντεῦθεν Ἀναύων χώρα τῆς Ἀρείας, σχοῖνοι νε', ἐν ἧι πόλις μεγίστη Φρὰ καὶ Βὶς πόλις καὶ Γαρὶ πόλις καὶ Νίη πόλις· κώμη δὲ οὐκ ἔστιν.

17: Ἐντεῦθεν Ζαραγγιανή, σχοῖνοι κα'. ἔνθα πόλις Πάριν καὶ Κορὸκ πόλις.

18: Ἐντεῦθεν Σακαστανὴ Σακῶν Σκυθῶν, ἡ καὶ Παραιτακηνή, σχοῖνοι ξγ'. ἔνθα Βαρδὰ πόλις καὶ Μὶν πόλις καὶ Παλακεντὶ πόλις καὶ Σιγὰλ πόλις· ἔνθα βασίλεια Σακῶν· καὶ πλησίον Ἀλεξάνδρεια πόλις (καὶ πλησίον Ἀλεξανδρόπολις)· κῶμαι δὲ ἔξ.

19: Ἐντεῦθεν Ἀραχωσία, σχοῖνοι λς'. ταύτην δὲ οἱ Πάρθοι Ἰνδικὴν Λευκὴν καλοῦσιν· ἔνθα Βιὺτ πόλις καὶ Φάρσανα πόλις καὶ Χοροχοὰδ πόλις καὶ Δημητριὰς πόλις εἶτα Ἀλεξανδρόπολις, μητρόπολις Ἀραχωσίας· ἔστι δὲ Ἑλληνίς, καὶ παραρρεῖ αὐτὴν ποταμὸς Ἀραχωτός. ἄχρι τούτων ἐστὶν ἡ τῶν Πάρθων ἐπικράτεια.

These sections introduce us to more than one new city. First we must note again Antiocheia in Margiana, which Pliny and Strabo state was founded by Alexander as an Alexandria, then destroyed by barbarians and then rebuilt by Antiochus I and called Antiocheia, while Martianus Capella and Solinus say that it was founded by Antiochus and called Seleukeia after his father Seleucus I.[28] After that, alongside Alexandria in Ariana, Isidore gives Kandak, an unknown locality, and Artakauan, the latter the Artacoana mentioned by Arrian as the place where the royal palace of the Arians (i.e. Achaemenids?) stood; it is familiar from other sources, all of which show that it still stood in the first century AD, quite distinct from Alexandria in Aria, which had replaced it as the chief city of the area.[29] In § 18 Isidore refers to an Alexandria and a nearby Alexandropolis in Sakastane, itself approximately equivalent to the early Hellenistic Drangiana. It has long been accepted that the double reference to πλησίον Ἀλεξάνδρεια πόλις (καὶ πλησίον Ἀλεξανδρόπολις) cannot be right, and must be emended. Exactly how, is not certain, and, as we shall see,

[28] Cf. above, p. 31; below, pp. 116-7.
[29] Cf. above, p. 30; below, pp. 109 ff.

it is possible that the corruption has spread into § 19, which contains a reference to Alexandropolis, the metropolis of Arachosia, 'a Greek city by which the Arachotos flows', which marks for Isidore the limits of Parthian power.[30]

One difficulty in interpreting Isidore's data should be mentioned. The epitome uses a number of different terms to describe localities, notably κώμη, κωμόπολις and πόλις, and we must beware of assuming that these terms can each be equated with one particular type of settlement, be it a Greek city (in whatever sense), a native Parthian city, an administrative centre, a village or a fort. Isidore is not writing a historical geography, but enumerating places, *Mansiones*, on a route. The word πόλις in particular is used of several different types of urban communities. Thus we find the expression πόλις Ἑλληνίς, Μακεδόνων κτίσμα, used to describe Ichnai (§1) (of which Stephanus s.v. Ἴχναι, πόλις Μακεδονίας, says ἔστι καὶ ἑτέρα τῆς Ἀνατολικῆς πόλις), Nikephorion described (ibid.) as παρ' Εὐφράτην πόλις Ἑλληνίς, κτίσμα Ἀλεξάνδρου βασιλέως, and Dura-Europus (ibid.) as Δοῦρα Νικάνορος πόλις, κτίσμα Μακεδόνων, ὑπὸ δὲ Ἑλλήνων Εὔρωπος καλεῖται, and again of the region of Apolloniatis he says (§ 2), ἔχει δὲ κώμας, ἐν αἷς σταθμός, πόλιν δὲ Ἑλληνίδα Ἄρτεμιτο . . . νῦν μέντοι ἡ πόλις καλεῖται Χαλάσαρ; but, by contrast, we find (§ 3) πόλις δὲ Ἑλληνὶς Χάλα, εἶτα Γάθαρ πόλις . . . εἶτα Σιρὼκ πόλις, and again (§ 17) Ἔνθα πόλις Πάριν καὶ Κόροκ πόλις, followed in the next section (§ 18) by the use of the word πόλις for four native cities and for Ἀλεξάνδρεια πόλις. It follows that in using Isidore we cannot take the word πόλις as a satisfactory criterion in itself for determining the origin or ethnic composition of a settlement. A native urban unit no less than a Μακεδόνων κτίσμα could be a πόλις. The use of the plain descriptions πόλις and πόλις Ἑλληνίς is characteristic of Περίπλους-literature already in the fourth century BC, e.g. in Pseudo-Scylax, where the formula is used both of Greek colonies and of dubiously Greek settlements,[31] and in the

---

[30] See further below pp. 136 ff. for the interpretation of the text of Isidore regarding the Alexandrias. As noted above, n. 26, the description of Arachosia as 'White India' indicates the extension of Scytho-Parthian power under the Azes dynasty to that region. 'Arachotoi' seems to have given Stephanus and his sources no less difficulty than they gave Isidore or his excerptor. Stephanus lists Alexandria ἐν Ἀραχώτοις (his (12)), while in the entries s.vv. Ἀραχωσία and Ἀραχωτοί both these are called πόλεις, the first repeating Eratosthenes' aberrant (or corrupt) reference to Ἀραχωτοὶ οὐκ ἄπωθεν Μασσαγετῶν (Str. 513 = IIIB, 63; cf. below, p. 139 n. 66, p. 144 n. 73), the second (Str. 516) describes it, like Isidore, as πόλις Ἰνδικῆς.

[31] See e.g. GGM i. 28 ff. §§ 22 ff., the περίπλους of the regions of the Ἰλλύριοι and

formula as preserved in Isidore the usage is equally ambiguous. A further complication in the use of Parthian evidence is the fact that, as noted above, the Parthians, like the Seleucids before them, renamed settlements on no principle known to us. It is wholly possible that the excess of Alexandrias in § 18 may arise from this cause.

Pliny's geographical books (notably v and vi) contain, as we have seen, much early matter relevant to the expedition of Alexander, and an occasional reference to Alexander-foundations, but our inability to penetrate the closed world of his sources, when unnamed, makes it impossible to assess fully the value of his evidence. When due allowance, however, is made for this, and for his own limited comprehension of the subject about which he was writing, he forms an essential link in the geographical tradition, in spite of the uncertainty which surrounds not only the question of his sources, but also the accuracy of the figures and facts transmitted by him. We have already seen that he quotes from both the bematists and Eratosthenes, and mostly agrees closely with the latter in regard to distances. We have also seen that he lists Isidore of Charax among his sources in the Index, and in the text of books ii and vi, and uses his larger geographical work, as well as Juba of Mauretania,[32] and also Artemidorus of Ephesus' Γεωγραφούμενα for continental measurements.[33] Unfortunately, most of Pliny's references to the settlements which he mentions—Antiocheia (Seleukeia) in Margiana, Alexandria in Sogdiana, Alexandria ad Caucasum, Ortospana, and Alexandria in Carmania—occur in sections of his text in which he does not name specific sources, so

---

Νέστοι, where there are several examples of the usage, noted by me in *Greek Historiography* (ed. S. Hornblower, Oxford, 1993), 186–7. For the ambiguities in the use of the term in the Seleucid Empire see now Grainger, *Seleukid Syria*, 63 ff., and P. Briant, in *Alexander the Great, Reality and Myth* (Anal. Rom, Inst. Danici, Suppl. xx, 1993).

[32] For Juba see *FGrH* 275, and Jacoby's excellent article, *RE* (2), and for Pliny's frequent use of him (see p. 88 n. 20, and cf. Juba F 28 ff (Arabia and Africa)) see Sallmann, 85 ff., esp. p. 85 n. 99. Pliny uses Juba for information about natural history (F 47, 54 ff.), plants (F 62 ff.), precious metals (F 70 ff.), and other topics, and the interests of the two men clearly coincided at many points. Pliny says of him, v. 16 (Juba, T 12b), *studiorum claritate memorabilior etiam quam regno*, while Plutarch, *Vit. Sert.* 9 (Juba, T 10) calls him ὁ πάντων ἱστορικώτατος βασιλέων.

[33] For Pliny's use of Artemidorus see Sallmann, 60 ff., who provides a very clear analysis of the problems relating to the Artemidoran element in Pliny and in other authors, and gives a list of all the passages in books ii and vi where Pliny quotes him.

that we are compelled, as so often, to fall back upon general considerations. The view that Isidore was Pliny's main source for the eastern geography is based on the assumption noted above, that his reference to 'Dionysius of Charax' as the most influential recent writer on the East should be altered to 'Isidorus', and although this change might be expected to provide us with a major source for Pliny's geographical material, it must be admitted that the actual quotations from Isidore in the text do little to strengthen the view that he used him in this capacity. At the same time the fragments of Juba are hardly more helpful in this respect; they too barely cover the relevant material in Pliny. Other Greek geographers used by Pliny are equally elusive, and have probably passed through Roman hands reflecting Roman conditions. Here M. Terentius Varro stands as the main figure in the background, though he too does not fit altogether in the role demanded of him as a major contributor to Pliny's geography.[34] We can only conclude that, while Pliny's distance-measurements show that he followed the Eratosthenic tradition based on the bematists, numerous other sources also contributed through unidentifiable intermediaries to his composite picture. Certainly in the present context, he has a place within the Hellenistic tradition, even if it is inconceivable that he knew at first hand all the Greek authors whom he quotes by name, either in the Index or in the text.

The evaluation of the information provided by Ammianus, who, though of the mid-fourth century, may be treated here, is far from easy. His notable chorographical excursus on Sassanian Persia,[35] contains a considerable amount of information on the regions of Drangiana and Arachosia which coincides especially with Strabo,[36]

[34] I refer here to Sallmann's detailed treatment of this topic. His view, as expressed in his conclusion (265 ff.), is that only two works of Varro, the *De Geometria* (which included the measurement of the *oikoumene*) and the *Libri legationum* come into count as geographical works, and that a Varronian 'chorographia', utilized by Pliny as a major source, is a chimera. No less fanciful is the attempt to identify the quotations of 'Varro' as referring not to the Reatine, but to Varro Atacinus, author of a metrical chorography of about the same time as his great namesake: see Sallmann, 37–9.

[35] xxiii. 6 §§ 54–72, *passim.*

[36] See Gardthausen, *Jahrb. f.Class. Philol.* vi(2) (1872/3), 509–56,' Die geographischen Quellen Ammians'. His view that Ammianus used Eratosthenes directly is based on the agreement of the terminal points of routes etc., for the main regions with which we are concerned, i.e. the distance from the Caspian Gates to India via Ortospana (Str. 514; cf. above, p. 84); Amm. Marc. loc. cit. § 70: *habent (sc. Paropanisadae) autem etiam civitates aliquas, quibus clariores sunt Agazaca et*

and, as Gardthausen saw over a century ago, probably indicates for this area a direct use of Eratosthenes, rather than of Strabo (who was little read in antiquity). However, while the Alexandrias mentioned by him—Alexandria in Arachosia, Alexandria Ariana, Alexandria in Carmania, and Alexandria in Sogdiana—are all to be found in Pliny,[37] and could be derived from an earlier source, it seems probable that some of the cities to which he refers were surviving in his own day. I revert to this question below (pp. 192 f.).

There consequently cannot be very much doubt that in general much of the material surviving in the geographical sources—in Eratosthenes-Strabo and in Pliny-Ammianus—ultimately goes back to Eratosthenes himself, at times directly, otherwise through intermediaries and, in some cases, to the bematists whom he used. From this it follows that the geographers form a no less valid source of information than the Alexander-historians—in some cases, it may be noted, Pliny quotes the historians—even though,

---

Naulibus et Ortospana, unde litorea navigatio ad usque Mediae fines, portis proximos Caspiis stadiorum sunt duo milia et ducenta. This is in excess of Strabo-Eratosthenes' 15,500 by some 270 m.p. See also Str. 513. For the Black Sea Ammianus (xxii. 8. 10; Erat. IIIB 79) quotes Eratosthenes and others: *omnis autem eius velut insularis circuitus litorea navigatio viginti tribus dimensa milibus stadiorum, ut Eratosthenes affirmat et Hecataeus et Ptolemaeus aliique huius modi*, which, as far as *stadiorum*, Gardthausen regarded as derived directly from Eratosthenes. Str. 125 gives the distance as 25,000 st. It is to be noticed that neither Strabo nor Ammianus quotes Eratosthenes by name in his section on Persia, and Gardthausen's view has been rejected as too unitarian. There can be no doubt that Ammianus also used many other sources, both Greek and Roman, including Isidore and Ptolemy. Mommsen, *Hermes*, 16 (1881), 602-36 = *GS* vii. 393-425, though in general critical of Gardthausen's view, accepted that Eratosthenes was the most probable ultimate source for Ammianus' geography of Arachosia etc.: see especially *GS* 415-16. For attempts to isolate the elements in the Roman geographical tradition between Pliny and Solinus, which are relevant to Ammianus, see the history of the problem in Sallmann, sect. I, E (esp. pp. 127-34). The summary given by J. Fontane, *Ammianus*, Budé edn., vol. iv(1), 54-64 (bibliography, p. 57 n. 1), illustrates the difficulty of determining Ammianus' sources.

[37] See Amm. xxiii. 6. 69: *abundat autem haec eadem Aria oppidis, inter quae sunt celebria Vitaxa Sarmatina et Sotira et Nisibis et Alexandria*; ibid. § 72: *post quos* (the Drangiani) *exadversum Arachosia visitur, dextrum vergens in latus, Indis obiecta, quam ab Indo fluviorum maximo* (*unde regiones cognominatae sunt*) *amnis multo minor exoriens aquarum alluit amplitudine, efficitque paludem quam Arachotoscrenen appellant. Hic quoque civitates sunt inter alias viles, Alexandria et Arbaca et Choaspis*; ibid. § 59: *Hic* (in Sogdiana) *inter alia oppida celebrantur et Cyreschata et Drepsa metropolis*; ibid. § 49: (in Carmania): *sunt etiam civitates, licet numero paucae, victu tamen et cultu perquam copiosae, inter quas nitet Carmana omnium mater et Portospana et Alexandria et Hermupolis.*

quite apart from the fundamental defects and uncertainties of Greek methods of mensuration, outlined at the beginning of this chapter, the derivative nature of much of the material that they provide indicates the existence of distance-variations that may have accumulated or occurred in the text on the way, for instance in the long span of time between Eratosthenes and Ammianus, either through accumulated scribal error or through variants due to the use of secondary sources, as when Pliny chooses to cite Nearchos and Onesikritos from Juba.[38] It is to be remembered that for the regions with which we are now dealing the problem of the possible 'modernization' of the information in the early sources hardly arises. Although it may have happened, by chance, as Pliny says,[39] that the ideas about Ceylon held by Eratosthenes and Megasthenes had been superseded by the journey of the freedman Annius Plocamus and by the voyage of the Sinhalese ambassadors to Rome, on the other hand knowledge of the geography of central Asia was still slight. The sketchy early Roman attempts at the mapping and chorography of the regions covered by Pliny's Book vi are recorded by him,[40] and he guarded himself to the best of his ability against the presentation of antiquated information by explicitly or tacitly using the latest available specialized sources, such as Isidore and Juba, while his frequent references to cities and tribes that had ceased to exist (particularly in the west) show his awareness of this problem; but little detailed information on such matters can have existed for the eastern regions.

There remains one geographical source of a very different type from the chorographers and from the authors of 'Stations':

[38] See Plin. vi. 96: *sed priusquam generatim haec persequamur indicari convenit quae prodidit Onesicritus classe Alexandri circumvectus in mediterranea Persidis ex India, enarrata proxime a Iuba* (FGrH 275 F28), *deinde eam navigationem quae his annis comperta servata hodie.* There follows the account of the narratives of Nearchos and Onesikritos (FGrH 133 F13; 134 F28).

[39] vi. 81-91. See also the graffito of Λυσᾶς Ποπλίου Ἀννίου Πλοκάμου, carved in the Wadi Menih, on the Berenike road, in the Eastern Desert of Egypt, JRS 43 (1953), 38 ff. (SEG xiii. 614; A. Bernand, Pan du Désert, no. 65; cf. Bingen in BE 1993, no. 685).

[40] 'Agrippa' gave overall measurements for India, Plin. vi. 57 (= fr. 32, Riese, op. cit. below), and for the region between the Indus and the Tigris, the Persian Gulf and the Taurus (ibid. 137 = fr. 33), as also for Asia Minor and Armenia (v. 102 = fr. 28). For attempts to elucidate the history of the geographical works, maps etc., that are attributed to Agrippa see the prolegomena to A. Riese, *Geographi Latini Minores* (1878 (repr. 1964)), and the detailed account of later theories in Sallmann, op. cit. 91 ff.

Claudius Ptolemy's *Geographical Guide*, the Γεωγραφικὴ Ὑφήγησις,[41] closely based on Marinus of Tyre's slightly earlier work, and consisting of a gazetteer to his projection of the *oikoumene*. Ptolemy's final figure for the length of the inhabited world towards the rising sun, as far as the Land of the Sinai, is, for reasons that are sufficiently well known, 72,000 st., instead of about 52,000 (180° 39' instead of approximately 126°), and the resulting co-ordinates are of little use in determining the true geographical location of sites not astronomically ascertained. In addition, however, to the list of places and their co-ordinates the gazetteer contains general statements of locations (θέσεις) and boundaries of regions and tribes in chorographical terms—as beyond the river, between rivers *x* and *y*, and so on—and these wider indications may be of value even within the framework of an erroneous projection. They are mostly given before the individual locations listed with their supposed co-ordinates, and, based as they are on the complex of sources used by Marinus and in part described by Ptolemy in the vigorous and critical first book of the *Geography*, from official Roman maps to (more especially) the information as to distances provided by travelling merchants (a source distrusted but used by Ptolemy), may be roughly correct in regard to general geographical features; but the individual locations within the regions, determined for the most part not by astronomical observation but by land measurements cannot be accepted in detail. The additional fact that a great many of the locations recorded by Ptolemy throughout the entire work are wholly unknown to other writers and to ourselves makes the task of utilizing his lists for true locations perilous, and is yet one more obstacle which any attempt to establish unknown locations has to overcome.

[41] I can only refer here to work on Ptolemy that is directly relevant to the regions of Central Asia. Polaschek's *RE* article (Suppbd. X, cols. 813 ff) provides an excellent *mise-au-point*. For a special edition with commentary of the portions of the text relevant to the present theme see I. Ronca's elaborate bilingual edition of the Central Asian section, *Ptolemaios, Geographie 6, 9-21* (IsMEO, Rome, 1971). In A. Berthelot's detailed reconstruction, *L'Asie ancienne centrale sud-orientale d'après Ptolémée* (Paris, 1930), 159-254, the locations given by Ptolemy are assigned with corrected co-ordinates to the modern map, which gives a false impression of the Ptolemaic map. McCrindle's veteran *Ancient India as described by Ptolemy* (Bombay, 1855, repr. with introd. and add. notes by S. M. Sastri, Calcutta, 1927) is still useful, while L. Renan's *La Géographie de Ptolemée, L'Inde*, vii. 1-4 (Paris, 1928) deals mainly with Gangetic India and further east. I may note here that the introd. to the Hildesheim reprint (1966) of Nobbe's Tauchnitz text contains a brief but authoritative statement of the chief manuscripts by the late Aubrey Diller.

In general there is no sign that he used Hellenistic material of the type provided by the bematists and the chorographers. The information available to him from travellers' reports of more recent date, whether derived directly from Marinus or not, clearly carries no warranty of the antiquity of a location, and it is matter for conjecture how many of the cities etc. existed at the time Ptolemy wrote.[42] He criticizes Marinus precisely for using unauthenticated and antiquated data, and makes a point of correcting his projection where better information was available to him, brief though the interval was between them.[43] However, he mentions (probably from Marinus) a number of defunct cities in Greece proper and Sicily, mostly, as with Stephanus, classical or pre-classical cities, without any indication that they had ceased to exist (unlike Strabo and Pliny, who drew attention to this historically significant element),[44] and the same may be true of little-known cities of the east.

[42] Ptolemy quotes some sources used by Marinus: Philemon (*RE* (11)), i. 11. 7, where Marinus criticizes his measurement of the width of Ireland because it was based on information supplied by merchants; i. 9, one Diogenes, for conditions in the region of Cape Guardafui: Διογένη μέν τινά φησι τῶν εἰς τὴν Ἰνδικὴν πλεόντων, κ.τ.λ.; ibid., in continuation, 'a certain Theophilos': Θεόφιλον δέ τινα τῶν εἰς τὴν Ἀφρικὴν πλεόντων ἀπὸ τῶν Ῥάπτων ἀναχθῆναι νότωι, καὶ εἰκοστῆι ἡμέραι ἐληλυθέναι εἰς τὰ Ἀρώματα. It is clear that such sources, used by Marinus, like the famous Maes Titianos, the Macedonian merchant who sent traders to the Serai along the Silk Route (i. 11. 7), have nothing in common with the Hellenistic sources from the bematists to Strabo. Note that each (including Maes) is referred to with a qualifying τις. As an example of reliable regional knowledge we may note Ptolemy's reference to Marinus' description of the route from the Caspian to Antiocheia Margiana by way of Ariana: i. 12. 7 πάλιν δὲ ἀπὸ ταύτης (sc. Ὑρκανίας) ὁδὸς εἰς τὴν Μαργιανὴν Ἀντιόχειαν διὰ τῆς Ἀρείας τὰ μὲν πρῶτα πρὸς μεσημβρίαν ἀποκλίνει, τῆς Ἀρείας ὑπὸ τὸ αὐτὸν ταῖς Κασπίαις Πύλαις κειμένης παράλληλον. This seems to be based on authentic reports, but it cannot be assigned beyond Marinus to any Hellenistic source of the type that we have been examining. For Ptolemy's own co-ordinates for Margiana and Aria see vi. 10 (Margiana) and vi. 17 (Aria).

[43] i. 6. 2: having admitted the care exercised by Marinus in most respects (§ 1) he goes on: ἐπεὶ δὲ φαίνεται καὶ αὐτὸς ἐνίοις τε μὴ μετὰ καταλήψεως ἀξιοπίστου συγκατατεθέμενος, καὶ ἔτι περὶ τὴν ἔφοδον τῆς καταγραφῆς πολλαχῆ μήτε τοῦ προχείρου, μήτε τοῦ συμμέτρου τὴν δέουσαν πρόνοιαν πεποιημένος, εἰκότως προήχθημεν, ὅσον ὠιόμεθα δεῖν, τῆι τἀνδρὸς πραγματείαι συνεισενεγκεῖν ἐπὶ τὸ εὐλογώτερον καὶ εὐχρηστότερον. Chs. 15-17 are particularly critical, and repay careful study. There is a German translation of them, with commentary by Mžik and Hopfner, *Klotho*, 5 (Vienna, 1938). *Des Klaudios Ptol. Einführung in die darstellende Erdkunde, I, Theorie und Grundlagen der darstellende Erdkunde.*

[44] See the list in Honigmann, *RE*, s.v. Marinos, col. 1769. It includes Megara Hyblaea, Gela, Megalopolis, Stymphalos, Haliartos, and others. For Pliny's *populi qui sunt aut fuerunt* see above, n. 4. Berthelot, op. cit. 113 ff. seems to underestimate the work of Marinus.

The chapters relevant to our purpose form most of bk. vi, namely: ch. 4 (Persis); 5 (Parthia); 6 (Carmanian Desert); 7 (Arabia); 8 (Carmania); 9 (Hyrcania); 10 (Margiana); 11 (Bactria); 12 (Sogdiana); 13 (Sakai); 14–15 (Scythia); 16 (Serica); 17 (Aria); 18 (Paropamisadai); 19 (Drangiana); 20 (Arachosia); 21 (Gedrosia), together with bk. vii, ch. 1 (India west of the Ganges). In the main regions listed, Margiana, Bactria, Drangiana, Arachosia, and Aria, Ptolemy records the following relevant cities, the actual location of which is considered in the next chapter: in Parthia, Hekatompylos (vi. 5. 2), in Carmania, Alexandria (vi. 8. 14), in Margiana, Antiochia Margiana (vi. 10. 4), in Bactria, Zariaspa (vi. 11. 7), in Sogdiana, Alexandria Oxiana (vi. 12. 6) and Alexandria Eschate (ibid.), in Aria, Artikaunda, and Alexandria (vi. 17. 6) and also apparently Areia (vi. 17. 7)—the order is Ptolemy's.

We may then add to our list of Alexandrias, and associated cities, the following, mostly mentioned neither by the historians, nor by the *Romance*, but drawn from the geographical sources considered in this chapter (Alexandria Troas being omitted):

Alexandria Ariana or 'among the Arians' (Bematists, Erat., Plin., Ptol.)
Alexandria in Margiana (Plin., Ptol.)
Alexandria Oxiana (in Sogdiana) (Ptol.)
Alexandria in Arachosia (Isid., Ptol., Amm. Marc.)
Arachotoi (Bematists, Erat., Plin.)

To these we may add from the historians (ch. iii):

Alexandria ad Aegyptum (Arr. etc.)
Alexandria ad Caucasum (Arr., Diod., Curt. Ruf. (Plin.))
Nikaia (1) ad Caucasum (Arr.)
Nikaia (2) and (Alexandria) (Bucephala) (Arr., Diod., Curt. Ruf.)
Alexandria at junction of Akesines and Indus (Arr., Diod., Curt. Ruf.)
Alexandria-Rambakia (Arr., Diod., Curt. Ruf. (Plin., Jub.))
Alexandria-Spasinou Charax (Arr. (Plin., Jub.))

From the historians and geographers we can, then, with some probability, extract some dozen Alexandrias and related foundations, such as the Nikaias, in the whole region between Hekatompylos and the eastern tributaries of the Indus. We may note that, except in Ammianus (who refers to Alexandria in Arachosia among the *civitates viles* of that area, a phrase that suggests some contemporary knowledge, and also refers to Alexandria in Aria and Alexandria in Sogdiana), there is no reference to any eponymous Alexander-city that can be assigned to a date later than Marinus–Ptolemy.[45]

At one important point, however, the evidence provided by the two Arabic adapters of Ptolemy, al-Khuwārizmī and Ṣuḥrāb (= 'Ibn Serapion'), both of the ninth century AD, the latter slightly the earlier of the two, enables us to proceed a little further. These texts, though not linguistically of any great difficulty, are totally unreliable within small margins in respect of the co-ordinates, which are provided with neither diacritical marks nor vowel-notation. Derived probably from a Syriac intermediary, they are extremely similar, though they appear to derive independently from an intermediate adaptor and translator. Their aim is to adapt Ptolemy's lists to the world of their own day by the improvement (for the most part) of his co-ordinates, and by the addition of Islamic locations. They consist of a preface (lacking, in fact, in the sole manuscript of al-Khuwārizmī), followed by a list of cities situated in the regions covered by them, namely the eastern *aqālim* (i.e. κλίματα), with their co-ordinates, followed in turn by a narrative description of the mountains, rivers, seas and islands within the *klimata*, each item with the area occupied or traversed by it, with all coordinates. In all sections considerable islamicization has taken place, and items recognizable from Ptolemy are interwoven with unrecognizable and indeed fabulous places.[46] This feature is analogous to the

---

[45] For the passages of Ammianus see above, n. 37.

[46] The two texts are published by H. v. Mžik, *Bibl. Arab. Hist. u. geogr.* 3 (1926), al-Khuwārizmī, and 5 (1930), Ṣuḥrāb), and the references are to that edition. Mžik's introductions give a brief analysis of the treatment of Ptolemy by these authors. A more general survey will be found in the translation of Barthold's preface to the *Ḥudūd al-'ālam*, printed in the prolegomena to Minorsky's edition of that work (2nd edn., as above, n. 16), pp. 10–12. For al-Khuwārizmī see also the detailed treatment by Nallino, *Mem. Linc.* 1894 = *Scritti Edite e Inedite* v (1944), 458–532 (with bibliographical addenda by his daughter), which analyses the relationship between Ptolemy's co-ordinates and those of al-Khuwārizmī, but does not print the Arabic text. Mžik has suggested in *Beiträge z. historischen Geographie, Kulturgeographie, Ethnographie u. Kartographie, vornehmlich des Orients* (ed. H. Mžik, Leipzig u. Wien, 1929), 186 ff., that the fabulous names on al-Khuwārizmī's map of the eastern and northern parts of the globe derive from the lost Arabic version of the *Romance*. He concludes: 'die [i.e. the Arabic *Romance*] aber in der einen oder anderen Bearbeitung wesentlich von der Fassung des Pseudo-Kallisthenes abgewichen sein muss, wie sich im folgenden noch deutlicher zeigen wird.' It is true that these place-names etc. link

presence in Ptolemy's lists of large numbers of non-Greek names, which, however, are not likely to be fabulous. The relevant information in al-Khuwārizmī is to be found in his entry among the Arachosian cities corresponding to Ptol. vi. 20. 4 (long. 114° o', lat. 31° 20'), Ἀράχωτος, which he gives as 'the Eastern Iskandarīya,[47] while Ṣuhrāb at the same point, by an illuminating oversight, has 'that is, Herāt'.[48] Both texts have Q.nd.h.r. among the towns of the region, and al-Khuwārizmī. says of the river adjacent to Iskandarīya that 'it flows by the city of Q.nd.h.r.,[49] exactly as Isidore says (§ 19, above, p. 91) that the Arachotos (the Arghandāb) flows by Alexandria in Arachosia, a Greek city'. This is by far the earliest Arab reference to Qandahar, and makes the equation Alexandria in Arachosia = Qandahar virtually certain. It also confirms the evidence for the continuous occupation of the site under the Qaitul ridge until the early Islamic period.

up with the al-Khḍr-legend and the exploits of Dhū'l-Qarnein, but a direct link with the *Romance* must remain, at least at present, very speculative. It is a matter of considerable interest that, as Honigmann (*RE*, Marinos (2), cols. 1795-6) points out, al-Masʿūdī is alone among the Arabs in referring to Marinus; cf. Dunlop, *Arab Civilization to AD 1500* (London and Beirut, 1971) 151 f., who quotes the relevant passage from his *Tanbīh*.

[47] See p. 132 (Ar. text), ll. 12-13, no. (1643 (Ar.)). Nallino lists the co-ordinates of Kandahar-Alexandria given by al-Khūwārizmī in his analysis of the text (see above, n. 46), p. 37 = *Scritti editi etc.*, p. 508.

[48] p. 29, no. [250] (Ar.)

[49] pp. 132-3 'wa yemurru biqurb madīnat al-Qandahar'. The whole phrase, under the general heading 'Known rivers of Islam in the East' reads 'a river rises in the region between Iskandarīya of the east and the mountains close by [co-ordinates], and runs between the city of Iskandarīya and the mountain, and close to Qandahar.' The co-ordinates of the Arabic adaptation are close to those of Ptolemy in the corresponding passages.

CHAPTER V

Identifications

THE purpose of this chapter is to consider the possible identification and location of the cities described as Alexandrias, or associated names, as recorded by the Alexander-historians and the geographers. No attempt is made to discuss the identifications proposed for cities recorded only in the Alexandrian or Iranian lists, which, for the reasons explained in Chapters I and II, I disregard in this context. The historicity of the foundations under consideration in this chapter does not depend on their exact locations, and it has not been my aim to undertake a fresh study of the material from that point of view, though I have naturally indicated my own views on some of these very perplexing and, for the most part, insoluble topographical questions. I must also stress that, at the expense perhaps of the coherence of the narrative, I have entered only where necessary into the difficult problems of movement and logistics which form an essential part of the history of the campaigns themselves, since my focus is not on Alexander's military operations but on his foundations.

The cities in question all lie, broadly speaking, within the region of Iran and Central Asia bounded on the west by the desert east of the Elburz Mountains, on the east by the Indus river, on the north by the Jaxartes-Tanais (Syr Darya), and on the south by the Persian Gulf. Within this vast region, embracing the later Muslim provinces of Khūzistān, Sijistān, Khorāsān, largely within the frontiers of modern Afghanistan, and 'Beyond the River (Oxus)', lie the chief cities associated with the name of Alexander. In terms of Hellenistic geography the area is covered by the first two 'Seals' of Eratosthenes (India and Ariana). The problem of their location and their identification with later cities is full of difficulties, of which the principal are as follows.

1. The total number of sites surveyed in Afghanistan, especially in the last fifty years, naturally far exceeds the number of cities that

we are seeking.[1] In particular the gazetteer of sites shows a heavy concentration of Achaemenid and Hellenistic sites (Seleucid, Bactrian, and, later, Kushan) in the area between the northern foothills of the Hindu Kush and the Oxus, especially along the valleys of the southern tributaries of the river, and along the course of the river itself, and another concentration, which includes more Parthian sites, in the lower Helmund valley between Lashkargar and Nad Ali (Zaranj). These sites are mostly unexcavated, and, in ancient terms, all of them unnamed. Some have been partially excavated, but for the most part they have only been superficially surveyed, and the historical chronology assigned to them is largely based on the collection of surface sherds and on the approximate date of surviving structures, if any. I shall have occasion to refer to some of these sites in due course.

2. Arrian and the other Alexander-historians rarely give distances in terms either of land-measurements or of day-marches, and their descriptions of natural features are not precise enough to enable us to identify anything other than the largest physical features such as mountain-ranges, the major rivers and the deserts. We have consequently very little information based on Alexander's bematists from our historical sources.

3. The geographers, to whom we owe our knowledge of the distances calculated by the bematists on whom they drew, though they provide distances, rarely agree with one another, and, as has already been emphasized, different manuscripts of the same passage may vary considerably, and already varied in antiquity. I have said enough about this in the previous chapter, so I may limit myself here to stressing that attempts to determine a location within a distance of even fifty miles on the basis of literary evidence, or

---

[1] For the study of the sites I rely on the invaluable *Gazetteer of Archaeological Sites in Afghanistan* by W. Ball and J.-C. Gardin (Paris, 1982), where every recorded site is given a serial number. I refer to this simply as 'Ball' followed by the number of the entry. *Archaeology in Afghanistan*, ed. F. R. Allchin and N. Hammond (London, 1978) refers to most of the sites in a historical and archaeological survey stretching from the earliest times to the Timurid period, and is an invaluable handbook. The historical geography of the region between the Oxus and the Indus is treated in A. Foucher's classic, if prolix, work, *La Vieille Route de l'Inde de Bactres à Taxila* (2 vols. Paris, 1942–7 (*Mém.* DAFA I)), based on the early researches of the DAFA, from 1922 to 1925. I refer to this as *Vieille Route*. The data provided by this admirable work are naturally in some respects superseded. The sober analysis given by Brunt in App. viii of his edition of Arrian (i. 487–509) provides an excellent guide to the chronology, logistics and geography of the whole campaign in the east; cf. also ibid. vol. ii, App. xviii.

of Ptolemy's co-ordinates, and corresponding attempts either to emend or to explain away discrepancies on the basis of modern measurements, cannot hope to succeed. Great help is provided by the Itineraries and records of routes and distances of the earliest Arab geographers and recorders of postal stages (*barīd*), especially for the provinces of Sijistān and Khorāsān, though they must be used with caution, on account of possible changes in natural conditions.

4. Although archaeological research has opened up new fields of study in Afghanistan and Pakistan, only three excavated sites play a significant role in this discussion—Aï Khanūm on the Oxus, Kandahar in the south of Afghanistan, and Begrām in the Kābul Kuhistān basin, at the southern foot of the Hindu Kush. The great progress resulting from the discovery of the first two sites—Aï Khanūm fairly thoroughly, Kandahar only very slightly, investigated—lies in the ascertained fact that both enjoyed a period of Greek occupation contemporary with the early Hellenistic Age in Greece, and both had previously been important Achaemenian centres. The third site, Begrām, though probably to be equated with Kapisanaki (Kapisa), an old Achaemenid settlement, which persisted till a late date, has not yielded significant evidence of the Hellenistic period or earlier. In general it has to be borne in mind that the effect of the Mongol invasions of the thirteenth century in Afghanistan was decisive: cities which had flourished in Sassanian and early Islamic times were utterly destroyed, and usually levelled to the ground—a fairly simple operation when the walls were for the most part of mud-brick. What now appears above ground in the form of citadels, forts, and mounds, when not crowned by a Buddhist stupa, represents mostly reconstructions of post-Mongol date. At Kandahar the pre-Islamic level at Shahr-i-Kuhna, the Old City, where ascertained, lies many metres below the present ground-level, and its discovery was made possible by the fact that the modern city of Kandahar is on a wholly different site. At Herāt, to take another major site, where the identification, though not the precise location, is certain, the Islamic city of today, or yesterday, stood where it had stood from early Islamic times, and if the pre-Islamic city, Alexander's foundation, was in the same immediate area, it must lie far below the present city. It follows that little is to be gained by associating any of the promising-looking mounds of Afghanistan or further north with this or that Hellenistic city

simply on the basis of approximate location. The mounds have to be excavated to determine their age, and indeed their authenticity as mounds with occupation levels; some may be artificial and erected for defensive purposes on some sort of scaffolding, others are simple earthworks. Identifications, then, must be established beyond all doubt, or otherwise treated with the greatest reserve. We shall see that, on closer scrutiny, the actual location even of a generally accepted identified site such as Alexandria in Aria–Herāt, may pose insoluble problems. Consequently the assignment of precise reasons of short-term strategy or long-term policy for the location of a foundation is hazardous unless, as with Alexandria on the Jaxartes, the purpose of the foundation is specified by our sources. We may contrast the case of Hellenistic foundations of which the precise site is known, and the significance of the choice of site can be determined by study of the map or by autopsy, as well as by an understanding of the general political and strategic advantages of a specific situation.

To these historical factors which create uncertainty, we must add the variations in climate and cultivation which complicate the argument at many points. There is, first of all, a man-made problem, that caused by the ruthless violence of the Mongols and the continued depredations of the nomad on the sown land. The problem of nomadism is certainly much older than the age of Alexander, who tried to cope with it, and it continued through-out antiquity and ever since. The eating out of cultivated land, particularly in Turkestan in the north and Sijistān in the south, has led to the increase of desert areas at the expense of oases and cultivatable land, which has to some extent been compensated in medieval and modern times by the extension of cultivation through the development of canal systems and other irrigational measures. Yet again, both to the south of the Hindu Kush and in the Indus Valley there has been considerable variation in drainage areas, so that, for instance, the lower reaches of the Helmund river run at some points by a different course from that which they followed in antiquity, while the whole map of the Lower Indus, its tributaries and its delta, was very different two thousand years ago.[2] Only the mountains and their passes have remained more or less (the latter by no means wholly) the same, and these, in the absence of surveying techniques, the ancients were unable to describe or

[2] See below, pp. 163-4.

orientate in a plausible form. In general we must think of movement and communication in terms not of roads, which as strictly
definable features are, for the most part, a late development, but of
tracks along river valleys, however narrow, and over passes, however precipitous. The mainly level route from Herāt to Kandahar,
which cuts across, and does not follow, the river valleys, is a major
exception to this pattern of communications.

In spite of these difficulties, however, it remains possible to
identify with a greater or less degree of probability, mainly by
the combination of the information provided by the geographers
and historians, the approximate location of some of Alexander's
authentic foundations. I propose to consider them in sequence from
the south-west to the north-east, that is, across the later route to
Khorāsān, and then from the northernmost point (Alexandria
Eschate) south-east to the Indus Valley and beyond, and then westward back to the head of the Persian Gulf. As already indicated, I
give only a few references to modern discussions, which, however
ingenious, cannot solve the problems inherent in the conflicting or
insufficient ancient literary evidence.

Our survey begins at the east end of the southern Caspian Gates,
the point of departure of the measurements of the bematists and
geographers,[3] but unfortunately not specifically mentioned by the
Alexander-historians. The first significant location to be noted is
Hekatompylos. The distance from the Gates to Hekatompylos given
by our sources varies considerably, and even if the stade used in
each case was certain, discrepancies would remain. As already
stated, Pliny gives the distance as 133 Roman miles (= approximately 1,064 stades), whereas Eratosthenes gives 1,960 stades

---

[3] See above, pp. 84-5, where the figures of the stages are tabulated. The reserva-
tions expressed about the figures must be borne in mind throughout. The southern
Caspian Gates are located beyond reasonable doubt at the Sar-Darrah valley which
slices through an eastern spur of the Elburz Mountains, and which is some six miles
long, its length being a physical factor which creates a basic margin of doubt in all
calculations based on distances from it; 6 miles = 50 stades, according to which end
of the pass was used as base-line, would account, for example, almost exactly for
the estimated discrepancy between Apollodorus of Artemita and Pliny (see below,
n. 7 and 11). Modern calculations are largely based on a base-line at the eastern
end, and this seems likely to be correct: see the discussions by Stahl, *Geogr. Journal*,
64 (1924), 318-20, and Hansman, *JRAS* (1968), 116-19 (with map on p. 117).
The fullest analysis of the geographical evidence relating to Alexander's movements
for the region between the Caspian and Herāt is that of Marquart, op. cit. below
(n. 11), pp. 60 ff., but his identifications are very uncertain, and involve numerous
emendations to Strabo and other writers, both Greek and Arabic.

or c.245 miles,[4] a variation that, it has been suggested, results from his having taken the northern Gates, a pass across the true Caucasus, west of the Caspian, as his starting-point. Apollodorus of Artemita, whom Strabo expressly quotes in an adjacent passage to that in which he quotes Eratosthenes,[5] gives the figure of 1,260 stades or c.157 miles, some 24 miles more than Pliny. The discrepancy can, however, be further reduced, since it can be established on independent grounds that Apollodorus used a short stade (i.e. of forty to the schoenus, like Eratosthenes) of 102 metres, and this figure, multiplied by 1,260, the distance in stades (at thirty to the Roman mile) from Hekatompylos to the Caspian Gates according to Apollodorus, gives a distance of just over 128 miles as compared with Pliny's figure of 133 Roman miles.[6] The agreement between Pliny and Apollodorus is thus sufficiently close to enable us, from a base-line at the Caspian Gates, to place Hekatompylos approximately 20 miles south-west of Damghān.[7]

This region has been investigated repeatedly, but it is only in recent years that a positive identification with preserved remains has been achieved at a point 20 miles (32 km.) south-west of Damghān called Shahr-i-Qūmis. Here, close to the line of the modern (and ancient) road into Khorāsān, in the area of the Persian Kumisene, a survey followed by an exploratory excavation (unfortunately incomplete) revealed a large complex of

---

[4] See above, p. 84, and below, n. 9. Strab. 514 (IIIB 20): λέγει δὲ καὶ οὕτω τὰ διαστήματα· ἀπὸ Κασπίων πυλῶν εἰς Ἰνδούς, εἰς μὲν Ἑκατόμπυλον χιλίους ἐννεακοσίους ἑξήκοντά φασιν, κ.τ.λ. (cf. below, n. 6).

[5] Strab. ibid. (ch. ix, init.): εἰσὶ δ' ἀπὸ Κασπίων πυλῶν εἰς μὲν Ῥάγας στάδιοι πεντακόσιοι, ὥς φησιν Ἀπολλόδωρος, εἰς δ' Ἑκατόμπυλον, τὸ τῶν Παρθυαίων βασίλειον, χίλιοι διακόσιοι ἑξήκοντα.

[6] Kiessling, *RE*, s.v. Hekatompylos, cols. 2794 ff., points out that Apollodorus' estimate of the *known* distance between Rhagai and the east end of the Sar-Darrah defile, 51 miles, is 500 stades (Strab. loc. cit.), which results in a stade of 102 m. However, he develops his argument in a direction that seems unacceptable, arguing that Eratosthenes and Apollodorus cannot have been at variance over such a fundamental measurement. He consequently proposes to emend Strabo (loc. cit. n. 5) to χίλιοι ἐννεακόσιοι, thus placing Seleucid–Parthian Hekatompylos at Shahr-Rūd, some two-thirds of the entire route further from Sar-Darrah, and assumes that the bematists' figure, 1,064 st., which gives a position near Damghān, refers to an earlier Achaemenid–Median site (in fact, Kiessling prefers Simnān), which was moved to Shahr-Rūd. This is an unnecessary complication, and is contradicted by the archaeological evidence: see n. 9.

[7] See the summary of investigations given by Hansman, loc. cit. pp. 116 ff. The failure of Damghān to yield pre-Islamic remains at levels below the present town-level leaves no room for doubt that the identification should be abandoned.

mounds dating from the Parthian period, with surface sherds of
Achaemenian date. The core of this complex the excavators propose to identify with Hekatompylos.[8] Even if this is not absolutely
certain, there can be no doubt that the site, the first large Parthian
settlement to be excavated in the area, and at the right distance,
according to the bematists' reckoning (Pliny), from the Caspian
Gates to Alexandria in Ariana, the first foundation after the Gates,
has much to commend it.[9] The difference between Damghān and
Shahr-i-Qūmis as candidates for Hekatompylos is less, it must be
emphasized, a matter of distance—for the distance between them
is only 20 miles, which can hardly be accounted significant on a
long stretch—than of archaeological evidence: Shahr-i-Qūmis,
whether Hekatompylos or not, is certainly a Parthian site with
evidence of Achaemenid antecedents, and no such site has been
scientifically recorded elsewhere in the region. Moreover, Polybius'
reference to Hekatompylos in connection with the expedition of
Antiochus III makes the old identification of Hekatompylos =

[8] See Hansman, loc. cit., and Hansman and Stronach, ibid. (1970), 28 ff. (cf. also
the summary by S. A. Matheson, *Persia: An Archaeological Guide*[2] (1976), 193 ff).
For the Parthian seals from the site see most recently A. D. H. Bivar, *Iran*, 20
(1982), 161 ff.

[9] The excavators rightly say, op. cit. (1970), p. 61, that on the basis of the
combination of distances and site-evidence, together with the absence of any
known alternative site providing the requisite evidence in the area, 'it would
seem not unreasonable to reaffirm . . . that the site of Shah-i-Qūmis Area B is, in
fact, Parthian Hecatompylos.' Brunt, *Arrian* (Loeb edn.), i (1976), 496, objects to
the identification on the ground that the calculation of distances is unsatisfactory,
and, like Kiessling, he prefers an identification closer to the 1,960 stades given by
Eratosthenes, regarding Apollodorus' 1,260 as a copyist's error; but to do this he
has to reject the figure of 500 stades given as the distance from Rhagai to the
Caspian Gates. Both figures could be accepted on the supposition that the longer
distance is from the northern 'Caspian Gates', as Engels (op. cit. below, n. 10)
pp. 81 n. 52; 83 n. 61; 157-8, suggested; but although Pliny vi. 30 says that
the two gates were frequently confused (*Ab iis sunt Portae Caucasiae magno errore
multis Caspiae dictae*, cf. Treidler, *RE*, s.v. Portae Caspiae, and Mittelhaus, ibid.
s.v. Kaukasiai Pylai) it is difficult to suppose that Eratosthenes made this error at a
time when the Caucasian Gates were much less known than they were in the
period of the early Empire (cf. Plin. vi. 40, on the confusion of name at the time
of Corbulo's expedition to Armenia: *sunt autem aliae Caspiis gentibus iunctae, quod
dinosci non potest nisi comitatu rerum Alexandri Magni*. In the surviving version of
Alexander's speech at Opis, Arr. vii. 10. 6, the same confusion may occur,
whatever its source; ὑπερβάντα δὲ τὸν Καύκασον ὑπὲρ τὰς Κασπίας πύλας, though
here the reference could be to the Paropamisadai; cf. Arr. iv. 22. 4, quoted below
n. 78 ὑπερβαλὼν δὲ τὸν Καύκασον). In any case the objections raised by Brunt on
account of the extremely vague and easily corrupted figures for distances do not out-
weigh the positive arguments provided by the evidence of the site of Shahr-i-Qūmis
itself.

Damghān untenable.[10] For our purpose the identification is of less significance than it might seem to be, for though it establishes the fixed location from which distances to Alexander's foundations in the Iranian provinces were originally calculated, the figures themselves after Herāt are so uncertain that the value of Hekatompylos as a cardinal point is much reduced. To these foundations I now turn.

I. ALEXANDRIA IN ARIA(NA)

A characteristic lacuna in our evidence is revealed in regard to this city. Its existence is attested by the bematists and by Eratosthenes, but, like other cities of less importance, it is not mentioned by the Alexander-historians. These agree in saying only that Alexander's route from Zadracarta in Hyrcania lay through Ariana,[11] and that having advanced from Ariana 'towards Bactra' he returned thither to subdue the rebellious Satibarzanes. Alexandria in Ariana is mentioned in the primary geographical sources (Eratosthenes,[12]

[10] See Polyb. x. 28. 7, with Walbank's very clear note and sketch-map, ad loc. An identification of Hekatompylos with Shahr-Rūd would have involved Antiochus in retracing his steps over a considerable distance. D. W. Engels, *Alexander the Great and the Logistics of the Macedonian Army* (California, 1978) 83, accepts this identification. For his analysis of the distances from the Caspian Gates see his Table 8, p. 157; his figures agree essentially with mine.

[11] Arr. iii. 25. 1; Diod. xvii. 78 (contracted account); Curt. Ruf. vi. 6. 33. The first location named in Ariana is Sousia: ἐπὶ τὰ τῆς Ἀρείας ὅρια καὶ Σουσίαν, πόλιν τῆς Ἀρείας. This may well be represented by the Arabic and later Ṭūs (for which see Le Strange, 388-9), which is in the right location, though the vowel-change is against it (cf. Marquart, *Untersuch. z. Gesch. Eran*, ii. 65, who has doubts about the 'Umformung').

[12] Strab. 514 = IIIB 63: τὰ δὲ διαστήματα οὕτω λέγει· ἀπὸ μὲν τοῦ Κασπίου ἐπὶ τὸν Κῦρον ὡς χιλίους ὀκτακοσίους σταδίους, ἔνθεν δ' ἐπὶ Κασπίας πύλας πεντακισχιλίους ἑξακοσίους, εἶτ' εἰς Ἀλεξάνδρειαν τὴν ἐν Ἀρίοις ἑξακισχιλίους τετρακοσίους, εἶτ' εἰς Βάκτραν τὴν πόλιν, ἣ καὶ Ζαρίασπα καλεῖται, τρισχιλίους ὀκτακοσίους ἑβδομήκοντα, εἶτ' ἐπὶ τὸν Ἰαξάρτην ποταμόν, ἐφ' ὃν Ἀλέξανδρος ἧκεν, ὡς πεντακισχιλίους· ὁμοῦ δισχίλιοι δισμύριοι ἑξακόσιοι ἑβδομήκοντα; cf. ibid. IIIB 20 (second excerpt): εἰς δ' Ἀλεξάνδρειαν τὴν ἐν Ἀρίοις τετρακισχιλίους πεντακοσίους τριάκοντα, εἶτ' εἰς Προφθασίαν τὴν ἐν Δραγγῆι χιλίους ἑξακοσίους, οἱ δὲ πεντακοσίους, κ.τ.λ. Berger, *Eratosth.* 248 n. 2, pointed out that the earlier modern geographers (Ritter etc.) had placed Alexandria in Ariana *north* of Eratosthenes' Taurus-line, and that is in fact a possible interpretation of the passage given by Strab. 68 = Berger, IIIA 2, where he associates Aria with the region of Hyrcania and says, of the route to Bactria, ἔπειτα ἡ ἐπὶ τὴν Ὑρκανίαν θάλατταν ὑπέρθεσις καὶ ἡ ἐφεξῆς ἡ ἐπὶ Βάκτρα καὶ τοὺς ἐπέκεινα Σκύθας ὁδὸς δεξιὰ ἔχοντι τὰ ὄρη, but in the fragments IIIB 20-3, dealing with the regions beyond Hekatompylos, he clearly associates Ariana throughout with the provinces south and east of the Elburz range, on the north with Bactria, on the south and east with Drangiana and Arachosia.

who was no doubt using the bematists quoted by Pliny,[13] and Pliny himself) and it is also in Stephanus' list.[14] Of its existence in the third century BC there can, then, be no doubt, but the failure of the historians, who describe Alexander's activities in and around the oasis in some detail, to mention that he built a city there, is undoubtedly surprising. Consequently, although, unlike Merv, discussed below, our ancient sources do not suggest that the foundation was of a later date than Alexander, the possibility exists. It was evidently built somewhere near the site of Artacoana, the capital or main citadel of the Achaemenid satrapy of Aria, which Alexander now conquered, though how near it is not possible to determine. The proximity and yet separateness of the two, is indicated by Pliny, who (not quoting the bematists) says *oppidum Artocoana, Arius amnis qui praefluit Alexandriam ab Alexandro conditam*, while he describes Artacabene as *multo pulchrius sicut antiquius* (than Artacoana) *Artacabene, iterum ab Antiocho munitum*. He adds that Artacoana had a circumference of 30 stades and Artacabene, the site and identity of which are unknown, of 50. Beyond this, however, we are left with some unanswerable questions concerning the location both of the new city and also of Artacoana, which survived to be mentioned by Strabo and others.[15]

---

[13] *NH* vi. 61 (cf. above, p. 79 n. 6): *Diognetus et Baeton itinerum eius mensores scripsere a portis Caspiis Hecatompylon Parthorum quot diximus milia esse, inde Alexandriam Arion, quam urbem is rex condidit, DLXXV mil.*, etc.

[14] ἑβδόμη ἐν Ἀρίοις ἔθνει Παρθυαίων κατὰ τὴν Ἰνδικήν.

[15] See below, n. 21. Engels, op. cit. 87 ff., who maintains that Alexander, on his first entry into Ariana, proceeded north from the modern Mashshad, not south-east, follows the narrative of Curtius (vi. 22 ff.) closely, and regards the isolated rock-girt plateau to which the Arians retreated as distinct from Artacoana, and identifies it with the remarkable natural redoubt of Kalāt-i-Nadir, which lies in an almost inaccessible area of the Persian–Russian frontier, on the edge of the Karakum desert. Although Curtius' account of the *praerupta rupes* is very graphic, I must confess that I find it very hard to believe that Alexander did not first enter the valley of the Hari-Rūd, and also that the plateau, described by Engels from Curzon, *Persia*, i. 133, as 'the most famous stronghold in the Near East, the "Gibraltar" of Persia', is that described by Curtius. Leaving on one side for the present the historical question whether Alexander originally intended to enter Bactria by a route north of Maimana to Merv Shāhijān, and evaluating the identification of the Kalāt with the *praerupta rupes* (Artacoana or not) on its physical merits, there is a very real difficulty about the dimensions of the remote retreat. Curtius vi. 6. 23 says *circuitus eius xxx et duo stadia comprehendit*, that is, something over four miles, and Engels p. 88 n. 81. provides a comparable figure for the perimeter of the interior plain based on the only measurements available to him, those of 'a Greek named Basil Batatzes' in 1728 (i.e. the remarkable metrical account of his mercantile journeys in Asia written by Vatatzes, and published by Legrand, *Publications de L'École des Langues Orientales Vivantes*, 2ᵉ sér. xix, Nouveaux Mélanges Orientaux (Paris, 1886),

Qodāma and Yākūt both identify Herāt as built by Alexander, saying that Alexander built Herāt when returning from his voyage to China, but the former does not say that it was called Iskandarīya, and Yākūt does not include the identification in his

185-295). C. E. Yate visited the site in 1885, and described it in *Khurasan and Sistan* (Edinburgh, 1900) 155 ff. (see below, n. 19), and gives it as 'some sixty miles in [external] circumference'. (He adds that his brother described the interior of the redoubt in detail in *The Daily Telegraph* of an unspecified date in August 1885, which I have not seen.) Curzon, who was prevented from entering the inner area, though he reached the southern entrance, describes it in his detailed narrative, loc. cit. 126-40 (with a clear panoramic sketch on p. 134), as 'some twenty miles in total length by five to seven in breadth', and he estimates the length of the steep southern face, by which he attempted to enter, as 'nearly twenty miles in a straight line', while his estimate of the total area is 'comprising a probable area of 150 square miles'. These figures are confirmed by C. M. McGregor, who entered the redoubt and traversed the whole plateau in 1875: see his *Narrative of a Journey through the Province of Khorassan in 1875* (London, 1879), ii. 52 ff. (p. 53: 'It is a district, or a basin fortified in the most wonderful manner by nature. In shape it is something like a foot, and it must have a length of twenty miles by a breadth of two to four miles'); and it is clear that, as McGregor says, the Kalāt is an entire district and not a single feature such as is indicated by Curtius, though in other ways (the abundant supply of water and timber) the plateau described by Curtius certainly resembles the Kalāt (for other visits to the Kalāt see the Index to A. Gabriel's useful summary of travellers' journeys, *Die Erforschung Persiens* (Vienna, 1952)). It is difficult to believe that Arrian's authorities, who described in detail Alexander's great achievement in scaling the Rocks of Chorienes and Aornos, would have passed over in silence the operation that would be required to capture the Kalāt. It is also hardly credible that the long and extremely arduous journey, for the most part of several days, required to reach the entrance to the Kalāt from any direction, except perhaps the east, which does not come into question, would have been undertaken simply to avoid a confrontation with Alexander's forces. Engels's view that Alexander's original route to Bactria lay through the Turkmen desert to Merv Shāhijān and thence to the Oxus, stands or falls on this identification. Following Curtius, he distinguishes this site from Artacoana, and places the latter at an unknown location in the Turkmen desert (p. 91): 'If Artacoana is located in the Soviet Union, it will only be a matter of time before the extensive excavations and survey work undertaken in Turkmenistan will uncover it. Khorasan in Iran, as was noted, has not yet received adequate attention from archaeologists, and if the city is located here, we will have to wait a good deal longer for its discovery.' It is worth calling attention here to the extraordinary similarity between the mountain retreat described by Curtius and the very similar locality, named Sirunka, utilized in like circumstances by the native inhabitants of Tambraka, in the neighbourhood of Astarabad (and therefore close to Kalāt-i-Nadir) on the occasion of Antiochus the Great's Hyrcanian expedition in 207 BC. See Polyb. x. 31. 6: συστησάμενος δὲ τὴν πορείαν ὡς ἐβούλετο καὶ παραγενόμενος ἐπὶ Τάμβρακα, πόλιν ἀτείχιστον, ἔχουσαν δὲ βασίλεια καὶ μέγεθος, αὐτοῦ κατεσκήνωσε. τῶν δὲ πλείστων πεποιημένων τὴν ἀποχώρησιν ἔκ τε τῆς μάχης καὶ τῆς περικειμένης χώρας εἰς τὴν προσαγορευομένην Σίρυγκα πόλιν— συνέβαινε κεῖσθαι (ἐκείνην), add. Büttner-Wobst) οὐ μακρὰν τῆς Τάμβρακος, εἶναι δὲ τῆς Ὑρκανίας ὡς ἂν εἰ βασιλήιον διά τε τὴν ὀχυρότητα καὶ τὴν ἄλλην εὐκαιρίαν—ἔκρινε ταύτην ἐξελεῖν μετὰ βίας. The issue was different, for the Hyrcanians slaughtered the Greeks in the city: in cont. . . . καὶ τοὺς μὲν Ἕλληνας κατασφάξαντες τοὺς ἐν τῆι πόλει,

list of cities of that name.[16] Ṭabārī also attributes the city to Alexander without giving it its pre-Islamic name.[17]

The location of Alexandria Ariana within the general area of Herāt has been accepted largely without debate.[18] The historic Islamic city lies at the centre of a large and very fertile oasis, and is described by the Arab geographers as offering (like so many other Islamic cities) the delights of civilized life, and a rich and luxurious vegetation. With the *Arius amnis*, the Hari-Rūd, running through the oasis in many channels and with many canals, it still forms the natural starting-point of all routes east to Arachosia and north-east to Balkh, skirting or penetrating the Hindu Kush. It is the natural site of a strategic urban settlement, and played a major role in political considerations of the area in the eighteenth and nineteenth centuries.[19]

τὰ δὲ ἐπιφανέστατα τῶν σκευῶν διαρπάσαντες νυκτὸς ἀπεχώρησαν. For the location see Walbank ad loc. who, however, does not call attention to the remarkable similarity between the two occasions, and the two locations; the latter suggests that unusual specific features such as mountain redoubts in these wild regions are not to be regarded as unique, as other events in Alexander's campaign showed.

[16] Qodāma, p. 265 (FT 207) (*BGA* vi) (see above, p. 56 n. 27); Yākūt, s.v. (cf. ibid. n. 26). In Qodāma the next city in geographical sequence founded by Alexander is Zaranj, for which see below, p. 126.

[17] See Ṭabārī, I. 2 702. Cf. also *Provincial Capitals*, § 12.

[18] See e.g. Droysen, *GE* iii. 215–16 = FT ii. 673–4; Tomaschek, *RE* (2); Tarn, *Alex.* ii. 234, 241; Tscherikower, 102.

[19] For descriptions of Herāt and its surroundings see, among many other accounts, those of G. B. Malleson, *Herat, The Granary and Garden of Central Asia* (London, 1880), 9 ff.; C. E. Yate, *Northern Afghanistan* (Edinburgh, 1888), ch. III, 'Herat and its Antiquities'; also his brother, A. C. Yate's (also a member of the Afghan Boundary Commission), *Travels with the Afghan Boundary Commission* (Edinburgh, 1887); he did not enter Herāt, but describes the valley of the Hari Rūd (pp. 133 ff.). The members of the Boundary Commission had unique opportunities of traversing the region between Herāt and the Russian frontier, and their accounts are invaluable (and sometimes surprising, as when C. E. Yate (p. 103) says that they observed tiger footprints in the Maruchak area, north of Herāt, in the valley of the Murghāb). The earlier travellers sometimes give fuller accounts; among the best is that of A. Conolly, *Journey to the North of India* (London, 1st edn. 1834; 2nd edn. 1838), part of which (ii. 1 ff.) is quoted by Malleson, op. cit. 37 ff. Substantial extracts from Malleson and C. E. Yate are reprinted in Nancy Dupree's *Afghanistan* (History and Geography of Central Asia, i (Buckhurst Hill, Essex, 1972), 74–132 and 133–53). Some other early travellers are quoted in the following notes. Among modern writings the most closely observed is the oecistic study by Abdul Wasay Najimi, *Herat, the Islamic City: A Study in Urban Conservation* (London, 1988), which is invaluable for a detailed study of the oasis and its present irrigation. Ibn Ḥawqal's description (2nd half of the 10th cent. AD) (*BGA* ii². 437 ff.; pp. 422 ff. trans. Kramers-Wiet) is quoted by numerous writers, notably by Le Strange, *LEC* 407 ff. (based on the first edition, published by De Goeje (1873); the longer text published by Kramers as the second edition (1938) is unaltered at this point). Ferrier, *Caravan*

Nevertheless the exact location of Alexander's city and its relation to Artacoana alike remain unknown, and unless excavations
in depth are ever undertaken at Herāt the first problem will remain
unsolved. The old city of Herāt lies some two miles north of the
Hari-Rūd, and approximately four miles from the mountain range
to the north, the rugged foothills of which overshadow the city. At
the north end, above the old city stands, or stood, the citadel, the
Kuhandiz, which was probably originally constructed in the early
Islamic period, when it was described by Ibn Ḥawqal, who states
that it had its own circuit of walls, quite separate from those of the
city itself, with four gates bearing the same names as the four gates
of the city. The citadel was destroyed during, and rebuilt after,
various conquests of the city over the succeeding centuries, and
today (or yesterday) what is left of it is Timurid.[20] It is natural to
suppose that Islamic Herāt stood on the site chosen by Alexander
for his new city, but there is no evidence that the citadel was in
existence before the Islamic period; its secrets, if it has any, lie deep
beneath what remains of its earthworks. We can only say that in
general terms the site of Herāt seems the most likely position for
the city, facing the river and protected by the mountains to the
north.

The previously existing city or fort, presumably the Persian
administrative centre for the province of Aria, called in our sources
Artacoana, or some variant of that name, comes into prominence
in the same context, with reference to the revolt of Satibarzanes,
and Alexander's precipitate return from the first stage of his
march to Bactria. It remains uncertain whether the high plateau
to which the local population fled on the news of his return, when
Satibarzanes left no less precipitately with his two thousand horse

Journeys and Wanderings in Persia, Afghanistan, etc. (London, 1856), 139, describes
the medicinal attraction of the river: 'The clear and limpid waters of the Heri are
pleasant, though aperient.' Experience has taught me that the same is true of the
waters of the Nile south of the dams. The same observer pointed out that the water-
level of Herāt was very high.

[20] See the references in n. 19. Photograph no. 10 in R. and S. Michaud's
Afghanistan (Eng. trans. London, 1980) taken from the north shows the Hari-Rūd
flowing in the distance south of the city. The archaeological evidence is provided
by Ball 428: 'a few chance finds of Sassanid seals and gems'. He does not refer to
Torrens, *JASB* 11 (1843), 316-21, who reports on an Elamite cylinder, found by
Pottinger, now vanished, and some chance finds of gems, some of which are from
further afield, e.g. Sistān. The Elamite text, if indeed of local origin, would have the
same importance as the text found in the excavations of Kandahar (see below,
n. 61) as indicating continuity in the area of Herāt.

for Bactra, is to be distinguished from Artacoana or not. This
plateau is described by Curtius Rufus as a high rock facing west,
with a circumference of thirty-two stades, that is approximately
four miles; and as 'planted with many trees and with a perennial
supply of water'. At a later point he refers to it specifically as a
'city' (*urbs*), though this hardly seems compatible with the description he has given of it earlier: it is strange to refer to a city simply
as *proximi montes* and *praerupta rupes*. But that may be only a
flourish, for Arrian's version of the event, adding the information
that Artacoana was the πόλις ἵνα τὸ βασίλειον ἦν τῶν Ἀρείων, at
least confirms that it was something more than a fort. At all
events, the two localities remained separate. Strabo, Isidore, and
Ptolemy all treat Artacoana as a separate native town, and it seems
likely that it continued in existence for some centuries after the
foundation of Alexandria.[21] The limited excavations that were
carried out at Kandahar suggests that there too the native settlement survived alongside the old, though there the Achaemenid

---

[21] The separate existence of the two cities was maintained by Droysen, *GA* ii. 8
n. 1 = FT i. p. 407 n. 1, and also accepted by Tarn, *Alex.* ii. 234 n. 5. Droysen
accepted the location of Artacoana given by Ptolemy, as NW of Herāt (see Table III
to Ronca's edn. of vi. 9–21, where the locations are clearly distinguished): vi. 17.
6: Ἀρτακαυάνα (X; Ἀρτικαύδνα: A, Nobbe, Wilberg) . . . ρθ γ´ λε̄ ϛ Ἀλεξάνδρεια ἐν
Ἀρείοις . . . ρῑ λϛ̄; Isid. § 15: ἐντεῦθεν Ἄρεια, σχοῖνοι λ. ἔνθα Κανδὰκ πόλις καὶ
Ἀτρακαύαν πόλις καὶ Ἀλεξάνδρεια ἡ ἐν Ἀρείοις· κῶμαι δὲ δ̄. Strab. 516 (not
Eratosthenes): πόλεις (of Aria) δὲ Ἀρτακάηνα καὶ Ἀλεξάνδρεια καὶ Ἀχαία, ἐπώνυμοι
τῶν κτισάντων· εὐοινεῖ δὲ σφόδρα ἡ γῆ· καὶ γὰρ εἰς τριγονίαν παραμένει ἐν ἀπιττώτοις
ἄγγεσι; 723 (= IIIB 20, first extract) does not refer to Artacoana, nor does 514 (IIIB
20, quoted above, n. 12, one of the distance-passages). It is to be noted that the co-
ordinates of Ptolemy place Artacoana and Alexandria south of the Hari-Rūd, which
is impossible if the identification with Herāt is maintained, and unlikely on more
general grounds of topography. Each of the Greek sources has a different spelling
for the native city. In his map *in calc.* of his edn. of Arrian, vol. i, Brunt prefers
Diodorus' form of the name (xvii. 78. 4): ὁ δὲ Σατιβαρζάνης τὴν μὲν δύναμιν ἤθροισεν
εἰς Χορτάκανα, πόλιν ἐπιφανεστάτην τῶν ἐν τούτοις τοῖς τόποις καὶ φυσικῆι διαφέρουσαν
ὀχυρότητι, κ.τ.λ. but Ἀρτακόανα seems the better-attested form. It was suggested by
Ferrier, op. cit. 165, that Artacoana was at Kussan, some 50 m. downstream from
Herāt, on the road to Mashshad. He put forward the notion that it might have been
the summer palace of the Achaemenian ruler of Herāt. The idea is appealing
because it emphasizes that we should not expect necessarily to find it in the immediate vicinity of Herāt, while its position on a hilltop indicates that it is not to be
sought south of the present city. Berthelot, *L'Asie ancienne*, 178, puts Artacoana at
Ghurian (= Fūshanj/Būshanj) some 50 km. west of Herāt, (see Le Strange, 411) and
about 50 m. south of Kussan (Kūhsan, Kūsūya), lying in a fertile plain, close to the
right bank of the Hari-Rūd, on the road to Khaff. It was a prosperous city in the
early Islamic period (see Le Strange, 411), but there seems no likelihood that
Artacoana was located there. For Engels's view that the *praerupta rupes* should be
identified with Kalāt-i-Nadir see n. 15.

citadel and the Macedonian settlement were close beside each other (see below, pp. 135-6), which may not have been the case with Artacoana and Alexandria in Aria.

The uncertainty surrounding this important city forms an excellent example of the impossibility of providing a wholly coherent account of the origin and history of Alexander's foundations. The historians give accounts of Alexander's activities at Artacoana, but do not mention the foundation of a new city. The only account of the new Alexandria, extremely brief, is that of Pliny, quoted above,[22] and though he certainly reproduces information found by his sources in the bematists, Eratosthenes (Strabo) refers to it only as a distance-point. Apart from Pliny, only Isidore refers to it as a city.[23] It figures in Stephanus' list (as his seventh Alexandria), but does not occur in any version of the Alexandrian tradition of the *Romance*; and we have to wait for Ṭabārī and Qodāma to give us the earliest equations with Herāt. It survived, at all events, through the centuries and served as the capital of the Parthian province of Hryw and Sassanian Harev, before it became Herāt, and firmly associated in the Arab and Persian mind with Iskander. Strictly speaking, our verdict in favour of the city having been founded by Alexander should be based exclusively on the explicit language of Pliny, where he quotes the bematists: *inde Alexandriam Arion, quam urbem is rex condidit DLXXV*, etc. Beyond that, we are left in the dark. We cannot determine when Alexander decided to build a new city here—not necessarily on his arrival or during his brief stay at the oasis, but possibly at some earlier time, after due consideration of the advantages of the site, on information supplied—nor what practical measures he took in planning, building, and populating the new city. Such details—and then only the scantiest—come to us from the narrative of Arrian, and are available only for Alexandria in Egypt and for his city in Sogdiana, Alexandria on the Jaxartes. Neither Alexandria in Egypt, founded on the shores of the Mediterranean, nor the city of Aï Khanūm, which was probably built in more settled circumstances a generation later, can safely

---

[22] See n. 13.

[23] Isidore (§ 15) is here, as frequently, elliptical. He says, Ἐντεῦθεν Ἄρεια σχοῖνοι λ'. ἔνθα Κανδὰκ πόλις καὶ Ἀρτακαυάν πόλις καὶ Ἀλεξάνδρεια ἡ ἐν Ἀρείοις· κῶμαι δὲ δ'. The entry cannot carry the weight assigned in this instance to Pliny. Even if Tarn were right in thinking that Isidore's text is a rehash of a 2nd-cent. BC original (see p. 89 n. 25), it has no claim to preference on chronological grounds over Pliny's sources and Eratosthenes.

be invoked as models for whatever town-planning there may have been during the actual campaign, at Herāt and elsewhere.

From the wide valley of the Hari-Rūd Alexander proceeded, on his second departure, after the defeat of Satibarzanes, through Drangiana and then, by way of Arachosia, marched on to the foot of the Indian Caucasus, the Hindu Kush. Timetable and routes are alike uncertain, and while the figures given by the bematists and the Σταθμοί may (if correctly transmitted) be roughly correct in themselves, we are not in a position to link them positively with the modern map. Arrian and the other historians, let it be repeated, mention no new foundations until this hard journey was over, and the foot of the mountain range was reached. Before following Alexander on this long detour, however, we must consider the possibility of his having founded a city at Merv, a problem which is itself closely bound up with his movements while in Aria.

The ancient evidence for this foundation has already been touched on.[24] Our major sources fail us, and we are once again dependent on Pliny; but an adulterated Pliny who is drawing not on the bematists, but on unspecified sources. Apart from Pliny the city only survives as an Alexander-foundation in the Iranian tradition, represented by Ṭabarī and the *Provincial Capitals of Erānshahr* (see Table at end), originally developed in the Parthian and Sassanian periods. The archaeological evidence from the vast site of Merv Shāhijān (which overshadowed its smaller homonym further down the Murghāb, Merv al-Rūdh, with which it is closely associated in the early Itineraries) is negatively against the supposition, for although parts of it have been frequently, but (inevitably) selectively, excavated over the years, and yielded remarkable material, it is all of the Parthian period or later, as at Nysa, further to the west, and though it was an Achaemenid centre, it has shown

---

[24] See above, p. 31 with note 67. The sources there analysed, which associate Alexander with 'Merv' are Pliny and his 'descendants' Solinus and Martianus Capella. The variant in Solinus' text (as between a city named Antiocheia and one named Seleukeia) is noted ibid. On the site and location of the Seleucid-Parthian city (Giaour-Kāla) see Strab. 516: παραπλησία δ᾽ ἐστι καὶ ἡ Μαργιανή, ἐρημίαις δὲ περιέχεται τὸ πεδίον. θαυμάσας δὲ τὴν εὐφυΐαν ὁ Σωτὴρ Ἀντίοχος τείχει περιέβαλε κύκλον ἔχοντα χιλίων καὶ πεντακοσίων σταδίων· πόλιν δ᾽ ἔκτισε Ἀντιόχειαν. Isid. § 14 has ἐντεῦθεν Μαργιανή, σχοῖνοι λ᾽: ἔνθα Ἀντιόχεια ἡ καλουμένη ἔνυδρος· κῶμαι δὲ οὐκ εἰσίν. For Curtius' description of Margiana see n. 26. There is no epigraphical evidence for either an Antiocheia or a Seleukeia in Margiana. The Σελευκεὺς ἀπὸ Μ . . . of IG ix(i)² 17. 100, restored hesitatingly by Hiller as ἀπὸ Μ[άργου] is rightly rejected by L. Robert, *OMS* ii. 1189 n. 3 (= *RPh.* 1934, p. 290) in favour of Σ. ἀπὸ Μ[αιάνδρ]ο[υ].

no specific traces up to the present of the Seleucid settlement.[25] Even if due allowance is made for the very large scale of the successive and adjacent city-sites—Achaemenid, Partho-Sassanian, and Seljuk—and the likely depth of unstratified levels, it remains wholly possible that there was a hiatus in occupation between the Achaemenid and the Seleucid-Parthian periods. Alexander had no occasion to visit the Merv oasis either at this juncture or later (unless the revolt in Aria had already broken out, to instruct him in the danger of leaving Achaemenid posts unsecured), and the suggestion that he arranged for the city to be founded there when he was elsewhere, for instance in Sogdiana or further away, goes against all that we know of Alexander's method of foundation.[26] Thus the evidence for the foundation by Alexander remains weak,

[25] A full account of Merv oasis, which covers some 50 square miles, as it was 100 years ago, will be found in E. O'Donovan, *The Merv Oasis* (London, 1882), ii, *passim*, esp. chs. 37 ff. Since then modern irrigation, mechanization, and other works have greatly altered the pattern of the whole oasis. For excavations see Knobloch, *Beyond the Oxus* (London, 1972), 174 ff.; Frumkin, *Archaeology in Soviet Central Asia* (Leiden, 1970), 146 ff. See also Ghirshman, *Iran sous les Parthes et Sassanides* (Paris, 1965), 29 ff. with plan 46. A brief account with a fuller plan will be found in Sherwin-White and Kuhrt, *From Samarkhand to Sardis*, 82–4. The polygonal fortress, Ak (Erk)-Kāla, within Giaour Kāla, is thought to occupy the site of the Achaemenid citadel, greatly extended by the Seleucids and Parthians, but no Achaemenid material is reported from the site. O'Donovan, 265, says that 'among the Vekil Turkomans [of the area immediately adjoining Old Merv] earthen lamps of the old Greek form are frequently met with in daily use'. The terracottas, seals, gems, etc. seem to be mostly of Buddhist and Manichaean date, but Pehlevi and other ostraca were also found (see *Iran*, loc. cit. below).

The city retained its importance as long as the Murghāb river and the Novur canal provided enough water, and the Seljuk Sultan Sanjar built the great dam at Bent-i-Kazaklī on the river. After the Mongol invasion the city then inhabited, Sultan Sanjar, was abandoned, and a new city was built to the south at Abdullah Khan Kāla, which regained its previous size and splendour; cf. Le Strange, 403. The final desolation of the site occurred when the Emir of Bokhārā destroyed the southern dam in 1795 (cf. Knobloch, op. cit. 176). Current excavations undertaken by a joint Turkmen-Russian-British expedition, are investigating the Sassanian and early Arab levels of Giaour Kāla, and as yet throw no light on the early history of the settlements (I am grateful to Dr St John Simpson for giving me this information: see now the report in *Iran*, 33 (1993), 39–62, with Plates xi–xviii). (The identification of Merv al-Rūdh with the actual site of Bālā Murghāb is not established: see Ball 198, who records no finds there.)

[26] This was the view of Droysen, *GE* iii. 215 = FT ii. 673, followed by Tarn, *Alex*, ii. 234–5, who says, 'even if he were really never there in person, could he not give orders?' Tscherikower, 105 (cf. p. 144), does not accept it. Curt. Ruf. vii. 15, records an expedition by Alexander to Margiana, in the course of which six cities were founded, two facing south, four facing east: *Superatis deinde amnibus Ocho et Oxo ad urbem Margianam pervenit. Circa eam VI oppidis condendis electa sedes est, duo ad meridiem versa, IIII spectantia orientem.* Engels, 105, accepts the evidence of Pliny and

and it is wiser to regard it as a Seleucid foundation. The broader
question of whether satisfactory evidence exists that the early
Seleucids built, or rebuilt, or renamed, where Alexander had preceded them, can hardly rest on this case (see above, pp. 35-6). We
may compare the case of Alexandria in Sakastane, at or near the
Arab capital of Sijistān, Zaranj, discussed below (pp. 127 ff.): there
the only evidence for its existence is to be found in Isidore (who
calls it Alexandria in Sakastane) and Qodāma, and while Arrian
states clearly that Alexander visited (i.e. took over) the Achaemenid
βασίλειον, there is no suggestion that he founded a city there.

One major problem needs consideration within the same geographical context. When Alexander left the region of Artacoana for
the first time, en route for Bactria, by which route did he proceed?
To that question our historical sources give no answer. Arrian only
says that he was recalled from his march towards Bactra by the
news of Satibarzanes' revolt, and that he accomplished the return
march of 600 stades (c. 75 miles) in two days.[27] We are not told
what route he and his forces had taken, but we may be fairly
certain, I believe, that he had not embarked on the long, but level,
detour through the southern desert which he took on his second
departure, and if that is accepted we may consider alternative
routes.

The first route is that of which the first part, as far as Bālā
Murghāb via the steep Subzak pass, has been already mentioned; it
continues through rough undulating country to Maimana, and so
to Balkh, a straightforward but long and arduous route. A second is
the hard haul up the Hari-Rūd, on a route which would eventually lead him to the area of Bāmiyān, then either down the Shībar

CR, and says, 'I fail to see how it is possible to maintain that Alexander was never
in Margiana, and did not found the city of Alexandria Margiana.' The virtual
impossibility of deciding whether such foundations, which the ancients themselves
claimed as first founded by Alexander, and then refounded by a Seleucid, is
illustrated by the independent evidence of Gerasa. Welles, *Inscr. of Gerasa*, 423, is a
dedication by the city of Gerasa of a statue of Perdiccas, presumably, therefore, its
founder, but the late Imperial bronzes of the city include an emission with a head
of Alexander and the legend Ἀλεξ(-) Μακ(-) κτί(στης) Γερασ(ηνῶν); he was perhaps
held at that time to have instructed Perdiccas to establish the city; cf. *EM*, s.v.
Γερασηνός and Seyrig, *Syria*, 42 (1965), 25 ff.

[27] iii. 25. 6: ταῦτα ὡς ἐξηγγέλθη αὐτῶι, τὴν μὲν ἐπὶ Βάκτρα ὁδὸν οὐκ ἦγεν,
ἀναλαβὼν δὲ τούς τε ἑταίρους ἱππέας καὶ τοὺς ἱππακοντιστὰς καὶ τοὺς τοξότας καὶ τοὺς
Ἀγριάνας καὶ τὴν Ἀμύντου τε καὶ Κοίνου τάξιν, τὴν δὲ ἄλλην δύναμιν αὐτοῦ καταλιπὼν
καὶ ἐπ' αὐτῆι Κρατερὸν ἡγεμόνα, σπουδῆι ἦγεν ὡς ἐπὶ Σατιβαρζάνην τε καὶ τοὺς Ἀρείους
καὶ διελθὼν ἐν δυσὶν ἡμέραις σταδίους ἐς ἑξακοσίους πρὸς Ἀρτακόανα ἧκεν.

pass to the south side of the Hindu Kush, or, by one of the northern passes or defiles out of the range, which would bring him directly into Turkestan, whence the road to Balkh and the valley of the Oxus provides no difficulties. This latter route, which passes through the wide fertile reaches of the Hari-Rūd, east of Herāt, and then climbs close to the river up to the enclosed valley of Bāmiyān, was later the central life-line of the Ghūrid kingdom, guarded by hilltop forts of Ghūrid date, and there are traces of Parthian and Sassanian presence. Though difficult, in its eastern stretches (which Alexander did not reach), the whole route was not impassible even in midwinter, though Bābur many centuries later found the snow a severe trial.[28] It was the recognized route in times of crisis for rapid communication between Ghazna and Nishapūr via Herāt during the Ghaznavid period,[29] and Ghenghis Khan later passed through it and laid it waste. Later travellers and Afghan armed units also frequently made use of it, and in due course the plateau of Bāmiyān became the great central stronghold of resistance against the rulers of Kābul. As between these two routes, it seems natural at first sight to suppose that Alexander would have been advised to take the external route, via Maimana, which enabled him to avoid crossing the entire range, by skirting its western end. However, there are two good reasons for believing that he took the other route, via Bāmiyān, and followed the Hari-Rūd some 75 miles up its course, before the news from Herāt forced him to turn in his tracks, apparently when he had reached the

---

[28] See A. S. Beveridge, *Memoirs of Bābur* (London, 1922; repr. Lahore, 1975), 307-9, a memorable narrative. Bābur left Herāt on 24 Dec. 1506, his destination being Kābul, and his route via the Ghorband valley, i.e. up the Hari-Rūd, and via Bāmiyān and the Unai pass to Kābul.

[29] See C. E. Bosworth, *The Ghaznavids*[2] (Beirut, 1973), 169, with reference to the trustworthy evidence of Baihāqī: 'The swiftest and most direct route between Nishapur and Ghazna, that via the Hari Rud valley and Ghūr, took fifteen days, but because of the difficult terrain, it was only used when exceptional haste was needed.' This is precisely true of Alexander in his pursuit of Bessus. For modern accounts of the route through the valley of the Hari-Rūd, where the remarkable minaret of Djām was discovered in 1943, see A. Maricq and G. Wiet, *Le Minaret de Djàm* (Paris, 1959) (*Mém.* DAFA 16), and for more popular accounts see Freya Stark, *The Minaret of Djam* (London, 1973), *passim*, and N. Dupree, *Afghanistan*[2], (Kābul, 1977), 461 ff. The two most detailed accounts of the area of Bāmiyān are those of General Josiah Harlan, in his *Central Asia, Personal Narrative of General Josiah Harlan, 1823-1841*, ed. F. E. Ross (London, 1939), 102 ff. (whose spelling of local names is, as frequently at that time, often based solely on the spoken sound), and of Masson, *Narrative*, ii. 324-455, an outstanding description of the area against the background of contemporary military operations.

vicinity of the modern Obeh, some sixty miles as the crow flies east of Herāt. First, if he had taken the other route, via Maimana, all the country south of the Hindu Kush would have been left unsecured behind him; and second, the inner route, passing through a wide and fertile valley for about the first hundred miles, though later narrow and precipitous, was shorter, and the swiftest link with Bactria, Alexander's goal in pursuit of Bessus, via the passes which led across the Hindu Kush, converging on Bāmiyān.[30] In fact, though seemingly isolated in its high valleys, the Bāmiyān plateau was the regular means of communication in the third century BC, and therefore probably known already to Alexander and to his Achaemenian predecessors. Eratosthenes, speaking in general geographical terms, but no doubt deriving his information from the bematists,[31] stated that from Alexandria of the Arians there were two ways to Bactria: one 'directly' (ἐπ' εὐθείας) across Bactria (i.e. the western end of the Hindu Kush, comprising the later Gharjistān and Ghūristān, at the head-waters of the Murghāb) and then over the mountain to Ortospana and the 'trifurcation from Bactra that lies in the Paropamisadae', and the other the longer route through the desert that eventually led to India.[32] Eratosthenes' indication of the two routes available for the

---

[30] Arr. iii. 25. 4: Ἀλέξανδρος δὲ ὁμοῦ ἤδη ἔχων τὴν πᾶσαν δύναμιν ἤιει ἐπὶ Βάκτραν, κ.τ.λ. The passes in question, the Hajigak and Unai passes, leading south to the Helmund valley and south-east to the area of Ghazna, the Shibar pass leading east down the Ghorband valley and emerging north of Charikar, and the two routes down the Balkh and the Darra Yusuf rivers to Turkestan, are discussed again below in the context of the location of Ortospana and Alexandria ad Caucasum: see pp. 140 ff.: see Map *at end*, and any large-scale map. e.g. the General Staff Map, 2149, 1934 edn., 'Afghanistan and adjacent Borderlands'. The main settlements in the western part of the valley of the Hari-Rūd are to be found on Ball's maps nos 102 ff. Remains at Obeh (Ball 781), 60 miles up-river from Herāt seem to be of Timurid date; Chist-i-Sharif (Ball 212, and Map 103) about 40 miles, by the line of the river (which the modern road follows, before debouching in a large curve to the south), has notable Ghūrid remains (cf. N. Dupree, *Afghanistan*, 265–7). It is a reasonable assumption that if Alexander did indeed take this route he reached the neighbourhood of Obeh.

[31] See above pp. 80 ff. Engels 90, n. 86, suggests that 'one of the reasons Alexander may have taken the road via Merv was to avoid the difficulties of crossing a mountain pass held by an enemy.' It is noteworthy that there are no references in the historical narrative to action against enemy troops between the revolt of Satibarzanes and arrival at the Oxus, save for the need to suppress the second revolt in Aria (Arr. iii. 28. 2–3). North of the Hindu Kush resistance recommences.

[32] Strab. 723 (= ΙΙΙB 20): μέχρι μὲν Ἀλεξανδρείας τῆς ἐν Ἀρίοις ἀπὸ Κασπίων πυλῶν διὰ τῆς Παρθυαίας μία καὶ ἡ αὐτὴ ὁδός· εἶθ' ἡ μὲν ἐπ' εὐθείας διὰ τῆς Βακτριανῆς καὶ τῆς ὑπερβάσεως τοῦ ὄρους εἰς Ὀρτόσπανα ἐπὶ τὴν ἐκ Βάκτρων τρίοδον ἥτις ἐστιν ἐν

expedition from Herāt onwards supports this interpretation of Alexander's first route, and, as we shall see, it appears likely that he eventually returned from Bactria via Bāmiyān and the Ghorband valley on his way to the Indus. I assume therefore that on his first departure from the city he did indeed move with his troops up the Hari-Rūd, intending to take one of the passes leading north from the bifurcation near Bāmiyān, to Turkestan, and on the second occasion took the southern, desert route (see below, pp. 122 ff.). We have already seen that the view that his intended original route had been through the Turkmen desert from Mashshad towards Merv, with the intention of reaching the Oxus and Balkh from the west, without taking in the oasis of the Hari-Rūd, based on the identification of the Kalāt-i-Nadir with the mountain refuge of the Arians, involves very considerable difficulties. If correct, it would naturally indicate that the decision to establish a city in the Herāt oasis was only taken after Alexander had retraced his steps.

The revolt of Satibarzanes apparently led Alexander to reconsider his general strategy and movements. He had learnt that Persian garrisons and fortresses could become centres of resistance, and that they must be captured and occupied as he continued on his

τοῖς Παροπαμισάδαις· ἡ δὲ ἐκτρέπεται μικρὸν ἀπὸ τῆς Ἀρίας πρὸς νότον εἰς Προφθασίαν τῆς Δραγγιανῆς· εἶτα πάλιν ἡ λοιπὴ (?αὐτὴ) μέχρι τῶν ὅρων τῆς Ἰνδικῆς καὶ τοῦ Ἰνδοῦ· ὥστε μακροτέρα ἐστὶν αὕτη ἡ διὰ τῶν Δραγγῶν καὶ Ἀραχωτῶν, σταδίων μυρίων πεντακισχιλίων τριακοσίων ἡ πᾶσα. This passage presents the strongest argument for supposing that Alexander had embarked on his first, thwarted, march from the oasis of Herāt up the course of the Hari-Rūd. There is no suggestion in the text that an alternative route lay across the Murghāb at Bālā Murghāb and so on to Maimana. His first route clearly includes the later Ghūristān under 'Bactria', and indicates that Alexander intended to follow the Hari-Rūd, through the Koh-i-Bābā, to Ortospana; and if we assign to the latter a location in the Bāmiyān valley, as I believe we must (see below, pp. 140 ff.), we can see that the route Alexander originally intended on his way to Bactria was the same as that he successfully accomplished (as far as Ortospana) on the way back. The words διὰ τῆς Βακτριανῆς are slightly anomalous, but the precise boundaries between Aria and Bactria cannot be determined on the western side, and καὶ τῆς ὑπερβάσεως τοῦ ὄρους provides the necessary orientation. I do not think there is any pre-Islamic evidence for the use of the 'external' route via Maimana, though it became the recognized route after the Islamic conquest: see the stages for the first part, Herāt–Merv al-Rūdh given by Le Strange, *LEC* 415 n. 1. Marquart (op.cit. above, n. 11), 67–71, believed that Alexander had advanced on his first departure by the 'external' route to Balkh, via Maimana, and had reached somewhere in the neighbourhood of the Murghāb river, and that Satibarzanes employed the inner route through Ghūr when he fled, and that the two met in the central reaches of the Hari-Rūd, east of Herāt. Satibarzanes' route of withdrawal from Artacoana is not given by Arrian in iii. 25, 7 but he reached Bactria and later returned to Artacoana where he caused a further revolt in the course of which he was eventually killed: ibid. 28. 2–3.

march. It thus became essential for him to subdue the southern satrapies and their capitals before he passed out of direct contact with the huge expanse of Persian territory that lay south of the Hindu Kush. To do this he had to take the alternative route through the southern deserts of Drangiana and Arachosia, not the best way to cross the Hindu Kush from Herāt. Arrian says little of this momentous change of plan, and what he does say gives no idea of the size of the undertaking: 'With the force left under Krateros, which had now joined him, he marched towards the territory of the Zarangaeans, and arrived at the place where their palace was.' There then follows the account of the conspiracy of Philotas, after which he continues: 'he proceeded towards Bactria and against Bessus and on his way won over the Drangians, the Gedrosians and . . . the Arachosians . . . and went against the Indians adjacent to the Arachotoi.' He adds that these operations caused considerable hardship to the troops and took place in deep snow, though snow does not lie long in the desert west and south of Kandahar.[33]

It is clear that in taking the long route to the oasis of Kandahar, and then following the courses of the Arghandāb and Tarnak rivers upstream northwards his intention was to neutralize any Achaemenian fortresses en route. The fact that, after completing his operations at Kandahar, he did not take the route across the Khojak and Bolān passes to the Lower Indus,[34] but continued on northwards, shows that he did not deviate from his purpose of conquering the Persian satrapies of the Paropamisos region

[33] iii. 28. 1 (after the conspiracy of Philotas): ταῦτα δὲ διαπραξάμενος προσῄει ὡς ἐπὶ Βάκτρα τε καὶ Βῆσσον, Δράγγας τε καὶ Γαδρωσοὺς ἐν τῆι παρόδωι παραστησάμενος. παρεστήσατο δὲ καὶ τοὺς Ἀραχώτας καὶ σατράπην κατέστησεν ἐπ' αὐτοῖς Μένωνα. ἐπῆλθε δὲ καὶ τῶν Ἰνδῶν τοὺς προσχώρους Ἀραχώταις. ξύμπαντα δὲ ταῦτα τὰ ἔθνη διὰ χιόνος τε πολλῆς καὶ ξὺν ἀπορίαι τῶν ἐπιτηδείων καὶ τῶν στρατιωτῶν ταλαιπωρίαι ἐπῆλθε. The reference to the Γαδρωσοί here is surprising, since the region of Gedrosia lay south of Arachosia, (Erat. IIIB 23). The tribal term may be employed in a wider significance than usual. For the lightness of snow at Kandahar (as opposed, especially, to Ghazna), see e.g. Masson, *Narrative*, ii. 189, 'Kandahar is esteemed felicitous in its winter climate, and snow, which remains on all the lands around, rarely falls on its favoured plains, or falls only to melt.'

[34] For this route see esp. Masson, ibid. i. 338–9, who describes it as the division of two climatic zones, the cooler country of Kandahar and the north-west, and the heat of Sind to the south-east. For the importance of this route see further below, p. 165. The climatic and physical characteristics of NW Pakistan in general are described in modern terms by D. Dichter (and Nathan S. Popkin), *The North-West Frontier of West Pakistan* (Oxford, 1967), 5 ff., but they do not touch on this feature.

and 'beyond the river' before advancing against the satrapy of Gandhara.

We must now consider that route, and the centres of habitation along the river-courses and small oases through Drangiana (roughly the southern drainage-area of the Helmund river, to Lake Zarah) and Arachosia, the area lying mainly east of the Helmund, and corresponding as a whole approximately to the modern provinces of Sijistān, Kandahar, Ghazni, and Lugar. Arrian does not help us with locations until we come to Alexandria ad Caucasum, and then only with a bare statement of fact.

The first problems arise in connection with Phrada-Prophthasia, the city so renamed by Alexander, and probably the place where the news of the conspiracy of Philotas was brought to him. Stephanus, s.v. *Φράδα*, has πόλις ἐν Δράγγαις, ἥν Ἀλέξανδρος Προφθασίαν μετωνόμασεν, ὡς Χάραξ ἐν ἕκτωι Χρονικῶν.[35] Eratosthenes calls the city, if such indeed it was at that time, Prophthasia, and locates it in Drangiana, on the southern route from Alexandria in Aria.[36] The figures for the distance from Herāt to Prophthasia given by Eratosthenes, quoted by Strabo as 1,600 stades (= *c*.200 miles) and by Pliny (who found discrepancies in his sources) as 198 Roman miles, accord closely.[37] Phrada-Phra, the

[35] Charax, *FGrH* 103 F20. Jacoby was inclined to date Charax to the early Byzantine period (*Komm.* 312), and dismissed the suggested identification with the Charax mentioned by M. Anton. *Comm.* viii. 25: οἱ δὲ δριμεῖς ἐκεῖνοι ἢ προγνωστικοὶ ἢ τετυφωμένοι πού; οἷον, δριμεῖς μὲν Χάραξ καὶ Δημήτριος [ὁ Πλατωνικὸς] καὶ Εὐδαίμων. Numerous inscriptions now show Charax to have been active in the reign of Antoninus Pius (cos. AD 147): see Habicht, *Istanb.Forsch.* 9/10 (1959/60), 109 ff., publishing an inscription in which Πατρέων ἡ πόλις dedicates a statue to A.Kl.Charax, on the base of which his public career is recorded (ending with τὸν συγγραφέα); for the pediment of the propylon now at the entrance to the sanctuary, with the inscription Κλ.Χάραξ τὸ πρόπυλον, see *AvonPerg.* viii. 3, *Das Asklepieion*, no. 141 (cf. Habicht, loc. cit. 118); cf. also ibid. no. 8. Habicht discusses all that is known of Charax's distinguished career, and stresses that the identification with the Charax referred to by Marcus Antoninus becomes virtually certain. Charax's information, whatever his immediate source, no doubt derived ultimately from Eratosthenes, though directly perhaps from a pinacographical source recording metonomasies (see above, pp. 5–6). For general discussions of the importance of Prophthasia see *RE* (2) (Treidler), who regards it as the main link in communications between Arachosia and Gedrosia (Arr. vi. 15. 5, with ibid. 27. 3). In early Islamic times Farah was the dividing point of the route from Greater Merv to Ḵarnīn and Zaranj, the capital of Sijistān.

[36] See above, p. 84.

[37] For Eratosthenes see the quotation from Strab. 514 (= IIIB 20(2); cf. also above, n. 32): λέγει δὲ (sc. Ἐρατοσθένης) καὶ οὕτω τὰ διαστήματα· ἀπὸ Κασπίων πυλῶν εἰς Ἰνδούς, εἰς μὲν Ἑκατόμπυλον χιλίους ἐννεακοσίους ἑξήκοντά φασιν, εἰς δ' Ἀλεξάνδρειαν τὴν ἐν Ἀρίοις τετρακισχιλίους πεντακοσίους τριάκοντα, εἶτ' εἰς Προφθασίαν

latter name used by Isidore, may have been an Achaemenian site,[38]
and it survived as the Arab-Persian Farah, which, a thousand
years after Isidore, Ibn Ḥawqal, before the Mongol invasion,
described as one of the largest cities in the area, after Bust and
Zaranj.[39] Does this square with an identification of Prophthasia
with Farah? Much depends on the route taken, and there is, as
always, uncertainty about this, but in this particular case the
deviations and alternatives are not great and are easily identifiable.
The ancient sources agree with a figure of c.200 miles (1600 st.)
from Alexandria in Aria to Prophthasia, while Farah is only c.160
miles from Herāt (via Sabzwar-Shindand).[40] That is sufficiently

τὴν ἐν Δραγγῆι χιλίους ἑξακοσίους, οἱ δὲ πεντακοσίους, εἶτ᾽ εἰς Ἀραχωτοὺς τὴν πόλιν
τετρακισχιλίους ἑκατὸν εἴκοσιν, εἶτ᾽ εἰς Ὀρτόσπανα, ἐπὶ τὴν ἐκ Βάκτρων τρίοδον,
δισχιλίους, εἶτ᾽ εἰς τὰ ὅρια τῆς Ἰνδικῆς χιλίους· ὁμοῦ μύριοι πεντακισχίλιοι τριακόσιοι. On
this passage see further below, pp. 140 ff. Plin. NH vi. 61 (= Eratosth. IIIB 21(2)):
inde Alexandriam Arion, quam urbem is rex condidit, DLXXV mil., Prophthasiam
Drangarum CXCVIIII mil., Arachosiorum oppidum DLXV mil., Ortospanum CCL mil.,
inde ad Alexandri oppidum L mil. In quibusdam exemplaribus diversi numeri reperiuntur.
Isidore § 16 has ἐντεῦθεν Ἀναύων χώρα τῆς Ἀρείας, σχοῖνοι ῑε̄, ἐν ἧι πόλις μεγίστη Φρὰ
καὶ Βὶς πόλις καὶ Γαρὶ πόλις καὶ Νίη πόλις· κώμη δὲ οὐκ ἔστιν. (17) ἐντεῦθεν
Ζαραγγιανή, σχοῖνοι κ̄ᾱ. καὶ ἔνθα πόλις Πάριν καὶ Κορὸκ πόλις. Unfortunately we do
not know the location of Ἀναύων χώρα so the distances cannot be controlled by
Isidore's measurements. If the forms of the name Δραγγή, Δραγγιανή have not been
contaminated by Strabo it must be assumed that Eratosthenes used the two forms
indiscriminately; in 723 Strabo gives Προφθασία τῆς Δραγγιανῆς and in 514
Προφθασία ἡ ἐν Δραγγῆι, both in direct quotation from Eratosthenes. In the former
passage Strab. also uses οἱ Δράγγαι. For further variants see Pape-Benseler, s.v.
Δράγγαι; Tomaschek, RE, s.v. Drangai. The variants Ζαράγγαι, Ζαραγγαῖοι seem to
be admitted by Arr. In iii. 21. 1 he has Βαρσαέντης ὁ Ἀραχωτῶν καὶ Δραγγιανῆς
σατράπης, and in iii. 28. 1, Δραγγαί, but in vii. 17. 3 ἐπ Ἀραχωτῶν καὶ Ζαράγγων,
and in vii. 27. 3. Στασάνωρ ὁ Ἀρείων καὶ [ὁ] Ζαράγγων σατράπης, while in vii. 6. 3
a long list of ἱππεῖς includes Ζαραγγῶν. Isid. 17 (above) has Ζαραγγιανή. For Zaranj
see further below, n. 41.

[38] The name Φράδα preserved by Charax seems preferable to the form Φρά given
by Isidore, which may represent local pronunciation. It is noteworthy that the
personal name Phrada was borne, among others, by a native of Margiana, who
revolted against Darius: see Kent, OP 198 for refs. In Hallock's Pers. Fortif. Tablets,
224 no. 744, the Elamite form Pirrada occurs in the text and glossary (p. 744),
which Hallock prefers to render as Fraċa (cf. p. 72). Cf. also Justi s.v. Frāda.

[39] For Ibn Ḥawqal's description of Farah see BGA ii². 420 (FT ii. 408). For its
condition in 1830 see Conolly, op. cit. ii. 59, and for its destruction shortly after
see Malleson, op. cit. 114-15.

[40] The calculation of the route Herāt-Kandahar is complicated by the discrepancies in distances and the number of routes available, but these do not affect
the direct route as far as Farah. The distance from Farah to Sabzwar (= Pusht.
Shindand) is 80 m, and from Sabzwar to Herāt another 80, on Malleson's measurements (op. cit. 107 ff.) on the flat main caravan route: this is 160 m. = c.256 km.
The point at which the modern road from Herāt to Dilarām comes closest to Farah,

short of 200 to have caused Droysen and Tarn to place
Prophthasia further from Herāt, the latter opting for a location in
the neighbourhood of Zaranj, the later capital of Sijistān, the
Parthian Sakastane, an area largely dominated by the delta of the
Helmund (Hamūn, Hilmand) and Lake Zarah, which has in recent
years revealed a considerable number of urban and palatial sites of
the Achaemenid period, when it was the centre of the satrapy or
province of Zra(n)ka.[41] Tarn argued that Prophthasia should be
located at or near Zaranj (which itself derives from the ancient
names of Zra(n)ka/Drangiana/Zarangiana), and that its true name
was Alexandria in Sakastane, for which Prophthasia was only a
nickname. We are thus plunged into a further sea of troubles.[42]
Alexandria in Sakastane is known only from Isidore's list of the
localities of Sakastane (the list itself undoubtedly corrupt) and

leaving it *c.*60 km. to the SW, is approximately 127 m. (203 km.) from Herāt, at
the crossing of the Farah-Rūd (the original city of Pul-i-Farah lay one stage south
of Farah: see Le Strange, 341). Fischer, *Bonn. Jahrb.* 167 (1967), 153, and Brunt,
Arrian, i. 501, reckon the distance Herāt-Farah as 270 km. (*c.*169 m.), by the
modern motor-road, which Brunt says 'must always have been in use'. He adds,
'this clearly points to Prophthasia being at or near Farah, 270 km. from Herat,
contra Droysen, [*GE* iii, 216], with the wrong distance.' Droysen, FT ii. 674 (cf. i.
409 n. 1), regards the distance as incompatible with a location of Prophthasia at
Farah, but offers no alternative, while Tarn, *GBI* 14 and 347, places it near Lake
Zarah, in the neighbourhood of Juwaiyn or Zaranj. See further, in the text, above.

[41] For Zranka (= Ζαραγγιανή/Δραγγιανή) in Old Persian texts see Kent, *Old
Persian,* DB i. 16; DPe 15 ff; XPh. 20, where it is closely associated with Parthava,
Haraira, and Harauvatis (Arachosia). For the 4th cent. see the texts of the time of
Artaxerxes II, ibid. 155-6. The excavations of the Italian Archaeological Delegation
under Professor Tucci in and around Lake Zarah have thrown a great deal of light
on the early history of Drangiana. There is a brief, provisional account of the
excavations in Matheson, 279 ff. (esp. pp. 281 ff., for the main site, Dahan i-
Ghulman). Fuller reports will be found in the various publications (Reports and
Memoirs) of IsMEO. No. 10 (1967) of this series, by G. Gnoli, *Ricerche storiche
sul Sistan,* deals both with the Avestan texts which refer to the area, which are of
particular significance in the growth of Zoroastrianism, and with the Greek texts
relevant to the use of the term Ζαραγγιανή: see esp. pp. 42 ff. The region and city
were known to Ctesias (*FGrH* 688(55)) F22: καὶ πόλιν Ζαριν καταλαβών, κ.τ.λ.

[42] Loc. cit. p. 14. Tarn says that Arr. iii. 25. 8, 'and all analogy' states that
Alexander founded a city among the Zarangians, but this is not so. Arr. in that passage says αὐτὸς (sc. ὁ Ἀλέξανδρος) δὲ ξὺν τοῖς ἀμφὶ Κράτερον ὑπολελειμμένοις, ὁμοῦ
οὖσιν ἤδη, ὡς ἐπὶ τὴν Ζαραγγαίων χώραν ἦγε· καὶ ἀφικνεῖται ἵνα τὰ βασίλεια τῶν
Ζαραγγαίων ἦν . . . (§ 26): Ἐνταῦθα καὶ τὴν Φιλώτα ἐπιβουλὴν τοῦ Παρμενίωνος ἔμαθεν
Ἀλέξανδρος κ.τ.λ. This palace of the Zarangians could (other things being equal)
have been at Phrada, and there is no suggestion 'by analogy' of a refoundation or
renaming such as is expressly testified by Charax for Phrada. Nevertheless, as I
show below, I regard it as likely that Alexandria in Sakastane was Zaranj, but that
it was not a foundation of Alexander.

(possibly) from a Chinese source.[43] It should be added that though Zaranj, the capital of the Ṣaffārid princes from the ninth to the end of the fourteenth century, when Sijistān was conquered by the Mongols and Zaranj destroyed, was accredited to Alexander by Qodāma at the end of his account of Alexander's conquest of China and Tibet, it is not taken as an Alexander-foundation by the other representatives of the Perso-Arab tradition of Alexandrias, perhaps because the city, though seemingly a centre of Zoroastrian activity in the early period, was not of much political importance until it became the capital of the Ṣaffārids.[44] The evidence seems

[43] Tarn, (ibid.) writes 'the official name, Alexandria, has been preserved by the Chinese historian Pan-Ku, who called Seistan O-ik-san-li, a word which has been shown to be Alexandria (see p. 347).' At p. 347, in discussion of the regions described by Pan-Ku, he says of the same region, 'it was suggested long ago that O-ik-san-li was Alexandria, and that seems now certain; but it has not been asked where an Alexandria could be found in Seistān. One can now see that it was the official name of Prophthasia, Alexander's capital of Seistān, which has perished in the Greek tradition, etc.' Unfortunately this statement begs the question, which is in fact insoluble. The relevant passage of the *Han Shu* of Pan-Ku is to be found in A. F. P. Hulsewé and M. A. N. Loewe's *China in Central Asia* (Sinica Leidensia, 14 (1979), 112 ff., with very valuable notes (Tarn used the text and commentary of de Groot, *Chinesische Urkunden zur Geschichte Asiens*, ii (Berlin, 1926), 91 ff., the translation of which is essentially the same). On p. 112 the translation reads: 'The state of Wu-i-shan-li . . . adjoins Chi-pin in the East, P'u t'ao in the north and Li-kan and T'iao-chih in the west . . . (p. 115) Wu-i is cut off and remote and Han envoys reach it only rarely. Proceeding from the Southern Route [i.e. south of the Taklamakan Desert] from the Yu-men and the Yang barriers, and travelling south through Shan-shan one reaches Wu-i-shan-li, which is the extreme point of the Southern Route; and turning north and then proceeding eastward one arrives at An-hsi [the Arsacid realm].' As n. 250 on p. 112 of Hulsewé and Loewe indicates, while Wu-i-shan-li is evidently a phonetic transliteration of Alexandria, there is no indication, beyond the words quoted above, which Alexandria Pan-Ku was referring to. Chavannes, *T'oung Pao*, 6 (1905), 555 n. 7 (quoted by Loewe, loc. cit.), identified it with Alexandria in Aria, as against Marquart's identification of it with Alexandria in Arachosia; the editors of the text do not commit themselves, while de Groot seems to have taken it to cover the whole of southern Afghanistan (see op. cit., loc. cit). Granted the uncertainty of frontiers in these provinces, it seems much more likely that the important centre in the valley of the Hari-Rūd should be picked out to express the region to the south of the Kushan kingdom than the almost unknown city of Alexandria in Sakastane. It is in any case doubtful to what extent the Chinese of the former Han dynasty had direct knowledge of the region. I do not think we are justified in accepting Prophthasia as an Alexandria on this basis, though it finally stood in the Index to Tarn's *Alexander*, ii. 455 as Alexandria (15).

[44] The fullest account of Sijistān under the early Arabs, before the time of the Ṣaffārids, is C. E. Bosworth's, *Sīstān under the Arabs* (IsMEO xi, 1968), summarized by him in *Islamic Dynasties* (2nd edn. Edinburgh, 1980), 103–6. Bosworth's account is based on a local anonymous chronicle, the *Tá'rīkh-i Sīstān*, of the 12th(?) cent. AD, first published in 1935. Balādhuri's account of the conquest of Sijistān now takes secondary place to this, though the importance assigned by the Persian

therefore insufficient for the identification both of Zaranj with Prophthasia and of Phra-Prophthasia with an Alexandria in Sakastane. The latter, if it can safely be extracted from the corrupt text of Isidore, is to be regarded as a name given to a city (perhaps Zaranj) at a later date, by a ruler (Parthian, no doubt) of Sakastane.[45] Nevertheless, Alexander is stated by Arrian to have visited the capital of the Zarangaioi (the accounts of the other Alexander-historians are dominated by the lengthy descriptions of the Philotas affair, and the geographical context is vague), and this divergence from the natural route across the Helmund in the direction of its egress was unnecessary, unless there was a bastion of Achaemenid power there, which it would be natural for Alexander to neutralize.

The sites in the neighbourhood of Lake Zarah have been intensively investigated on the Afghan side of the border, notably by K. Fischer, while the excavations of Italian and Persian teams in Iran, on the Persian side, in and around the lake, notably at Dahan-i-Ghulman, close to the medieval Zaranj, have, as already mentioned above, also brought to light important Achaemenid as well as Parthian and Sassanian settlements. The whole area watered by the streams and canals of the Helmund made the region between Zaranj and Bust a fertile zone, known as the Zamīn-Dāwar, noted for its peacocks.[46] Alexander had learnt of the need to

Anonymus to e.g. the Zoroastrian element may be excessive. For the historical geography see Le Strange's account of Sijistān, *LEC* 334 ff. Qodāma says (*BGA* vi. 265 (= FT 207)) that Dhū'l Qarnein-Iskander returned from China, and after founding Alexandria Eschate in Sugd went to Bokhārā, and Merv, and founded Herāt and Zaranj. This is a stray piece of the legends about Alexander, and does not link up obviously with the regular lists. The Anonymus quotes an earlier source for the statement that Alexander was one of those who contributed to the fortifications of Zaranj (Bosworth, 7). *The Provincial Capitals of Erānshahr*, § 18, speaks of Zaranj as the capital of the province, but does not associate it with Alexander. For the Zoroastrian traditions regarding Zaranj see Bosworth, ch. 1, and Gnoli, loc. cit.

[45] The complicated problems regarding Sakastane in the Hellenistic age were discussed by me in *Afghan Studies*, 2 (1979), 13 (and nn. 25-6), with especial reference to the work of Daffinà, *L'immigrazione dei Saka nella Drangiana* (IsMEO, Reports and Memoirs, 9 (Rome, 1967)), which contains an extremely detailed discussion of all aspects of the problem. My final views regarding the identity of Kandahar with Alexandria in Sakastane have changed, since I now regard it as to be identified with Alexandria in Arachosia. See below, pp. 132 ff. For the various Muslim names of the region see Minorsky, *Ḥudūd al-ʿālām*, 344 ff.

[46] Of the older accounts of Sijistān the most important is that of G. E. Tait, *Seistan* (2 vols., Calcutta, 1911), which provides a picture of the area before the almost complete submergence of the standing remains. His photographs of Nād Ali = Zaranj

neutralize all Achaemenid fortified posts, provincial capitals etc., and was for that reason, as we have seen, advancing to Bactria by the great arc through the southern desert and Arachosia by Kandahar and Ghazna. It is therefore unlikely that he would not have taken the extra detour to the area of the lake to cover his position. Nevertheless, it would have been contrary to his overall plan for new foundations to build a city (more especially an eponymous city) for which he could not see a great future, which would fulfil neither a military nor an economic role. This basic consideration, and the absence of any historical reference to a foundation (as opposed to the entry in Isidore's schedule), suffice to discredit the suggestion that Alexandria in Sakastane should be regarded as a city founded by Alexander. It is true that Arrian does not record the foundation of Alexandria in Aria either, but that is established beyond reasonable doubt by its early appearance in the bematists and geographers, while Alexandria in Sakastane has to wait until Isidore, and finds no support as an Alexander-foundation until the reference to it by Qodāma. The closest analogy, simply in terms of evidence, is that provided by Alexandria in Margiana. As we have already seen (above, pp. 31 ff.), apart from the ambiguous passage in Pliny, the only evidence for Merv lies in the Iranian tradition represented by Ṭabārī and *The Provincial Capitals of Erānshahr*, and that is not enough. As I explain below, I believe that the site at Zaranj was Alexandria in Sakastane, but that it was not founded by Alexander.

The concatenation of evidence that speaks in favour of the historical sequence on the one site of Phrada-Prophthasia-(Phra)-Farah, may be further supported by the notice in Pliny in which he places *flumen Ophradus* next to Prophthasia,[47] a pointer which

are particularly valuable (the site (Ball 752) is now 'covered in alluvial deposit'). For the recent surveys and other investigations carried out by Fischer and others see Ball, nos. 502, 595, 597, 601, 608, 708, and many more sites. For the peacocks of Zamīn-Dāwar see Minorsky, *Ḥudūd al-ʿālam*, 345. Le Strange, 334 ff., gives a graphic picture of the branching canals and dams of the Helmund in his description of Sijistān as it was at the time of Ṣaffārid rule and later. The quantity of flowing water in the city is described by Ibn Ḥawqal, *BGA* i², pp. 414 ff. (= FT 401 ff.).

[47] Plin. vi. 94, after describing Aria and regions adjacent to Alexandria in Aria, adds, among other items, *amnes Pharnacotis, Ophradus*. Herzfeld, *Arch. Mitt. Iran*, 2 (1930), 92 f. pointed out that the latter word corresponded closely to ὁ Φράδος; cf. J. Schmidt, *RE*, s.v. Phrada. The resemblance is very close, and I incline to accept that the name of the river and that of the city are in one way or another interdependent. The *Tabula Peut.* has a name Propasta, which resembles Prophthasia, but

seems valid, and may be accepted. Our prime concern is not with the site itself, but with the change in its ancient name. Only Isidore calls it Phra, while Ptolemy, who includes it in the inhabited localities of Drangiana (he has no Sakastane), and Ammianus (who, though mostly using much earlier sources, seems here to have adorned his narrative) retain its new name.[48] There remains the problem why Alexander (if it was he) should have renamed Phrada Prophthasia, 'Anticipation'. Abstract substantives or personifications are otherwise rarely attested as city names, and an especial explanation is needed of this one.[49] A similar form,

which Tarn says (ibid.), following Tomaschek, *SBWien.Akad.* 102 (1883), 213, 'may be a Persian term meaning "seen from afar"'. That seems unlikely in itself, but the readings of the texts are doubtful. The Ravenna Cosmographer also refers to Propasta (cf. Markwart's note (p. 88) to § 38 Paspora: see (ed. Schnetz, *Itin. Rom.* ii (1940)), II, 3, p. 16, § 3, 18 (= Pinder and Parthey, 42), ibid. II, 10, p. 21, 2 (Proptas Prostas); II, 3, p. 17, 7 (Tropsasia); II, 12, p. 23, 4 (Oroppa). The notices in these late itineraries cannot be traced to any specific source. The Ravenna Cosmogr. also has several references to Alexandrias in India: p. 16, 1 (PP 42), sub. Palanda: no. 5, Alexandria, no. 10, Alexandrium, no. 12, Alexandria Bucephalos; no. 13, Albi Alexandri. Though no. 12 is historical I do not feel that the others qualify for consideration, and have therefore not included them in the Table of Alexandrias. We may recall the Seleucid 'Alexandropolis' in India recorded by Appian (above p. 38)

[48] Ptol vi. 19. 4: πόλεις δὲ καὶ κῶμαι φέρονται τῆς Δραγγιανῆς αἵδε· Προφθασία . . . ρῑ . . . λβ γ´. In this list of eleven localities in Drangiana, headed by Prophthasia, Ptolemy, as usual, does not indicate which locations he classes as πόλεις and which as κῶμαι. Amm. xxiii 6 71: *Ante dictis continui sunt Drangianai collibus cohaerentes, quos flumen alluit Arabium nomine ideo appellatum, quod inde exoritur, interque alia duobus municipiis exultantes, Prophthasia et Ariaspe, ut opulentis et claris.* The contrast with Ammianus's description of Alexandria in Arachosia (see below, p. 142) is striking, if not illuminating.

[49] Such derivative and probably fictitious forms found in Stephanus, e.g. Ἀγαθοῦσσα (= Telos), Ἀγάθεια (πόλις Φωκίδος), Ἀγάθη (πόλις Λιγυῶν ἢ Κέλτων) do not come into consideration. As personified names we may note Ἀδράστεια (from Charax, *FGrH* 103 F1), but here the cult-title has been personified into a king: Ἄδραστος Νεμέσεως ἱερὸν ἱδρύσας; to the same category belongs Ἐπιφάνεια, in effect a dynastic eponymous name. More directly analogous are Πονηρόπολις, allegedly the original name of Philippopolis (Thcop. *FGrH* 115 F 110; cf. Plin. iv. 41, Plut. *Mor.* 520 B, and *RE*, s.v. Philippopolis, col. 2244; L. Robert, *EEP* p. 171), Εὐκαρπία in Phrygia, and Εὐπορία in Macedonia (Steph. s.v., ἣν Ἀλέξανδρος τάξεως νικήσας(?) ἔκτισε καὶ ὠνόμασε διὰ τὸ εὔπορον; cf. Ptol. iii. 13. 35) = Gazoros, E. of Heracleia Sintica (see Hammond, *Macedonia*, i. 197 and map 17, opp. p. 181), no doubt an imaginary foundation of Alexander's, unless a duplication of Alexandria in Thrace (cf. above, pp. 26, 29-30), and Σωτείρα, allegedly founded by Antiochus I in Aria or Parthyene (App. *Syr.* 57), if understood as commemorating an actual 'salvation' rather than as deriving from the cult-title of its founder (cf. Tscherikower, 102). Note also (App. ibid.) Χάρις, for whose existence no other testimony exists. (For the Seleucid foundations listed by Appian in *Syr.* 57 see above, pp. 36 ff.), Droysen, *GE* iii. p 242 = FT 692, suggested that the Ὀσονόη of Ptol. vi. 1. 5 in the neighbourhood of

Prophthasia, occurs as the name of a festival at Klazomenai in 382 BC, where the noun is, of course, a neuter plural, Προφθάσια; there is, in any case, no reason to link the two words historically. The most likely explanation is, as Droysen suggested, that Alexander bestowed the name in commemoration of the anticipation there of the conspiracy of Philotas. Alexander, we may suppose, took over the old Achaemenian capital of Drangiana, reorganized it and renamed it Prophthasia, before he marched further south, and followed the direct route until he reached the capital of the Zarangians in the neighbourhood of Lake Zarah. The distance given by Ibn Khordādhbeh (p. 50) for Zaranj to Herāt is 80 farsakhs, or *c.* 240 miles, and since Farah to Herāt is 160 miles, the distance from Farah to Zaranj by the route that lay east of the present road, was, on this reckoning, approximately 80 miles. His subsequent route is discussed below. The latest historical reference to Prophthasia is by Ammianus, who describes it, along with Ariaspe, as flourishing and wealthy; we have already seen that in his chorographical excursus, though modernizing on occasion, he generally reproduces the substance of Eratosthenes or Pliny without significant variation; on this, as on other occasions, he may have been drawing on his imagination. Collectively the evidence shows that the city preserved the name that Alexander gave it for many centuries, and that it is, to that extent, hardly correct to describe it as a 'nickname'.[50]

Ecbatana, which appears as Εἰσόνη ἢ Ἰσονόη in the cod.Pal. might be another such abstract name given by Alexander to commemorate the healing of the rupture between Eumenes and Hephaestion (Arr. vii. 13. 1: τούτωι τῶι λόγωι ὑποπτήξαντα Ἡφαιστίωνα συναλλαγῆναι Εὐμενεῖ, οὐχ ἑκόντα ἑκόντι; cf. Plut. *Eumen.* 2): 'le nom véritable doit avoir été Ὁμονόη ου Ἰσονόη. De même qu'Alexandre, après avoir prévenu la conjuration de Philotas, donna à une localité le nom de Prophthasia, il a bien pu attacher assez d'importance à la réconciliation de deux personnages considérables pour en fixer le souvenir dans le nom d'une ville'. Tarn, *GBI* 472, who does not believe that the name Prophthasia was bestowed on the city by Alexander, gives an amusing list of place-names generated by linguistic misunderstandings, of which the most pleasing is Ptol. ii. 11. 27 (not, as Tarn, iii. 2. 27), Σιατούτανδα in Germania = 'ad sua tutanda', Tac. *Ann.* iv. 73). Von Gutschmid, *Kl. Schr.* v. 228 ff. listed some noteworthy examples of Latin misunderstandings of an orginal (lost) Greek text Latinized in the *Ravenna Cosmogr.*, esp. concerning Egypt: *ambo Aegyptus id est inferior et superior, hoc est Anocura et Mareoton* = (presumably), ἡ ἑκατέρα Αἴγυπτος, τουτέστιν ἡ κάτω καὶ ἡ ἄνω ἤτοι ἡ ἄνω χώρα. For Ptolemy's Σκαβίωσα Λαοδίκεια see above, p. 23.

[50] Plut. *De Alex. Virt.* 328 F, justifies Alexander's conquests thus: οὐκ ἂν ἡμερώθησαν εἰ μὴ ἐκρατήθησαν· οὐκ ἂν εἶχεν Ἀλεξάνδρειαν Αἴγυπτος, οὐδὲ Μεσοποταμία Σελεύκειαν, οὐδὲ Προφθασίαν Σογδιανή, οὐδ' Ἰνδία Βουκεφαλίαν, οὐδὲ πόλιν Ἑλλάδα Καύκασος †παροικοῦσαν αἷς ἐμποδισθείσαν ἐσβέσθη τὸ ἄγριον καὶ μετέβαλε τὸ χεῖρον ὑπὸ τοῦ κρείττονος ἐθιζόμενον. The whole passage is difficult, and corrupt, and it is not

The assumption that on leaving Zaranj Alexander took the route across the great chord of the southern bow of the Helmund, and reached that river, via the area of the modern Khast, somewhere in the neighbourhood of Lashkari Bazār (Bust), and thence attained the main through-route at Giriskh, and thence to Kandahar, makes the distances given by Eratosthenes and Pliny for this stretch, (4,120 stades and 565 miles = 4,120 stades, respectively) not unreasonable. We have seen that they both put the distance from Herāt to Kandahar at well over 700 miles, the first at about 720, the latter at about 745, and that the distance, if measured from Herāt via the old route to Farah and thence direct to Kandahar, is only about 375-400 miles; that is, little more than one-half of their figure. The distance from Zaranj through the Zamīn-Dāwar to Bust is given by the early Arab geographers, notably Iṣṭakhrī in his description of Sijistān, as five day-marches, *c.*150 miles, on a level route, and this figure, on the present hypothesis, will have been included by the bematists in their original measurement. To it must also be added the distance from Farah to the area of Zaranj, again a straight and level route of about 80 miles (3 farsakhs, according to Ibn Khordāhbeh), giving a total corresponding roughly to that required by the omission from the calculation of the northern side of the triangle formed by Farah, Zaranj, and Bust; the distance from Farah to the crossing of the Helmund at or near Giriskh, on the 'regular' route, being some hundred miles. The Zamīn-Dāwar was still fertile in pre-Mongol times, and the lower course of the Helmund supported a large population. Lashkari Bazār itself, the imposing remains of which are so prominent today, was the summer residence of the Ghaznavid rulers. We learn from Iṣṭakhrī and Ibn Ḥawqal that when the Helmund was in spate there was a regular route by river between Bust and Zaranj along the Sanā-Rūd, and this waterway still forms the focus of life for the whole area.[51]

easy (and perhaps not necessary) to set the geography in order. The detailed treatment by Tarn, *Alex.* ii. 255-9, is characteristically brilliant (and dogmatic), but will not persuade everybody. As far as Prophthasia in Sogdiana is concerned Treidel's claim, *RE*, s.v. Prophthasia, col. 821, that this refers to the inclusion by Darius of the Sogdians and Arians along with the Chorasmians and Parthians in a single tribute-area (Hdt. iii. 93) is not convincing. Tarn's explanation is based on historical considerations which result in (or from) a substantial rewriting of the whole passage. See also below, p. 194 n. 4. For Ammianus' looseness in his descriptions of localities in this region see below, p. 142, and n. 71.

[51] For Lashkari Bazār see D. Schlumberger *et al.*, *Lashkari Bazar*, IA-IB (*Mém.*

2. ALEXANDRIA IN ARACHOSIA

Arrian tells us in a few words that after the termination of the Philotas affair Alexander proceeded towards Bactra, and 'won over' the Drangians and the Gedrosians on the way, also (almost as a grammatical afterthought) the Arachosians, and then marched north to the Paropamisadae.[52] Neither the Alexander-historians, who seem to have been little interested in this stretch of Alexander's advance, nor the earlier Hellenistic geographers, refer to a city called Alexandria in Arachosia (see Table); the name occurs only in Isidore, Ammianus, Ptolemy, and Stephanus. On the other hand, Eratosthenes, the bematists (Pliny), Stephanus, and Ptolemy all refer to a city called variously Arachotoi or Arachotos, and Pliny also refers to *Arachosiorum oppidum*, to which Isidore and Ammianus do not refer. Since our early sources do not attest a city called Alexandria in Arachosia, or 'among the Arachosians', it has been much debated whether, if it existed, it was founded by Alexander, and what relation, if any, it bore to the city named Arachotoi, etc., and, inevitably, the uncompleted excavations on the site of the Old City of Kandahar, one of the localities most involved in the discussion, have thrown the matter open to further debate.[53]

We must first remark that the western literary evidence for a foundation by Alexander in Arachosia is only stronger than

DAFA 18, Paris, 1978); II, do. by J.-C. Gardin (Paris, 1963); *Archaeology of Afghanistan*, 311 ff. For the route by river see Iṣṭakhrī, BGA i. 243 (p. 141, top, Cairo edn.); Ibn Ḥawqal, ibid. ii². 417-18. Few travellers in the 19th cent. took the route from Lake Zarah to Lashkari Bazar, though C. E. Yate traversed the ground at the time of the Afghan Boundary Commission. In his later travels, recorded in great detail in his *Khūrasan and Sistan* (cf. above, n. 15), Yate studied the frontier area on the Persian side, i.e. in the neighbourhood of Zābul. The distance from Zaranj to Lashkari Bazar, on the direct route via Ḥarūrī, on the left bank where the Khwash turns south-west, is given as five marches i.e. about 150 miles, but it involved a double crossing of the river before reaching Ḥarūrī, and the route may more safely be reckoned at *c.*200 m.: the marches are given by Iṣṭakhrī, Ibn Ḥawqal and Muḳaddasī: see Le Strange, op. cit. pp. 343, 351. For the survival of the river route see Ferrier, op. cit. 428 ff. The numerous pre-Islamic sites along the lower Helmund are given by Ball, op. cit. There is a particular cluster, usually on the left bank, around Kuchnay Darwishan (Ball 595, 709, 1250) and further down river, west of Rudbar (Ball 849, 863).

[52] Arr. iii. 28. 1, quoted above, n. 33.

[53] Though I may refer the reader here to my discussion of the Greco-Roman geographical evidence in my article in *Afghan Studies*, loc. cit. the discussion that follows reaches a different conclusion: see above, n. 45. Kandahar is Ball 522.

that for an Alexandria in Sakastane if we accept that when Eratosthenes and Pliny, the latter clearly deriving from the bematists, speak of a city called 'the city Arachotoi' and *Arachosiorum oppidum* they are referring to the city called Ἀλεξάνδρεια or Ἀλεξανδρόπολις, μητρόπολις Ἀραχωσίας by Isidore. If that equation does not hold, there is no peg available in the literary wardrobe on which to hang an Alexandria of Arachosia founded by Alexander. If the literary sources were all, the name, if not the foundation, could, like Alexandria in Sakastane, be regarded as of Parthian or even later date; its attestation by the later authorities, Ptolemy, Ammianus (if he is not reproducing Eratosthenes or Pliny), and Stephanus is of course compatible with that.

Although there are a number of cities named Q.nd.h.r in the eastern Muslim world, and identification of any particular one is frequently difficult on account of the negligent and carefree descriptions of the military operations of the early Muslim conquests in the region given by the Arab writers, it seems probable that, contrary to received opinion, Alexandria in Arachosia was already known as Kandahar by the ninth century at the latest. We have already seen that it is used as equivalent to 'Alexandria of the east' in Arachosia by the earliest Islamic adapters of Ptolemy's geography, al-Khuwārizmī and Ṣuhrāb, and that identification, which stands quite outside the Iranian tradition regarding Iskander = Dhu'l-Qarnein, is of great importance.[54] Our first concern, now, is with the Hellenistic site known to have existed at Kandahar, as a point from which to reckon distances northwards.

In one respect the transmitted distances, although they still present formidable difficulties, are less open to doubt than those affecting the route from Herāt south-eastwards up to this point.

[54] For a very full, occasionally fanciful and uncritical, account of the various cities named Kandahar in Islamic sources, and of the bestowal of the name on the city of Afghanistan, see W. Ball *South Asian Studies*, 4 (1988), 115-42, 'The seven Qandahārs', which contains an analysis of the sources, which frequently confused the various cities of that name, with a very full modern bibliography. There seems little doubt that the original Arab name was al-Rukhkhaj, itself probably a corruption of some form of Arachosia. This city, and Banjaway are clearly located in the Itineraries and early geographers, as east of Bust and near the Arghandāb: see Le Strange, *LEC* 346-7, largely from Muḳaddasī. Unfortunately Le Strange did not distinguish between the various Kandahars, and the texts of the 9th-cent. adapters of Ptolemy who already identify Kandahar specifically with Iskandarīya (see above, pp. 100-1), had not been published when he wrote, though Nallino's analysis of the text of al-Khuwārizmī was available.

Though doubts may exist, or have existed, as to the identification of Kandahar, Ḳalāt-i-Ghilzai or Ghazna as the site of an Alexander-foundation, there can be no doubt as to the general direction of the route followed by Alexander's forces.[55] From Drangiana to the Indian Caucasus the most direct route northwards is that which follows the valleys of the Arghandāb and Tarnak, as far as the approximate latitude of Ghazna, at which point Alexander could have turned westwards, and crossed the Unai and Hajigak passes into the valley of Bāmiyān; this, though unlikely, is not impossible. Consequently, though the distances given by our sources and the identification of the places mentioned by them cause major problems, the general direction of the march of the army, at least as far as Ghazna, and probably beyond, is not in doubt. The distances, already noted (pp. 83–5), are as follows:[56] Eratosthenes gives 4,120 stades (515 m.) as the distance from Prophthasia εἰς Ἀραχωτούς, then another 2,000 stades (250 m.) to Ortospana and

[55] Ball, op. cit. 132–3, raises the possibility that 'Alexandria in Arachosia' should be identified with the modern Sikandarabad in the middle Helmund valley. But though the adjacent citadel, Shahr-i-Kohna, has yielded Achaemenian material (see Ball, ibid.), there can be no question of continuity in the name, which, as Ball is prepared to grant, is of modern origin, like many other Iskandarīyas, Alexandrias, etc.

[56] Droysen's discussion of the problem of the location of Alexandria in Arachosia and Arachotoi in *GE* iii. 217–20 = FT ii. 674–7, is fundamental as regards the ancient sources, but difficult to follow for a variety of reasons (notably changes of names of localities and uncertainty as to the accuracy of the modern sources used by him), and a correct understanding of the routes is best obtained by study of the day-diaries of early travellers, notably A. Conolly and Ferrier, and the summary provided by Malleson, though they were not concerned with associating the modern routes with the ancient evidence. The article of J. Fischer, (above, n. 40), should also be consulted. On the problem of the route Droysen (*GE* iii. 219 = FT ii. 676) says: 'Entweder hat dieser Weg von Prophthasia nach Arachotos eine sehr bedeutende südliche Ausbiegung (dem Lauf des Etymandros [i.e. the Helmund] folgend), so dass dann die Lage von Arachotoi 50 geogr. Meilen von Kabul auf Kelat-i-Gildschi [i.e. Ḳalāt-i-Ghilzai] fällt—oder es lag Arachotoi bedeutend oestlicher, etwa wo im Afghanenkrieg auf der Marschroute der Bombayer Colonne von Kabul nach Kalat (bei Zimmermann S. 35), der Ort Speenwarree verzeichnet ist [i.e. Spin Boldak, Ball 1108] mit der Bemerkung: Ruinen einer Stadt [mound] an einem Flusse in einem angebauten Thal (dieser Fluss heisst Argesan [i.e. Arghastan] und fliesst westlich zum Tarnak).' Though the second alternative, which involves an easterly detour almost as far as the Khojak Pass, is to be rejected, Droysen was right in seeing that the distances required a substantial extension of Alexander's route from Prophthasia, as I have indicated in the text above. Tarn's map at the back of *Alexander*, ii, correctly marks the essential diversion to Lake Zarah (cf. p. 236, and *GBI* 14, 470) for he identifies his Alexandria-Prophthasia with the site of Zaranj; cf. above, p. 131. Brunt's map at the back of his Loeb *Arrian* ii, shows the conventional route from (presumably) Farah direct to Kandahar.

the Bactrian 'trifurcation'.[57] Pliny's bematists give 565 Roman miles from Prophthasia to *Arachosiorum oppidum*, and 175 Roman miles from there to Ortospana.[58] The cumulative figures given by these two sources are, then: (*a*) Eratosthenes: Herāt–Prophthasia, 1,6(5)0 st. = *c*.200 m.; Prophthasia–Arachotoi, 4,120 st. = *c*.515 m, Arachotoi–Ortospana 2,000 st. = 250 m.: total 7,770 st. = *c*.965 miles; (*b*) Pliny (bematists): Herāt–Prophthasia 199, Prophthasia–*Arachosiorum oppidum*–*Ortospana*, 989 Roman miles (but he adds after these figures, *in quibusdam exemplaribus diversi numeri reperiuntur*). The excessive distances given for the stretch from Prophthasia to 'Arachotoi', are only, if at all, acceptable on the assumption that they include the deviation via Zaranj and Bust en route to Kandahar. In the absence of this explanation, it has hitherto been necessary to locate sites in the Arghandab valley closer to Kābul than Kandahār, on the traditional route between Sijistān and the Hindu Kush, notably at Kalāt-i-Ghilzai and Ghazna, the former some 85, the latter some 220 miles north of Kandahar, and thus *c*.590 miles from Herāt. On the above calculation this is not necessary, even though the precise distance of the additional stretch cannot be determined on the ground accurately owing to the variety of march-routes available. If we accept that Isidore's 'Alexandria in Arachosia' is correctly identified with ἡ πόλις Ἀραχωτῶν and with *Arachosiorum oppidum*, and that this is the early Hellenistic city located at Kandahar, it is not possible to assign an ancient identity to either Kalāt-i-Ghilzai or Ghazna, since neither satisfies the geographical requirement for identification with Alexandria ad Caucasum.[59] We may leave for the moment the distance-calculation for the final stretch, Alexandria in Arachosia to Alexandria ad Caucasum, while we consider the confirmation of the identification of Kandahar with Alexandria in Arachosia.

The discovery in 1958 of a rock edict of Asoka, inscribed on a fallen boulder in Greek and Aramaic, near the Qaitul ridge rising behind the Old City of Kandahar (Zor Shahr or Shahr-i-Kohna), and of a second Asokan text in Greek alone, indicated the likely

---

[57] See the passage of Eratosthenes quoted above, n. 37. Engels, op. cit. App. 5, gives a table of the bematists' measurements, which approximately coincide with the figures given here. His note to the table, on p. 158, gives the rationale of his identification of the relevant sites.

[58] See above, n. 32.

[59] See below, n. 67.

existence of a Greek community, or, at the least, of a direct line of communication with the Greek-speaking world, in that region, in the middle of the third century BC, and at the same time emphasized the importance that the Maurya king attached to the route and locality.[60] In addition the recent, and very limited, excavation of the area of the Old City brought to light both an Elamite cuneiform and an early Hellenistic Greek inscription.[61] There can be no doubt therefore that Old Kandahar, lying beside the Arghandāb, is on the site of an early Hellenistic settlement, itself on the site of an earlier Achaemenid fortress, and at present the only solidly authenticated one in southern Afghanistan, which formed the province of Harawaitha, well attested in Old Persian documents. The case for its being Alexandria in Arachosia, 'Alexandria of the East', probable in itself, is ultimately clinched, as already stated, by the explicit identification in the Arab adapters of Ptolemy. On the assumption that that identification is correct, we may look at the geographical evidence a little more closely.

Isidore, whose text, whether written in the second or first century BC,[62] certainly reflects a period when the historical topography and nomenclature of the region had changed from the earlier Hellenistic period, gives the route from Drangiana to the confines of India thus:[63] '(§ 18) Thence Sakastane of the Saka

[60] For this well-known discovery see Schlumberger, Dupont-Sommer, and Benveniste, *JA* (1958), 1 ff., and many subsequent discussions; the Greek text is reprinted as *SEG* xx. 326, with bibliography. For the second edict on a plaque, the exact provenance of which is not known, see Schlumberger, *CRAI* (1964), 126–40.

[61] These items were found in the excavations of the British Institute at Kābul in the mid-1970s, of which the final report has not yet been published. For the cuneiform inscription see *Afghan Studies*, 3–4 (1982), 53; for the Greek inscription, published originally by me in *Afghan Studies*, 2 (1979), 9 ff., see *SEG* xxx. 1664. For subsequent attempts to reconstruct the poem see *ZPE* 56 (1984), 145–7, and ibid. 60 (1985), 76 (*SEG* xxxiv. 1434). As I explain in my article, there are no positive grounds for restoring Ἀλεξ[ανδρεύς] in the lacuna in line 2 of the text. It would be exceptional (but not unparalleled) for a dedicant to refer to himself by his ethnic in making a dedication in his home-town. The supplement therefore cannot be used as a confirmation of the identification of the city.

[62] See above, pp. 88 ff. Note also Ammianus' obscure information, which can hardly be based in this instance on Eratosthenes (cf. above, pp. 94–5, for his regular use of Eratosthenes), in xxiii. 6. 72, below, p. 142, with n. 71.

[63] § 18: Ἐντεῦθεν Σακαστάνη Σακῶν Σκυθῶν, ἡ καὶ Παραιτακηνή, σχοῖνοι ξγ΄. ἔνθα Βαρδὰ πόλις καὶ Μὶν πόλις καὶ Παλακεντὶ πόλις, καὶ Σιγάλ πόλις· ἔνθα βασίλεια Σακῶν· καὶ πλησίον Ἀλεξάνδρεια πόλις (καὶ πλησίον Ἀλεξανδρόπολις πόλις). κῶμαι δὲ ἕξ. (19) Ἐντεῦθεν Ἀραχωσία, σχοῖνοι λς΄. ταύτην δὲ οἱ Πάρθοι Ἰνδικὴν Λευκὴν καλοῦσιν. ἔνθα Βιὺτ πόλις καὶ Φάρσανα πόλις καὶ Χοροχοὰδ πόλις καὶ Δημητριὰς πόλις. εἶτα Ἀλεξανδρόπολις, μητρόπολις Ἀραχωσίας· ἔστι δὲ Ἑλληνίς, καὶ παραρρεῖ αὐτὴν ποταμὸς

Scythians, also called Paraitakene, 63 schoeni (c.315 m.); there
are Barda, a city, and Min, a city, and Palakenti, a city, and Sígal,
a city; there is the capital of the Sakai; and nearby is Alexandria,
a city [and nearby is Alexandropolis, a city: *see below*], and
six villages . . . (§ 19) . . . Then Alexandropolis, metropolis of
Arachosia; and this is a Greek city, and by it flows (παραρρεῖ)
the river Arachotos. To this limit extends the Kingdom of the
Parthians.' In a previous section (§ 16) he gave his distances,
which throughout are calculated only in *schoinoi*, from Aria to the
Parthian frontier, and it is clear that the route followed is that from
Herāt to the region of Ghazna, via Kandahar and the course of the
Arghandāb river, and that the contents of both sections must be
accommodated within that geographical framework.[64]

Ἀράχωτος. ἄχρι τούτου ἐστὶν ἡ τῶν Πάρθων ἐπικράτεια. Of this whole section Ch.
Müller rightly said (ad loc., GGM i. 254), 'Pro libitu haec impune cuique adornare licet',
a warning not always heeded.

[64] Since Isidore's total measurement from the eastern frontier of Aria (§ 16) to
the Parthian frontier is 175 sch. = c.600 miles, which is approximately the distance
from Herāt to Ghazna on the direct road (reckoned above, by the modern road, at
c.590 miles; reckoned by Droysen for the same route at 120 geogr. miles = c.600
(stat). miles) Droysen (loc. cit. above, n. 56) concluded that Isidore's description
followed the direct route to India, without divergences. On the basis of this
measurement he placed the territory of Ἀναύ(β)ων χώρα (55 sch. = c.210 m.) some
30 stat. m. east of Farah, i.e. at Siahab; then 21 sch. = c.90 m. to Schorab (see
below); then began Sakastane, which, with a length of 63 sch. = c.240 m., extended to Ḳalāt-i-Ghilzai, in which overall area he placed both Alexandria and
Alexandropolis (§ 18). Sakastane is followed by Arachosia (§ 19), with a length of
36 sch. = c.135 m., in which lay Alexandropolis, the metropolis of Arachosia, and
the river Arachotos, which he (wrongly) identified with the Ghazna river, on the
basis of Ptolemy's statement that it had its outlet in a lake (vi. 20. 2: τὸ δὲ κατὰ τὴν
γινομένην ὑπ᾽ αὐτοῦ λίμνην, ἥτις καλεῖται Ἀράχωτος κρήνη, μέρος ἐπέχει μοίρας ρῖε, κῆ,
γο'), i.e. the lake Ab-Istadeh, east of Ghazna, into which the Ghazna river falls. He
therefore concluded that Isidore's Alexandria or Alexandropolis in Sakastane was
Kandahar—placing one of the two, if it had a separate existence, alternatively, at
Giriskh—while Alexandria in Arachosia-Alexandropolis, the most extreme part of
the Parthian realm, was at or near Ghazna. Though the boundaries of Sakastane
are conjectural, it is to be noted that Isidore equates it with Paraitakene, and Strabo
(522; 524) locates the latter far to the west, comprising the eastern flank of the
Zagros Mts. as also in general terms does Ptol. vi. 4. 3, ἡ μὲν παρὰ τὴν Μηδίαν πᾶσαν
Παραιτακηνή; cf. Treidler, RE, Suppbd. X, s.v. Paraitakene, cols. 478 ff. If we are to
accept Isidore's equation of Sakastane and Paraitakene we must regard (as does
Herrmann, loc. cit. below, n. 66) the area as including much of the lower Helmund
valley. Droysen's interpretation is open to fundamental criticism (see esp. Bernard,
Stud. Iran. 3 (1974), 182-3, for his error in identifying the Arachotos river with
the Ghazna river), but his approach to the text is straightforward—too straightforward for Tarn, whose picture starts from plausible emendations in the text of
Isidore, but in other respects little in his highly complex and ingenious, but
uncoordinated, argument can be accepted as reasonably substantiated.

Tarn rearranged the confused, or at least repetitive, entries in Isidore so that § 18 should read ἔνθα βασίλεια Σακῶν καὶ πλησίον Ἀλεξανδρόπολις, κῶμαι δὲ ἕξ (omitting the duplicated πλησίον Ἀλεξανδρόπολις πόλις), and § 19 Ἀλεξάνδρεια μητρόπολις Ἀραχωτῶν.[65] The argument is complex, for it involves transferring Ἀλεξάνδρεια in § 18 to § 19, and Ἀλεξανδρόπολις in § 19 back to § 18, as well as deleting the bracketed phrase, which can only be an erroneous addition. Only the deletion of this redundant phrase can be regarded as certain, but the argument for the transfer of the two names is probably also correct. His further claim that 'Alexandropolis near Sakastene' could only be Kandahar, and that by reason of its -πολις termination it could not have been founded by Alexander, but must have been attributed to him at a later date, is probably only true as far as the second part of the proposition is concerned.[66]

[65] See GBI 469 ff., esp. p. 471 n. 1.

[66] As always, Tarn's statements have to be scrutinized carefully. His almost stray remark (p. 471, top) that πλησίον in § 18 means 'near the province of Sakastene', and therefore outside it, is clearly incorrect, not only because if Alexandria was not in Sakastane, it was in Arachosia, but also because if πλησίον bore that meaning it would also apply to the following κῶμαι δὲ ἕξ, and it clearly does not; or, to put it another way, for his argument to hold water, πλησίον Ἀλεξάνδρεια should come *after* κῶμαι δὲ ἕξ (cf. below in this note for the significance of πλησίον). The problem is rather to determine where the frontier between 'Sakastane' and Arachosia lay, and that must depend, for this period, on the text of Isidore, who is the only writer (other than Ptolemy, who gives it in a corrupt form: see below, in this note) to employ the specifically Parthian term. Droysen, loc. cit., showed that the distance-figures point to a western boundary somewhere west of Girishk (between it and Wahir), and with this determination, imprecise though it is, we must be satisfied. The province or principality, then, probably occupied much of the valley of the Helmund river (cf. Herrmann, RE, s.v. Sakastene, cols. 1807 ff.; Herzfeld, Sakastan (Arch. Mitt. Iran, 4 (1931)), 1 ff. Daffinà, op. cit. passim). Droysen included Kalāt-i-Ghilzai in Sakastane, but Kiepert (ap. Droysen) thought this was too far east for that province. In any case, the important point is that Sakastane itself is a Parthian administrative unit (i.e. of the end of the 2nd cent. (cf. Hermann, loc. cit.)), and cannot have been the original name of the Alexandria so called in § 18, if that was an early foundation. It should be noted that Tarn, loc. cit. and elsewhere, always refers to the province as Σακαστηνή, but the superior MS of Isidore, A (Paris 443), has Σακαστάνη, as with some other locations which may thereby reveal their Parthian origin; the form with two etas is found in the second MS (Paris 571), which was followed by Fabricius in his edition of 1849. Müller commented, ad loc., 'Σακαστηνῆς temere, ut solet, B; Fabricius'. (Schoff retains the form in alpha.) In Ptol. vi. 19. 3, Σακαστάνη has become Τατακηνή, correctly described as the χώρα between Drangiana and Arachosia. The location in Sakastane, then, is a good, but not a conclusive, reason for regarding the foundation as late, as Tarn urged on account of its -πολις termination. Tarn was content that Alexandria (Alexandropolis) in Sakastane should be Kandahar, but his argument has to be wholly reconsidered in the light of the excavation of Kandahar, which shows that

However, his conclusion, essentially that of Droysen, that Alexandria in Arachosia was to be placed at Ghazna, can hardly stand.[67] In view of the undoubted presence of both Achaemenid

Old Kandahar was both an Achaemenid and an early Hellenistic centre. Isidore says clearly that the Parthians did not call Arachosia by that name; they called it 'White India'. I no longer believe that the site at Kandahar can convincingly be equated with Alexandria in Sakastane, as I suggested in *Afghan Studies*, 2 (1979), 13, with notes, with reference to the recent discussions of Fischer and Brunt. As indicated in the text, the case for Alexandria in Arachosia seems to be as strong as could be expected, from a combination of the excavation and the Arab adapters of Ptolemy (whom I had not studied when I wrote my article), while Alexandria in Sakastane = Alexandropolis can be conveniently accommodated, as a foundation of a later date, or as a renaming of a site in the area of Zaranj. This interpretation is substantiated by the repetition of the preposition πλησίον, which does not otherwise occur in the text of Isidore. His Stations are invariably indicated by ἐντεῦθεν and εἶτα to mark sequences of distance and ἔνθα to mark location. The repetition confirms Tarn's view that one of the two clauses is an interpolation, since the word would be most unlikely to be used in two successive clauses. That being so, it is most likely that the 'correction' is due to someone (the excerptor, no doubt) who was aware of the error over Ἀλεξάνδρεια in §18 and Ἀλεξανδρόπολις in §19. The use of πλησίον in §18 is an indication that the site in question lay off the main route of the Σταθμοί, for if it had been on the through-route either ἐντεῦθεν (εἶτα) or ἔνθα would have been used. This fits well with the location of Alexandreia (Alexandropolis) at or near Zaranj, which lay off the main route from Aria (§16) to Arachosia (§19). Bernard, loc. cit. maintained that the city of Arachotoi and Alexandropolis referred to the same place, the capital of Arachosia, also Alexandria in Arachosia, Alexandropolis simply representing a change of name in the Parthian period, and that Kandahar was the only site involved. The evident corruption in the text of Isidore makes this very uncertain. That there are two Arachosian Alexandrias in Stephanus' list (12 and 15) derives probably ultimately from the fact that according to Strabo Eratosthenes (513 = Erat. IIIB 63 quoted above, p. 92 n. 30) placed an Arachosia along the Oxus. But the attribution to Eratosthenes can hardly stand, whether the mistake be Strabo's or another's, for Eratosthenes knew very well that Arachosia was south of the Hindu Kush (see IIIB 23). Several explanations have been offered (see Berger, 318-19), of which the most simple is to read Ἀρ(ε)ίους for Ἀραχωτούς, but the emendation has no textual justification.

[67] See Tarn, 470-1. Tarn says that this foundation [that of Alexandria in Arachosia] was made '*before* (Tarn's italics) Alexander crossed the Caucasus into the Kābul valley, but when he was already in the hills', quoting Arr. iii. 28. 4; whereas in his discussion of Alexandria ad Caucasum, pp. 461 ff., which, he accepts, lay near the junction of the Panshir and Ghorband rivers, 'in radicibus montis' (Curt. Ruf. vii. 3. 23), he does not quote Arrian. If this is a correct interpretation of his views it is clear that he is mistaken, for the hills north of Ghazna could hardly be described as forming part of the Caucasus-Hindu Kush range, from which, on the direct route, they are separated by the winding course of the Lugar valley and the whole plain of Kābul itself. It is true that Ghazna lies at a higher altitude than Kābul, but its position, in my opinion, does not permit its identification with Alexandria ad Caucasum. The Arab texts, followed by many European travellers, emphasize the extremes of climate, especially the extreme cold, prevailing at Ghazna (see e.g. Yākūt s.v.; Elphinstone, *Account of the Kingdom of Caubul* (3rd. edn.,

and early Hellenistic material at Kandahar, it is impossible to deny that this too was an Achaemenid settlement developed either by Alexander or (less probably) by Seleucus Nicator. Excavations at Ghazna have not penetrated to pre-Islamic levels, and it is therefore impossible to say what might lie beneath the great mound. The most straightforward solution of the problem seems to be that Alexandria (or Alexandropolis) in Sakastane lay at or near Zaranj, and was a later foundation, while Alexandria the metropolis of Arachosia, Alexander's foundation, was indeed the excavated site of Kandahar. At present there seems to be no role, or evidence, for Ghazna as an early foundation. It is regrettable in this context that the Arab Itineraries, so valuable for routes from Herāt to the valley of the Helmund, largely cease for the route from Kandahar northwards: we do not have their guidance in locating the cities on the northern and southern faces of the Hindu Kush. The post-antique routes taken to reach Transoxiana from Mashshad passed north of Herāt by the route to the greater Merv, or via Maimana to Balkh, and not by the eastern river-valleys, which would have added greatly to their journey.[68] Consequently we must rely on modern estimates, which are not infrequently based on inapplicable data, notably those associated with modern routes. To assess their value we must turn to the next city on our roster, Alexandria ad Caucasum, to which the major distances were reckoned in our ancient Greek and Latin sources.

3. ALEXANDRIA ἐν Παροπαμισάδαις or ἐν Ὠπιανῆι

Arrian describes the position of this foundation in very general terms. After leaving Prophthasia (having despatched a force back to deal with a further insurrection of the Arians under Satibarzanes) Ἀλέξανδρος πρὸς Καύκασον τὸ ὄρος ἦγεν, ἵνα καὶ πόλιν

London, 1839; repr. Karachi, ed. O. Caroe, 1972), i. 181–2: 'Ascending the valley of the Turnuk, we at last reach the level of Ghuznee, which is generally mentioned as the coldest part of the plain country in the Caubul dominions . . . For the greater part of the winter the inhabitants seldom quit their houses; and even in the city of Ghuznee the snow has been known to lie deep for some time after the vernal equinox . . . Caubul itself, being lower than Ghuznee, and more enclosed by hills, appears not to suffer so much from cold.'). For the archaeological evidence from Ghazna see Ball 358 (cf. 385: nothing pre-Ghūrid/Ghaznavid).

[68] For this northern route see the map given in A. Sprenger's *Post-und Reiserouten des Orients*, Map 1, and the accompanying text in ch. 1.

ἔκτισε καὶ ὠνόμασεν Ἀλεξάνδρειαν. That is all that he tells us, but Diodorus adds that the city stood at the 'entrance' (εἰσβολή), which led into 'Media'.[69] The geographical sources, that is, the bematists represented by Pliny, following the southern route from Alexandria in Ariana = Herāt via 'Prophthasia of Drangiana' attest an 'Alexandri oppidum' fifty miles north of Ortospana, itself 175 miles from 'Arachosiorum oppidum' = Alexandria in Arachosia = Kandahar, therefore 225 miles in all from Kandahar; while Eratosthenes places 'Arachotoi the city', to which we have given the same ancient equation, 4,120 stades' (515 miles) beyond 'Prophthasia of Drangiana', and Ortospana 2,000 stades (250 miles) north of Ἀραχωτοί. In effect, these two strands of the bematists' measurements, which, as we have seen, differ by fifty miles for the distance from Prophthasia to Alexandria in Arachosia, differ by only twenty-five miles for the total distance from Alexandria in Ariana to Ortospana. In view of the possibility of variations in routes on the one hand and of discrepancies in the transmission of the figures, mentioned by Pliny, that is a reasonable congruence. Eratosthenes does not mention Alexandria ad Caucasum, since after referring to the Bactrian τρίοδος at Ortospana he diverges to give the measurements eastwards to τὰ ὅρια τῆς Ἰνδικῆς, whereas Pliny includes the distance to Alexandria before branching off to the Kophen river. In another passage, however, speaking of the route from Aria to Bactria Eratosthenes says that one direct route lay 'through Bactria and the crossing of the mountain to Ortospana and to the trifurcation of the ways from Bactra which is in the Paropamisadai', while the other 'diverged a little' passing via Prophthasia (see p. 120). Unfortunately he, or at least Strabo, gives no distances in this passage, but the natural interpretation is that Ortospana lay within the east–west orientation of the Hindu Kush, as reached from Herāt via the course of the Hari-Rūd along the foothills of the Koh-i-Bābā and the valley

---

[69] Arr. iii. 28.4; Diod. xvii. 83. 1: πόλιν ἔκτισε κατὰ τὴν εἰσβολὴν τὴν φέρουσαν εἰς τὴν Μηδικήν, ἣν ὠνόμασεν Ἀλεξάνδρειαν. The interpretation of the erroneous Μηδικήν is not of great importance, since it cannot be correct, but the use of εἰσβολήν is of significance as indicating that the ultimate source, whatever that was, thought that the city stood close to the entrance, that is, a pass of the Hindu Kush, to the region in question. Bernard, *JS* (1982), 217 ff., accepting Reiske's probable emendation of Μηδικήν to Ἰνδικήν, rightly rejects the view of Goukowsky, Diod. xvii (Budé edn.), 236–7, that Diodorus is referring to Alexandria Oxiana here; cf. below, n. 93. Nobody can assess the extent of error that may lie behind Diodorus, who places Alexandria ad Caucasum north of the mountain.

of Bāmiyān, where Ortospana lay at the trifurcation from Bactra. The trifurcation has been understood to be at or near the point where the Ghorband and the Panshir valleys from the west and north meet, and their combined rivers flow south to meet the Kābul valley near Charikar, forty miles north of Kābul, at (H)Opiān or Begrām-Kapisa.[70] If that description is correct, Ortospana must have been close to Begrām, and Alexander's new city will have been some fifty miles north of it. However, a site fifty miles north from Opiān or Begrām in the direction of Bactria, by any of the direct north-south passes, would lie on the northern slopes of the mountain, which is clearly unsuitable from the description given of its location. We must look elsewhere for the solution, which is provided both by the second passage of Eratosthenes quoted above, relating to Ortospana, and by the distance of fifty miles between 'Alexandri Oppidum' and Ortospana given by Pliny. The natural interpretation of Eratosthenes' description of Ortospana is that it lay where three roads met, en route to Bactria. We must, then, seek a place where three routes, including passes, and defiles and river-valleys, not only the latter, meet. That requirement is best met by a point in the area of Bāmiyān where the route via the Hajigak pass from the south joins that valley, and almost opposite it on the north, the passes and valleys lead down to Turkestan, while the road from the west, from Herāt, which joins them at this point, continues its traverse over the Shībar pass down to the Kūhistān, 'high land', the mountain-ringed basin north of Kābul. Ortospana is called a city (even a *'clara urbs'*) only by Ammianus, and we may wonder what authority and pedigree this strange statement (a striking contrast to his description of Alexandria in Arachosia as a *'civitas vilis'*) has;[71] it can hardly reflect Eratos-

---

[70] See e.g. Tarn, *GBI* 460-1. Foucher, *Vieille Route*, i. 21, fig. 6, has a clear schematic plan of the routes involved.

[71] xxiii. 6. 70: *habent autem* (the grammatical subject is *Paropanisadae* in the previous sentence) *etiam civitates aliquas, quibus clariores sunt Agazaca et Naulibus et Orthospana, unde litorea navigatio ad usque Mediae fines, portis proximos Caspiis stadiorum sunt duo milia et ducenta.* The description is hardly compatible (even if it were true) with Eratosthenes' bare statement of distances, for these are measured from the south, as described in the text. Ammianus, whose description of Alexandria in Egypt, discussed above, p. 18 n. 37, shows his power of fantasy, seems to have invented his descriptions of the 'cities' in the eastern provinces, perhaps assisted by scrutiny of a schematic illustrated itinerary. Ibid. § 71, he says that Prophthasia and Ariaspe were the pride of the Drangians *'ut opulenta et clara'*. For Alexandria in Arachosia, *civitas vilis*, see ibid. 72: *'hic* [in Arachosia] *quoque civitates sunt inter alias*

thenes' description of it, for he calls it only a trifurcation, though, of course, it may naturally have become a city of some sort in the course of time. It was in his time a strategic crossroads, which may have been guarded by a fort, and its position must have been almost identical with, or close to either the site of the striking Muslim fortress of Shahr-i-Zuhak, which stands precisely where the Hajigak pass debouches on the plain of Bāmiyān, or slightly further west in the plain itself, at the fortress site of Shahr-i-Ghulghula, probably the Ghūrid capital of the region, close to the two northern transits of the mountain via the Balkh and the Dara Yusuf rivers. Unfortunately, neither fort has been more than superficially excavated, and the earliest recorded finds are of the Kushan period or later.[72] We must examine the implications and consequences of this location for Ortospana more closely.

In his list of the πόλεις καὶ κῶμαι of the Paropamisadai Ptolemy identifies Ortospana with Kaboura, *Κάβουρα ἡ καὶ Ὀρτόσπανα*, and on that account the location has been identified with Kābul, but to accomodate that solution the text of Eratosthenes must be emended so that the fifty miles given by Pliny for the distance from Ortospana to 'Alexandri Oppidum' are taken to represent the distance between Kābul and (H)Opiān-Begrām. Though no excavated archaeological remains of the pre-Kushan period have been found in or near Kābul, a coin-hoard of the fourth century BC found on the outskirts of the city itself, though of uncertain significance, suggests some link with the trading pattern of the area, of which Begrām-Kapisa was later the focal point.[73] However, another city,

---

viles, Alexandria et Arbaca et Choaspa'. (For the locations assigned to them by Ptolemy see vi. 20. 4, among the πόλεις καὶ κῶμαι of Arachosia.)

[72] See Ball 1042 (Shahr-i-Ghulghula: the earliest material observed is said to be late Sassanian, and very little is pre-Islamic. There was a trial excavation by Allchin and Codrington in 1951, but it is apparently unpublished); 1052 (Shahr-i-Zuhak, no record of anything pre-Hephthalite). The identification of Ortospana with the Sanskrit Urddhasthana (*vel sim.*), argued by Cunningham, *Ancient Geography of India*, i (London, 1871), 35, and accepted by Foucher, *VR* 213 f. has not found other supporters. Even if it happened to be correct, it would not affect the argument advanced in the text here. W. Aly, *Strabon von Amaseia* (Antiquitas, Reihe 1 (5), Bonn, 1957), 147, broadly shares my view as to the role of Ortospana: 'Es war das Posthaus, wo die Strasse die von Baktra herkam, nach Indien einmündete, so wie das Posthaus Spondinig an den Vintschgaustrasse dort liegt, wo die Stilfserjochstrasse einmündet, kein Ort, sondern nur ein Haus.'

[73] The name Kaboura is transmitted under various forms in the MSS of Ptol. vi. 18. 5: *Κάβουρα, Καρούρα, Καβούρα, Κανούπα* etc, of which the first has the best authority.: see Ronca's edn. ad loc.. The identification of Ortospana with either Kābul itself, or the Bālā Hissar close to it, was put forward by Cunningham, op. cit.

itself called Kophen, referred to only by Stephanus, who identifies it with 'Arachosia', apparently stood close to the Kābul (Kophen) river, on or near the site of Kābul, and Ptolemy's identification of Ortospana with the otherwise unknown Kaboura or Karoura is problematical.[74] In these circumstances the description given by

35 and accepted by Foucher, *VR* 213 f., who was keen to emphasize that Ortospana was a significant city ('Bornons-nous à saluer pour l'instant l'avènement de cette ville dans l'histoire . . . et acceptons-en les conséquences immédiates'), Ghirshman, *Begram* (see below, n. 80), p. 9, and Tarn, *GBI* loc. cit. and p. 471, who accepted the identification with the Bālā Hissar, and emended the relevant passage of Eratosthenes in Strab. 514 (Erat. IIIB 20), which reads as follows: εἶτ' εἰς Ἀραχωτοὺς τὴν πόλιν τετρακισχιλίους ἑκατὸν εἴκοσιν, εἶτ' εἰς Ὀρτόσπανα, ἐπὶ τὴν ἐκ Βάκτρων τρίοδον, δισχιλίους, κ.τ.λ. to εἶτ' εἰς Ὀρτόσπανα [. . . (figure) εἶτ'] ἐπὶ τὴν ἐκ Βάκτρων τρίοδον, thus avoiding the difficulty regarding the position of Ortospana (p. 461: 'Ortospana-Kabul was nowhere near the τρίοδος.'). The basis for this 'certainty' is that Kophen must be Kābul (see n. 74). For obvious reasons, I do not accept this reasoning, or his characteristically swift dismissal of the parallel passage, Str. 724 (Erat. ibid.): ἡ μὲν ἐπ' εὐθείας διὰ τῆς Βακτριανῆς καὶ τῆς ὑπερβάσεως τοῦ ὄρους εἰς Ὀρτόσπανα ἐπὶ τὴν ἐκ Βάκτρων τρίοδον ἥτις ἐστὶν ἐν τοῖς Παροπαμισάδαις: 'The words εἰς Ὀρτόσπανα, which have got in from xi. 514, make nonsense and should be omitted; the meaning is quite simple, "the direct road through Bactria and across the Hindu Kush to the τρίοδος in the Paropamisadae".' The archaeological material from Kābul is meagre. Kushan or Sassanian coins were found in 1933 at Tepe Maranjan, where a Buddhist monastery was excavated (see J. Hackin and J. Carl, *Nouvelles recherches archéologiques à Bāmiyān* (*Mém.* DAFA 3 (Paris, 1933)). The main find has been that of a 4th-century BC coin-hoard at Chaman-i-Houzouri in 1933, pub. Schlumberger, *Mém.* DAFA 14 (Paris, 1953), 1–64, 'L'Argent grec dans l'empire achéménide' (cf. the summary in *Archaeology in Afghanistan*, 202–3). The hoard contained a number of Greek, especially Athenian, coins, and a few *sigloi*, thus conforming to the general pattern of such hoards (e.g. from the Oxus Treasure and Balkh). No late Achaemenian hoard of this type has been found at Aï Khanūm. There is no material evidence for any pre-Muslim settlement in the plain of Kābul (see Ball 483), and Foucher, *VR* ii. 202, well described the area as lying outside the early network of communications: 'la situation de cette ville à l'écart de la grande artère Nord–Sud nous explicerait du même coup pourquoi il est si peu question d'elle dans les textes anciens.' The earliest Arab names for the chief city of this area, Kābulistān, are Jurwas(h) (Ja'qūbī, *BGA* vii. 290) or Jarwīn (see Wiet's trans., p. 106 n. 5), and Ṭābān (Iṣṭakhrī, *BGA* i. 280 + vol. iv. 424 = Yākūt, ii. 454, s.v. Ṭābān: qarīya bil-Khābūr), names of uncertain origin: see Le Strange, *LEC* 349.

[74] For Kophen see Steph. s.v. Ἀραχωσία, πόλις οὐκ ἄπωθεν Μασσαγετῶν, Στράβων ἑνδεκάτηι, ὑπὸ Σεμιράμεως κτισθεῖσα, ἥτις καὶ Κωφὴν ἐκαλεῖτο. οἱ πολῖται Ἀραχώσιοι, τῆς δὲ Κωφῆνος Κωφήνιοι. Meineke ad loc. refers this quotation to Str. 516, but though Strabo there and in 513 talks about the Massegetai (513 = Erat. IIIB 63; cf. above, n. 66), he does not mention Kophen, unrecorded outside Stephanus, whose identification of it with 'the city Arachosia, not far from the Massegetai', which we have encountered more than once (see n. 66) is not reassuring. Ptol. vi. 18. 3, does not list Κωφήν. Cunningham, loc. cit. n. 72, identified Kābul itself with Nikaia (see below, n. 79), and assigned Kaboura to an unspecified location in the Lugar valley. I do not believe that Kābul can meet the very specific requirements of Eratosthenes' description of the location of Ortospana, for the reasons indicated. It is a puzzling

Eratosthenes of the position of Ortospana must be left to speak for itself, which it does very eloquently. As we shall see, it was probably by way of, or close to, Ortospana that Alexander returned to the south side of the Hindu Kush after his campaigns in Bactria and Sogdiana, but the route had no doubt been located on the way north, perhaps even before he left Herāt for the first time.

It may be helpful at this point to remind readers that the Paropamisadai formed the northern boundary of Eratosthenes' second Sphragis, and that he has no information about Bactria or Sogdiana. At the same time, the other end of the chain of evidence, consisting of the Itineraries and other early Arab geographical texts, has little to say about Bactria south of the Oxus, since the natural route from Mashshad to Balkh, and thence eastward and northward, was, as I have noted above, either by Maimana or Merv Shāhijān. It is consequently the more to be regretted that Arrian refers only briefly to Alexander's movements in the area between the mountain and the river Oxus. However, with one possible exception, that of Alexandria in Oxiana, there is no suggestion in any of our sources that any cities founded by him, or named after him, lay in this area, though survey shows that it was well supplied with Achaemenid settlements and strongpoints.[75]

Arrian says that on his return journey two years later, before reaching the Kābul (Kophen) river, the course of which he subsequently followed in a general easterly direction at least to its junction with the Kunar river, Alexander 'came to the city Nikaia, and sacrificed to Athena'.[76] Though he does not specifically say so,

feature of Ptolemy's text that he should here use the double nomenclature, K. ἡ καὶ Ὀρτόσπανα, a formula which occurs nowhere else in bk. vi (it is common enough in bk. v). It cannot be a simple case of a foreign name used alongside a Greek one, as in v. 4. 8, Ἀλεξάνδρου νῆσος ἡ καὶ Ἀρακία, since neither name is Greek. The introduction of Kophen into the story increases the obscurity of the whole matter, but, if it has any real existence apart from the river-name, it encourages one to seek for independent locations for Kaboura and Ortospana.

[75] For these see e.g. Ball, 611 (Kirghiz Tepe, map 85); 666 (Kutlug Tepe, map 80); 745 (Mundik Tepe, map 83); 741 (Mullah Quli, map 85); 927 (Quchi, map 85); 930–1 (Kundūz, map 85); 933 (Qunza, map 85); 959 (Rud-i Shahrawan, maps. 87–9, sites in the river valley north of Taluqan); 1086 (Shish-Tepe, map 88, west of Taluqan); 1225 (Uvlia Tepe, map 80, c. 40 km. NW of Balkh). They lie especially in the valleys formed by the southern tributaries of the Oxus, north of the main road between Kundūz and Taluqan, and between the Rostaq range and the Oxus, on both sides of Aï Khanūm. They are especially clustered in the region of Kundūz (see Ball, map 85).

[76] iv. 22. 6: ἀφικόμενος δὲ ἐς Νίκαιαν πόλιν καὶ τῆι Ἀθηνᾶι θύσας προὐχώρει ὡς ἐπὶ τὸν Κωφῆνα, κ.τ.λ.

his language suggests that the city was already in existence, and
was therefore perhaps one of the subsidiary foundations ('other
cities') made by Alexander before he crossed the mountain northwards, which are mentioned by Diodorus.[77] It is perhaps unlikely
that he would have undertaken the establishment of two cities
close together in the relatively small pocket of land between the
confluence of the Kābul and the Ghorband rivers and the foot of
the mountain, and the site should probably be looked for further
east, in the Laghman area: the language of Arrian is imprecise at
this point.[78] Many suggestions have been made as to its location,
but it remains quite uncertain.[79]

We must now consider the site at the modern Begrām, 'the
ruins', one of the most notable archaeological sites in Afghanistan.
Situated at the junction of the Ghorband and the Panjshir rivers,
some ten kilometres north of Charikar, on the south bank of
the united rivers, the excavation of the site, consisting of two

[77] xvii, 83, 2: Ὁ δ' Ἀλέξανδρος καὶ ἄλλας πόλεις ἔκτισεν, ἡμέρας ὁδὸν ἀπεχούσας τῆς
Ἀλεξανδρείας; cf. Brunt on Arr. iii. 28. 4 (n. 6).
[78] iv. 22. 4: ὑπερβαλὼν δὲ τὸν Καύκασον ἐν δέκα ἡμέραις ἀφίκετο εἰς Ἀλεξάνδρειαν
πόλιν κτισθεῖσαν ἐν Παραπαμισάδαις, ὅτε τὸ πρῶτον ἐπὶ Βάκτρων ἐστέλλετο . . . (6)
ἀφικόμενος δὲ ἐς Νίκαιαν πόλιν καὶ τῆι Ἀθηνᾶι θύσας προὐχώρει ὡς ἐπὶ τὸν Κωφῆνα,
προπέμψας κήρυκα ὡς Ταξίλην, κ.τ.λ.. Nikaia is mentioned in Itin. Alex. civ: undecima
die quam super molitus est illic Alexandriam venit. Transmissis inde regionibus
Parapapisamidium (sic) perque Nicaeam oppidum et Cophaena flumen Indum petere
contendit, etc., reflecting Arrian's narrative.
[79] O. Stein, RE, s.v. Nikaia (8), gives a list of suggested identifications,
whose diversity shows the impossibility of reaching any conclusion: Ritter and
Cunningham chose Kābul, Smith, Early Hist. of India, 53, and Foucher (CRAI
(1939), 435 ff.; id. Vieille Route, ii. 205 (cf. his map, ibid. fig. 36)) a site some
15 m. NW of Jalalabad; others (Trinkler, Petermann's Mitth. 196 (1928), 58)
Begrām itself (there is, of course, nothing in the literary evidence that suggests that
Begrām was Alexandria ad Caucasum, likely though that is on other grounds: see
below). If we bear in mind that the Kophen river would end its long course in the
Indus and therefore that a reference to it might be to a point considerably to the
east of its junction with the Panjshir, the reference to the dispatch of a herald to
Taxiles might indicate that a site somewhere in the Laghman area, as suggested by
Smith and Foucher, cannot be excluded. It is true that Alexander's own route
skirted the southern side of the Kafiristān range, north of the Kābul river and therefore to the north of Jalalabad, but the general direction of his movements was
towards the Indus valley, which figures as the next main focus of Arrian's narrative. The precise site selected on topographical grounds by Foucher, Mandawara, just
north of the Kābul river before it is joined by the Alinghar and Alishang rivers,
flowing down from the Kafiristān mountains, has not been investigated in detail:
Ball's account of it (705, and map 112) is not encouraging: 'Many mounds in and
around the village. On a hill to the north are some petroglyphs of ibex.' In any case,
as Bevan, in CHI i. 348 n. 3, rightly saw, Nikaia was not itself on the river:
Alexander advanced on there to the river; cf. Arrian, quoted above, n. 76.

complexes, lying on a north–south orientation on a low plateau, by the French Archaeological Mission in the years 1936 to 1946, though only partial, yielded splendid treasures of both eastern and western art, which testified to its role as the centre of a wealthy state, indeed empire, in the early Roman Imperial period.[80] The French excavators concluded that the site was that of the Kushan 'summer capital', the 'Capisa', mentioned by Pliny as the capital of 'Capisene', and by Ptolemy as a city or village of the Paropamisadai.[81] That Kapisa had been in existence in the Achaemenid period is clear from the reference in the Behistūn inscription to 'a fort named Kapisakani (in Arachosia)', where a battle was fought which finds an echo in Pliny and Solinus.[82] The site itself has not vouchsafed its Greek name, and the question naturally arises whether this rich site of the Kushan period, sitting at the junction of the great rivers, was originally Alexandria ad Caucasum, or, more accurately, originally Kapisakani, then Alexandria ad Caucasum, before becoming the summer capital of the Kushan and eventually the Hephthalite kings, the Kapisa of the western traditions. Other possibilities exist.

Neither the literary sources nor the archaeological evidence

[80] For the excavations see J. and J.-R. Hackin, *Mém.* DAFA 9(1) and 9(2) (1939), *Recherches Archéologiques à Begram (Chantier no.* 2,); ibid. 11 (2 vols.) (1954), by J. Hackin, *Nouvelles recherches archéologiques à Begram*; ibid. 12 (1946), Ghirshman, *Begram, Recherches archéologiques et historiques* (ibid 79 (1946) p. 2+pls. i.-ii. For a summary see *Archaeology in Afghanistan*, 275 ff.; Ball 122 (with plan, map 9). Begrām is a Turki(?) word simply meaning 'city', and there are other Begrāms in the region between the Hindu Kush and the Indus and in Gandhara. Foucher, p. 140 etc., rightly refers to the excavated Begrām as 'Le Begram de Kapisa', and (see Index, p. 409, and cf. p. 152, and his map, fig. 7, p. 31)), to 'the Begram of Nagarahara' (i.e. Haḍḍa); cf. Beal, *Buddhist Records of the Western World* (see below, p. 220 n. 8) i. 95. n. 48); Holdich, *Gates of India* p. 394.

[81] *NH* vi. 92: *A proximis Indo gentibus montana. Capisene habuit Capisam urbem quam diruit Cyrus.* cf. Solin. 211. 11: *Proximam Indo flumini urbem habuere Caphisam, quam Cyrus diruit;* Ptol. vi. 18, 4: πόλεις δέ εἰσιν ἐν τοῖς Παροπανισάδαις καὶ κῶμαι αἵδε . . . Κάπισα (Κάτισα al.) . . . ριῆ γο′ λζ̄.

[82] See Kent, *Old Pers. Gram.* DBIII 126 1. 60: 'A fortress by name Kapishakani— there they joined battle.' Cf. previous note. Bernard, *Studia Iranica*, 3 (1974), 177 ff., stressed that there was another Kapisa, mentioned in the Behistūn inscription, in the area of Kandahar, which may have been the city destroyed by Cyrus, and it must be admitted that since the Old City of Kandahar was undoubtedly an Achaemenian fortress before it was an Alexander-foundation, this is not impossible, but it involves the supposition of deep-seated corruption and confusion in the text of Pliny (itself by no means an impossibility). This does not directly affect the possible identification of Alexandria ad Caucasum with Begrām, even if no identifiable Achaemenian level has been found there. Pliny-Solinus' *proximam Indo flumini urbem* (cf. Pliny quoted above (n. 81)) fits Kandahar less well than Begrām.

provide any information on this particular score. The excavations
have yielded no small finds that can be dated earlier, on comparative grounds, than the first century AD, and though Masson
acquired thousands of coins there, none was of pre-Bactrian date.
The oldest structural remains, such as they are, hardly do more
than indicate the existence of a pre-Kushan occupation. It is therefore not surprising that the excavators themselves did not identify
the site with Alexandria, for which they proposed as possible
candidates a number of unexcavated sites in the Kūhistān, in the
general area of the junction of the rivers, both to the west and the
east of the junction.

A different, possibly more plausible, identification of the site of
Alexandria ad Caucasum is reached by another argument, which
was put forward by Cunningham, and elaborated by Tarn.[83]
Stephanus' fifth Alexandria is ἡ ἐν τῆι Ὠπιανῆι κατὰ τὴν Ἰνδικήν, and
a village north of Charikar bears, or bore, the name (H)Opiān or
(H)Upiān. The site is still identifiable by a small tel, with the ruins of
a stupa, which stands at the mouth of the Ghorband valley (to the
west of the modern motor road), and facing Begrām, which lies
a few miles east at the junction of the Ghorband and Panjshir
rivers. Opiane is otherwise unknown in ancient sources,[84] and

[83] See Cunningham, op. cit. 25 ff.; Tarn, *GBI* 96-7, 460-1. The location of
(H)Opiān is frequently referred to in modern discussions of the historical topography
of the area (see e.g. Foucher, *VR* 143, 203) without a specific identification with an
ancient site. Masson, *Narrative*, iii. 148-70 (a chapter which contains his views on
the antiquities of the Kūhistān of Kābul) was already aware of the possibilities of
Upiān. He writes (p. 161) 'without affecting the probability that at Begram, or
in its immediate neighbourhood, was the site of Alexandria ad Caucasum, it will
be remembered that the narratives of Chinese travellers expressly state that,
subsequently, there was a capital city in this part of the country called Hu'pi'ān. A
locality of this name still exists between Cha'r'ika'r and Tu'tam Dā; and I have noted
many vestiges of antiquity, yet, as they are, exclusively, of a sepulchral and
religious character, the site of the city to which they refer may rather be looked for
at the actual village of Malek H'upi'ān, on the plain below, and near Cha'ri'ka'r, by
which it may have been replaced as the principal town, as, more anciently, it superseded another, perhaps Alexandria itself.' Cf. below, n. 88.

[84] Not quite, perhaps. Hecataeus knew of a tribe called the Ὠπίαι, and refers to
a τεῖχος βασιλήϊον, an Achaemenian fort, in their territory, which he places on the
west bank of the Indus. Hec. *FGrH* 1 F299 (Steph. s.v. Ὠπίαι) ἔθνος Ἰνδικόν. Ἑκαταῖος
Ἀσίαι· ἐν δὲ αὐτοῖσι οἰκέουσι ἄνθρωποι παρὰ τὸν Ἰνδὸν ποταμόν, ἐν δὲ τεῖχος βασιλήϊον.
μέχρι τούτου Ὠπίαι, ἀπὸ δὲ τούτων ἐρημίη μέχρις Ἰνδῶν. On account of this Stein,
RE, s.v. Opiai and Opiane, leaves the location of Opiāne open, as between the
neighbourhood of the modern Hopiān and the Indus valley. The presence of a τεῖχος
βασιλήϊον suggests that the Opiai must have had some permanent settlement in the
form either of an Achaemenian garrison or that of a local chieftain (for the term

perhaps the presumed survival of the place-name over so long a period is an insufficient foundation for the identification. Its absence from the passages of Eratosthenes quoted by Strabo is worth noting, since the geographer knew Ariana, Drangiana, and Arachosia, but that argument cannot be decisive against the historicity of the name, both because the city might originally have been called ἐν Παροπαμισάδαις, and only later ἐν Ὠπιανῆι, and because there can be no guarantee that the text of Eratosthenes, as transmitted by Strabo, is complete in this respect. Stephanus' list of Alexandrias shows some signs of confusion in the Asiatic items, and the presence of both Ἀλεξάνδρεια ἐν Ὠπιανῆι and (as no. 17) Ἀλεξάνδρεια ἐν Παροπαμισάδαις may have arisen from a failure to identify the two cities. It is also a difficulty that Pliny, clearly referring to the region in question, calls it Capisene.[85] Moreover, while it is true that Masson saw abundant signs of ancient occupation at Opiān[86], and that, like Begrām, it stands at the parting of the ways between Bactria and the route to the Indus and to Arachosia (at the crossing of a land-route, whereas Begrām is at the nodal point of the river-system), the site seems in itself too small for a substantial city.[87] There seems, then, no decisive reason to prefer H(O)piān to Begrām as the most probable site for Alexander's city.[88] At the same

cf. Hdt. vii. 59). For Hsüan-Tsang's reference to Ho-pi-na see below, n. 88 and p. 230 n. 8.

[85] Freinshe(i)m (see Meineke, ad loc.) proposed Ὀξιανῆι, which cuts the knot since ἐν Ὠξιανῆι is not listed by Stephanus (see below, p. 155). Note that his sixth city, ἕκτη πάλιν (?πόλις) Ἰνδικῆς is the only item without further specification, and could derive from an erroneous entry at some stage. For Capisene see Pliny, vi. 92, (quoted) above, n. 81 and below, n. 88.

[86] See Masson, quoted in n. 83; Cunningham, loc. cit. Although it is true that some provincial regional names survived as townships (for instance Aria ⟩ Herāt, Arachosia ⟩ Rhukhkhaj), and in those cases the linguistic link with early Arab forms is perfectly comprehensible, it seems unlikely that the term could survive, vowels, root and stem all unchanged, until modern times.

[87] Cunningham loc. cit. supposed that in due course H(O)piān and Begrām, which he supposed to be Pliny's Cartana (vi, 23: *Cartana oppidum sub Caucaso, quod postea Tetragonis dictum. Haec regio est ex adverso Bactriae. Opiorum (regio) deinde cuius oppidum Alexandria a conditore dictum*), Ptolemy's Καίσανα or Κάρνασα (vii. 1. 43), were merged, but modern excavation of Begrām and investigations in the area do nothing to support that hypothesis. Tarn's view (*GBI* 97–8, 460) that the native Kapisa on the east bank, and the new Alexandria on the west, constituted a double city, Alexandria-Kapisa, was abandoned by him in the Addenda to the 2nd edn. (p. 540, and p. 460), because of the uncertainty of the outcome of the French excavations at Begrām.

[88] Hsüan-Tsang, ii. p. 285 (cf. i. 55 n. 198.), describes U-pi-na (Hupiân) as the capital of the region round Kapisa, now commonly accepted to be Begrām. For

time it remains possible that, as Cunningham maintained, the two sites, originally separate, were merged by the Kushan period, if not earlier. At all events, we may say with some degree of certainty that Alexandria in the Paropamisadai, Alexandria of Opiane, if we feel that is a valid equation, lay within the wide basin between the southern foot of the Hindu Kush, in the Kūhistān, somewhere between the modern Charikar and the junction of the Ghorband and the Panjshir. The city did not survive to be recorded in the Iranian tradition (see Table), though it has been claimed (on dis-

Opiān cf. Foucher, 'Notes sur l'itinéraire de Hiuan-Tsang en Afghanistan', in *Étud. asiat. publ. à l'occas. du 25ᵉ anniv. de l'École franç. d'Extrême-Orient*, i (1925), 257, and his *Vieille Route*, where he makes general use of the narrative at many points: see App. 3, below p. 235 no. 8. Tarn 96-7, 460-1, claims that Alexandria in Opiane is the correct name of Alexandria ad Caucasum, 'if it had an official name it is lost'. He also claims that Plin. vi. 92, describing the provinces bordering on India, is referring to Opiane, though Pliny calls the region of Capisa Capisene (which Tarn, *GBI* 96, regards simply as Pliny's name for Opiane). He says, 'Pliny's sixth book is only a collection of notes very briefly transcribed; but vi. 92, the Paropamisadae, is good stuff if properly construed.' Good stuff or not, the text is very unhelpful as transmitted: *haec regio est ex adverso Bactrianorum, deinde cuius oppidum Alexandria a conditore dictum . . . ad Caucasum Cadrusi, oppidum ab Alexandro conditum* (Mayhoff; *haec regio est ex adverso Bactriae; Arianorum deinde cuius oppidum Alexandria a conditore dictum . . . ad Caucasum Cadrusi, oppidum ab Alexandro conditum*, Loeb). *Arianorum*, the emendation of the Loeb text, is hardly justified; in any case the reference seems to be to Alexandria in Ariana, while Alexandria ad Caucasum is separately mentioned in the second clause. Tarn (p. 76 n. 6; cf. p. 460) says that Pliny in the first clause is referring to Alexandria in Opiane, but since on his hypothesis Alexandria in Opiane is Alexandria ad Caucasum, and he (Pliny) refers to the latter town in the second clause (without a specific name) the problem (if I understand it correctly) is not solved. Cunningham's emendation of the text (p. 22) from *ex adverso Bactrianorum* to *ex adverso Opiorum* is clearly unacceptable. The ruins of Opiān near Charikar are not now easily identifiable, since there have been many changes in the approach to the road in the last generation with the construction of the Sarlang tunnel, but they seem to have been on a small scale. Ball 435 says only 'Some large mounds built up from ancient deposits, built over by a modern village. Many antiquities are reported to have been found here.' There are other sites in the same area, the Kūh Daman, and the whole Kūhistān basin, but they are largely unexplored; see Masson's excellent account of the area, and the sites marked on Ball, map 111. Cunningham, *AGI* 26-8, argued with great ingenuity that the 'Square City' referred to by Pliny vi. 92, *Cartana oppidum sub Caucaso, quod postea Tetragonis dictum* was itself Begrām, on the basis of Masson's description of the unexcavated site as 'accurately describing a square of considerable magnitude'; the area of the site is drawn within a rectangle by Cunningham on his map opp. p. 17. That the site of Burg al-Abdullah, the excavated Begrām, is indeed approximately quadrilateral in shape is certainly true: see the maps referred to, above n. 80. Cunningham further thought that Pliny's Cartana was Ptolemy's Κάρσανα (see above, n. 87). Tarn, *GBI* 96 ff., thought that there was little doubt that Kartana-Tetragonis was Bāmiyān. Such conjectures illustrate very clearly the uncertainties regarding precise identifications within the general area of the Hindu Kush.

putable grounds) as the birthplace of the great Indo-Greek conqueror, Menander.

4. ALEXANDRIA ESCHATE

For the next two years Alexander was campaigning in the region of Turkestan, north of the Hindu Kush, and across the Oxus in Sogdiana, extending his control as far as the Jaxartes (Syr Darya), on the lower reaches of which he founded 'the city called after him in a region suitable for development into a large city, and well situated to defend the area from the Scythians'.[89] This city is no doubt that called by Ptolemy Ἀλεξάνδρεια Ἐσχάτη, by Appian Ἀλεξανδρέσχατα, and by Qodāma 'the furthest Alexandria'.[90] It has traditionally been identified with Khojend (subsequently Leninabad, now again known by its old name), recorded by the early Arab Itineraries under that name, which stands where the Syr Darya reaches the southernmost point of its winding course, at the western end of the Farghāna oasis,[91] and excavations of the old citadel suggest, if they do not prove, that the site, like Kandahar, was occupied from Achaemenid times through the Hellenistic period and later.[92] The city and citadel occupy a position close to

[89] Arr iv. 1. 3–4: Αὐτὸς δὲ πρὸς τῶι Τανάϊδι ποταμῶι ἐπενόει πόλιν οἰκίσαι, καὶ ταύτην ἑαυτοῦ ἐπώνυμον. ὅ τε γὰρ χῶρος ἐπιτήδειος αὐτῶι ἐφαίνετο αὐξῆσαι ἐπὶ μέγα τὴν πόλιν καὶ ἐν καλῶι οἰκισθήσεσθαι τῆς ἐπὶ Σκύθας, εἴποτε ξυμβαίνοι, ἐλάσεως καὶ τῆς προφυλακῆς τῆς χώρας πρὸς τὰς καταδρομὰς τῶν πέραν τοῦ ποταμοῦ ἐποικούντων βαρβάρων. ἐδόκει δ' ἂν καὶ μεγάλη γενέσθαι ἡ πόλις πλήθει τε τῶν ἐς αὐτὴν ξυνοικιζομένων καὶ τοῦ ὀνόματος τῆι λαμπρότητι.

[90] See Ptol. vi. 12.6: μεταξὺ δὲ καὶ ἀνωτέρω τῶν ποταμῶν ; . . . Ἀλεξάνδρεια Ὠξειανή . . . Ἀλεξάνδρεια Ἐσχάτη cf. viii. 23. 14: ἡ ἐσχάτη Ἀλεξάνδρεια; cf. App. *Syr.* 57, at the end of his list of Macedonian-named cities, ἐν δὲ Σκύθαις Ἀλεξανδρέσχατα: for this list see above, pp. 36 ff. Plin. vi. 49 has *Ultra Sogdiani, oppidum Panda in ultimis eorum finibus Alexandria ab Alexandro Magno conditum, etc.; Itin. Alex.* ch. xxxvi (81 Hausmann), echoes Arrian (above, n. 89): *Ipse progressus ad Tanaim illic quoque urbem sibi instituit haud disparem magnitudine cognominibus Alexandriis, idque usui cavens, si quando post id eadem militaretur.* For Iskandariya al-qaṣwā see Qodāma, *BGA* vi. 265 (FT ibid. 206) (in Sugd, i.e. Sogdiana). No source uses the expression ἡ Σογδιανή, though of course it was recognized that it was in Sogdiana. Tarn, *Alex.*, ii. 243–4, claims that Alexandreschata was the equivalent of Alexandria in Scythia, known exclusively from the *Romance* tradition (Table 23; cf. p. 21, n. 43), since he believed that Alexandria in Sogdiana was on the Oxus at Termez. This was a mare's nest (see below, n. 97). For Ptolemy's location of Alexandria Eschate and Alexandria Oxiana see below, n. 93.

[91] For the Arab Itineraries see Iṣṭakhrī (*BGA* i), p. 328, ll. 4 ff; Ibn Ḥawqal, *BGA* ii², pp. 511 f. = FT 489 f. the fullest account.

[92] See reports in (1) A. J. Bilalov and T. V. Belyaeva, *Issledovania kreposti Khodjenta* (*Investigations of the Fortress of Khodjent*), *Arkheologiskia Otkrytia*, 1975 (*Archaeological*

the river, as Arrian's narrative requires, in a long stretch without left-hand tributaries, and in a key position in the fertile oasis of Farghāna, on what was later the main caravan-route from Bokhārā via Samarkand (which Alexander had captured shortly before) to Khawak and Akhsikath on the north bank of the river. Ibn Ḥawqal, who visited Khojend in the tenth century, describes the city as spread out along the banks of the river, and rich in fruits and other natural products. Thus, all told, although, as at Kandahar, Begrām and Ai-Khanūm, the excavations have not yet, so far as is known, yielded the ancient name of Khojend, it is reasonable to accept an overall identification with Alexandria Eschate, though, as at Alexandria in Aria, the new city was probably not on precisely the same site as the old. In fact, it seems probable that the Achaemenid settlement was at Cyropolis, or τὰ Κῦρα, which Alexander is said to have captured and perhaps destroyed before building Alexandria Eschate.[93] The new settlement was constructed, according to Arrian, as a walled city, and it was populated by Greek mercenaries, local tribesmen who volunteered to settle there, and even some time-expired Macedonians. This was perhaps the most politically significant settlement made by Alexander since he had founded Alexandria in Egypt—the fortification took only three weeks, it is true, but we are not told how many hands were set to work—for although he carried out

Discoveries, 1975, Moscow, 1976), 562; (2) N. N. Negmatov, *Arkheologiska Otkrytia*, 1976 (Moscow, 1977), 569; (3) *Raskopki v. tsitadeli Leninabada i lokalisatsia Alexandrii Eskhaty* (*Excavations of the citadel of Leninabad, and the localization of Alexandria Eschate*). I am extremely grateful to Mr S. Hornblower for translating these two reports for me (in 1979). As may be seen from G. Frumkin, *Archaeology in Soviet Central Asia* (Leiden, 1970), 54-5 and map, there is now a vast water-basin between Khojend and Farghāna; cf. also Frye, *Ancient Iran*, 147 with n. 22.

[93] For Cyropolis see Arr. iv. 3. 1 ff.: οὕτω δὴ τὰς πέντε πόλεις ἐν δυσὶν ἡμέραις ἑλών τε καὶ ἐξανδραποδισάμενος ᾔει ἐπὶ τὴν μεγίστην αὐτῶν, τὴν Κύρου πόλιν. Arr. seems to distinguish between Cyropolis, which surrendered, and Alexandria Eschate, which he built afterwards (§ 4) on the river bank. Strab. 517 (not Erat.) says καὶ τὰ Κῦρα, ἔσχατον ὂν Κύρου κτίσμα, ἐπὶ τῶι Ἰαξάρτηι ποταμῶι κείμενον, ὅπερ ἦν ὅριον τῆς Περσῶν ἀρχῆς· κατασκάψαι δὲ τὸ κτίσμα τοῦτο, καίπερ ὄντα φιλόκυρον, διὰ τὰς πυκνὰς ἀποστάσεις. This is presumably to be understood as referring to a period subsequent to his foundation of the adjacent Alexandria. Κυρέσχατα occurs in Ptol. vi. 12. 5 ὀρειναὶ δέ εἰσι πόλεις τῶν Σογδιανῶν παρὰ τὸν Ἰαξάρτην αἵδε· Κυρέσχατα ρκδ ... μγ γο' ... § 6 μεταξὺ δὲ καὶ ἀνωτέρω τῶν ποταμῶν ... Ἀλεξάνδρεια Ὠξειανή ... Ἀλεξάνδρεια Ἐσχάτη ... ρκβ ... μα, i.e. Kyreschata is between five and six parallels of latitude north of Alexandreschata, almost on the same meridian: the positions on his projection are indicated on Ronco's Table I. The city is also listed by Steph. s.v. Κύρου πόλις· ἢ καὶ Κυρέσχατα καλεῖται, πόλις πρὸς τοῖς ἐσχάτοις Περσίδος, but he has no Ἀλεξανδρέσχατα vel sim.

operations north of the river until forced to withdraw by illness, it seems probable not only that it was intended as a permanent base on the northern marches of the Empire, for both military and trading purposes, but also that for Alexander, φιλόκυρος, it symbolized the identification of the old Cyrus with the new. It is significant that this remote city is the only Alexander-foundation (Alexandria in Egypt, naturally, excepted) to appear in a documentary record of the Greek world in the third century BC. In the *Marmor Parium* under the date 328/7 BC the entry occurs: ὠικίσθη δὲ πρὸς Τανάι πόλις Ἑλληνίς.[94] It is likely that this city was among the first to be submerged by the Saka inroads from the north, even though its name survived in Pliny and Ptolemy (whose coordinates place it in an impossible position), and, surprisingly, in Qodāma.

The foundation of Alexandria Eschate marked, or coincided with, a turning-point in the campaign. After relieving Marakanda-Samarkand (Arr. iv. 5-6), Alexander recrossed the Oxus and wintered in 329/8 in Zariaspa (iv. 7. 1), then returned in spring 328 to Sogdiana (iv. 17.), where he dispatched Hephaestion 'to synoecize the cities in Sogdiana'—that is, presumably, to consolidate scattered villages in the oases—and spent the following winter, that of 328/7, at Nautaka (iv. 18. 1), somewhere between the Upper Oxus and the Polytimetus (Sugd) rivers; in spring 327 he made his assault on 'the Rock of Sogdiana', i.e. Baisun-tan, east of Derbent (iv. 18. 4-20), and the 'Rock of Chorienes' in the Pareitakai, and then returned to Bactra (iv. 22).

It is in the context of the last phase of these operations that the foundation of Ἀλεξάνδρεια κατὰ Βάκτρα, perhaps to be identified with Ἀλεξάνδρεια Ὠξιανή, must be considered. Ἀ. κατὰ Βάκτρα is known by name only from Stephanus' list, in which it appears as the eleventh city. It is perhaps a reflection of the tradition, which is found in Diodorus and Justin, that Alexander built 'some' (ἄλλας, Diodorus), eight (Strabo), or twelve (Justin) cities in Bactria and

---

[94] *FGrH* 239 B7. The event is dated by the archonship at Athens of Euthykritos (328/7 BC). The Marble's source for this entry is unknown, but it must be an almost contemporary historical source, or other documentation. We may wonder whether an official list of the dates of foundations existed, starting with that of Alexandria of Egypt, in 331 BC. Appian, loc. cit., erroneously lists Alexandreschata among Seleucid foundations, ἐν δὲ Σκύθαις Ἀλεξανδρέσχατα, and it may be, as Tscherikower, 106, suggests, that it was refounded by Seleucus after the withdrawal of the Greek settlers after the death of Alexander. But it is even more likely to be an error of Appian, or transmitted by him in a context where such an error was not difficult and perhaps deliberate: see above pp. 36 ff., 151, n. 90.

Sogdiana.[95] This tradition finds no support in Arrian or the geographers, and may be regarded as part of the highly coloured picture found, with a larger sweep, in Plutarch's famous description of Alexander's activity.[96] On the other hand Alexandria in Oxiana has acquired a substantial role in modern studies of Alexander, and the outlines of the problem must be given here. The argument turns largely on the evidence from Aï Khanūm, the Achaemenid-Hellenistic city excavated by the French Archaeological Mission on the promontory at the confluence of the Kokcha and Oxus rivers, on the south bank of the river, north-east of Kundūz. Before the excavation of that city, Alexandria Oxiana had received the attention of Tarn, who, with characteristic ingenuity and intrepidity, had identified it, by means of a supposed Tibetan translation of a Sanskrit work, which provided the intermediate form Tarmita, with the modern city of Termez on the north bank of the Oxus, that is, in Sogdiana. According to Tarn the city was later refounded by Demetrius of Bactria as a Demetrias. This seductive story was decisively rejected by orientalists, and need not be further considered.[97] With the chance discovery and excavation of Aï Khanūm the problem found a new context inevitably unknown to Tarn, for

[95] Diod. xvii, 84, where the reference is, of course, to the cities allegedly close to Alexandria ad Caucasum, i.e. south of the Hindu Kush: Ἀλέξανδρος καὶ ἄλλας πόλεις ἔκτισεν, ἡμέρας ὁδὸν ἀπεχούσας τῆς Ἀλεξανδρείας, κατώικισε δ' εἰς ταύτας τῶν μὲν βαρβάρων ἑπτακισχιλίους, τῶν δ' ἐκτὸς τάξεως συνακολουθούντων τρισχιλίους καὶ τῶν μισθοφόρων τοὺς βουλομένους. Strab 517: φασὶ δ' οὖν ὀκτὼ πόλεις Ἀλέξανδρον ἔν τε τῆι Βακτριανῆι καὶ τῆι Σογδιανῆι κτίσαι, τινὰς δὲ κατασκάψαι, ὧν Καριάτας μὲν τῆς Βακτριανῆς, ἐν ἧι Καλλισθένης συνελήφθη καὶ παρεδόθη φυλακῆι, Μαράκανδα δὲ τῆς Σογδιανῆς καὶ τὰ Κῦρα (cf. above, n. 93). Just. xii. 5. 12-13: *Et ut his terris nomen relinqueret, urbem Alexandream super amnem Tanaim condidit, intra diem septimum decimum muro sex milium passuum consummato, translatis earum civitatium populis, quas Cyrus condiderat. In Bactrianis quoque Sogdianisque xii urbes condidit, distributis his, quoscumque in exercitu seditiosos habebat.*

[96] See the passage of Plutarch quoted above, p. 130 n. 50; below, pp. 188 ff. Tarn, *GBI* 115, n. 1 stated that the Chinese Lan-chi mentioned in the *Hu-Han-shu* 'historically cannot possibly be anything but Bactra'—but the interpretation of the name, which is transmitted in the form Chien-Shih, is uncertain, as usual. See n. 278 of Hulsewé and Loewe (op. cit. p. 119). They consider the possibility, on linguistic grounds, of an identification with Khulm, and, on general grounds, with Aï Khanūm, but do not accept either alternative. Ἀ. κατὰ Βάκτρα itself remains in limbo.

[97] Tarn unfolded this story in *GBI* 118 ff.; cf. *JHS* 60 (1940), 89 ff. It is reproduced in *Alex.* ii. 235. Narain, *The Indo-Greeks*, 40-1, summarizes the discussions of Whitehead, *NC* (1947), 35 and (1950), 213-4, and H. W. Bailey, *BSOAS* 13 (1950), 400-3. This view was revived on different grounds by Goukowsky, in his Budé edn. of Diod. xvii (236-7; cf. above, n. 69). He is answered by P. Bernard, in *JS* (1982), 217 ff.

it has been maintained that this uniquely preserved city, which succeeded an adjacent Achaemenian settlement, should be identified with Alexandria Oxiana, mentioned only by Ptolemy, and placed by him between the Oxus and the Jaxartes.[98] In spite of the obvious overall attraction of the identification, I do not feel that, for the present at least, we are entitled to take that step. The epigraphical record indicates without any doubt that the inhabitants of the city, at the beginning of their civic history, in the early third century BC, regarded a Thessalian or Macedonian, Kineas, otherwise unknown to history, as their founder.[99] That the city, after a history as a busy emporium, had ceased to exist by the end of the second century BC, having been destroyed by the Sakai on their route southwards, is also undoubtedly true. Ptolemy's, or Marinus', list represents, as so often, tralaticial information, and, standing unsupported as it does, its faulty coordinates and location are open to a variety of interpretations. It is obviously possible that the city

[98] vi. 12. 6: quoted above, n. 93 (cf. note 85). Alexandreschata is placed nearly four degrees south of Alexandria in Oxiana: see Ronca's Map I. I cannot give here a full account of the many discussions concerning the ancient name of Aï Khanūm. A full bibliography of the site will be found in Ball, no. 18 (113 items). Apart from the final reports (*Fouilles d'Aï Khanoum*, (*Mém. DAFA*), i (vol. xxi (1973, 2 vols.)), *Campagnes 1965-1968*, by P. Bernard; ii (vol. xxvi (1983)), *Les Propylées de la rue principale*, by O. Guillaume; iii (vol. xxvii (1984)), *Le Sanctuaire du temple à niches indentées*, 2, *Les Trouvailles*, by H.-P. Francfort; iv (vol. xxviii (1985), *Les Monnaies hors trésors*, by P. Bernard; v (vol. xxix (1986)), *Les Remparts et les monuments associés*, by P. Leriche; vi (vol. xxx (1987)), *Le Gymnase, architecture etc.*, by S. Veuve; vii, O. Guillaume and A. Rouquelle (vol. xxxi (1987)), Les petits objets; viii, Cl. Rapin (vol. xxxiii (1992)), *La trésorerie du palais hellénistique d'Aï Khanoum*) see Bernard, opp. citt. below, nn. 98-9; id. *JS* (1982), 219 ff.; id. *et al. BÉFÉO* 68 (1980), 1-75, 'Campagne de Fouille 1978 à Aï Khanoum'; id. and H. Francfort, *Études de géographie historique sur la plaine d'Aï Khanoum* (1978), 3-17.

[99] The inscription, originally published by L. Robert in *CRAI* (1968), 416 ff., was republished by him in *Aï Khanoum*, i. 207 ff., in the same terms. The theme is by now well known. An epigram by Klearchos, probably the Peripatetic, commemorates the erection of his personal copy of the Delphic Maxims at the site Κινέου ἐν τεμένει. Robert and Bernard, locc. citt., stated clearly that the reference to the sanctuary could only mean that Kineas was the founder of the city. Robert, *CRAI* 431-2: 'il ne me paraît point douteux que Kinéas ait été le fondateur, l'οἰκιστής, de notre ville sur l'Oxus, enterré, à l'intérieur même de la ville, sur l'agora. Un homme de ce nom n'est point connu parmi les compagnons d'Alexandre. etc.' This may be accepted, and discussion of the name of the city must start from there. The lettering of the inscription, and the link with Clearchus, favour a date at the end of the fourth or the beginning of the 3rd cent. BC for the foundation, and thus make it probable that the city was a Seleucid foundation. The preponderance of early Seleucid bronzes, especially those of Antiochus I, among the coins found on the site, supports but does not prove the Seleucid origin of the city: see Bernard, *Fouilles d' Aï Khanoum*, vi (1985), 5 ff.

was named by Kineas, or by someone else, after Alexander, but the 'sanctuary of Kineas' argues, against that. On the other hand, to regard it as an otherwise unrecorded Seleucid foundation called Alexandria would involve the postulation of a metonomasy of the type that there is no good evidence that the early Seleucid rulers adopted. Moreover, the absence of any reference to such a conspicuous foundation in the surviving Alexander-historians, though obviously not of great weight, should be borne in mind. At present, then, the arguments against the identification seem strong. The name Alexandria Oxiana may itself be a confusion, as has been suggested, with the other Alexandria in Sogdiana, Alexandreschata on the banks of the Jaxartes,[100] but the discovery in recent years at a site to the north of the Oxus, almost opposite Aï Khanūm, of a dedication in Greek to the river-god Oxus, probably of the Kushan or Saka period,[101] seems to indicate that Oxiana at that time included an area considerably north of the river and that therefore the text of Ptolemy should not be tampered with. That a city so named once existed, in historical circumstances unknown to us, may indeed be true, but the evidence at present available does not sustain its identification with Aï Khanūm, the importance of which as the prime witness to the Hellenic–Macedonian surge in Central Asia is not thereby affected.

To return to our main narrative. In summer of 327 BC Alexander moved back across the Hindu Kush, passed by Alexandria ad Caucasum, where he established some more settlers (Arr. iv. 22. 5), and reached the junction of the Panjshir and Kābul rivers. His route from Turkestan back to the south of the mountain range is

---

[100] See Bernard, *Proc. Brit. Acad.* (1967), 92 n. 4. He points out that Ptolemy uses the phrase (vi. 12. 4) παρὰ τὸν Ὦξον as he does (ibid. 5) παρὰ τὸν Ἰαξάρτην. For the role of Aï Khanūm in the integrated Seleucid Empire the reader should now also consult Sherwin-White and Kuhrt, *From Samarkhand to Sardis, passim* (see Index, p. 251).

[101] For this inscription, from Takht-i-Sangin, now *SEG* xxxi. 1381, see *Afghan Studies*, 2 (1979), 17 n. 31. The name of the dedicant is Atrosokes. For a photograph see Sherwin-White and Kuhrt, pl. 16. The lettering is un-Hellenic in style, and resembles most the Greek lettering of the Bactrian inscription from Sirkh Khotal, published by D. Schlumberger, *Proc. Brit. Acad.* 47 (1961), 77 ff., with pl. ix (b), and by Schlumberger *et al.*, *Sirkh Khotal en Bactriane* (1 vol. in 2, *Mém. DAFA* xxv, 1983), 1(2) pl. 72, and frequently elsewhere (e.g. in *Archaeology in Afghanistan*, 235 f.). The Greek inscription of Palamedes (ibid. pl. 71; republished by myself, *Afghan Studies*, 3–4, pp. 7–8) is also in the same style. Vinogradov, *VDI* 1985(4), 99 (see *SEG* xxxv. 1479), apropos of subsequent discoveries in the Oxus area, has suggested a date for it in the 2nd cent. BC. The style is clearly local, and may well have earlier antecedents, so I would regard this date as perfectly possible.

not specified by Arrian, but is said by Strabo (not from
Eratosthenes) to have been by a shorter transit than that by which
he had traversed the range in the opposite direction.[102] This is an
indication of some significance. It has already been suggested above
(pp. 118 ff.) that when Alexander left Herāt for the first time he did
so by following the Hari-Rūd upstream towards Bāmiyān, but that
he was forced to abandon this project of a swift transit to Bactria,
and on his second departure he followed the great curve of the
desert route to Zaranj and Kandahar. It is clear that the 'shorter
routes' mentioned by Strabo represent the itinerary via Bāmiyān in
the reverse direction, and it follows that (as might be expected)
Alexander did not take that route on his journey north, on leaving
the Kūhistān basin. We may therefore regard it as certain that he
traversed the main range northwards by one of the main passes,
more arduous than that via the defiles accessible by way of the
Bāmiyān plateau, but more immediately at hand, once he was in
the Kūhistān basin. Which of the passes he followed we cannot be
certain, but it is natural to suppose that it was one of the main
western passes, either the Kushan pass (ht. 15,000 ft.) or the
Sarlang (12,000 ft.), where the modern motor road runs through
the tunnel, or else (less probably in my opinion) by the Khawak
pass (13,000 ft.) that turns at an abrupt angle at a high altitude
at the watershed of the Panjshir valley, and debouches further east,
outside the range of Alexander's subsequent movements.[103] All

---

[102] Str. 697: ἀνέστρεψε δ᾽ οὖν ὑπερθεὶς τὰ αὐτὰ ὄρη κατ᾽ ἄλλας ὁδοὺς ἐπιτομωτέρας,
ἐν ἀριστερᾶι ἔχων τὴν Ἰνδικήν, κ.τ.λ. Tarn, *GBI*, 139-40, correctly evaluates the
difference between the route via Bāmiyān and those over the main passes, but in
his narrative of Alexander's route from Bactria to the south he does not refer to
Strabo's significant and decisive observation; he says only (*Alex.* i. 87-8), 'Local
tradition says that he recrossed the Hindu Kush by the lofty Koashan pass, 14,300
ft. high, but doubtless he took the usual route by Bamyan and the Ghorband
valley, which turned the range.' Engels, op. cit. 107, identifies the shorter route
as that of the Salang, and regards the Shibar route as longer. However, that is
not so with a starting-point at Balkh. It is unfortunate that in this section Strabo
gives a general geographical sketch of Alexander's activity in Ariana and the
Paropamisadai without quoting his authority.

[103] A full account of the passes, which have been described by many writers and
travellers, cannot be given here. Apart from the standard modern maps, the reader
will find a graphic sketch of all the passes in the map accompanying C. R.
Markham's excellent papers on the passes in the *Proc. Roy. Geogr. Soc.* 1 (1879),
38 ff., 110 ff., cf. ibid. 191 ff. (reprinted in N. Dupree's *Afghanistan* (see above, n. 19),
252-93 (in continuous numeration)), and, in a very clear form, by Holdich, 410 ff.
with map opp. p. 500; see also Bernard *JS* (1982), 224-5, who also has a clear
account of the various passes, and a map based on that of Markham; cf. also
Foucher, *Vieille Route*, 17 ff. and fig 5 (based on that of Holdich). Markham gives

these passes (and others: Markham lists seventeen between the
Anjuman pass on the east and the Shībar pass in the Ghorband
valley in the west) were usually closed by snow from October
onwards, as was the route via the Hari-Rūd to Bāmiyān, and we
cannot determine which pass Alexander used on his northward
march, though one of the three mentioned above seems most
probable. On his return his force apparently moved by more than
one route, for Strabo in the passage under discussion says 'by
shorter routes', an indication, perhaps, if the plural noun is to be
taken at its natural face-value, of the problem facing those who
first made use of the bematists for distances, and one possible
explanation of the variations in distances recorded in Pliny and
Eratosthenes; for Alexander, we know, did not move his troops en
bloc over large distances, and, that being so, we cannot identify
one rather than another. However, both the route which follows
the Balkh river and the Darra Yusuf and the alternative, more
easterly, one which follows the course of the Tashkhurgan river via
Haibak to the Ak Robat, reach the plain of Bāmiyān—where, I
have suggested, Ortospana should probably be located—and merge
easily with the Shībar pass, whence there is a straightforward
route down the Ghorband river to the plain of Kūhistān and
Alexandria ad Caucasum, and thence eastwards. By traversing one
(or, more strictly, speaking of his entire force, both of
them) Alexander completed the circle of his traverse of the
Paropamisadai. This was the regular route to the south from
Turkestan followed centuries later by the Mongols and their predecessors, and by the pilgrim Hsüan-Tsang, when he was crossing

the approximate height of the individual passes from east to west on p. 283, as also
does Holdich, on his excellent map. Tarn, *GBI* loc. cit. seems certain that he took
the Khawak pass 'The central route, over one of the lofty Kaoshan passes, does not
come into question; it rises too high, though local tradition believes that Alexander
used it for one of his crossings.' Engels, op. cit. 94–5, also says that the
Macedonians 'undoubtedly used' the Khawak pass. This is far from certain. The
Khawak pass is the furthest route, for the Panjshir valley describes a great curve to
the east, and would have taken Alexander out of the direct road to Bactra. Moreover
(as the Russians found out in recent years) it possesses a number of tributary defiles,
which could be very dangerous to troops attempting to force the pass. The Sarlang
and (less probably) the Kushan remain serious candidates: see Holdich, loc. cit.;
Bernard, loc. cit. 228–9, agrees that the reverse route was via the Shībar pass, but
maintains that he took the Khawak on his way north. We cannot tell what immediately relevant factors—trouble, potential or actual, from hill-tribes, climatic conditions, available information—may have determined Alexander's final choice,
whichever it was.

the Hindu Kush southwards from Balkh, on his way to Kapisa and Laghman, that is to say, the same route as that followed by Alexander, when he passed by Alexandria ad Caucasum on his way to the Indus valley (see below, App. 3).

His route from Alexandria to the area of Laghman (Lampaka), of which the centre is Jalalabad, is fairly certain. It seems clear that he did not follow the course of the Kābul river, which would have required him to retrace his steps southwards, but that he took the route along the southern skirts of the Kafiristān ranges, by the Panjshir and Kunar rivers.[104] Hephaestion and Perdiccas, whom he sent with a substantial mixed force by a more southernly line of march, may have followed the line of the Kābul river, at least from the Lataband pass (Sarobi), where the Panshir flows into the Kābul, onwards, passing the neighbourhood of Jalalabad. The matter perhaps is not of great importance to us here, since the role of Alexander as city-builder does not recommence until he has passed beyond the Indus; but it may at least be noted that the latter forces were sent in advance to prepare for the crossing of the Indus, while Alexander probably took the longer, more mountainous and more difficult route and followed the Kunar (Choaspes) river northwards, then crossed the Shawāl or Mandal pass into Upper Swat, thence descending during the winter of 327/6 into the plain of Peshawar (Gandhara) by the Malakand pass to Taxila.[105] On this route, somewhere among the distant hills of Swat, he established a new fortified settlement at Arigaion (iv. 24. 6), which had been set on fire at his approach by its inhabitants, and which he now repopulated with unfit soldiers and local tribesmen. Then, captur-

---

[104] This 'old route' was traced by Foucher in his study of the route of Hsüan-Tsang, *Étude Asiatiques*, i (1925), 257-84, 'Notes sur l'Itineraire de Hiuan-Tsang en Afghanistan', esp. pp. 273 ff. The map of Hsüan-Tsang's route given by Foucher on p. 278 shows very clearly the route from Kūhistān to the Kunar river, which Alexander also took. Foucher covered the same topic in much greater detail in *Vieille Route*, *passim*, esp. pp. 34 ff. Masson gives an excellent account of the landscape of the same route (*Memoirs*, iii. 171 ff.), travelled by him in the opposite direction.

[105] For the route (given in Arr. iv. 23-8) via the Kunar river and the Malakand pass see Aurel Stein, *Geogr. Journ.* 101 (1942), 49-56, with excellent photographs of the Upper Indus gorge; id. *On Alexander's Path to the Indus* (London, 1929), 10, with photograph of the Malakand pass. Malakand itself lies some way to the west, closer to the river; cf. Smith, *Early History of India*⁴ (Oxford, 1924), 54. For the crossing of the Indus at Ohind, the later capital of the Hindu Shāhis, after their rule in Kābul had been suppressed by the Ghaznavid Mahmoud, see Cunningham, pp. 52 ff., Smith, p. 63, who also discusses the various forms of the name. See also next note.

ing and fortifying the mountain strongholds of Massaga, Ora, and Bazire, he marched down to Peucelaotis (Charsadda), which surrendered to him. He then turned back and captured the famous Rock of Aornos in southern Swat, returned once more to the plain, crossed the Indus north of the present Attock, at or near 'Ohind',[106] and reached Taxila, the capital of the satrapy of Ghandara, and accepted its surrender from its client ruler, 'Taxiles'. Equestrian and athletic contests were held by the river.

The bematists' measurements continue as far as Taxila by the main route (that is, that followed by Hephaestion), but beyond this we have (Bucephala-Alexandria apart) only the evidence of the Alexander-historians for the foundation of cities, and though these are precise as to the occasion of foundations they do not assist in determining exact locations. Furthermore, the early Hellenistic chorographers of India were interested in the general native habits, political and social, of the strange new subcontinent, and were seemingly not concerned with any Greek cities, or cities with Greek inhabitants (if such there were), that they encountered. Thus of the fragments of Megasthenes and Eratosthenes which form the basis of Strabo's knowledge of northern India, the former omits Pataliputra, the Gangetic capital of the Mauryas, while the quotations from Eratosthenes are strictly geographical. At the same time, the horizon of the Arab geographers did not normally extend to India (Hindustān and Sind) before al-Bīrūnī, and the only references to an Alexandria are those by Yākūt in the *Mushtarik* where he refers to Bucephala-Alexandria, though he does not record this among his Alexandrias in the *Mu'jam* (see Table at end), and by al-Farghānī who called Wayhind (Ohind) a foundation of Alexander.[107] Apart from Bucephala, and its twin-foundation Nikaia there is little that can be said of the Indian foundations in general. In western sources outside the pages of

---

[106] al-Farghānī (p. 34, Gol.) gives among the cities of his third *aqlīm* in balād al-Hind the city of Qandahar, then, to the north, the country of Sind, and the country of Kābul, and Kerman and Alexandria and Sijistān. For al-Bīrūnī see *Alberuni's India*, ed. Sachau, (ET, 2 vols., London, 1888), p. 206, who calls Wayhind 'the capital of Kandahar, west of the Indus'; it is not clear that he is referring to Kandahar of Arachosia, rather than another one of several places so named in the general area, particularly Gandhara: see Ball, *South Asian Studies*, 4 (1988), 130. 2, for Gandhara = Qandahar.

[107] See al-Farghānī, loc. cit. who replaces the Wayhind of Iṣṭakhrī by Iskandarīya, in the sequence quoted in the previous note This may be only an error of transmission, rather than an independent attestation.

the Alexander-historians themselves we have only an occasional reference in Pliny and (for Bucephala) Ptolemy, and the entries in Stephanus under Bucephala and Nikaia (the latter including 'a fourth in India'), and a passage in the *Periplus Maris Erythraei*.

5. BUCEPHALA (OR BUCEPHALA-ALEXANDRIA) AND NIKAIA

The twin foundations on the Jhelum commemorated respectively the death of Bucephalus, Alexander's beloved horse, and the victory over Porus. These were founded on either bank of the Jhelum, Bucephala apparently on the west bank and Nikaia on the east, where the battle was fought. The former has been set by many investigators at Jhelum itself, while others prefer to place it some thirty miles south of Jhelum at Jalalpur. These sites have not been excavated, and, given their position on the edge of a changing river-bed and (on the eastern side) in marshy land, and the repeated action of the monsoon, it is unlikely that early remains survive at either site even at a great depth.[108] It will be remembered that Arrian tells us that at the very outset both cities suffered from the rains during the brief period in which Alexander had advanced further east and returned to the Jhelum: 'on reaching the Hydaspes, where the cities of Nikaia and Bucephala were, he employed his army to repair damage caused by the rains'.[109] Nevertheless Bucephala-Alexandria (or simply 'Bucephala' as it was known to most of our sources) apparently survived at least until the early Imperial period, under Indo-Greek rulers. It was presumably for some time under the rule of the Mauryas from their

[108] The topography of the crossing of the Jhelum, and consequently of the likely site of Bucephala were studied in detail by Aurel Stein, *Geogr. Journ.* 80 (1932), 32–46. He devoted a considerable amount of study to the area between the river and the Salt Range to the west, at this point, and provides very strong reasons for believing that Bucephala lies below the modern Jalalpur. I assume this to be correct. The sites have not been excavated, and the matter is of no great importance in the present context. See further below, n. 111. Alexander entrusted the supervision of the building of the cities to Craterus (Arr. v. 20. 1): see below, p. 226.

[109] Ibid. 19. 4: ἵνα δὲ ἡ μάχη ξυνέβη καὶ ἔνθεν ὁρμηθεὶς ἐπέρασε τὸν Ὑδάσπην ποταμὸν πόλεις ἔκτισεν Ἀλέξανδρος. καὶ τὴν μὲν Νίκαιαν τῆς νίκης τῆς κατ' Ἰνδῶν ἐπώνυμον ὠνόμασε, τὴν δὲ Βουκεφάλαν ἐς τοῦ ἵππου τοῦ Βουκεφάλα τὴν μνήμην, ὃς ἀπέθανεν αὐτοῦ, οὐ βληθεὶς πρὸς οὐδενός, ἀλλὰ ὑπὸ καύματός τε καὶ ἡλικίας, κ.τ.λ. For the damage ibid. 29. 5: καὶ τὸν Ἀκεσίνην αὖ διαβὰς ἐπὶ τὸν Ὑδάσπην ἧκεν, ἵνα καὶ τῶν πόλεων τῆς τε Νικαίας καὶ τῶν Βουκεφάλων ὅσα πρὸς ὄμβρων πεπονηκότα ἦν ξὺν τῆι στρατιᾶι ἐπεσκεύασε καὶ τὰ ἄλλα τὰ κατὰ τὴν χώραν ἐκόσμει.

capital at Pataliputra,[110] and no doubt the later presence of the Indo-Greek rulers contributed to its survival as an urban centre of some importance.[111]

---

[110] See R. Mukerji, *Asoka* (London, 1928), 94 ff.

[111] The essential text for the survival of the city is *Peripl. Mar. Erythr.* § 47: ἐπίκειται δὲ κατὰ νώτου (?) τῆι Βαρυγάζηι μεσόγεια πλείονα ἔθνη, τό τε τῶν Ἀρατρίων καὶ ⟨Ἀ⟩ραχουσ(ί)ων καὶ Γανδαραίων καὶ τῆς Προκλ(α)ΐδος, ἐν οἷς ἡ Βουκέφαλος Ἀλεξάνδρεια. καὶ τούτων ἐπάνω μαχιμώτατον ἔθνος Βακτριανῶν, ὑπὸ βασιλέα ὄντων ἴδιον [τόπον?, see Müller, ad loc.]. It is doubtful if the author knew more of Bucephala than he might learn at Barygaza, or perhaps Kalliena; cf. § 52 of Kalliena: καὶ γὰρ τὰ ἐκ τύχης εἰς τούτους τοὺς τόπους ἐσβάλλοντα πλοῖα Ἑλληνικὰ μετὰ φυλακῆς εἰς Βαρύγαζαν εἰσάγεται. Narain, *Indo-Greeks*, 81, is surely over-cautious to say 'we have no means of verifying whether Bucephala still existed in the hostile Punjab at this time (i.e. in the time of Menander)': the *Periplus* is clear on that point. The precise location of Nikaia, on the east bank of the river, is quite uncertain, but it was probably as nearly opposite Bucephala as possible. Arr. v. 19. 4 (cf. Curt. Ruf. ix. 1. 6) makes it clear that the cities were founded on opposite sides of the Hydaspes, and that Nikaia was on the east bank, and Bucephala therefore on the west side. Tarn, *Alex.* ii. 236 ff. places Bucephala east of the river, and claims that Ptolemy supports him, but this cannot be the correct interpretation of Ptolemy who in vii. 1. 46 and 47 (46) has περὶ (emended, probably correctly, by Tarn to παρὰ) δὲ τὸν Βιδάσπην (= Arr.'s Ὑδάσπην; cf. McCrindle, *Ancient India, as described by Megasthenes and Arrian* (Calcutta, 1877; 2nd edn. rev. R. C. Majumdar, 1960, 197 n.)), with the cities of Sagala and Bucephala; that this refers to the west of the river seems clear; in § 47 he goes on τὰ δὲ ἐντεῦθεν πρὸς ἀνατολὰς κατέχουσι Κασπειραῖοι. Tarn, ibid. claims that the phrase of the *Last Days* (see below, pp. 212 f., for this work), p. 20. § 62, *item equi occisi multi, in quibus equus Alexandri nomine Bucephalus occisus est, quo equo omnibus proeliis semper vicerat. igitur in eo loco oppidum eo cognomine condidit, quod nunc Bucephala nominatur. post, ut solitus erat, mortuos sepeliri iussit suos atque hostium fortissimos*, supports his location of Bucephala east of the river, where the battle was fought, but the text is too divorced from events to carry weight on this point. Other *Romance* texts do not refer to the building of the city. A has only the death of Bucephalus: iii. 3. 6 (p. 102.8-10): πίπτει δὲ ὁ Ἀλεξάνδρου ἵππος ὁ Βουκέφαλος διαληφθεὶς ὑπὸ τοῦ Πώρου, καὶ ἐξησθένησε τὴν γνώμην· τούτου δὲ γενομένου ἀμελήσας τῆς μάχης αὐτὸς ἑαυτῶι ἔσυρε τὸν ἵππον, μὴ ἀρθῆι ὑπὸ τῶν πολεμίων. In *GBI* 326-7, Tarn claimed that Bucephala was the capital of the Indo-Greek King Hippostratos, on the basis of the City-Tyche on his coins, which he claimed could only come from a Greek city, which could only be Bucephala. But (as he himself, *Alex.* ii, Addenda, p. 451 (on p. 236) noted), this was based on an incomplete scrutiny of the numismatic material (cf. Narain, *Indo-Greeks*, 150), which does not support this claim. Ptolemy, it may be observed, calls the city simply Βουκέφαλα; so also Plin. *NH* vi. 20 of the tribes round the Indus: *caput eorum Bucephala, Alexandri regis equo cui fuerat hoc nomen ibi sepulto conditum*. Plut. *De Fort. Alex.* 328 F (see above, n. 50), who calls the city Βουκεφαλία, no doubt had derived his information from some of the literary sources known to him. Yākūt lists Bucephala in the *Mushtarik* p. 23: *wa minhā al-Iskandarīya allatī banāhā 'alā ismi farasihi almusammī būqefalūs wa tefsīrhu ra's al-thawri.*

6. FOUNDATIONS ESTABLISHED BY ALEXANDER ON THE LOWER INDUS

These seem to have been intended mainly as temporary forts and garrison-posts, and they do not appear to have received an urban structure. Here, too, in any case, the enormous changes in the course of the southern stretch of the Indus and its Delta, combined with monsoon rains and extensive flooding, are sufficient to have overwhelmed any riparian settlements at a very early stage.[112]

Nor is that the end of our difficulties. At the time of Alexander's campaign the area between the Kori creek, at the north end of the Rann of Katch, and Karachi, now consisting, apart from the main courses of the Indus, of dessicated channels, canals, and alluvial land, was open sea for a depth of some eight to ten miles, and attempts to identify the maritime locations in Nearchus' abbreviated narrative serve no useful purpose. Further inland, the total and sudden change in the course of the Lower Indus, near Hyderabad, in 1758, excludes the possibility of accurate identifications. It is only to the west of Karachi, in the neighbourhood where the Arabios (Hab) river empties into the Indian Ocean, that we find ourselves on terra firma.[113] Here we have the narratives of the journey, by sea and land, to aid us, but still no archaeological

---

[112] For these changes, and the courses of the 'forsaken rivers' of Sind see the lucid description by M. R. Haig, *The Indus Delta Country* (London, 1894; repr. Karachi, 1972), 1 ff. and recent studies, esp. those by the geologist H. Wilhelmy, listed in P. H. L. Eggermont's *Alexander's Campaigns in Sind and Baluchistan*, (Louvain, 1975), p. xx (a work that in spite of its obvious defects, nevertheless contains a number of useful suggestions (and a very large bibliography)). See also H. T. Lambrick, *Sind, A General Introduction* (Hyderabad, 1st edn. 1964, 2nd edn. [little changed, save for an additional preface] 1975), *passim*, and esp. ch. 7, 'Sind in Ancient Historical Times', pp. 100 ff. A number of subsidiary topographical problems arise in connection with Alexander's descent of the Indus, but I leave them out of account. H. Wilhelmy's description of the Delta in *Erdkunde*, 20 (1966), 276 ff., gives a good general survey, based on previous topographical accounts (Cunningham, Haig, Lambrick) and on his own recent observations. On p. 269 he gives a useful set of plans of the courses of the river over the millennium between the 8th and the 18th cents., and on p. 274 shows very clearly the change of course after 1758. (A second article in *Die Erde*, 99 (1968), 132–62, 'Karachi, Pakistans Tor zur Welt', is a popular account of the growth of the city from its origins in the mid-18th cent. (when it was a fishing village dependent on the khanate of Kalāt).)

[113] For the lost coast of Sind see the works mentioned in the previous note. Haig's narrative, loc. cit., is cogent, except for occasional details, and exposes the weaknesses of several of Cunningham's identifications. His map in frontispiece shows the change in the coast-line very clearly; see also the map in Lambrick, facing p. 132.

evidence of settlement of the relevant period on or near the coast. Aurel Stein's reports on archaeological remains in the area are valuable (though inevitably imprecise in the absence of a identifiable chronological framework) for that part of the coastal zone west of Gwadar, just east of Tiz, where he recorded 'burial grounds comprising the first few centuries of our era', but we have no help for the stretch of the coast east of this, the land of the Ichthyophagi. A particular difficulty occurs where the rivers of Baluchistan empty into the Indian Ocean, for the water-supply has suffered basic diminution with corresponding changes in settlement-areas. On the other hand some of the long inland valleys and plateaus parallel to the sea seem to remain relatively fertile, and support some agricultural activity.[114]

7. ALEXANDRIA–RAMBAKIA, OR ALEXANDRIA AMONG THE OREITAI

Arrian tells us that in the first part of this journey, having left Pattala in the winter of 325/4, Alexander, moving, presumably, through the pass at the south end of the Kirthar range, advanced as far as the river Arabios, the modern Hab, and then entered the territory of the Oreitai, and reached Rambakia, 'the largest village of the ethnos of the Oreitai', a locality to be set at, or near, Las Bela, at the head of the basin through which the Porali and its tributaries run, formed by the Mor and Haro ranges. He expressed satisfaction at the location, and considered that a city built in that

[114] The best general account of the coastal zone is that of Holdich, *The Gates of India* (London, 1910), 145 ff., but his account of the movements of Alexander's army is based on the view (shared by many, not least by Eggermont, op. cit. 57 ff.) that the army travelled along the coast, after crossing the Porali, by-passing Rās Mālān, and not along the natural inner route from Las Bela to Turbat. I have followed the convincing account of the route given by Stein, *Georg. Journ.* 102 (1943), 193–227, 'On Alexander's Route into Gedrosia: An Archaeological Tour in Las Bela' (Stein's last article; he died in Kābul in the winter of 1943, the tour described in the article having been made in January to March of that year), according to which Alexander marched up the estuary of the Porali to Las Bela (a shorter route by some miles than the present distance), before turning west along the inland route. Stein's article contains a full account, with excellent photographs, of the wild and arduous territory; see also Goukowsky, *Essai sur les origines du mythe d'Alexandre*, i (Nancy, 1981), 97 ff. (Kokala the port in Diod., Kambali the town); Tarn, *Alex.* ii. 249 ff. (cf. below n. 115). Certainty is unattainable. I may note that D. T. Potts, *The Arabian Gulf* (Oxford, 1990, 2 vols.), ii, contains an exhaustive account of the archaeological evidence of the Arabian side of the Gulf itself and its islands; cf. below, p. 180, n. 13.

neighbourhood would prosper, would, in words by now familiar, 'become large and prosperous'—the same words used by Arrian of the foundations on the Nile and the Jaxartes, and surely representing an authentic formula attributable to the basic conceptions of Alexander himself. In other words, Alexandria-Rambakia was to be the main new emporium, with access both to the southern sea, less distant then than now, and to the passes to Kandahar (Alexandria in Arachosia), for purposes of trade and for military requirements, a role performed over many subsequent centuries by Las Bela.[115] Viewed from this point of view the foundation must be

---

[115] See Arr. vi. 21. 5: ἀφικόμενος δὲ ἐς κώμην ἥπερ ἦν μεγίστη τοῦ ἔθνους τοῦ Ὠρειτῶν, Ῥαμβάκια ἐκαλεῖτο ἡ κώμη, τόν τε χῶρον ἐπήινεσε καὶ ἐδόκει ἂν αὐτῶι πόλις ξυνοικισθεῖσα μεγάλη καὶ εὐδαίμων γένεσθαι. Ἡφαιστίωνα μὲν δὴ ἐπὶ τούτου ὑπελείπετο; cf. ibid. 22. 3: ἀπολείπει Λεόννατον . . . τὴν πόλιν ξυνοικίζειν καὶ τὰ κατὰ τοὺς Ὠρείτας κοσμεῖν, κ.τ.λ.; cf. Diod. xvii. 104. 8: ὁ δ' Ἀλέξανδρος παρὰ θάλατταν ἐφιλοτιμήθη κτίσαι πόλιν καὶ λιμένα μὲν εὑρὼν ἄκλυστον ἔκτισεν ἐν αὐτῶι πόλιν Ἀλεξάνδρειαν. For Leonnatus' role cf. Juba, quoted by Plin. NH, vi. 97 (FGrH 275 F28 = ibid. 134 F28 (Onesicritus)): Alexandria condita a Leonnato iussu Alexandri in finibus gentis; Argennus portu salubri . . . (98) Ori gens; flumen Carmaniae Hyctanis portuosum et auro fertile. Steph. places Ἀλεξάνδρεια τῶν Ὠρειτῶν (4) (Νεαρτῶν, MSS, already corrected in early edns., followed by Mein., to Ὠριτῶν, ex Arr.; Diod. xvii. 105. 1 also has Νεαρτῶν: see Welles ad loc., Loeb) in the land of the Ichthyophagi, a characteristic elaboration, which over-simplifies the geographical reality. The land of the Ichthyophagi naturally lay on the narrow strip of coast west of the mouth of the Hingol river, and not inland, at Las Bela. The Ἀλεξάνδρου νῆσος mentioned by Ptol. vi. 8, 15 νῆσοι δὲ παράκεινται τῆι Περσίδι . . . Ἀλεξάνδρου ἡ καὶ Ἀρακία (cf. Marcian., § 24: ἀπὸ δὲ Ῥογομάνιος ποταμοῦ εἰς Χερσόνησον στάδιοι φ'. ἐνταῦθα παράκειται νῆσος Ἀλεξάνδρου καλουμένη), whatever the historical origin of the name, is included in the Περσίδος θέσις, and therefore not relevant in this context. I accept Stein's identification of Alexandria-Rambakia as lying near or at Las Bela, at the north end of the fertile triangle, in the area known as Welpat, through which the Porali runs. The site has not been investigated, but Stein describes the refuse dumps on which it is built, and which were then continually growing, op. cit. 215 (Brunt, on Arr. vi. 21.5, says 'Las Bela, where ancient remains have been found', but Stein refers to none). There is no indication in Arrian, as quoted above, that Alexandria-Rambakia was on the coast, and while Diodorus loc. cit. states that it was a harbour he cannot be trusted on the precise location. The view, therefore, that it lay at Somniani on the coast, at the eastern end of the great inlet of Miani-Hor, satisfies the phraseology of Diodorus, but otherwise has nothing in its favour, though it is frequently maintained, e.g. by Tomaschek, SB Wien. Akad. 1890 (121), pp. 19-20. Eggermont, 77, places it at the western end of Miani-Hor, Hamilton, loc. cit. (below note 117), p. 608, 'not far from the northern shore of the Miani Hor'. In any case the basin of the Porali has undergone substantial changes since antiquity, as a result of the accumulation of silt from the river: see Haig, Indus Delta, 136 ff. Las Bela was known to the Arabs as Armabil or (less correctly) as Armayil and the Hudūd al-'ālam, p. 123, refers to Armabil as 'situated close to the sea on the edge of the desert': see Le Strange, op. cit. 330 n. 3, and Holdich, op. cit. 304 ff. It formed a station on the route between the Makrān and Sind through the region known in the early Arab writers as Turān. In later times, until the construction of the railway from Karachi

judged no less significant than those in central Asia, an indication of the range of Alexander's vision. The next city in Stephanus's list (10), Ἀλεξάνδρεια ἐν Μακαρηνῆι, otherwise unattested and perhaps a corrupt form, but provided with the localization, ἣν παραρρεῖ ποταμὸς Μαξάτης, an unknown river, may perhaps be the same city.[116] We may also note that Pliny, Ptolemy, and Ammianus

to Quetta, it was the first major stage on the route to Kalāt after leaving Somniani, where the caravans collected: see Masson, *Narrative*, ii. 164-5, on the regular caravan route to Kalāt, which for most of the way followed the course of the Porali. Masson says that the *kāfila* consisted of merchants from Sind, Bombay and Kandahar, thus illustrating the vital link between the Lower Indus valley and Central Asia provided by the Porali; cf. also Mohan Lal, *Travel in the Punjab* (London, 1846; repr. Calcutta, 1977) pp. 192 ff. O. Caroe, *The Pathans* (London, 1958), 370 ff., has a general account of the strategical and commercial role of Kalāt and Quetta as key points between India and Kandahar.

[116] Μακαρήνη is entered in Pape's *Wörterbuch* with a question mark, repeating perhaps the doubts expressed by Saumaise, who proposed Σακασ(τ?)ήνηι, while Holsten preferred Μαξαρηνῆι, no doubt because of the river Μαξάτης, which Saumaise emended to Ἰαξάρτης: see Meineke's note ad loc. Tarn, *Alex.* ii. 249-55, who rightly dismisses Saumaise' efforts to transform Makarene into something 'which he happened to have heard of', has a long section in which he attempts to establish that this city 'in Makarene' is no other than Alexandria among the Oreitai, Arrian's Ora (vi. 22.3), which he regards as the capital of the Oreitai and the true site of the new Alexandria, while Rambakia 'was only a village'. The natural reading of Arrian is that the new city was built at or near Rambakia, and that Ora was an alternative name for it, used, as Tarn emphasized, by Aristobulus, *FGrH* 139 F49 = Strab. 723, where see Kramer's note). Tarn claims that the form Μακαρηνή is a true 'eparchic' form (following his theory regarding geographical forms in -ηνή), and that it is the direct antecedent of the word Makrān, 'an eparchy of Gedrosia' (so also Tomaschek, *RE* (10)). The term Makrān/Mukrān is attested in the accounts of the earliest Arab conquests of the area (see the summary of these events in Holdich, 291 ff.), and it is possible that the term survived. But I do not feel confident about it (Eggermont, p. 64, offers a different etymology). It is any case clear that there was only one city in the area, Rambakia, as Hamilton has shown, *Historia*, 21 (1972), 604-6, cf. Goukowsky, *Mythe d'Alexandre*, ii (Nancy, 1981), 96 ff. who also (pp. 99-100) discusses A. in Makarene, which he regards as a separate foundation by Leonnatos, in the hinterland of Gedrosia. Cunningham, p. 309, suggested that Alexandria-Rambakia was the Ἀλ. κατὰ τὸν μέλανα κόλπον, of Stephanus (16: see above, pp. 26-7), on the basis of the resemblance of the Greek word 'to the bay of Malan, to the east of Rās Mālān of the present day', the ancient Μάλανα, which Arrian describes as the westernmost point of the territory of the Oreitai (see Arr. *Ind.* 27. 1: ἀφικνέονται ἐς χῶρον, ὃς δὴ ἔσχατος ἦν τῆς Ὠρειτῶν γῆς, Μάλανα τῶι χώρωι ὄνομα). The location in very general terms would suit that Alexandria not too badly (better than some suggestions that have been made), for it comes in Stephanus' list after Ἀλ. παρὰ τοῖς Ἀραχώτοις (see above, pp. 2 ff.), but, even if there were any evidence that Alexander built a further, otherwise unrecorded, city in this area, the great bare headland, described by Holdich (p. 161) as 'the huge barrier of the Malān range, abutting direct on the sea' could not be the potential site of a 'large and prosperous city': see also Stein's account of the ascent of the Mālān pass, op. cit. 204-5. The name of the headland is given by Pliny as *mons Maleus*, and a connection with the Greek μέλας may be discounted; cf. Tarn, ibid. 253-4.

refer to an Alexandria in Carmania, unknown, like that of Makarene, to historians, the tradition of the *Romance*, and the Arab geographers.[117] These perplexing Alexandrias of the area of Baluchistan, which lack the authentic testimony of Alexandria-Rambakia, cannot be identified.

On leaving his new city Alexander marched on the natural (but very strenuous) line of communication via Turbat down to Gwadar, and then moved into the heart of Gedrosia, to reach Pura, sixty marches from Ora-Rambakia. Pura itself probably lay close to Bampur, on the Bampur river, some 150 miles inland.[118] After a period of rest he advanced into southern Carmania, where Craterus and other commanders joined him from the Indian regions to the north bordering on Sijistān, and thence moved across Fars to Pasargadai and Persepolis, and thence to Susa. From there he sailed down the Eulaios to its junction with the Koprates (Karūn), and thence to the open sea, and round to the (then separate) mouth of the Tigris. He then sailed up the Tigris to Opis, probably half-way between Baghdad and Sāmarrāh. After that he returned across Iran to Ecbatana in Media, where Hephaestion died, made his expedition against the Kossaians in the mountains of Luristān (winter 324), and then returned to Babylon. Here his plans for the 'colonization' of the head of the Persian Gulf and its islands were formulated—Arrian uses the word κατοικίζειν[119]—for, Arrian says, Alexander thought that this region would be no less prosperous than Phoenicia; once more the emphasis is on regional (and ultimately 'global') prosperity, which, in this context, presumably indicates that Alexander envisaged the development of communications and trade between the Middle East and India via the Persian Gulf. Moreover, the eastern coast of Arabia further south offered similar attractions: numerous offshore islands such as Tylos

---

[117] Tarn, 239, accepts the Carmanian Alexandria, in the region of Hormūz (for which see his detailed study, *GBI* 481 ff.), as a foundation of Alexander himself, but its attestation is weak.

[118] The details of this part of the route are excellently worked out by Stein, loc. cit. 193; cf. Tarn, *Alex.* ii. 251. As far as Gwadar the route is clear, as described above; beyond that, in Kirmān, identifications become more difficult, the location of Pura itself, the capital of Gedrosia, usually located at Bampur, being conjectural, but likely. For a closely argued discussion of the entire route, in essential agreement with Stein's exposition, see Brunt's *Arrian*, ii. 474 ff., esp. pp. 478 ff.

[119] vii. 19.6: τήν τε γὰρ παραλίαν τὴν πρὸς τῶι κόλπωι τῶι Περσικῶι κατοικίζειν ἐπενόει καὶ τὰς νήσους τὰς ταύτηι. ἐδόκει γὰρ αὐτῶι οὐ μεῖον ⟨ἂν⟩ Φοινίκης εὐδαίμων ἡ χώρα αὕτη γενέσθαι.

and Ikaros, and abundant harbours to provide anchorage for his fleet and suitable locations for settlements likely to enjoy a prosperous future. With these settlements in mind Alexander sent Archias to Tylos, and also investigated Ikaros (Failaka), both off the Kuwaiti coast, and other commanders were dispatched further south. He himself sailed south from Babylon down the Pallacopas canal on the west side of the Euphrates, and reached the 'land of the Arabs', on the edge of the cultivation, and here founded his last city, perhaps to be identified with Spasinou Charax, a fortified site which he populated with some Greek mercenaries (never his favourite troops), some of whom were volunteers and others time-expired and sick men (how sick troops were likely to survive in that unhealthy spot he perhaps did not consider).

8. THE LATER SPASINOU CHARAX

Also supposedly founded by Alexander, this is placed by Pliny, following Juba, to the east of the Tigris, between the mouths of the Eulaios (Karūn, Dujayl) and the Tigris; once ten stades from the coast, this distance by Juba's time had become 50, and by Pliny's 120, miles.[120]

According to Pliny the city was destroyed in due course by the

---

[120] Plin. vi. 138-40 (*FGrH* 275 F1): *Charax oppidum Persici sinus intimum, a quo Arabia Eudaemon cognominata excurrit, habitatur in colle manu facto inter confluentes dextra Tigrim, laeva Eulaeum IIp. laxitate. conditum est primum ab Alexandro Magno, colonis ex urbe regia Durine quae interiit deductis militum inutilibus ibi relictis; Alexandriam appellari iusserat, pagumque Pellaeum a patria sua quem proprie Macedonum fecerat. flumina id oppidum expugnavere. postea restituit Antiochus quintus regum et suo nomine appellavit; iterum quoque infestatum Spaosines Sagdodonaci filius, rex finitorum Arabum, quam Iuba satrapen Antiochi fuisse falso tradit, oppositis molibus restituit nomenque suum dedit, emunito situ iuxta in longitudinem vi p., in latitudine paulo minus. primo afuit a litore stadios x et maritimum etiam ipsa portum habuit, Iuba vero prodente L p.; nunc abesse a litore cxx legati Arabum nostrique negotiatores qui inde venere adfirmant.* Arr. vii. 21. 7, gives the settlement with his usual brevity: τούτων ἕνεκα ἐπί τε τὸν Παλλακόπαν ἔπλευσε καὶ κατ᾽ αὐτὸν καταπλεῖ ἐς τὰς λίμνας ὡς ἐπὶ τὴν Ἀράβων γῆν. ἔνθα χωρόν τινα ἐν καλῶι ἰδὼν πόλιν ἐξωικοδόμησέ τε καὶ ἐτείχισε, καὶ ἐν ταύτηι κατώικισε τῶν Ἑλλήνων τινὰς τῶν μισθοφόρων, ὅσοι τε ἑκόντες καὶ ὅσοι ὑπὸ γήρως ἢ κατὰ πήρωσιν ἀπόλεμοι ἦσαν. In vii. 7. 2, Arrian refers to Alexander sailing down the Eulaios from Susa to the mouth of the Tigris, but there is no reference to a foundation of a city, although this passage has usually been quoted in support of the location: see next note. The Alexander-foundation, wherever it was, has been identified with Stephanus' Ἀλεξάνδρεια ἐπὶ τοῦ Τίγριδος (see above, p. 32 n. 69) but no historian or geographer makes the identification, or (Pliny apart) indeed calls the city an Alexandria. The site at the mouth of the Pallacopas is said to be Teredon (Diridotes), Arr. *Ind.* xli, 6, cf. Tomaschek, loc. cit. 79-80.

flooding of the Euphrates, and refounded by Antiochus Epiphanes; and, finally, once more destroyed, rebuilt by Spasines, the neighbouring Arab ruler, who took the precaution of surrounding it with moles. From that time onwards it was known as Spasinou Charax (its ethnic Χαρακηνός, the home of Isidore), and probably survived either as the independent centre of the principality of Mesene or as a Parthian subject state until absorbed in the Sassanian kingdom in the third century AD. However, though Juba and Pliny agree that Spasinou Charax was originally a foundation of Alexander, and although its site has now been established beyond reasonable doubt at the Arab Karkh Maisān (now Naisan)', it is possible that its identification as an Alexander-foundation is erroneous. Arrian has two accounts of Alexander's activities in the area of the modern Shaṭṭ al-'Arab, one in 324 BC and one in the following year; in the first of these there is no mention of a foundation, and it is in the second, which refers to a point further west than that now established for Spasinou Charax, that he is expressly said to have founded his city. Thus though there is good reason to believe that the site of Spasinou Charax has been correctly identified, and that Alexander founded a city somewhere in the neighbourhood of the Lower Tigris, the identity of the two must turn on preference for the testimony of Pliny and Juba over the unspecific account of Arrian.[121]

---

[121] The problem of the location of Spasinou Charax is very complex, turning to a large extent on the determination of the almost continuous hydrographic changes of Lower Mesopotamia. The very full study of these and of visible remains in the water-logged region, by J. Hansman, recorded in *Iranica Antiqua*, 7 (1967) pp. 21-58 (cf. id. *Iran*, 22 (1984), pp. 161 ff.) seems to have settled the location. But it is unfortunate that in his opening study of the ancient sources (pp. 21-2) he has conflated the two passages of Arrian with that of Pliny to make one event of Alexander's activities, namely when he sailed down the Eulaios as described in Arr. vii. 7. 2, where there is no reference to a foundation (see previous note). The important article of P. Bernard, *JS* (1990), 3-68, traces the later history of Mesene in the light of the remarkable inscription carved on the thigh of the bronze statue of Herakles found at Seleukeia-on-Tigris, which describes the conquest of Mesene by 'Arsakes Vologases', and the removal of the statue to Seleukeia (as it were, the Palladium of Spasinou Charax), *SEG* xxxvii. 1403; cf. further, D. Potter, *ZPE* 88 (1991) 277 ff. Detailed maps of the waterways, ancient and modern, are provided by Hansman, locc. citt., cf. Bernard, 29. The νόμιμον ἐμπόριον λεγόμενον ἡ Ἀπολόγου, κειμένη κατὰ ⟨Σ⟩πασίνου Χάρακα of *Peripl. Mar. Erythr.* § 35, was evidently close to the latter, but distinct from it. There is no reference to it elsewhere, so its location and its role in the general pattern of harbours etc. in the region of the Shaṭṭ al-'Arab remain wholly uncertain. It is identified (on grounds of linguistic continuity) by Le Strange, *LEC* 19, cf. p. 47, with Ab-Ubullah or Obolla on the Baṣra Canal, at its junction with the Tigris (see map II, ibid.). Hansman, *Iranica Antiqua*, loc. cit. 25,

From Egypt to Susiana we have enumerated the foundations of cities that the historians ascribe to Alexander in their accounts of his campaigns, and it now behoves us to consider what conclusions, if any, we may draw from their evidence, in spite of all the limitations on our knowledge regarding their identity and location, and the almost total absence of directly relevant archaeological evidence in the whole vast region that he traversed and conquered. Before turning, however, to that task, the reader may be reminded here, of a major consideration explored at an earlier phase of this enquiry. The cities discussed in this chapter, of whose historical existence, whatever their precise location, there can be no serious doubt, do not overlap at all with those listed in the α-tradition of the *Romance*. The two lists represent separate worlds, one real, one fabricated, the only members common to both being Alexandria ad Aegyptum and Alexandria-Bucephala.

regards it as the successor of Spasinou Charax in the 2nd cent. AD (perhaps after the Parthian conquest described in the inscription on the thigh of Herakles?). What noun are we to supply with the article ἡ? πόλις seems the most popular candidate, but the personification of Ἀπόλογος may be deemed rather improbable until a further instance of the personal name is found. Ἡ τοῦ ἀπολογ(ισμ)οῦ ἀπόστασις or ἀποθήκη, referring to customs' or other quays at this point on the river, seems to combine best with ἐμπόριον, and might have stood in the original Greek text, though if the Arabic equation is correct the shorter form must have been the current Greek one in early Islamic times. Parallels for the use of a plain genitive for the name of a locality are given by Meineke in Steph., note on Μενέλαος (p. 445), but these are compounded of proper names. Tarn, *GBI* 13, adds some more, notably Διαδόχου, Steph. s.v., πόλις Περσικὴ οὐ πόρρω Κτησιφῶντος. For the particular meaning to be given to νόμιμον ἐμπόριον see L. Casson, *Periplus Maris Erythraei* (Princeton, 1989), 275-6.

CHAPTER VI

General Assessment of Alexander's Foundations

SEVERAL features seem to recur constantly as factors in the foundations, which provide us with an indication of Alexander's purpose in founding cities. In assessing this evidence we leave on one side the numerous forts and temporary garrisons, the construction of which was a recurrent feature of operations throughout the years of campaigning, and which are frequently referred to by the historians. There is no suggestion in our sources that these were planned as urban communities, and they may be omitted from our discussion. In general it seems clear that Alexander's urban settlements—sometimes, but not always, named by himself after himself—fall into specific groups, or fulfil certain regular functions, in the whole region which he traversed in a vast arc between the first eastern settlement at Herāt to the last, near the emergence of the Tigris and Euphrates. It is naturally uncertain how much we can discover of the intentions of an individual of such unique energy and purpose, when they go largely unrecorded, but it is legitimate to draw conclusions from the few motives attributed to him by his historians, and to infer some general principles from what appear to be constant features of his activities in this connection.

Before doing this, however, we must stress that it is a fundamental weakness of the Classical writers (historians and geographers alike), in so far as a modern assessment is required, that the civilization of which they formed part had no sense of the historical, geographical, or cultural significance of landscape. In Arrian or Eratosthenes, as preserved in Strabo, or any of the other sources utilized in this book (save only occasionally in Strabo himself and, in his fanciful, elaborate way, Ammianus), we do not read of the oases that must have gladdened the hearts of Alexander's men from the Caspian to the Jaxartes and to the Indus; and the mountains, deserts, and rivers which dominate Central Asia, and which they crossed, are barely noticed. The lack of descriptive writing in the surviving sources (for some at least of the original sources seem to have been more informative) is a fundamental defect in our appreciation of Alexander's motives for founding cities, for choice of location and so on. For the most part we have to rely on later accounts. Who could guess from Arrian of the magnificent richness of the oasis of Herāt, through which so many waterways ran, and made it so natural a site for Alexandria in Aria, or of the oasis of Kandahar where two great rivers converged? Nobody. It is as if, except for a few mountains and rivers that are but names in the text, Alexander marched over a college lawn. Yet the physical characteristics (which, even in the account of his harrowing journey back through the Makrān desert, are given no real dimensions) are vital to our assessment of his intentions and discernment in selecting this rather than that site. Whoever wishes to understand the riches of the landscape two thousand, no less than one thousand years ago, and to grasp the 'human geography' of the region must turn to the Arabs, and use their accounts, with due regard to changed circumstances, to give flesh and blood to the dry bones of the Classical topographers. Nevertheless, in spite of this limitation of our vision we can apprehend that Alexander followed certain procedures with sufficient frequency for us to call them a policy.

(1) The first feature we can observe is that, with the exception of Bucephala, he chose to establish his new cities on the site of, or very close to, existing Achaemenid fortresses and perhaps satrapal capitals. This may have been for the obvious reason that these lay for the most part in large and rich oases, adapted to intensive agricultural activity, with convenient access to the main river-systems and valley-routes. Thus Alexandria in Ariana was built in the Herāt oasis, close to the Hari-Rūd, near, though not on, the site of the Achaemenian Artacoana; Alexandria in Arachosia probably in the oasis of Kandahar, virtually on a pre-existing Achaemenian site; Alexandria ad Caucasum in the Kūhistān basin north of Charikar, probably on or near the site of the Achaemenian Kapisakani-Begrām, at the confluence of the Ghorband and Panjshir rivers, close to the junction of the three ways from Bactria and the Indus valley; and Alexandreschata near Cyropolis, Cyrus'

own foundation on the banks of the Jaxartes. This general pattern was, as noted, probably in part the result of the natural policy of occupying and settling the best land in the oases, but it is also to be noted that only in one instance, Cyropolis, are we told that Alexander destroyed one of the Achaemenian cities, nor is there any archaeological evidence that he did so. It must therefore be remembered both that Alexander was φιλόκυρος, and also that he had no wish to destroy the Iranian traditions and way of life; on the contrary, he absorbed them himself to a degree that alienated his Macedonians; and once the Achaemenid dynasty was destroyed, he proposed, as his publicly proclaimed ultimate aim, the union of the two peoples, Persian and Macedonian, in joint rule over the conquered territories. It was, then, only natural that, so far as was possible, he would wish to emphasize and perpetuate this Iranian–Macedonian continuity in his foundations. In Gandhara and the Indus Valley and beyond, the nineteenth Achaemenian satrapy, the rule of the Achaemenids had sat more lightly and less effectively than in the Iranian world and Transoxiana, and here Alexander found local rulers who, once the victory over Porus was achieved, could offer little co-ordinated resistance. In the place of Achaemenian fortresses and satrapal centres he found small princely capitals, such as Taxila and Charsadda-Peukelaotis, and rulers such as Taxiles and Porus himself. It was a natural consequence of this situation that Alexander had less need here to stress the continuity of rule than in the Iranian provinces, and that in the Punjab he marked his victory over Porus with the foundation of Nikaia, and did not call attention to the origin of other cities, by giving them an eponymous name; Bucephala-Alexandria commemorated the loved companion of his many struggles and journeys from his youth till the time of the horse's death. Whether, at the beginning of the homeward journey, the foundation of Alexandria at Rambakia in the Makrān lay within organized and effectively governed Achaemenian territory we are not in a position to say.

This characteristic of Alexander's foundations, that the new cities by their names proclaimed the new world created by him, and by their proximity to Achaemenian centres emphasized the continuity of urban and military settlement, as opposed to the destructive passage of armies, may be said, without undue rigidity of formulation, to represent the political aspect of his foundations.

(2) No less significant a factor, perhaps even paramount where appropriate, although Alexander did not formulate the aim in modern terms, was the appreciation of the need to stimulate the expansion of contacts between peoples and regions, both to develop trading and commercial activity in its widest sense, and to encourage the natural growth of a settled agricultural way of life. It had not escaped the notice of the Greeks that, in spite of its wealth in treasure, the Achaemenid Empire was economically stagnant. Isocrates, the shrewdest surviving observer of the dying Empire, had referred a generation before Alexander's birth, in 387 BC, to the wealth of Asia, which was waiting to be brought to Europe to work;[1] in 346 he identified not Artaxerxes, but Idrieus, the Carian satrap, as 'the richest man in Asia',[2] and had described the economic distress of the Persian Empire as remediable only through Greek initiative, and in particular through the foundation of new cities to absorb and settle the brigands and other human by-products of the economic distress of Greece itself, who (it was to be hoped) would exploit the land profitably. It was, said Isocrates, the duty of a high-minded philhellene—he was thinking of Alexander's father—'with a wider vision than other men', to use this human material also for warlike purposes against Persia, to achieve this end.[3] The second point was perhaps now obsolete, or, at least, dealt with, for Alexander had indeed used available mercenary man-power in his campaign, and had also settled some of them in his new colonies; he could not foresee how unsuccessful an experiment this would turn out to be. But the wider issue of the incorporation of the potential economic productivity and range of the Persian Empire into the new empire of which the commercial pivot would be Alexandria in Egypt, and which would embrace the Aegean, with its enormous market potential—the transference of Achaemenian wealth both to the revitalized centres of the east and to Europe—could only be effected in lasting terms by the development of new centres of trade, as then understood. It seems likely

---

[1] *Paneg.* 187: Αὐτοὺς οὖν χρὴ συνδιορᾶν, ὅσης ἂν εὐδαιμονίας τύχοιμεν εἰ τὸν μὲν πόλεμον τὸν νῦν ὄντα περὶ ἡμᾶς πρὸς τοὺς ἠπειρώτας ποιησαίμεθα, τὴν δ' εὐδαιμονίαν τὴν ἐκ τῆς Ἀσίας εἰς τὴν Εὐρώπην διακομίσαιμεν.

[2] *Philip*, 103: καὶ μὴν Ἰδριέα γε τὸν εὐπορώτατον τῶν νῦν περὶ τὴν ἤπειρον προσήκει δυσμενέστερον εἶναι τούτων τῶν ἐθνῶν χρήσιμον. σοὶ δ' ἦν πολεμεῖν πρὸς αὐτὸν βουληθῆις συμφόρως ἕξειν.

[3] *Ibid.* 122: Ἔστιν οὖν ἀνδρὸς μέγα φρονοῦντος καὶ φιλέλληνος καὶ πορρωτέρω τῶν ἄλλων τῆι διανοίαι καθορῶντος, ἀποχρησάμενον τοὺς τοιούτους πρὸς τοὺς βαρβάρους καὶ χώραν ἀποτεμόμενον τοσαύτην ὅσην ὀλίγωι πρότερον εἰρήκαμεν, κ.τ.λ.

that, although Alexander can hardly be credited with any general conception of co-ordinated economic growth throughout his new empire, he at least appreciated the need for lines of communication both with the Mediterranean world, and internally across the land-routes; and the stimulus for that could be provided, not by Persians, nor even by Macedonians, but by the Greeks whom he, paradoxically, distrusted. It is in such questions of psychological understanding as to what Alexander actually intended that the absence of informed and independent contemporary comment, in orators or historians, and the survival only of military accounts of his expedition as our primary sources, is most felt.

It is nevertheless apparent that from the outset, with the foundation of Alexandria in Egypt, that was to outlive all other Alexandrias, such was his intention. There already he or his advisers (notably the devious Cleomenes of Naucratis) envisaged the fillip likely to be given to both Aegean and eastern trade by the establishment of a great port on the south Aegean shore, to take the place of the declining (but by no means defunct) Naucratis, to establish links through the Nile valley with the eastern and southern markets, which the Ptolemies were later to tap, and to establish a firm commercial base to reap the harvest of expanding Asiatic, Aegean and eventually Mediterranean trade. His purpose here was essentially commercial; he thought that the city would prosper—καὶ ἔδοξεν αὐτῶι ὁ χῶρος κάλλιστος κτίσαι ἐν αὐτῶι πόλιν καὶ γενέσθαι ἂν εὐδαίμονα τὴν πόλιν—and would bring the wealth of Asia to Europe. Whether he also envisaged the exploitation of the land of Egypt itself, in the Pharaonic manner that the Ptolemies were to perpetuate and develop, we cannot tell, but it is natural to suppose that he did. Certainly no Greek settlers, from the Nile to the Jaxartes, would settle happily into a life which did not also include the normal opportunities of small-scale agricultural activity and enjoyment of the resulting produce, notably the grape, the olive, and the fig. No rural territory would satisfy the demands of settlement unless it was εὔοινος and ἐλαιοφόρος—terms frequently used by Strabo to indicate the best and most characteristic features of a region—and we know that these fruits, essential to the Greek way of life, were and remained available, either as indigenous growth or after acclimatization by the Greeks, not only in Egypt, but also in Khorāsān, Sijistān, and Transoxiana.

The same pattern is noticeable in the other descriptions of

foundations authenticated by the historians, though it is only natural that the bematists, writers of *stathmoi*, and geographers do not provide such information. A mercantile motive is understandably not stated for Alexandria ad Caucasum, at the foot of the Hindu Kush, because even if its (re)foundation may have facilitated the safe passage of goods from the Ghorband valley, Turkestan, and Transoxiana into the Indus plain, that is unlikely to have been a primary consideration: Alexander was here concerned to establish a firm base for the transit of the mountain and the control of the difficult mountain-country to the west, the area of Bāmiyān and the later Ghūristān. With a new foundation in the oasis of Herāt and another at or near Begrām, Alexander could hope to dominate the entire east–west axis of the western Hindu Kush. However, at the most northern point of his main theatre of operations, in Sogdiana, the commercial motive is once more apparent. The foundation of Alexandria Eschate on the Jaxartes, probably at Khojend, not only indicated that to Alexander, as to his Achaemenid predecessors, the river-valleys and fertile areas of Sogdiana were part of his empire, beyond which lay the foreign outer world, and were therefore to be placed under the protection of a strong settlement at the river-frontier; but the same settlement was also envisaged as developing into a prosperous trading-centre (ὅ τε γὰρ χῶρος ἐπιτήδειος αὐτῶι ἐφαίνετο αὐξῆσαι ἐπὶ μέγα τὴν πόλιν), which, given its location, would be based on the caravan-trade from the north and east and on the local trading operations of the oases and river-valleys of Sogdiana, which later produced the opulent culture of the Polytimetos (Zeravshan; Sugd) river.[4] On the military side it is to be stressed that the Oxus was, for Alexander, as for the Persians, part of an internal, and not of a frontier, river-system, and to that extent it would be in keeping with the hypothesis here advanced that the greatest Achaemenian city on the south bank, Bactra, seems to have owed much of its importance to its significant role as a centre of Zoroastrianism. Bactria itself probably included the territory north of the river as far as the Hissar (Gissar) range which forms the natural barrier between the region dominated by the Oxus, and the Sogdian river-system beyond.[5] It

---

[4] On the culture of the region, centred on Pendzhikent, on the Zeravshan, see the account by Frumkin, op. cit. 72–80. The Sogdian civilization belongs to the 7th-8th cents. AD, and was finally destroyed by the Turks in the middle of the 8th cent.

[5] See Tarn *GBI* 102–3.

is only in very modern times that the Oxus has been an international frontier, and as late as the mid-nineteenth century the Emirate of Bokhārā held land south of the river, between Charzui and Termez and as far east as Kundūz. The internal trade-routes of this area, from the Hindu Kush to the Hissar range, were already determined by long usage, and, the *limes* of the Empire once fixed at the Jaxartes, the strategic importance of Bactria was essentially as a passage to the distant frontier. It is possible that the main importance of the site at Aï Khanūm was also commercial rather than military.[6] The inhabitants of the new Alexandria, that succeeded the Achaemenian Cyropolis (its Iranian name is unknown) were largely isolated from the rest of Alexander's empire, linked to it only by the passes of the Hissar range or by the long route from Samarkand; but compensation was to be found in the extraordinary fertility of the region, and of Khojend in particular, to which both Iṣṭakhrī and the author of the *Hudūd al-ʿālam* and, centuries later, Bābur, bear witness. It was famed above all for its pomegranates; Bābur tells us that the excellence of the pomegranates of Khojend and of the apples of Samarkand was proverbial, and he adds with his customary enthusiasm, that it was excellent sporting country.[7] Iṣṭakhrī at an earlier date dilates on the varied mineral wealth of the adjacent mountains to the south.[8] Here, then, at the farthest point of his empire, Alexander left his mixed community of farmers, traders and guardians of the marches, Greeks, Macedonians, and natives; the Iskander Kāl of Turkish times recalling, through who knows how many meandering divagations of legend and tradition, the man who came and saw the possibilities of the place.

(3) We may turn now to the other foundations of Alexander that seem to point to a clear policy of settlement on his part. These lie in a totally different region, some eleven hundred miles almost due

---

[6] The commercial activity at Aï Khanūm is well attested by the amphorae and other containers, inscribed with measures and other details of content, published by P. Bernard, especially in *BEFEO* 68 (1980), 1–75, and Cl. Rapin, *BCH* (1983), 315–72. These seem to belong mostly to the first half of the second cent. BC., cf. above, p. 155 n. 98.

[7] For Bābur's description see p. 7, Beveridge: 'Khujand is one of the ancient towns . . . Fruit grows well there; its pomegranates are renowned for their excellence; people talk of a Khujand pomegranate as they do of a Samarkand apple . . . The hunting and fowling-grounds of Khujand are first-rate; pheasant and hare are all had in great plenty. The climate is very malarious; in autumn there is much fever . . .'   [8] p. 332 (*BGA* i).

south of Khojend, on the shores of the Indian Ocean, and form part of the pattern of settlement that developed on his journey homewards from Patala to the head of the Persian Gulf. As we have seen, the first settlement lay at Rambakia, in the territory of the Oreitai, probably at the head of the plain of Las Bela, at the northern end of the estuary of the Porali river. Here Alexander decided to found a large city by the synoecism of the local population; it would, he believed, as he believed of Alexandria in Egypt and Alexandria on the Jaxartes, become great and prosperous.[9] It was here, then, in the heat of Baluchistan that Alexander saw the main base for his coastal trade, and possibly also the strategic base for lasting control of northern Gedrosia and Arachosia, by way of the well-worn tracks over which caravans and armies have marched over the centuries, up the Porali valley to Kalāt in the Harboi Hills and Quetta, and through the Bolān and Khojak passes to Kandahar, the circle of his empire thus completed. Here, too, then, a commercial and a military purpose may be seen operating simultaneously, and the potential significance of this site at the 'Western Gate of India' should not, indeed cannot, be overlooked. Holdich called Quetta, Kalāt and Las Bela 'the watch-towers of the western marches', and stressed the vital importance of the maintenance of this route as the ultimate key to the road to Herāt; he added of this link-route between the coast and the interior, 'until quite lately these seaboard approaches to India have been almost wholly ignored by historians and military strategists',[10] Alexander, whose knowledge of this inland route, which he had not himself traversed, must have come from the leaders of caravans and others who journeyed over the land-route from the coast to the world beyond the northern passes to Arachosia and Ariana, was here establishing a vital link for his empire, and one which, so far as we are able to tell, had little Achaemenian precedent. To us it may seem unlikely that a commander oppressed, as Alexander was at this point, with problems of commissariat and indeed of

---

[9] Arr. vi. 21. 5: ἀφικόμενος δὲ εἰς κώμην, ἥπερ ἦν μεγίστη τοῦ ἔθνους τοῦ Ὠρειτῶν, Ῥαμβακία ἐκαλεῖτο ἡ κώμη, τόν τε χῶρον ἐπήινεσε καὶ ἐδόκει ἂν αὐτῶι πόλις ξυνοικισθεῖσα μεγάλη καὶ εὐδαίμων γενέσθαι. Ἡφαιστίωνα μὲν δὴ ἐπὶ τούτοις ὑπελείπετο. Diod. xvii. 104. 8, is more circumstantial: ὁ δ᾽ Ἀλέξανδρος παρὰ θάλατταν ἐφιλοτιμήθη κτίσαι πόλιν ⟨καὶ⟩ λιμένα μὲν εὑρὼν ἄκλυστον, πλησίον δ᾽ αὐτοῦ τόπον εὔθετον ἔκτισεν ἐν αὐτῶι πόλιν Ἀλεξάνδρειαν. Cf. above, p. 165 with n. 115.

[10] *Gates of India*, 138–9, 141. See also ch. 8, on the Arab exploration of the Makrān, which is among the finest in that admirable book.

survival and extrication, should have thought along these lines, but the question of the overland route from the region of Sijistān to the coast of the Persian Gulf was probably in his mind the previous year when he despatched Craterus from the Indus through Arachosia and Drangiana; for Craterus rejoined Alexander in Carmania, thereby demonstrating the feasibility for men and elephants of the land-route via Kalāt, which later became a main route for trade and caravans.[11] It is perhaps ironic that the only surviving reference to a deliberate policy on the part of Alexander in respect of road-building lies in the fabulous proclamation that the *Romance* puts into his mouth after the death of Darius; he says in this proclamation that he will build measured roads throughout the empire that he has taken from Darius to promote trade and safe communications.[12]

However, the periplous that was about to begin showed that the commercial significance of the Gulf was of prime importance in Alexander's plans for an eastern trade route. When, his gruelling march through southern Persia over, towards the end of his life, Alexander looked ahead to the next stage in the long years that he might presume to lie before him, it is clear that his interest was |centred on exploration, both for its own sake, in the interests of further knowledge, that is to say, and also to investigate the prospects of an extension of maritime trade; and though not all, indeed only a small part, of these projects were completed, or even put in hand, his intention was evidently to develop the mercantile potential of the communities of the Gulf and its islands. In due course, we know that one or two of the northern Gulf islands were brought within the sphere of Seleucid administration, though we cannot determine whether that was a continuation of Alexander's

[11] Arr. vi. 15. 4; cf. vi. 27. 3. There are difficulties about Craterus' movements at this time (see Brunt on vi. 15. 5), but his subsequent instructions to take the route via Arachosia and Drangiana to a meeting-point in Carmania, and to take the elephants with him, are expressly stated in vi. 17. 3, and the reunion equally explicitly in vi. 27. 3; for further details see Brunt, App. xvii. 29 [not 31, as stated ibid. n. 4 on p. 183] Cf. also Berve, ii. 224–5. For the importance of the trade route, Somniani-Kalāt-Bolān pass-Kandahar-Ghazna see the accounts in the 19th-cent. travellers, esp. Masson, noted above, p. 165 n. 115, and for its strategic potential, Holdich, *Gates*, loc. cit.

[12] ii. 21. 10–11: τὰς δὲ ὁδοὺς τῆς Περσίδος πραγματεύεσθαι εἰρηνικῶς, ὅπως καὶ οἱ ἀπὸ τῆς Ἑλλάδος εὐκόπως εἰς ὁποίαν ἐὰν βούλωνται πόλιν τῆς Περσίδος πορεύωνται. ἀπὸ γὰρ τοῦ Εὐφράτου ποταμοῦ [καὶ] τῆς διαβάσεως καὶ τῆς ἀρχῆς τῆς ὁδοῦ διὰ ἡμισχοίνου ἑκάστωι σατράπηι ἀπέστειλα ὁδὸν ποιῆσαι καὶ διὰ σχοίνου ἐγγράψαι, ὅπου ἡ ὁδὸς φέρει.

earlier plans, or the result of direct Seleucid initiative.[13] It remains at all events clear that he established one new foundation, possibly two, at this time; the one, unnamed, perhaps the later Spasinou Charax, at Maisān, and the other, closely connected with it (but not specifically associated with Alexander, and probably of Hellenistic origin) 'the emporion called ἡ Ἀπολόγου named in the *Periplous*.[14] It is obvious both from the context in which Arrian describes Alexander's plans for the region, and from the location of Spasinou Charax, if that was indeed a foundation of Alexander (though not an Alexandria), that it was intended to open a new phase in the development of the harbourage facilities in the continuously changing course of the Euphrates and the united Eulaios and Tigris (the two main rivers had not yet joined to form the Shaṭṭ al-'Arab), and to provide opportunities for the Gulf trade; an early forerunner of Sassanian and Arab Sirāf and Arab Hormūz. These final plans were not to be matured by Alexander, but they were developed gradually from Seleucid times onwards. We may see the result as developed over three or four centuries in the text of the *Periplous*.

The various motives for Alexander's foundations, as described here, are clearly partly hypothetical, but nevertheless they seem to correspond to what little we can learn of them from our literary sources, from archaeology and from reasonable conjecture as to their general geographical location. If, then, it is correct to regard Alexander as essentially concerned, in his foundations, on the one hand with the preservation and continuation of the Achaemenian pattern of life in his new Macedonian–Iranian Empire, and with the

---

[13] On the history of Failaka (Ikaros) and the other islands in the Seleucid period see the very full paper by C. Roueché and S. M. Sherwin-White, *Chiron*, 15 (1985), 1 ff. where all the evidence is analysed, and a revised text of the Letter of Antiochus III to the inhabitants of Ikaros provided (*SEG* xxxv. 1476). The dedication to Helios by a military party of the late 4th or early 3rd cent. BC (*SEG* xxxv. 1477), is too isolated to form a significant item in the argument. (It is worth pointing out here, as an epigraphical curiosity, that the doubt that exists in regard to the latter inscription as to whether Soteles is an Athenian or the son of Athenaios, the stone having *AΘHNAIO.*, is exactly paralleled by a lost inscription of the early Ptolemaic period from Abukir, *OGIS* 18 = *SB* 8847: Ἀρτέμιδι Σωτείραι | ὑπὲρ βασιλέως | Πτολεμαίου | Ἐπικράτης Ἀθηναι[.]. (An analysis of the ambiguities of the word Ἀθηναιος in Egyptian documents is given in *Ancient Society*, 20 (1989), 169 ff.)). The material is now presented against the background of the development of the Seleucid colonial administration by S. M. Sherwin-White and A. Kuhrt in *From Samarkhand to Sardis*, 170 ff. Cf. also D. T. Potts, *The Arabian Gulf in Antiquity* (see above, p. 164 n. 114), ii. 1 ff., 10 ff., 154 ff., where all the material relevant to Ikaros is listed.

[14] *Perip.* 35: cf. above, p. 169 n. 121.

establishment of the centres necessary for its military protection, and, on the other, with the creation of a new framework for the revival and development of trade and communications within the Empire and beyond its frontiers, what, we may ask, is left for Alexander as founder of cities intended to be vehicles for the spread of Greek culture? What, if the phrase be permissible, becomes of Alexander, the torch-bearer of Greek culture to the non-Greek, oriental world? It is beyond all doubt that within a generation or so of his death Greek civic life and traditional Greek culture had spread to some remote corners of the Iranian world; so much has been revealed by the spectacular excavations on the south bank of the Oxus and by finds in Transoxiana and at Kandahar. Are these manifestations of early Hellenistic culture to be attributed to Alexander's own activity, and, if so, do they reflect a deliberate policy of the diffusion of Greek culture through the cities he founded, or are they, rather, casual products either of his own activity in building the cities and of taking over Achaemenian fortresses for this purpose, or of that of his Seleucid successors operating from secure bases in the new world that he had created? Or, in the remoter places, are the artefacts and written records simply chance records of Greeks, perhaps long after his time, who travelled in distant parts for commerce, as Claudius Ptolemy described in the first book of his geographical work, leaving behind some casual sign of their passage?

The weight of informed opinion, influenced in no small degree by the rhetorical epideictic picture of Alexander as the civilizer of mankind given by Plutarch in his essay *On the Fortune of Alexander*, inclines to the view that Alexander was indeed anxious, for various reasons, to see the spread of Greek culture, and was the pioneer in that process by design. I find it difficult to accept this notion. His highest concept of government, as far as the evidence at our disposal permits us to see, was the Macedonian–Persian Empire embracing geographically Greece proper, the Balkans to the Danube (as a deep frontier-zone) and the satrapies of the Persian Empire, from Egypt to the Jaxartes and the Indus. That was no mean concept, no mean ambition. It was, perhaps, a vast revolution of political thought, for it rose above conquest (in a way that the Achaemenids, when they sought the destruction, later the attrition, of Greece, never did) to an articulated unity of rule. But it was based on, though not necessarily inspired by, a distrust of the Greek element in his Empire that shows itself in almost all the political and administrative measures recorded as having been taken by him. In a different perspective we may perhaps say that, just as his father's aim, successfully accomplished, had been the subjugation of Greece to Macedon, the imposition of Macedonian control in Greece and the southern Balkans, his own aim was the creation of a Macedonian Empire over the lands of the Achaemenian Empire, in addition to the already accomplished rule of Macedon over Greece. In this new world the Persians would have an active role, already expressed by his appointment and reappointment of Persian satraps.

The evidence for his coolness towards the Greeks, on whose culture he had inevitably been nourished, encounters us at every turn, and we may enumerate the more significant general and particular aspects of this anti-Hellenism, so markedly in contrast with the pro-Persian feelings of the 'admirer of Cyrus'. That the Greeks, in the final result, 'conquered' the Macedonians over much of Greek and Iranian Asia, in spite of the differently conceived and executed 'ancestral Macedonism' of the Seleucids, was due both to their ever-increasing superiority in numbers, and to the qualities of administrative and commercial ability—in a phrase, practical initiative and skills, their inheritance from a distant past, and still today developed in a changed civilization—which placed them head and shoulders above the Macedonian military at that time (the dynasties naturally excepted), and led ultimately to the survival of the latter, outside the frontiers of Macedonia, only as a dwindling military element in the later Hellenistic age, while the Greeks survived all conquests, to become the essential intellectual, European element in the Ottoman world.

In the speech that he made to the Macedonians at the Beas, if Arrian's record of it is to be trusted as at least in part historical, Alexander expressly divided the Greeks into two groups—those who were friendly to him, and those who were not.[15] Even though

---

[15] v. 26. 6: ἐπεὶ καὶ ἡμῖν αὐτοῖς τί ἂν μέγα καὶ καλὸν κατεπέπρακτο, εἰ ἐν Μακεδονίαι καθήμενοι ἱκανὸν ἐποιούμεθα ἀπόνως τὴν οἰκείαν διασώιζειν, Θρᾶικας τοὺς ὁμόρους ἢ Ἰλλυρίους ἢ Τριβαλλοὺς ἢ καὶ τῶν Ἑλλήνων, ὅσοι οὐκ ἐπιτήδειοι ἐς τὰ ἡμέτερα, ἀναστέλλοντες; Much of this speech (which Arrian glosses, v. 27. 1 with the words ταῦτα καὶ τοιαῦτα εἰπόντος Ἀλεξάνδρου) is demonstrably unhistorical: see already Tarn, *Alex.* ii. 287 ff., who says 'scarcely any document we possess is more obviously a late patchwork than the boastful oration which Arrian has put into Alexander's mouth at the Beas. Why he did so is quite obscure.' Cf. also A. B. Bosworth, *From Arrian to Alexander* (Oxford, 1988), 123 ff., in the same sense. But

this cannot be taken as his *ipsissima verba*, it corresponds historically to the fact that he used Greeks only when necessary and then
those he could trust, for instance Greek naval commanders for
maritime operations during the war in the Aegean, at the beginning of his campaigns, and again at the end for the investigation
and reconnaissances of the Persian Gulf; in this capacity
Macedonians could not assist him. At the same time only two
Greeks seem ever to have been really close to him during the long
years of the campaign, Eumenes, the astute man of affairs, who
acted as his confidential secretary, and was murdered after
Alexander's death by a Macedonian general because of his popu-
larity with the Macedonians in his army, and Nearchus, the Cretan
admiral of his fleet, whose account of his voyage up the Persian
Gulf, in parallel with Alexander's land-march, survives as one of
the most precious fragments of authentic Alexander-literature. For
the rest, his attitude to the Greek troops on his campaign was, for
the most part, derogatory, and it seems probable that, although
they were bound to him as subordinate but allied members of the
League of Corinth, he regarded them rather in the light of
hostages, to guarantee the quiescence of Greece during his absence.
This attitude is not surprising. On every battlefield the Macedonian
phalanx, which formed the core of his army, confronted the Greek
mercenaries who opposed him in the front line of Darius' forces,
and in his account of the Battle of Issos Arrian emphasizes that
some of the fierceness of the struggle between the Greek mercenaries of Darius and Alexander's Macedonians was due to racial
rivalry; and the Greek prisoners who were captured by the
Macedonians in the first encounter on the Granicus were sent back
to Macedonia in chains.[16]

while the geographical terminology (as quoted in the passage above) and some of
the concepts undoubtedly demonstrate this, it is improbable (though not impossible)
that the whole address is a fabrication.

[16] ii. 10. 6: καὶ τὸ ἔργον ἐνταῦθα καρτερὸν ἦν, τῶν μὲν ἐς τὸν ποταμὸν ἀπώσασθαι
τοὺς Μακεδόνας καὶ τὴν νίκην τοῖς ἤδη φεύγουσι σφῶν ἀνασώσασθαι, τῶν Μακεδόνων δὲ
τῆς τε Ἀλεξάνδρου ἤδη φαινομένης εὐπραγίας μὴ λειφθῆναι καὶ τὴν δόξαν τῆς φάλαγγος,
ὡς ἀμάχου δὴ ἐς τὸ τότε διαβεβοημένης, μὴ ἀφανίσαι. καί τι καὶ τοῖς γένεσι τῶι τε
Ἑλληνικῶι καὶ τῶι Μακεδονικῶι φιλοτιμίας ἐνέπεσεν ἐς ἀλλήλους; cf. Brunt, *Arrian*, i,
p. xxxvii. For the political distinction between the Macedonian kingdom and the
Greek states in the Common Peace of 337 see the remarks of Hammond, *Macedonia*,
iii (1988), 571 ff. For the return of the Greek prisoners to Macedonia see Arr. ibid.
i, 16. 6: ὁ δὲ (Ἀλέξανδρος) καὶ τῶν Περσῶν τοὺς ἡγεμόνας ἔθαψεν· ἔθαψε δὲ καὶ τοὺς
μισθοφόρους Ἕλληνας, οἳ ξὺν τοῖς πολεμίοις στρατεύοντες ἀπέθανον· ὅσους δὲ αὐτῶν
αἰχμαλώτους ἔλαβε, τούτους δὲ (?δὴ) δήσας ἐν πέδαις εἰς Μακεδονίαν ἀπέπεμψεν

Correspondingly it is to be noted that when Alexander appointed someone other than a Macedonian to govern a satrapy, as occasionally happened, it was usually a Persian, and not a Greek, unless it was a Greek from a city already incorporated within the Macedonian kingdom. And it is for this reason that the Hellenistic kingdoms, founded by Alexander's military leaders, are not of Greek descent; the great dynasties are, and remain, Macedonian, the lesser Iranian, or quasi-Iranian. The Seleucids, in whom Persian blood was intermingled from the outset, provide the exception, but confirm the phenomenon. It was perhaps with this ultimate evolution in mind that, shortly before his death, in his speech at Opis, when he decided to send back to Macedon from Babylon some time-expired men who were the fathers of children by Asiatic women, and made them leave their children behind, he promised to see that they were brought up in the Macedonian way, as befitted the leaders of the future, against the day when he would bring them back in person to their fathers.[17] It was fitting that when his toil-worn body eventually found rest in Egypt, Ptolemy, his old companion-in-arms, and chronicler of his deeds, buried him first at Memphis Μακεδόνων νόμωι, 'in the Macedonian way'.[18]

Nevertheless, the active element of the world of Alexander's day in the eastern Mediterranean regions was the Greek population, and his own upbringing and education had inevitably been in the Greek tradition, and common Greek, we cannot doubt, was his natural language. The dichotomy that existed between Macedonian and Greek in Alexander's army is therefore not easily explained except on the basis of a national, or patriotic, feeling, (akin to the not wholly unknown antipathy between Celts and Anglo-Saxons), and so it remained throughout the early Hellenistic age.[19] To this

ἐργάζεσθαι, ὅτι παρὰ τὰ κοινῆι δόξαντα τοῖς Ἕλλησιν Ἕλληνες ὄντες ἐναντία τῆι Ἑλλάδι ὑπὲρ τῶν βαρβάρων ἐμάχοντο. I owe to Christian Habicht a reference to the fact that the eight or so manacled skeletons found in tombs at Akanthos (and elsewhere) may be such Greek prisoners, retained in shackles till their death: see Phaklares, *AAA* 19 (1986), 178-84.

[17] vii. 12. 2: αὐτὸς δὲ ἐπιμελήσεσθαι ὡς ἐκτρέφοιντο Μακεδονικῶς τά τε ἄλλα καὶ ἐς τὰ πολέμια κοσμούμενοι, γενομένους δὲ ἄνδρας ἄξειν αὐτὸς ἐς Μακεδονίαν καὶ παραδώσειν τοῖς πατράσιν. The promise contained in the second half of the sentence is surprising, if true. Are we to suppose that Alexander was proposing at that point to remain in Asia until these small children had reached the age of ἄνδρες?

[18] Paus. i. 6. 3: τὸν μὲν νόμωι τῶι Μακεδόνων ἔθαπτεν ἐν Μέμφει; cf. Ptol. *Alex.* ii. 31-2 n. 79.

[19] Note e.g. Seleucus' remark about Eumenes in Diod. xix. 13. 1, in 317 BC, when he tried to persuade the Macedonians to replace him as their commander:

may be added a consciousness of political subordination which probably stemmed from two causes. On the Greek side, Philip II's conquest of Greece, in spite of his construction of the League of Corinth, with its unequal terms, fostered a feeling of inferiority, while it seems probable that among the Macedonian military élite, the ἑταῖροι and others, after Philip's conquests, a very strong sense of Macedonian unity, of which Alexander became the leader and the symbol, prevailed. But the Greeks were to hand everywhere in Alexander's army, and in the cities on his early lines of communication, and it was inevitable that they should form a part of the population of his new foundations. It may be that he regarded it as a misfortune that he could not populate these new (or renewed) foundations entirely with Macedonians, on the European side, but military exigencies permitted him to assign this role only to time-expired and discharged Macedonians. What the Greek troops, left behind as settlers in the remote areas of the Upper Satrapies during the campaign, thought of their situation may be judged from the fact that once news of Alexander's death reached them they immediately packed their bags and began that journey home that soon ended in disaster.

Alexander's foundations seem, in terms of the original settlers, to form a uniform pattern throughout. With the possible exception of Alexandria in Egypt the foundations were synoecisms of the classic type—concentrations of population from the surrounding neighbourhood together with new Greek or Macedonian settlers; the local population seems in some cases to have consisted of nomads seasonally settled in the area, and this reminds us of the great importance attached by all conquerors and rulers of Central Asia to settling nomads and thus reducing the damage done to agriculture and livestock by nomadic movements across fertile arable land. Such measures were in the long run usually ineffective, but they testify to the importance attached to finding a solution to the problem even at that date.

ταῦτα (sc. boats for crossing the Tigris) δὲ προσαγαγόντες πρὸς τὴν ἔκβασιν πάλιν ἐπεχείρουν (sc. Seleucus and Peithon) τοὺς Μακεδόνας πείθειν ἀποστῆσαι τὸν Εὐμένη τῆς στρατηγίας καὶ μὴ προάγειν καθ᾽ αὑτῶν ἄνδρα ξένον καὶ πλείστους Μακεδόνας ἀνῃρηκότα (cf. xviii, 37. 2). Much later App. *Mithr.* 17. 118, speaking of Rome's reconquest of territory captured by Mithridates, includes καὶ τὴν ἀρχαίαν Ἑλλάδα καὶ Μακεδονίαν. The original occurrence of that formula cannot be determined. It is hardly Appian's own. But cf. below, p. 195 n. 4 The passage of Arr. (Nearch.) *Ind.* 2. 7, is curious: τὰ μὲν πρὸς μεσημβρίαν κατὰ Πάταλά τε καὶ τοῦ Ἰνδοῦ τὰς ἐκβολὰς ὤφθη πρός τε Ἀλεξάνδρου καὶ Μακεδόνων καὶ πολλῶν Ἑλλήνων.

We may examine the procedure in more detail as it is recounted by the Alexander-historians and other reliable sources which provide an account of Alexander's measures. Arrian's narrative gives no indication for Alexandria in Egypt, but the other evidence, notably that provided by Strabo, strongly suggests that the settlement was on a previously largely unpopulated site. Curtius Rufus seems to produce only a stereotype when he says *ex finitimis urbibus commigrare Alexandream iussis, novam urbem magno multitu-dine implevit.*[20] and it seems probable that in the first place the inhabitants came from Greece itself and the islands, Magna Graecia and Macedonia. Plutarch says picturesquely that Alexander's seers told him that the city would be 'a nurse to men from all regions',[21] and no doubt immigration was encouraged, even if full citizenship was restricted. In the remoter regions, however, where his other foundations lay, Alexander can hardly have failed to realize that the options were strictly limited, that he was unlikely to find large bodies or groups of volunteers from Greek lands, and that it was as desirable as it was necessary to make use of the local population as settlers, and to bring them within the orbit of an orderly society. Nevertheless, that Alexander intended that the 'barbarians' were to be integrated into city-life, were to be πολῖται, if not δημόται, seems unlikely; for when he spoke of a new Macedonian–Persian world it may be doubted whether he saw this communion as operating within his new *poleis*; that new system was to be essentially at the imperial and administrative, not the civic, level.

This procedure is clearly expressed, even if in the usual laconic language accorded such events, in regard to the furthest of Alexander's foundations, Alexandria Eschate, the frontier-city on the Jaxartes. Of it we are told that the site was chosen for its position as a defence against the barbarians, and that Alexander thought that it would develop into a prosperous city on account of the number of communities synoecized to form it. To this end he settled in it those with whom he could most easily dispense—Greek mercenaries, time-expired Macedonians, and volunteers from the adjacent tribes.[22] Two years later, in 327, once more south of the

---

[20] iv. 8. 5.

[21] *Alex.* 26. 6 οὐ μὴν ἀλλὰ τῶν μάντεων θαρρεῖν παραινούντων (πολυαρκεστάτην γὰρ οἰκίζεσθαι πόλιν ὑπ᾽ αὐτοῦ, καὶ παντοδαπῶν ἀνθρώπων ἐσομένην τρόφον) ἔργου κελεύσας ἔχεσθαι τοὺς ἐπιμελητὰς αὐτὸς ὥρμησεν εἰς Ἄμμωνος, κ.τ.λ.

[22] Arr. iv. 4. 1: αὐτὸς δὲ τὴν πόλιν, ἣν ἐπενόει, τειχίσας ἐν ἡμέραις εἴκοσι καὶ ξυνοικίσας ἐς αὐτὴν τῶν τε Ἑλλήνων μισθοφόρων καὶ ὅστις τῶν προσοικούντων βαρβάρων

Hindu Kush, he saw to the settlement of Alexandria ad Caucasum, which he had established on his way towards Bactria. To the original population (the composition of which is unknown) he now 'added others of the local population and all time-expired men'.[23]

In India, though on a smaller scale, the procedure was similar for the permanent defensive forts which were not intended as cities. When campaigning in Swat or Waziristān, east of the upper waters of the Kunar river, Alexander established a large garrison with a civilian settlement on the site of the native Arigaion, which the population had burnt before fleeing,[24] and this, though not a full-scale city in intention (unlike the native town whose place it took), but a fortified settlement, drew its population once again from local material. So too the unnamed settlement on the Akesines-Chenab, which Hephaestion was left behind to fortify, was populated with local volunteers and expendable time-expired Greek mercenaries.[25] Of the population of Bucephala and Nikaia on the Hydaspes we know nothing. Finally, the Alexandria founded on or near the site of the later Spasinou Charax at the head of the Persian Gulf, the local population in the area of which was probably very small and scattered, he populated with Greek mercenary volunteers, along with time-expired and invalided troops.[26] It is regrettable that, for the other cities founded by Alexander, notably Alexandria in Ariana and Alexandria in Arachosia, two pivotal cities, no details survive, where most one might wish them. One can only suppose that in addition to the surviving population of the previous settlement of Achaemenian times once more a military nucleus was left behind, to guarantee the security of the regions in question. In

ἐθελοντὴς μέτεσχε τῆς ξυνοικήσεως καί τινας καὶ τῶν ἐκ τοῦ στρατοπέδου Μακεδόνων, ὅσοι ἀπόμαχοι ἤδη ἦσαν, κ.τ.λ.

[23] iv. 22. 5: προσκατοικίσας δὲ καὶ ἄλλους τῶν περιοίκων τε καὶ ὅσοι τῶν στρατιωτῶν ἀπόμαχοι ἦσαν, κ.τ.λ.

[24] iv. 24. 7: ταύτην μὲν δὴ τὴν πόλιν, ὅτι ἐν ἐπικαίρωι χωρίωι ἐδόκει ὠικίσθαι (a new formulation of the familiar phrase regarding the suitability of the site), ἐκτειχίσαι τε προστάσσει Κρατερῶι καὶ ξυνοικίσαι ἐς αὐτὴν τούς τε προσχώρους ὅσοι ἐθελονταὶ καὶ εἰ δή τινες ἀπόμαχοι τῆς στρατιᾶς.

[25] v. 29. 3: διαβὰς δὲ τὸν Ὑδραώτην, ἐπὶ τὸν Ἀκεσίνην αὖ ἐπανήιει ὀπίσω καὶ ἐνταῦθα καταλαμβάνει τὴν πόλιν ἐξωικοδομημένην, ἥντινα Ἡφαιστίων αὐτῶι ἐκτειχίσαι ἐτάχθη· (in fact Arr. had not previously referred to this instruction) καὶ ἐς ταύτην ξυνοικίσας τῶν τε προσχώρων ὅσοι ἐθελονταὶ κατωικίζοντο καὶ τῶν μισθοφόρων ὅ τι περ ἀπόμαχον, αὐτὸς τὰ ἐπὶ τῶι κατάπλωι παρεσκευάζετο τῶι ἐς τὴν μεγάλην θάλασσαν.

[26] vii. 21. 7 quoted above, p. 168 n. 120.

addition the oases themselves would attract and provide a settled agricultural element.

It is of interest to observe that there seems to be no instance, with the possible exception of Alexandria in Egypt, in which it is stated that the settlement included civilian Greeks, of which there were presumably considerable numbers, male and female, in the train of the army. If the silence on this point is significant, it too suggests that technically the settlements, or at least the Greek element in them, were more in the nature of the later catoecic settlements than *poleis* in the conventional sense, and we are left to wonder what, if that is so, the nature of their civil government was.

Plutarch claimed that Alexander 'founded over seventy cities and sowed Greek governments throughout Asia',[27] but certainly he was either speaking irresponsibly, as elsewhere, or attributing to Alexander the formal urban developments that are characteristic of the early Seleucid foundations. He is, in fact, a suspect source in more than one respect. It is to be remembered that there is no evidence as to the form of constitution imposed by Alexander himself on his Egyptian foundation.[28] The suggestion that Aristotle in bk. vii of the *Politics*, when drawing up the conditions requisite for the best form of government, which contains a polarization between the Greek citizen-body and the barbarian tillers of the soil, was in fact providing a special blueprint for Alexander's Asiatic foundations, is hardly acceptable in view of Aristotle's known hostility to Alexander's idea of a world empire superimposed on the polis.[29] In any case, his imposition of democratic regimes on Chios and in other Greek cities in the early part of his operations

---

[27] *De Alex. Fort.* 328: Ἀλέξανδρος δ' ὑπὲρ ἑβδομήκοντα πόλεις βαρβάροις ἔθνεσιν ἐγκτίσας καὶ κατασπείρας τὴν Ἀσίαν Ἑλληνικοῖς τέλεσι, τῆς ἀνημέρου καὶ θηριώδους ἐκράτησε διαίτης. What follows, τοὺς μὲν Πλάτωνος ὀλίγοι νόμους ἀναγιγνώσκαμεν, τοῖς δ' Ἀλεξάνδρου μυριάδας ἀνθρώπων ἐχρήσαντο καὶ χρῶνται, has the same historical value as the description of the cities of Asia as μέχρι τοῦ νῦν κατοικοῦνται καὶ εἰρηνεύονται, at the head of the list of Alexander's foundations in the A-text of the *Romance*; see above, pp. 40 ff.

[28] See *Ptol. Alex.* i. 93 ff.

[29] For this view see E. von Ivanka, op. cit. p. 80 above, n. 7, who maintains with some apparent plausibility that the section in bk. vii, of the *Politics*, 1329a–1330b, which deals with the best composition for a citizen-body, reveals by the contrast it makes between citizens and perioecic barbarians, that it was advice addressed to Alexander as to how he should regulate his newly founded cities, in which the contrast between Greek and barbarian would be real in a way that it could not be in the old Greek world (except partially in the coastal cities of Asia Minor). See esp.

should not lead us to suppose that he imposed, or intended to impose, a similar form of government on the mixed populations of his new foundations established in wholly different contexts, 'from scratch'.

The picture drawn here of Alexander's foundations as authenticated by the Alexander-historians, notably Arrian, is that of a policy of commercial and strategical consolidation such as might be expected from a leader of outstanding insight and boundless purpose. It does nothing to support the view that he was anxious to nourish the adoption of Greek culture as a convenient commodity for the improvement of natives, in the manner of a mandatory power. For him, as for all his contemporaries in the Greek world, Greek culture was the accepted framework of life, but his own aim, the creation of a single empire harmoniously ruled by Macedonians and Iranians, linked by a concatenated system of settlements, fortresses, and trading-centres, was pragmatic and realistic, and based, in part, on inherited ideas. That the foundations of this system were purposefully laid by him is clear. He could not foresee that the next fifty years would witness not the Macedonian–Iranian development that he had hoped, but a no less purposeful, and more lasting Hellenization by his Macedonian generals, who were able to build their cities in a world that Alexander had created.

To conclude. Once we have reduced 'Alexander's Foundations' to their true historical scale, we see how clearly they dominate the map of central Asia, both geophysically and militarily. Based in part on existing Achaemenian administrative and military organization, they foreshadow the strategic requirements and economic potential on which, centuries later, the Imperial strategists of British India, from Masson (and even his predecessors) to Curzon

---

1329^a 25: φανερὸν δὲ καὶ ὅτι δεῖ τὰς κτήσεις εἶναι τούτων, εἴπερ ἀναγκαῖον εἶναι τοὺς γεωργοὺς δούλους ἢ βαρβάρους περιοίκους. He suggests that this may in fact be the tract listed in Diogenes (v. 22) as Ἀλέξανδρος ἢ περὶ ἀποικιῶν, and further argues that this reflects the difference of outlook as between Aristotle and his pupil, which is more clearly stated in 1252^b 9, and 1285^a 20, and the passages are not indeed compatible. Leaving out of account the two subsidiary points, it must be clear that the argument stands or falls by the date that we assign to bk. vii, which, on Ivanka's hypothesis, must be of very late date. Jaeger, *Aristotle*,[2] 263 ff., believed bks. vii and viii to be of an early date, and written under the influence of Hermias, to whom the same blueprint might have been offered (Ivanka took issue with this view as expressed by Jaeger in the 1st edn. of his book). For Aristotle's views see esp. Tarn, *Alex.* ii. 400 ff., and numerous subsequent discussions.

and Holdich insisted. From Herāt to Las Bela, from Alexandria in Ariana to Alexandria-Rambakia, and from Alexandria in Arachosia to Alexandria Eschate, from Kandahar to Khojend, the locations of Alexander's cities testify that the requirements of imperial rule in Central Asia are laid down by nature, and were as valid in the time of Alexander (and earlier) as in that of Queen Victoria.

CHAPTER VII
Epilogue

A BRIEF assessment of the various data concerning Alexander's foundations may be summarily presented here, before turning to consider the immediately subsequent history of the cities he founded. By way of recapitulation, then, it may be stated, as the central thesis of this study, that the lists of cities named Alexandria as recorded in the *Romance* and texts which derive from it, either through use of it in a different context (as the *Excerpta Barbari* and the *Paschal Chronicle*) or in directly derived versions of the *Romance* itself, are independent material belonging to an earlier period than the α-version of the *Romance*, like the Corpus of Letters of Alexander, the *Testament*, the Rhodian pamphlet, and one or two other elements, and to be regarded as essentially fabrications which were inserted into the α-version when that was compiled from the various fictitious and tendentious Alexander-pamphlets circulating in Alexandria, of which this list of Alexandrias was one. At a later date, the Iranian tradition emerges, both in the *Romance* and outside it, in which Alexander is credited with the foundation both of cities known from Sassanian sources and, later, of other cities notable in the early history of Muslim culture. If we reject these lists, and also some (but not all) of the Alexandrias recorded by Stephanus of Byzantium, we are left, for historical consideration, with those recorded by the Alexander-historians and the geographers whose sources are either derived from the bematists and writers of *stathmoi*, or (and here we think particularly of Eratosthenes) combine their information with other Hellenistic material.

From that basic position we advanced to consider the claims of the individual cities recorded by the historians and the geographers, and we found that here too major difficulties exist. The historians, notably Arrian, provide us with what may be considered reliable information regarding the foundation of settlements

by Alexander during his years of campaigning, but the attempt to
identify these on the ground within very narrow limits, has shown
itself to be, save in three or four instances, an unrewarding
exercise. In spite of the intensive investigations that have been
devoted to this topic since Droysen initiated critical study of the
question, it is evident that in most cases the vital factors which
would enable us to identify this or that ancient site with a modern
locality simply do not exist, and to debate the preference between
two or more unexcavated sites, none of which is fixed by an exact
correspondence of mileage as given in the geographers (themselves
aware of potential dangers in this field on account of variations in
units of measurements and transmitted distances, large and small)
is fruitless. In almost every case any attempt to be more precise
than the ancient source leads to a dead end, since we lack the
necessary information to carry the identification further.

Yet even so, if we confine ourselves (Alexandria in Egypt always
excluded) to Alexandria in Ariana, Alexandria in Margiana (a very
doubtful runner in any case), Alexandria Eschate, Alexandria-
Rambakia, and the rather different cases of Alexandria Spasinou
Charax and Bucephala, we note that these cities never appear in
ancient epigraphical evidence in the form, for example, of ethnics
assigned to individuals, and we are therefore entirely dependent
on historical arguments for their existence.[1] One question, then,
remains to be considered, the answer to which constitutes the final
phase of our examination of Alexander's foundations in Asia. We
have seen that there is reason to suppose that several of the cities
noted in Chapter V survived into the Parthian period (as attested
by Isidore), even the Sassanid period (as apparently attested,
among western writers by Ammianus Marcellinus). What do we
know of their later history over the years, even the centuries, after
their foundation? What happened to them within the frequently
changing context of Asian conquests and invasion, by Parthians,

---

[1] It is unfortunately not possible to assign a civic identity to the ethnics noted,
probably from Oros, sometimes supposedly from reputable sources, by Stephanus,
s.v. Ἀλεξάνδρεια. He links none with a specific city in his list, but adds them in the
philological part of the entry: Δίδυμος δὲ παρατίθεται χρῆσιν ἐξ Ἐρατοσθένους τοῦ
Ἀλεξανδρίτης. Φαβωρῖνος δὲ ἐν τῶι Περὶ Κυρηναϊκῆς πόλεως Ἀλεξανδρειώτην φησί παρὰ
τὴν . . . Ἀλεξανδρειανός. The passage regarding Kyrenaika from Favorinus' *Mirabilia*
does not constitute historical evidence (even if it was intelligible) for it owes its existence to the pre-*a*-version of the *Romance*: see above, pp. 27–8. The location of the
indirect quotation from Eratosthenes cannot be determined (cf. Schmidt, *Didymi
fragm.* 51, *c*).

Scythians, Kushans, and others, in the long centuries between Alexander's brief association with them and the end of Greco-Roman and Sassanian rule in the Middle East and beyond, and the emergence of the Islamic world?

The first change of circumstance in the pattern created by Alexander took place almost immediately after his death in Babylon. We are told by Diodorus, whose information derives from Hieronymus of Cardia, our primary source for these events, who was closely associated with his fellow-countryman Eumenes, the confidant of Alexander, that as soon as news of Alexander's death in Babylon reached the distant settlements in the Upper Satrapies the Greeks who had been settled there 'in their longing for Greek customs and the Greek way of life, rose in revolt when his death was known'.[2] They appointed a general named Philon, a Thessalian, to lead them home, and they mustered in military formation, some twenty thousand infantry and three thousand cavalry. One has the impression of a tragic and desperate determination by these men with their families to break away from the remote life to which Alexander had condemned them, and to find their way back to the Greece where they would once more be at home, among their own kith and kin. Better the hot plains of Thessaly or the rocky villages of Boeotia than the valleys of the Oxus and the Jaxartes, for all their wealth in fruit and vine. A tragic outcome followed a desperate decision.

Perdiccas, who was in charge of the central administration at Babylon after Alexander's death, sent the Macedonian general Peithon with a wholly Macedonian force to suppress the movement. Peithon, unfortunately, was over-ambitious, and thought that he might win the loyalty of these distant rebels, and with their support set himself up as a petty king—as later happened when Bactria broke away from the Seleucid Empire. Perdiccas, a very shrewd Macedonian, judged his man's intentions correctly (one wonders why he chose him for the task), and to forestall his plans ordered him to put to death all the rebels after he had defeated them, and to distribute their property among his troops. Peithon corrupted a Greek, and with his aid defeated the rebels, but he was unable to resist his ambition; having disarmed them he was preparing to enter into negotiations with them to return to their settlements, when the Macedonians, aware of Perdiccas' order,

---

[2] For this well-known episode see Diod. xviii. 7, which I paraphrase here.

moved in among them, butchered them and looted their posses-sions.[3] That very revealing story is significant in two ways. Looking backwards we can see that we are witnesses of the culmination of that hostility between Greek and Macedonian which smouldered throughout the campaign; the Macedonians had fought (and quarrelled) with their beloved king and leader, wherever he led them, and had won the Persian Empire for him. So they saw it, forgetting, no doubt, the increasing tension between themselves and him as a result of his adoption of Persian *mores* and their own refusal to cross the Beas. In their view the Greeks had had no part in this, save as subordinate members of the League of Corinth or as mercenaries, and their attempt to nullify one aspect of their master's achievement by rebellion was brutally suppressed. The massacre, instigated by Perdiccas himself, was a human hecatomb, to propitiate the spirit of their lost, loved leader. But, of course, though that is of great interest as showing once again how dia-metrically opposed the Greeks and the Macedonians in this context were, and how wrong it is to speak of the latter as if they formed a uniform force with the Greeks, the main point is that which concerns the future. By this one act the active Greek population of Alexander's settlements was virtually wiped out by the Macedonians. A force of nearly twenty-five thousand active, or once active, soldiers, must have comprised most of the Greek population settled in the 'Upper Satrapies'. We may further be fairly sure that the Macedonians did not settle down in the places left vacant by those whom they had massacred, for as many as were entitled were discharged after Alexander's death, and others were sent home to join the Macedonian forces left in Greece, where at the news of Alexander's death the whole Greek nation had sprung to arms against Macedon; another facet of that same bane-ful hostility. The Macedonians who remained in the East, probably a substantial element of Alexander's whole force, were fully occupied in the next generation or so in serving as fighting material in the long, drawn-out struggles between Alexander's generals, which had begun almost immediately after the massacre of the Greeks, and they did not adopt a sedentary, urban, or semi-urban existence.[4] At the same time new settlements in the Iranian

---

[3] Ibid. 9: ἀπροσδοκήτως γὰρ αὐτοῖς ἐπιθέμενοι (οἱ Μακεδόνες) καὶ λαβόντες ἀφυλάκτους ἅπαντας κατηκόντισαν καὶ τὰ χρήματα διήρπασαν.

[4] For troops and continued military organization in what are perhaps anachro-

provinces had, for the most part, to wait until after Ipsos, or even Corupedion. We should, then, probably suppose either that Alexander's settlements virtually died out, and were abandoned, or that, only a few non-active members of the Macedonian and Greek population having remained behind, these were absorbed in due course in the native background, and that the oasis-dwellers and even nomads moved in to fill the vacuum and maintain their native way of life. In other words, the decline of these cities began very soon after Alexander's death, though no doubt it proceeded unequally in different places.

If that is correct, we have to ask ourselves about the historical role of Alexander's cities. To do this satisfactorily we must consider what corroborative evidence we can find for their survival, and also how many of the cities that we have regarded as founded by him are likely to have lost their Hellenic identity.

The approach through archaeology, using the evidence discussed in Chapter V, does not solve the problem for us, for, as we have seen, in the whole of the Iranian region none of the sites excavated which have yielded Greek material, notably Aï Khanūm, has provided direct first-hand information as to their identity. Aï Khanūm may have been founded by Alexander—though I do not myself think so—and, if it was, and if it was destroyed as late as *c.*130 BC, in the invasion of the Sakai or Scythians, then we might hope to find evidence for the survival of Greek culture in a city founded by Alexander, until the Parthian period. That remarkable city, with its substantial Greek-speaking element, which honoured Kineas, the Thessalian, as its founder, is, however, probably of Seleucid date, and thus does not contribute to the solution of the question, how long the cities founded by Alexander survived after his death. That some Seleucid cities certainly did survive in the Iranian and Semitic parts of the Seleucid kingdom is not in doubt; several of them, notably Seleukeia-on-Tigris, survived with a Greek population, and a Greek administrative and municipal system through the Parthian and Sassanian period. As far as Alexandrias are concerned, however, there is almost no evidence, and the

nistically called αἱ ἄνω σατραπεῖαι in 317 BC see Diod. xix. 13. 6: (Eumenes) πρὸς δὲ τοὺς ἐν ταῖς ἄνω σατραπείαις ἡγεμόνας ἦν μὲν καὶ πρότερον ἀπεσταλκὼς τὰς παρὰ τῶν βασιλέων ἐπιστολάς, ἐν αἷς ἦν γεγραμμένον πάντα πειθαρχεῖν Εὐμένει. That the troops involved were Macedonian is not expressly stated, but seems to follow essentially from the massacre of the Greeks on the earlier occasion. Cf. also App. *Mithr.* 8: Εὐμένους δὲ ἀναιρεθέντος ὅτε αὐτὸν οἱ Μακεδόνες εἵλοντο εἶναι πολέμιον.

impression that not much was left of the Greek population of his settlements in the Iranian world is strong, though not conclusive. It does not, of course, follow from this that the cities which we have included in our short list ceased to exist; we have seen that that is not so, but, if the picture drawn is correct, it must be accepted that, where they survived, they played little or no part in the activities of the Hellenistic world as we understand that term. The same is true, for the most part, of the Bactrian cities, of which we hear nothing in external documentation.

This silence requires further consideration. Of prime importance is the undoubted fact that in the mass of documentation from inscriptions from all parts of the Greek world, and of papyri from Egypt, there is not a single reference to any of the eastern Alexandrias with which we are here concerned. Though we have tombstones and other documents—honorary decrees and similar texts, especially lists of competitors in the festivals of the Greek mainland, in which citizens of the authentic Seleucid foundations seem to have been especially active, as if to demonstrate their membership of the world of traditional Greek culture—from all over the Greek world, there is no reference to an Alexandrian other than to a native of Alexandria in Egypt or Alexandria Troas. At the same time it is noticeable that none of the Alexandrias listed in our sources is stated by Stephanus to have undergone a change of name at a later date (exception being made for the early and doubtful cases of Seleucid refoundations), which might make their disappearance from the historical arena more apparent than real. If, then, the inhabitants of these cities survived with Greek-speaking populations into the Hellenistic Age, they seem to have stayed in the East, and not to have ventured into the distant Greek homeland, for the sake of returning to which the first military settlers had been massacred. It may be maintained that the evidence has simply not come to light, despite the innumerable tombstones of immigrant Greeks found in cities such as Athens, Rhodes, and Demetrias, and the honorific statues on their bases set up by the Delphians, Athenians, and others in the Hellenistic and Imperial periods. However, the universal silence makes that familiar line of argument more difficult to accept than that here proposed. No wonder that Plutarch, referring, in rhetorical vein, to the seventy cities founded by Alexander, should have incautiously included Seleukeia-on-Tigris among them. In this respect, as in other ways, he shows an affinity with the *Romance* tradition, for the only parallel for this regrettable oversight occurs in a spurious letter of Alexander to his satraps in Syria, Cilicia, Cappadocia, and elsewhere, that they should dispatch to 'Antioch of Syria' various pieces of equipment and clothing.[5]

Second, we must consider the possible relevance of the numismatic evidence to our problem. It is well known that the extensive unspecified coinage of the Seleucids was assigned by Newell to specific eastern and western mints on the basis, primarily, of the monograms on the coins and on more general considerations of find-spots etc. Among the eastern mints, in addition to the well-attested Seleukeia-on-Tigris and Susa-Seleukeia-on-Eulaios, and other possible cities, Newell identified that of Alexandria in Aria. According to Newell, the Seleucids struck silver coinage at Herāt until they lost the region of Ariana to the expanding Bactrian power, when it crossed the Hindu Kush. It would then be a reasonable assumption that this Alexandria at least remained an active Greek-controlled city (though not, of course, necessarily, a free *polis*; rather a minting centre for the central authority) till the end of Seleucid rule in that area. Newell says, 'A more appropriate situation for an important mint could hardly be conceived. Artacoana-Alexandria[6] constituted the central metropolis of a large and fertile region through which passed several busy trade routes, its mint was in a position to supply with a circulating medium not only its own immediate vicinity but also the adjacent regions not so conveniently to be supplied from either Ecbatana or Bactra.'[7] The general appreciation of the importance of the oasis is certainly correct (see above, p. 109 ff.), but that does not establish the correctness of Newell's attribution in this case. His arguments rest, as often, on general hypothetical assessments, rather than on specific evidence, and the identification of the eastern Seleucid mints, outside those determined by scientific excavation and study, notably Seleukeia-on-Tigris, is recognized to be extremely

---

[5] *De Fort. Alex.* 328–9, quoted above, p. 130 n. 50. That Plutarch is not here including the foundation of Seleukeia as a postponed achievement of Alexander in the sense that, if Alexander had not founded his cities, the Seleucids would not have founded theirs, is, I think, obvious. For Alexander's instructions to his satraps regarding the dispatch of tunics etc. to Antioch see Ps.-Call. ii. 11. Merkelbach, 208, ad loc., rightly says of the reference to Antioch here, 'nil mutandum'. [See Addenda]

[6] We have seen that this equation is probably unacceptable: see above, p. 109 ff.

[7] *Eastern Seleucid Mints* (Numismatic Studies, i, New York, 1938), 256.

hazardous. Whether, even if the existence of a mint at Alexandria Ariana or Alexandria in Arachosia could be regarded as established beyond reasonable doubt, that would constitute evidence for a substantial Greek population, is another question that we cannot answer. Certainly silver had once been mined in the mountains west of Herāt. The coinage of the dynasty that succeeded Alexander does not, then, help us in our search for the survival of the Alexander-foundations in the Iranian provinces.[8]

Finally, literary evidence lends support to the view that most of the settlements Alexander founded had ceased to exist as active centres of Greek civic life before the later Imperial period, or at least were virtually unknown even to the geographers of the Iranian regions. We have seen that Pliny speaks in general terms in his geographical books of cities that had existed once, but had perished before his day.[9] Strabo confirms this, almost *en passant*, with reference to Alexander's own supposed foundations. In his eleventh book, which contains his geography of central Asia, discussing Alexander's operations in Bactria and modern Afghanistan, on the basis, largely, of earlier writers who had been with Alexander on his campaign or of geographers of the third century BC, notably, of course, Eratosthenes, he says abruptly, 'In any case they say that Alexander founded eight cities in Bactria and Sogdiana . . .', and he goes on to explain that he destroyed others, including one founded by Cyrus, Cyropolis, because of its frequent revolts, though he was a great admirer of Cyrus.[10] It is quite clear from the manner in which Strabo expresses himself—'they say that

---

[8] The unreliability of Alexander mint-locations based on geographical probability is stressed by M. J. Price in his *The Coinage in the Names of Alexander the Great and Philip Arrhidaeus* (London and Zurich, 1991) [British Museum Catalogue]; see esp. p. 37: 'When other evidence failed, Newell sometimes resorted to the geographical position of the city as a criterion for deciding whether it might have possessed a mint of Alexander coinage . . . This should be resisted, since the pattern of mints must have followed the sources of silver rather than the trade-routes.' The silver mines west of Herāt, at a mountain called Jebel al-Fiḍa, are recorded by Iṣṭakhri, *BGA* i. 269, who states that they had fallen into disuse through lack of timber for fuel. (For this region, near Ghurian, see above, p. 114 n. 21.)

[9] See e.g. Plin. iii. 116; cf. above, p. 78 n. 4.

[10] Str. 517: φασὶ δ' οὖν ὀκτὼ πόλεις τὸν Ἀλέξανδρον ἔν τε τῆι Βακτριανῆι καὶ τῆι Σογδιανῆι κτίσαι, τινὰς δὲ κατασκάψαι, ὧν Καριάτας μὲν τῆς Βακτριανῆς. ἐν ἧι Καλλισθένης συνελήφθη καὶ παρεδόθη φυλακῆι, Μαράκανδα δὲ τῆς Σογδιανῆς καὶ τὰ Κῦρα, ἔσχατον ὂν Κύρου κτίσμα, ἐπὶ τῶι Ἰαξάρτηι ποταμῶι κείμενον, ὅπερ ἦν ὅριον τῆς Περσῶν ἀρχῆς· κατασκάψαι δὲ τὸ κτίσμα τοῦτο, καίπερ ὄντα φιλόκυρον, διὰ τὰς πυκνὰς ἀποστάσεις; cf. above, p. 154. The fact that Alexander himself destroyed the Achaemenid Cyropolis is of course irrelevant to the argument here advanced.

he founded eight cities'—that these πόλεις (Strabo uses this word of any settlement larger than a few isolated hutments), these settlements, had ceased to exist by his time, and even, perhaps, by the time that his sources wrote, for 'they say' seems to refer to a vague tradition, and not, as is customary with him, to a specific source such as Eratosthenes or Apollodorus of Artemita. To appreciate this obviously incorrect generalization it is only necessary to compare the manner in which he speaks of the Seleucid foundations that were still flourishing in his day—the Antiochs and Seleucias that formed the basis of the Seleucid urbanization of the Middle East; they are to him living urban entities, of whose history and cultural role he gives an account. What his sources for this statement were we cannot tell, but its very vagueness betrays the fact that the foundations, though they may have survived, were no longer recognized as Macedonian–Hellenic colonies. Strabo, speaking on his own authority, cannot always be trusted.[11]

Nevertheless, we cannot wipe the slate entirely clean. Some authentic eastern Alexandria-names occur at a later date, and we must consider how they are to be interpreted. These are confined to the few instances in which a writer, notably Isidore, Ptolemy or Ammianus, seems to speak of an Alexandria as a contemporary city. The most natural explanation, in view of very strong negative evidence, if they are not among the authenticated Alexander foundations (Alexandria in Oxiana is a case in point) is that these names were adopted at a later date; but after examining the general probabilities, and bearing in mind that by the time of Ptolemy the Parthian Empire was nearing its final phase, we shall feel that the mere statement of the supposed location of an Alexandria in Ptolemy's geographical lists does not suffice to prove its antiquity, and that, if it survived, it was probably as, in the words used by Ammianus of Alexandria in Arachosia, which Alexander undoubtedly founded, a *civitas vilis*.[12] With Isidore the

---

Contrast Strabo's account of the Seleucid foundations of Media (from Apollodorus of Artemita), 524, fin. = FGrH 779 F5(b): εἰσὶ δὲ καὶ Ἑλληνίδες πόλεις, κτίσματα τῶν Μακεδόνων ἐν τῆι Μηδίαι, ὧν Λαοδίκειά τε καὶ Ἀπάμεια καὶ [Ἡράκλεια? ; cf. Kramer, ad loc.] ἡ πρὸς Ῥάγαις καὶ αὐτὴ Ῥάγα, τὸ τοῦ Νικάτορος κτίσμα· ὃ ἐκεῖνος μὲν Εὐρωπὸν ὠνόμασε, Πάρθοι δὲ Ἀρσακίαν, νοτιωτέραν οὖσαν τῶν Κασπίων πυλῶν πεντακοσίοις που σταδίοις, ὥς φησιν Ἀπολλόδωρος Ἀρταμιτηνός.

[11] Compare his remark in 593, apropos of Alexandria Troas, which he regarded as a metonomasy by Lysimachus: ἔδοξε γὰρ εὐσεβὲς εἶναι τοὺς Ἀλεξάνδρου διαδεξαμένους ἐκείνου πρότερον κτίζειν ἐπωνύμους πόλεις, εἶθ' ἑαυτῶν.

[12] See above, p. 142 n. 71.

situation is slightly different. He described the same Alexandria in
Arachosia as μητρόπολις Ἀραχωσίας· ἔστι δὲ Ἑλληνίς,[13] and though
it might be maintained that by that he meant no more than
that it had a Greek name, by contrast to the native κῶμαι to which
he frequently refers, it seems more natural to suppose that, at
that time, in the age of Augustus, this city at least had retained
its Greek character, as Seleukeia-on-Tigris did for many centuries.
Ammianus' description of it as a miserable community is
probably to be regarded as a statement of a contemporary or
near-contemporary, even though in other passages he seems to be
basically dependent on Eratosthenes.[14] A passage of Theophylact
referring to a locality in Persia in the sixth century AD known as
Ἀλεξανδρινά is a possible example of such a later survival claiming
not indeed to have been founded by the conqueror, but to have
been named after him, in the heart of Sassanian territory.[15]

The occasional survival or revival of such a Greek community is
not surprising. It was inevitable, after Alexander's conquests, and
the stabilization of the Middle East by the Seleucids, and later by
the Romans and the Parthians, that Greeks would settle in close
proximity with natives wherever a suitable situation presented
itself, along the river valleys and in the oases, just as they did long
afterwards when Islam had supplanted Byzantine rule in the
Middle East and Egypt, and continued to do until the twentieth
century. In such circumstances 'Greek cities' could survive on
the fringes of the oriental world. What happened to those foundations that were not involved, first in the disastrous retreat of
the original Greek settlers, and then in the invasions of Sakas,
Kushans, and others, foundations such as Rambakia in the
Makrān, which Alexander had seemingly planned with thought for
its future as a fixed point in a network of communications, we
cannot tell. They do not appear again in our sources, and they

[13] Isid. § 19; cf. above, pp. 91 ff.
[14] See above, pp. 94 ff. with n. 36. Curt. Ruf.'s statement, vii. 10. 16, *Tunc velut
freni domitarum gentium, nunc originis suae oblita serviunt, quibus imperaverunt*, would,
if true, point to a similar state of affairs.
[15] Theophyl, v. 7: (p. 219, Bonn.): οἱ μὲν οὖν ἀμφὶ τὸν Χοσρόην Ῥωμαῖοί τε καὶ
Πέρσαι ἐν Ἀλεξανδρινοῖς, οὕτω καλουμένωι χώρωι, τέσσαρσιν ἡμέραις ἀφίκοντο. τὴν δὲ
προσηγορίαν ὁ χῶρος ἀπὸ τῶν πράξεων τοῦ Μακεδόνος Ἀλεξάνδρου κατεκληρώσατο· ὁ
τοῦ Φιλίππου γὰρ ἐκεῖσε γενόμενος ἅμα τῆι Μακεδονικῆι δυνάμει τῆι τε Ἑλληνικῆι
ξυμμαχίαι ἐρυμνότατον κατέσκαψατο φρούριον, τούς τε ἐν αὐτῶι βαρβάρους διώλεσεν. Cf.
Theoph. Chr. p. 266. 9: ὁ δὲ Βαρὰμ τοῦτο μαθών, τάς περὶ αὐτὸν δυνάμεις ἀναλαβὼν
ἐν τόπωι Ἀλεξανδρινοῖς ὀνομαζομένωι, κ.τ.λ.

probably reverted within a few generations (if they were not abandoned) to the state of semi-barbarism in which Alexander had found them, with a small surviving core of those descended from early settlers along with some newcomers. The fact that no citizens of any of these Alexandrias ever appear in any epigraphical source in the way that so many of the Antiochs and Seleucias do is thus to be explained, not only, perhaps not primarily, by geographical remoteness from the main centres of the Mediterranean basin—the Hellenistic Age was one of intensive and extensive travel, as we can see precisely from epigraphical records—but by the 'cultural gap' which separated the inhabitants of the surviving cities founded by Alexander from the Greek motherland. Their communities had become one with their oriental milieu. That they did not survive within the new world of Christendom is clear from their absence (Alexandria of Egypt and Alexandria Troas excepted) from the Conciliar lists between Nikaia and Chalcedon.[16]

We must then leave Alexander as the actual founder of only the following cities: Alexandria in Egypt, Alexandria in Aria, Alexandria Eschate, Alexandria in Susiana, Alexandria-Bucephala and Alexandria among the Oreitai (Rambakia), and, if that seems to diminish his achievement in one respect, in others what was accomplished was sufficiently overwhelming not to suffer diminution through the removal of some artificial accretions.

[16] The lists of Nikaia I are conveniently collected by Gelzer, *Patrum Nicaenorum Nomina* (Teubner, 1898), whose Index, pp. 232 ff., gives a full conspectus of the signatories according to the different traditions (for the significance of the Roman figures after each entry see his 'Siglorum tabula' at the end of the preface) but details must be sought in the complex tomes of Schwartz's *ACO*. The comparative lists given by Jones, *CERP* ii. 522 ff., specifically relate, on the ecclesiastical side, only to participation at Chalcedon (and unfortunately not in the original Greek or other language); ibid., p. 522-3, he gives a useful guide to the publication of the Councils in Mansi and *ACO*. The lists do not include the episcopal seats of the Monophysite faith after Chalcedon, and similarly the Sassanian world is unrepresented. For a recent bibliography of Christianity in that state see A. J. Butler, *Arab Conquest of Egypt*[2] (Oxford, 1978), p. lviii.; see also S. P. Brock, *Studies in Church History*, 18 (1982), 1-19, with particular reference to the role of the Christians deported from the Roman provinces after Sassanian victories.

APPENDIX I
The Principal Texts

The passages which follow are only intended to make available in convenient form the main lists of Alexandrias. I have printed the texts from the available editions, without apparatus criticus because my discussions in the text cover the relevant textual-historical points. In particular:

1. The edn. of Steph. Byz. is 150 years old, and a modern app. crit. would look very different in some respects, which do not affect the main entry s.v. Ἀλεξάνδρεια.
2. The app. crit. of the *Romance* text consists of records of the various collateral and derived versions in a number of texts in different languages, amd the whole apparatus is in need of reformulation.
3. The *Excerpta* and the *Paschal Chronicle* have no textual apparatus of significance.
4. I have not reprinted in this Appendix the relevant passages from Eratosthenes-Strabo and Strabo himself, because the number of passages quoted throughout the book is substantial and discontinuous. The text of Isidore is also quoted and discussed in the text and notes.

(a) Stephanus of Byzantium, s.v. Ἀλεξάνδρεια.

Ἀλεξάνδρειαι πόλεις ὀκτωκαίδεκα. πρώτη ἡ Αἰγυπτία ἤτοι Λίβυσσα, ὡς οἱ πολλοί, ἀπὸ Ἀλεξάνδρου τοῦ Φιλίππου. Ἰάσων δὲ ὁ τὸν βίον τῆς Ἑλλάδος γράψας ἐν δ΄ βιβλίῳ φησί "τὸν μὲν οὖν τόπον τῆς πόλεως ὄναρ ἐχρησμοδοτήθη οὕτως

νῆσος ἔπειτά τις ἐστὶ πολυκλύστῳ ἐνὶ πόντῳ,
Αἰγύπτου προπάροιθε, Φάρον δέ ἑ κικλήσκουσιν.

ἐκέλευσε δὲ διαγράφειν τὸ σχῆμα τοὺς ἀρχιτέκτονας· οὐκ ἔχοντες δὲ λευκὴν γῆν ἀλφίτοις διέγραφον, ὄρνιθες δὲ καταπτάντες τὰ ἄλφιτα αἴφνης διήρπασαν· ταραχθεὶς οὖν Ἀλέξανδρος, οἱ μάντεις θαρρεῖν ἔλεγον· πάντων γὰρ τὴν πόλιν τροφὸν γενήσεσθαι". ταῦτα καὶ Ἀρριανός. ἐκλήθη δὲ Ῥακῶτις καὶ Φάρος καὶ Λεοντόπολις, διὰ τὸ τὴν τῆς Ὀλυμπιάδος γαστέρα ἐσφραγίσθαι λέοντος εἰκόνι. ἐλέγετο δὲ κατ' ἐξοχὴν πόλις καὶ πολῖται ἐξ αὐτοῦ, ὡς ἄστυ αἱ Ἀθῆναι καὶ ἀστοί καὶ ἀστικοί οἱ Ἀθηναῖοι [ὡς καὶ ἐπὶ Ῥώμης λέγεται οὐρψ]. ἐκλήθη δὲ ἐπὶ τῶν Ῥωμαϊκῶν Σεβαστή καὶ Ἰουλία καὶ Κλαυδία καὶ Δομετιανή καὶ Ἀλεξεντηρία. τῷ δὲ συνοικισμῷ τριακοντατεσσάρων ἐστὶ σταδίων τὸ μῆκος, ὀκτὼ δὲ τὸ πλάτος, ἡ δὲ ὅλη περίμετρος σταδίων ἑκατὸν δέκα. δευτέρα ἐστὶ πόλις Τροίας, ἐν ᾗ ἐγένετο Ἡγήμων ἐποποιός, ὃς ἔγραψε τὸν Λευκτρικὸν πόλεμον τῶν Θηβαίων καὶ Λακεδαιμονίων. περὶ ἧς Δημοσθένης ἐν τετάρτῳ Βιθυνιακῶν. τρίτη Θρᾴκης πρὸς τῇ Μακεδονίᾳ, ἣν ἔκτισε πρὸ τῆς μεγάλης Ἀλεξανδρείας ἑπτακαίδεκα ὢν ἐτῶν. τετάρτη πόλις Ὠριτῶν, ἔθνους Ἰχθυοφάγων, κατὰ τὸν περίπλουν τῆς Ἰνδικῆς. πέμπτη ἐν τῇ Ὠπιανῇ, κατὰ τὴν Ἰνδικήν. ἕκτη πάλιν Ἰνδικῆς. ἑβδόμη ἐν Ἀρίοις, ἔθνει Παρθυαίων κατὰ τὴν Ἰνδικήν. ὀγδόη τῆς Κιλικίας. ἐνάτη ἐν Κύπρῳ. δεκάτη πρὸς τῷ Λάτμῳ τῆς Καρίας, ἐν ᾗ Ἀδώνιον ἦν ἔχον Πραξιτέλους Ἀφροδίτην. ἑνδεκάτη κατὰ Βάκτρα. δωδεκάτη ἐν Ἀραχώτοις. τρισκαιδεκάτη ἐν Μακαρήνῃ, ἣν παραρρεῖ ποταμὸς Μαξάτης. τεσσαρεσκαιδεκάτη παρὰ Σωριανοῖς, Ἰνδικῷ ἔθνει. πεντεκαιδεκάτη παρὰ τοῖς Ἀραχώτοις, ὁμοροῦσα τῇ Ἰνδικῇ. ἑκκαιδεκάτη κατὰ τὸν Μέλανα κόλπον. ἑπτακαιδεκάτη ἐν τῇ Σογδιανῇ παρὰ Παροπαμισάδαις. ὀκτωκαιδεκάτη ἐπὶ τοῦ Τανάιδος αὐτοῦ κτίσμα, ὡς ἐν τῷ τρίτῳ Πτολεμαῖος ἀποφαίνεται. ἔστι καὶ τόπος ἐν τῇ Ἴδῃ τῇ Τρωικῇ Ἀλεξάνδρεια λεγόμενος, ἐν ᾧ φασι τὸν Πάριν διακρῖναι τὰς θεάς, ὡς Τιμοσθένης. τὸ ἐθνικὸν Ἀλεξανδρεύς ἐκ τῆς Ἀλεξάνδρου γενικῆς. τὸ θηλυκόν, ὡς ἀπὸ τοῦ Σινωπεύς Σινωπίς, οὕτως ἀπὸ τοῦ Ἀλεξανδρεύς Ἀλεξανδρίς. Δίδυμος δὲ παρατίθεται χρῆσιν ἐξ Ἐρατοσθένους τοῦ Ἀλεξανδρίτης. Φαβωρῖνος δὲ ἐν τῷ περὶ Κυρηναϊκῆς πόλεως Ἀλεξανδρειώτην φησὶ παρὰ τὴν . . . Ἀλεξανδρειανός, ὡς Μύρλεια Μυρλειανός, Ἡράκλεια Ἡρακλειανός. λέγεται καὶ Ἀλεξάνδρειος κτητικόν. Νικάνωρ δὲ ὁ Ἑρμείου ἐν τῇ περὶ Ἀλεξανδρείας πρώτῃ ταῦτα πάντα κυροῖ, καὶ τὸ Ἀλεξανδρῖνος καὶ τὸ Ἀλεξανδρίνης, οὐ μέντοι τὸ Ἀλεξανδρεώτης. ἔστι καὶ ἀλεξάνδρεια βοτάνη καὶ φυτόν, παρ᾽ ἄλλοις δὲ ἀλεξάνδρα, ἐξ ἧς ἐστέφετο Ἀλέξανδρος ἐν τοῖς ἀγῶσι. τινὲς δὲ δανάην αὐτὴν καλοῦσιν, οἱ δὲ χαμαιδάφνην, οἱ δὲ ἐπιφυλλάκανθον ἢ φυλλόκαρπον.

(b) Romance A-text iii. 35.

Οὐ τοσούτους δὲ βασιλεῖς Ἀλέξανδρος πολεμῶν ἐνίκησεν, ὅσους τελευτῶν κατέλειψεν. ἐβίωσε μὲν οὖν Ἀλέξανδρος ἔτη λ'. ἀπὸ ιε' ἐτῶν ἀρξάμενος πολεμεῖν ἐπολέμησε ἔτη ζ', μέχρι κ' ἐτῶν γεγένηται· τὰ δὲ ἄλλα λ' ἐν εἰρήνηι καὶ ἀμεριμνίαι καὶ εὐφροσύνηι ἔζησεν. ὑπέταξεν ἔθνη βαρβάρων κβ', Ἑλλήνων ι'· ἔκτισε δὲ πόλεις ιγ', αἵτινες μέχρι τοῦ νῦν κατοικοῦνται καὶ εἰρηνεύονται· Ἀλεξάνδρειαν τὴν ἐπὶ Βουκεφάλωι ἵππωι, Ἀλεξάνδρειαν τὴν πρὸς Πέρσας, Ἀλεξάνδρειαν τὴν ἐπὶ Πώρωι, Ἀλεξάνδρειαν τὴν ἐν Σκυθίαι, Ἀλεξάνδρειαν τὴν ἐπὶ τοῦ Τίγριδος, Ἀλεξάνδρειαν τὴν ἐπὶ Βαβυλῶνος, Ἀλεξάνδρειαν τὴν πρὸς Τρωάδα, Ἀλεξάνδρειαν τὴν ἐπὶ Σούσοις, Ἀλεξάνδρειαν τὴν πρὸς Αἴγυπτον.

ἐγεννήθη μὲν οὖν Τύβι τῆι νεομηνίαι ἀνατολῆς οὔσης, ἐτελεύτησε δὲ Φαρμοῦθι τετράδι δύσεως.

(c) *Excerpta Latina Barbari* fos. 34a (fin.)-34b

34*a* Vixit autem Alexander annos XXXVI
Regnauit quidem annos XVII   sic.
Pugnauit enim annos VIIII usque dum fac
tus est annorum XXVIII Illos autem alios oc
to annos uixit in pace et securitate   subiuga
uit autem gentes barbaras XXII et Grecorum
tribus XIII   Condidit autem Alexander
ciuitates XII
Qui usque nunc inhabitantur

34*b* Alexandriam qui in pentapolim
Alexandriam qui in Aegyptum
Alexandriam qui ad arpam
Alexandriam qui cabiosum
Alexandriam Scythiam in Egeis
Alexandriam qui in poro
Alexandriam qui super Cypridum fluuium
Alexandriam qui in Troada
Alexandriam qui in Babylonia
Alexandriam qui in mesas gyges
Alexandriam qui in Persida
Alexandriam fortissimam et mortuus est.

(d) *Paschal Chronicle* p. 321 (Bonn.)

Ἀλέξανδρος ἔκτισε πόλεις ιβ΄, ὧν αἱ προσηγορίαι αὗται·
Ἀλεξάνδρειαν τὴν παρὰ Πεντάπολιν, πρότερον Χεττοῦν καλουμένην, Μέμφεως
οὖσαν ἐμπόριον.
Ἀλεξάνδρειαν τὴν πρὸς Αἴγυπτον.
Ἀλεξάνδρειαν τὴν πρὸς Ἄρπαν.
Ἀλεξάνδρειαν τὴν Καβίωσαν.
Ἀλεξάνδρειαν τὴν καὶ Σκυθίαν ἐν Αἰγαίοις.
Ἀλεξάνδρειαν τὴν ἐπὶ Πώρωι.
Ἀλεξάνδρειαν τὴν περὶ Κύπριδος ποταμόν.
Ἀλεξάνδρειαν τὴν ἐπὶ Τρωιάδος.
Ἀλεξάνδρειαν τὴν ἐπὶ Βαβυλῶνος.
Ἀλεξάνδρειαν τὴν ἐπὶ Μεσασγαγές.
Ἀλεξάνδρειαν τὴν ἐπὶ Πέρσας.
Ἀλεξάνδρειαν τὴν Κάσον.
Ἀλέξανδρος λβ΄ ἔτος ἄγων ἀναιρεθεὶς φαρμάκωι τελευτᾶι ἐν Βαβυλῶνι.

APPENDIX 2
The Alexander-Romance

SINCE the *Romance* has played a considerable part in the argument of the preceding chapters, and especially of Chapter I, it may assist the reader if I give here a brief account of what the Greek version of the *Romance* in essence is, and how it reached the form in which it survives in the earliest Greek text. The theme has been the subject of much detailed research from the time of Charles Müller's *Editio princeps* in 1846, through Ausfeld's fundamental study of the whole tradition and Kroll's admirable edition of the text, to the works of R. Merkelbach and his school.[1] I am concerned to give here only sufficient background to enable the reader to follow my use of the evidence in the body of the book.

Three different traditions of the Greek *Romance* survive, generally known by the capital italic letters *A*, *B*, and *Γ* (or A, B, C, *latine*), of which we

---

[1] Published in the same volume as the Didot Arrian ed. Ch. Dübner, Müller's pioneer study provided a composite text, based on the Parisinus 1685, the chief representative of the *B*-tradition, in which the different versions were combined to create a continuous text. Müller's failure to base his text on Parisinus 1711 is pungently criticized by Ausfeld, *Rh.Mus.* 52 (1898), 435, but the edition perforce served two generations of students. Like all who have occasion to study the *Romance*, I am much indebted to Ausfeld's posthumous *Der Griechische Alexanderroman* (Leipzig, 1907. ed. W. Kroll). Kroll's edition, with a valuable preface, *Historia Alexandri Magni*, i, Berlin, 1926, is the standard text. In the apparatus Kroll makes full use of the subsidiary Greek and oriental traditions in his attempt to reconstruct the oldest version of the work. His edition is hardly antiquated as a text, but the discovery of a considerable amount of associated material, notably in papyri, has put the earliest history of the *Romance* in a different light, and it was the achievement of R. Merkelbach in his *Die Quellen des Griechischen Alexanderroman* (Zetemata, H.9, Munich, 1954; 2nd edn. J. Trumpf, 1977) to utilize all this subsequent material, and on the basis of it to expound a comprehensive, though to my mind only partially successful, explanation of the origin of the whole work, starting with an epistolary novel composed of letters of Alexander to Olympias, Aristotle, and his other known correspondents. I need say little about the subsequent editions of the later Greek traditions, *B* and *Γ*, since I have already given a full bibliography in *Ptolemaic Alexandria*, ii. 944 n. 8, and I have noted in Chs. I and II above items which have superseded those given in that note. I may note, however, the recent publication of an English translation of the *Romance* by R. Stoneman, *The Greek Alexander Romance* (Penguin Books, 1991), which is based on the Leiden MS (L), filled in with other elements; it has a valuable introduction. If anyone chooses to consult my analysis in *Ptolemaic Alexandria* they will find that my views have been considerably modified in the last twenty years, though not in any fundamental respect. I hope that I have succeeded in penetrating further into the original Alexandrian background.

are only concerned with the first, represented (in Greek) by a single manuscript, A. The two later traditions, *B* and *Γ*, include a number of manuscripts which differ individually in detail and completeness, but are all considerably longer than A and other texts of the *A*-tradition, and still more fabulous in content. The single manuscript, A, Paris 1711, of the eleventh century, bears the heading Βίος Ἀλεξάνδρου τοῦ Μακεδόνος, while the Paris representative of the *B* class, Paris 1685, of AD 1468, has the incipit Καλλισθένης ἱστοριογράφος ὁ τὰ περὶ τῶν Ἑλλήνων συγγραψάμενος· οὗτος ἱστορεῖ Ἀλεξάνδρου πράξεις, whence the familiar title 'pseudo-Callisthenes' loosely used as a label for the Greek version(s). The text has, of course, nothing to do with Callisthenes and other MSS give other notable writers as the author.[2] The name of the original work and of its author were clearly lost at an early date (the Heracleides whom Plutarch quotes as an authority on early Alexandrian legends cannot, for chronological reasons, be the author),[3] and the fabrications of authorship thereby facilitated. The correct title for the work is the *Life*, but the term *Romance* is firmly embedded in modern scholarship and so I have designated it. It is possible that the original title given it by the author emphasized the link between Alexander and the city of Alexandria, and was called something like 'The Life of King Alexander the Founder (Κτίστης)'.[4]

It is essential to distinguish between the Paris MS 1711, A, and the lost original *Romance* of seven or eight hundred years earlier, designated in this book, as elsewhere, as α. It is this lost original that we have to try to recreate, mainly from A, but, where A fails us—as is not infrequently the case, for it is ill-written, lacunose, and interpolated—also from derived sources that represent the same tradition *A*. Beyond that, we have to look behind α, and try to discover what sources it used. A itself is distinguished from all the Greek MSS of the other classes by its (relative) simplicity of narrative, and by the absence (relative, again) of elaborated versions of many legends which occur in it in a simpler form. The relationship of the various versions is schematically reproduced in the stemma (Fig. 2).[5] A is divided into three parts (μέρη), and the main elements of the narrative— the fabulous framework—are as follows:

[2] See Kroll, pp. xv–xvi: Onesikritos and Aesop are other honorands.

[3] See below, p. 223 n. 44.

[4] For this title as applied to Alexander see above, p. 14. Some such title for the *Romance* was suggested by Ausfeld, *Alexanderroman*, 233, since he felt it was required to substantiate the reference to τούτου τοῦ ἐδάφους (see below, p. 215). No version offers a hint of such a title, but the hypothesis is plausible.

[5] Full stemmata of both the *A*- and *B*-traditions will be found in D. J. A. Ross's *Alexander Historiatus* (Warburg Inst. Surveys, i, 1968), an excellent introduction to the whole topic, though Ross is specifically concerned with medieval illustrated Alexander-texts. He gives a full stemma of the later *A*-tradition on p. 26, and of *B* and its descendants on p. 46. My own stemma aims at showing the pre-texts of α,

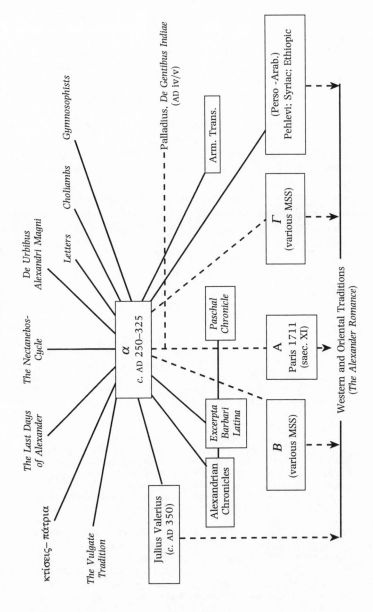

Fig. 2. *The Life of Alexander*

1. The story of the birth of Alexander in Pella from the surreptitious union of Olympias and Nectanebos, the last Egyptian Pharaoh, who is portrayed as a magician who appears to Olympias in the form of a snake, and seduces her while Philip is away on a campaign. In due course Alexander murders Nectanebos, and Philip takes over. He too in due course is murdered by Pausanias, who desires to gain possession of Olympias (i. 1-24).

2. On his accession Alexander mounts his expedition against Persia. His route is: from Macedonia to Lykaonia,[6] via Thrace, thence to Italy, where he finds the Romans engaged in a war against Carthage—they would, we are told, have paid him more tribute if they had not been engaged in this costly undertaking—and he crosses to Carthage, and from there passes through the desert to Siwa, to consult the oracle of Ammon, which instructs him to found the city of Alexandria in Egypt, and he comes to the isle of Pharos from the west. The foundation of the city is then described at length (i. 25-33), with a wealth of details, some authentic, some fictitious, some suspect, and far surpassing anything that we know from any other source, including Strabo's detailed description of the city as he knew it.

3. From Alexandria Alexander advances against Persia, and the Battle

and does not develop the derivatives of the *B*- and *Γ*-traditions. Two small excerpts from texts which show a mixed allegiance but whose primary links, as indicated mainly by extremely brief lemmata, are with *A*, have been published, one by G. Ballaira in *Frammenti Inediti della perduta recensione δ del romanzo di Alessandro in un codice Vaticano* [1700, 14th cent.], *Bolletino del Comitato per la preparazione della Edizione nazionale dei classici greci e latini.* NS 13 (Accad. Lincei, 1965) 27-59, the other, by J. Trumpf. *Classica et Mediaevalia* 24, (1965) 83-100, of a Paris MS, Suppl. gr. 689 (15th cent) which consists of twenty-two lemmata. Variations from the *A*-tradition are mostly small and insignificant and do not merit discussion here, save that it may be noted that the author of the Vatican excerpts contributes one surprising novelty; he claims (Trumpf, p. 99) that Alexander subdued thirteen Greek 'tribes' (as in A) and instead of the reference to the cities 'being still at peace' the statement that he also 'founded seventeen cities all called Alexandrias, all of which "had a distinctive title"': ἔκτισε μέντοι πόλεις ιη΄ Ἀλεξανδρείας ἁπάσας ὀνομασθείσας πλὴν μέντοι προσθήκης διαφόρου (πλὴν μέντοι προσθήκης διαφόρου is a comment not otherwise encountered in this context and is slightly ambiguous. It could mean 'without however a distinctive addition', or 'except however that each city had a distinctive title'. The μέντοι strongly favours the latter interpretation). The number is one less than that provided by Stephanus and there may be some association between the two texts. The relevant lines of Vat. 1700 and A are printed in parallel on pp. 39-40 of Ballaira's article. Those of the former, as quoted above, provide only, as Ballaira says (p. 32), 'an vago riscontro con tutte le recensioni: termini diversi e nuovi: μέντοι ed ιη΄.

[6] The Latin translator, Julius Valerius, a conscientious man, rebelled at this, and after *pergit ad Lycaoniam* went on (i. 22): *cui nunc aetas recens nomen Lucaniae dedit* and Λευκανίαν was preferred here by Ausfeld, ad loc. Kroll keeps the reading of A, Λυκαονίαν, on the sound guiding principle that A must not be emended in the interests of historical or geographical sense.

of Issos is briefly described. After that he proceeds to Achaia, then to Pieria, and then to Phrygia, where he visits Troy and sacrifices to Hector, Achilles, and other heroes. Thereafter he continues his journey—to Locris and to Boeotian Thebes, of the capture of which there is a long but unhistorical description. He then arrives in Corinth, where he presides at the Isthmian Games, and presents the prizes (i. 34-7).

4. Book ii opens with a sketch of Alexander's relations with Athens, in which Demosthenes figures largely; a lengthy speech by him refers to Alexander's application to the oracle at Siwa: where should he found a city named after him, the name of which would last for ever?[7] Demosthenes dwells on the wealth and abundance of Egypt as providing the best location for Alexander's city. Alexander then moves down to Laconia, which he leaves ἀπολέμητον καὶ ἀφορολόγητον, and passes on to Cilicia, where he catches a severe cold, and is tended by Philippus, his Acarnanian doctor. He then traverses Armenia, crosses the Euphrates at Zeugma, and moves into Bactria and eventually into . . . Media. This is followed by the execution of Darius by Bessus and Ariobarzanes (ii, *in toto*).

5. Book iii begins with the march to India, which brings him into contact with the Brahman gymnosophists. Alexander's dialogue with them originally occupied only a short section of the text, but, as we shall see, additional matter has been added. Alexander's impressions of the wonders of India are contained in a long letter to Aristotle, one of a number of such letters to his teacher. He then establishes contact with Kandake, Queen of Meroe, and her son Kandaules, after which he moves on to the land of the Amazons, where he makes a considerable impression. He describes his subsequent adventures in a letter to Olympias, and we next find him in Babylon, where the last phase of his life begins (iii, 1-29).

6. The *Romance* substitutes for the traditional account of Alexander's death as we read it in Arrian the version (known to and rejected by Arrian) in which he is poisoned by his seneschal, Iollas, on the instructions of Antipater, the poison having been provided by Cassander.[8] This is followed by a letter of Alexander to the Rhodians, and by his Will and final instructions. Finally we are given details regarding his age, statistics of his conquests and of the eponymous cities that he founded, and the dates of his birth and death (iii. 30-5).

Such is the outline of the *Romance* as contained in A. We must now try to discover how this strange narrative came into existence—what the pre-texts of which it is formed are. Our concern in this study is not with most of the numerous later versions of the *Romance*, western and oriental,

---

[7] II. 4. 5: ποῦ τῆς ὀνομασίας ἑαυτοῦ ἀείμνηστον πόλιν κτίσει;

[8] For an attempt to interpret this version of his death as historically true see Bosworth, *CQ* ns 21 (1971), 112-36. Arr. vii. 27, having given a number of transmitted stories about the cause of Alexander's death, concludes καὶ ταῦτα ἐμοὶ ὡς μὴ ἀγνοεῖν δόξαιμι, μᾶλλον ὅτι λεγόμενά ἐστιν ἢ ὡς πιστὰ ἐς ἀφήγησιν ἀναγεγράφθω.

except for the Latin and Armenian versions, which help us to reconstruct α. The Latin translation is that of Julius Valerius, of the middle of the fourth century or earlier, the Armenian, perhaps by Moses of Chorene, written some time between the fifth and seventh centuries.[9] In general it is a beguiling pastime to sort out the relationship of these later versions to the Greek text(s), but they hardly help us to unravel the pre-history of the *Romance*, that is, to lead us to the sources that were used by the original author.

We must not approach the analysis of the *Romance* with the idea that we are looking for direct sources. Even the basic historical narrative, as summarized above, is as unlike the Alexander-historians as it could be, and though it is commonly regarded as having some affinity with the style and matter of Alexander-history popularized by Clitarchus, probably an Alexandrian of the early Ptolemaic period, it is so grotesquely transformed and caricatured that all that need be said is that, with certain specific and clear exceptions, it represents the sort of unhistorical, popular style of writing, and the extent of knowledge about Alexander himself that was available at the date, and in the place, where α was composed, put together, or whatever term we choose to use; the sort of fanciful history, perhaps, that Palladas spent so many weary years teaching. In any case, the actual 'historical' narrative is, even in A, only a very flimsy continuum to which are attached a number of quite separate elements that have been pretty clumsily welded on to it.

What, then, are the constituent 'pre-texts', and what belongs to the original finished work, α? Several aspects of this problem have been investigated in the course of this work, and for that reason will be passed over briefly. We may note first a few general considerations, both negative and positive. We may begin by excluding a popular, folk-origin for it. That the original version of the *Romance* did not consist of any form of ballad verse may be regarded as certain. Formal epics about Alexander may have been written, Ἀλεξανδριάδες, known only by their title, but no 'ballads', folk-poetry about Alexander, are known to have existed in the way that in the Byzantine age the Akritic ballads probably preceded the actual Akritic epics, which in their turn foreshadow the λαϊκά τραγούδια of a later date. Subsequently the long tradition of the Byzantine *Alexander-Romance*, as it is preserved in more than one MS, in political verse, or in the later ριμάδα, is also literary and not popular. It is not until the eighteenth century, with the publication of the various Greek φυλλάδια in Venice that the by then

---

[9] The Latin translation by Julius Valerius edited by Kuebler (Teubner, 1888) has now been re-edited in the same series by M. Rosellini (Teubner, 1993). This new edition makes no change in the list of Alexandrias, but in general provides a full text based on a far larger manuscript tradition: see Rosellini, pp. v ff. I have retained the numeration of Kuebler, which is given by Rosellini in the margin of her edition. For the Armenian version, trans. A. M. Wolohojian, see above, p. 21 n. 44.

very changed *B* and *Γ* traditions—largely the latter—become part of a popular literature, and then, popular *printed* literature, which is something very different from what we mean by 'folk-traditions'. Of course, Alexander also appears in the *Καραγκιόζη* puppet-plays, but these too have an identifiable written origin. In other words, the *Romance* is not a prose version of early ballads of the type that Niebuhr and Macaulay thought lay behind the prose versions of the legends of early Rome in Livy, or, in modern terms, as the Robin Hood cycle of ballads lies behind the Scottish prose chronicles. It is work of the same general character as Sir John Mandeville's *Travels*, a conglomerate of earlier heterogeneous prose material. With the Mandeville tradition the *Romance* has many similarities, including the existence of a metrical version.[10]

We are concerned then not with sources in the commonly accepted sense, but with pre-texts, as I have called them, earlier items of different types which the unknown author of α selected to suit his own taste and that of his public. I have dealt above with the crucial question for us, that of the origin of the list of Alexandrias at the end of the *Romance*, and we have seen that it is very probably an invention of the Ptolemaic period, to which the author of α added an additional clause which reflects conditions of a much later date. Before reverting to this 'Alexandrian' element I shall analyse five separate sections of the text, which are similar, easily identifiable 'implants'.

1. The role of Alexander as the son of Olympias and Nectanebos, the last Pharaoh of Egypt. Nectanebos played an important part in native conceptions of Egyptian history of the period just before the Macedonian conquest of Egypt—as the king who will return, or, alternatively, whose son will return, and Macedonian rule will thus be transformed into a new Pharaonic rule.[11] In the *Romance*, after Nectanebos has left Egypt—an event also recorded by Diodorus[12]—the Egyptians ask Hephaestus who will become King of Egypt, and the reply (once in verse) is, 'He who flees Egypt in strength and valour, old, and a King and Ruler, will return as a young man after an interval, casting off old age, and he will circle the earth, and here on the soil of Egypt he will subject our enemies to us.' We know that a cycle of Nectanebos-tales existed in Demotic in the second century BC, and we possess the text of a remarkable dream relating to him which is preserved in Greek among the papers of Apollonius, one of the *Κάτοχοι* of the Serapeum at Memphis, dated to the middle of the second century

[10] Those interested in pursuing the history of *Mandeville's Travels* will find full information in M. Letts, *Sir John Mandeville, The Man and his Book* (London, 1949), and in *The Travels of Sir John Mandeville*, translated with an introduction by C. W. R. D. Moseley (London, Penguin, 1983).
[11] For the role of Nectanebos in contemporary literature see in general *Ptol. Alex.* i. 680 ff., with notes.
[12] xvi. 51. 1.

BC.[13] There can be no serious doubt that this section of the *Romance* was adapted by the author of α, or by some earlier writer, from an item of the Nectanebos-cycle. It is therefore a very early piece of Egyptian, not Greek, material in the text. We may note that this nationalistic Egyptian element is closely paralleled in the Iranian tradition transmitted by Ṭabārī and Dīnawārī on the authority of 'some scholars', that Alexander was the brother of Darius III. The central feature of that episode is the marriage of Darius' daughter with Philip II, as a result of diplomatic negotiations, and Philip's rejection of her because her breath smelt, in spite of the cure for this found in the herb 'skadr'. On her return home pregnant, she gave birth to a son whom she called Iskander after the herb that had cured her (but not saved her marriage). The story varies a little: in Ṭabārī and Ibn al-Athīr, Darius II married Olympias, who was daughter of the King of Rumi, and she was sent home because her breath stank, and gave birth to Alexander in Greece, whereas in Dīnawārī the unnamed daughter of Darius marries Philip. But in both versions Alexander addresses Darius III as 'my brother' when he reaches him only to find him dying of his wounds.[14]

This 'nationalistic' fiction in which Nectanebos appears as the father of Alexander may have been grafted on to the story of Ammon's paternity, which Plutarch found in Eratosthenes (who, surprisingly, accepted it), and which involves Ammon appearing as a snake to Olympias, but the purpose of the variation is not to establish the divinity of Alexander himself (as his Macedonian troops saw it), but to vindicate the continuation of Pharaonic rule through Alexander, and is thus a natural development of the Nectanebos-cycle.

2. The story of Alexander's Dialogue with the Gymnosophists. This is known in various forms in the historical tradition, and it also occurs as a separate item in a Greek papyrus of about 100 BC. I discuss it further below; here it is enough to note that it too was available to the author of α in some form or other.

3. The most significant identifiable element for the student of the Hellenistic world is the section contained at the end of the entire work, iii. 31-4. This consists of a self-contained narrative of Alexander's 'Last Days' and his testamentary dispositions. Having been poisoned (see above, p. 209), he dictates his will on his death-bed. In A the text of the will is merged with a Letter to the Boule and Demos of the Rhodians, which contains provisions some of which reflect the struggles of the Diadochi immediately after the death of Alexander, and which originally can only have been contemporary with those events. These magnify in particular the role assigned to Perdiccas, who was murdered in 321, and to a lesser

[13] UPZ 81.
[14] For these stories see Ṭabārī, I. 2 694 ff.; Dīnawārī, 31 ff.

degree Ptolemy.[15] Other provisions, insertions of a later date, stress Alexander's concern for Rhodes, a concern that was not evident in his lifetime. The Will was to be deposited in Rhodes—a very important factor in any claims the Rhodians might make concerning Alexander in the Hellenistic world. In a Latin text corresponding to this concluding section of A, which stands as a separate work entitled *Liber de Morte Alexandri Testamentoque Alexandri Magni* (the title is in an Escorial MS), the Letter and the Will are separate, but both contain items favourable to Rhodes. Again, a papyrus of the late Ptolemaic period, c.100 BC, contains a fragment of the Will, with variant passages also favourable to Rhodes. These passages must all reflect the tendentious purpose of a politically motivated narrative written by a Rhodian at a time when Rhodes was mistress of the Aegean, for one of the clauses of the Will is that Alexander τοὺς νησιώτας ἀφίησιν ἐλευθέρους, καὶ ἐπιτρόπους αὐτῶν Ῥοδίους εἶναι. The prominence accorded to Ptolemy and to the burial of Alexander in Egypt, following his own instructions,[16] also indicates a time when Rhodes was not disposed to dispute—was even inclined to further—the role of the Ptolemies as principal successors of Alexander. Both features suggest some time in the third century BC. It would not be difficult to find, among the many Rhodian chroniclers and historians mentioned by Polybius and in the *Lindian Chronicle* and elsewhere, several candidates for the authorship of such a work. Since the claim that Alexander deposited his will in Rhodes occurs also in Diodorus, in the eulogistic prelude to the account of the siege of Rhodes,[17] it would be natural to assign to the admittedly Rhodian section of Diodorus (excluding, of course, the account of the actual siege) and the

[15] See the detailed discussion of the whole document, and particularly the elements referring to the roles of Perdikkas and Ptolemy, by Merkelbach, op. cit. 121–51, and for a possible reflection (outside the *Romance*) of the role of Craterus see below, Additional Note, p. 224. For the details of the Rhodian insertion, and the brief summary of it given here, see *Ptol. Alex.* ii. 947 n. 16, reference to which removes the necessity of repeating the evidence here, though the new piece of Rhodian evidence, *POxy* 3823, referred to below, n. 28, must now be added to those already known. The nomination of Ptolemy as the husband of Alexander's sister Kleopatra in Ps. Call. iii. 33 = Jul. Val. ii. 58, cf. Diod. xx. 37. 3, (where the decision comes from Kleopatra), is rightly described by Berve, *Alexanderreich*, ii. 213 n. 2, as 'eine Erfindung in gloriam Ptolemaei'; cf. below, p. 226, n. 56.

[16] iii. 33. 10, the very positive statement, Πτολεμαῖος δὲ τοῦ ἐμοῦ σώματος γενόμενος φύλαξ. The link between Rhodes and Ptolemy is emphasized in the new Rhodian fragment.

[17] Diod. xx. 81. 3: διόπερ συνέβαινεν αὐτὴν [SC. τὴν Ῥόδον] τιμᾶσθαι μὲν ὑφ' ἑκάστου βασιλικαῖς δωρεαῖς, ἄγουσαν δὲ πολὺν χρόνον εἰρήνην μεγάλην ἐπίδοσιν λαβεῖν πρὸς αὔξησιν· ἐπὶ τοσοῦτον γὰρ προεληλύθει δυνάμεως ὥσθ' ὑπὲρ μὲν τῶν ἄλλων Ἑλλήνων ἰδίαι τὸν πρὸς τοὺς πειρατὰς πόλεμον ἐπαναιρεῖσθαι καὶ καθαρὰν παρέχεσθαι τῶν κακούργων τὴν θάλατταν, τὸν δὲ πλεῖστον ἰσχύσαντα τῶν μνημονευομένων Ἀλέξανδρον προτιμήσαντ' αὐτὴν μάλιστα τῶν πόλεων καὶ τὴν ὑπὲρ ὅλης τῆς βασιλείας διαθήκην ἐκεῖ θέσθαι καὶ τἆλλα θαυμάζειν καὶ προάγειν εἰς ὑπεροχήν. Ammianus also knew of the Will, perhaps from the *Romance*: see p. 18 n. 37.

Alexander-text a common source. This view, however, is not without its difficulties, and from the point of the view of the *Romance* it is sufficient that the beginning and the end of the work as they stand in A, and as they no doubt stood in α, the Nectanebos story and the Letter and the Will, are historically separate and identifiable items of Hellenistic date, in the first case of a date almost immediately after Alexander's death, in the second probably in the third century.

4. I naturally include in this list of early material in the *Romance* the list of Alexandrias, to which I have devoted considerable space above, in Chapter I. Here it suffices to repeat the conclusion reached there, that the list of cities in the *Romance*, subsequently reproduced in the *Excerpta Barbari Latina* and other late Imperial annals, is of Ptolemaic origin, and probably of the later third century BC. The final *enjambement* with the list is provided by the reference to the cities being 'still at this time inhabited and at peace', a reflection, it is suggested, of the lack of knowledge of the trans-Euphratic world in the late third or early fourth century AD, when the α-version was completed.

5. A further item, which forms a separate and distinct element in the *Romance* is a long account of the foundation of Alexandria in Egypt. It may be argued that this is a natural topic to be treated at length by an Alexandrian author of a supposed Life of Alexander, but here too there are grounds for supposing that the account was lifted bodily from an earlier source, though not necessarily one of Hellenistic (that is, Ptolemaic) date. We saw above that the tradition of foundation-legends, Κτίσεις, regarding Alexandria appears to have originated in the third century BC at the latest, as soon, perhaps, as direct, living memory of that event had passed away, and is attested by the title of a poem by Apollonius Rhodius, of which one fragment survives.[18] Apollonius specialized in such Κτίσις-literature—apart from the Ἀλεξανδρείας κτίσις, we know of a Ναυκράτεως κτίσις, a Καύνου κτίσις, a Κνίδου κτίσις and a Ῥόδου κτίσις written by him, all of which have been lost except for tiny fragments—and it seems likely that the tradition owed something to his example. It is natural to suppose that the long section on the foundation of Alexandria contained in the *Romance* derived from a work in that tradition, even if it is not a complete reproduction of any particular work.[19] The substance differs from that of Arrian in almost every way, and cannot be regarded as itself of historical value, although it contains precious isolated pieces of information, with

---

[18] See J. Michaelis, *De Apollonii Rhodii Fragmentis* (diss. Hal. 1885), 6. II (cf. Powell, *Coll. Alex.* 5 ff.) = Schol. Nicand. *Ther.* 11: Περὶ γοῦν τῆς τῶν δακνόντων θηρίων γενέσεως, ὅτι ἐστὶν ἐκ τῶν Τιτάνων τοῦ αἵματος . . . Ἀπολλώνιος ὁ Ῥόδιος ἐν τῆι τῆς Ἀλεξανδρείας κτίσει ἀπὸ τῶν σταγόνων τοῦ τῆς Γόργονος αἵματος. Cf. above, pp. 44–5.

[19] i. 30–3 (pp. 27–37). For the references to τοῦτο τὸ ἔδαφος (cf. below, p. 215) see 31. 2, παραγεναμενος δὲ ἐπὶ τούτου τοῦ ἐδάφους, κ.τ.λ.; ibid. 32, παραγενόμενος οὖν ὁ Ἀλέξανδρος εἰς τοῦτο τὸ ἔδαφος.

which it is possible to supplement both that account and the detailed account of the topography by Strabo. It is therefore worth looking at it more closely. First we may notice that it is in this section that the author explicitly acknowledges that he is writing in Alexandria for Alexandrians: he says, with reference to the future site of the city, that Alexander arrived εἰς τοῦτο τὸ ἔδαφος, 'this place of ours'. It is at the same time clear, when we look at the topographical details themselves, that these are not of Ptolemaic date, but unmistakably Imperial. Although neither Ptolemies nor emperors are mentioned in it the author is continually calling attention to the fact that some local topographical names, supposedly, and probably actually, of early date, are 'still surviving today': the sixteen villages with their canals which had been blocked up at the foundation, 'and are still blocked up to-day';[20] of the two villages named after the two eponymous (and surely early Ptolemaic, or pre-Ptolemaic, if the term may be used) komarchs, Eurylochus and Melanthius, he says again, 'the names of these villages still survive';[21] and of a cult-practice supposedly inaugurated by Alexander the author says, 'whence the Alexandrians preserve this practice even until now'.[22] This perspective of Imperial date is fully supported by

[20] i. 31. 3: αἱ δὲ ις΄ κῶμαι εἶχον ποταμοὺς ιβ΄ ἐξερευγομένους εἰς τὴν θάλασσαν· καὶ μέχρι νῦν αἱ διεκδρομαὶ ἀναπεφραγμέναι εἰσίν. ἐχώσθησαν οἱ ποταμοὶ καὶ ἀγυιαὶ τῆς πόλεως καὶ πλατεῖαι ἐγενήθησαν. δύο δὲ μόνοι διέμειναν, οἳ καὶ ἀπορρέουσιν εἰς τὴν θάλασσαν.

[21] i. 31. 7–8: εἴξας τοῖς ἀρχιτέκτοσιν ὁ Ἀλέξανδρος ἐπιτρέψων αὐτοῖς, οἷς βούλονται μέτροις τὴν πόλιν κτίζειν. οἱ δὲ χωρογραφοῦσι τὸ μῆκος τῆς πόλεως ἀπὸ τοῦ Δράκοντος τοῦ κατὰ τὴν Ταφοσιριακὴν ταινίαν μέχρι τοῦ Ἀγαθοδαίμονος τοῦ κατὰ τὸν Κάνωπον, καὶ ἀπὸ τοῦ Μενδησίου ἕως τῆς (?τῶν) Εὐρυλόχου καὶ Μελανθίου τὸ πλάτος. καὶ κελεύει τοῖς κατοικοῦσι κωμαίοις μεταβαίνειν ἀπὸ λ΄ μιλίων τῆς πόλεως ἔξω, χώρημα αὐτοῖς χαρισάμενος, προσαγορεύσας αὐτοὺς Ἀλεξανδρεῖς. ἦσαν δὲ ἀρχέφοδοι τῶν κωμῶν τότε Εὐρύλοχος καὶ Μελάνθιος· ὅθεν καὶ ἡ ὀνομασία ἔμεινεν. It seems natural to suppose, both because of the names themselves, of which Eurylochus is characteristic of Macedonia and Thessaly in the 4th and 3rd cents BC, and also because their names 'survived until the present' that the two individuals belonged to the early days of the city (in view of the plural κωμῶν the correction τῶν for τῆς seems desirable). The area 'of Eurylochus', no doubt the same village, is referred to in a papyrus of 5 BC, *BGU* 1121 (*Sel. Pap.* 41), linked with a locality called Ἀρσινοῖς: see the passage quoted in full in *Ptol. Alex.* ii. 251 n. 82. Schubart, ad loc., identified Eurylochus with the Magnesian mercenary leader mentioned by Polyb. v. 63 as commanding some Ptolemaic troops at Raphia (*PP* 2160); but the prevalence of the name in 4th-cent. Macedonia makes the alternative suggested here preferable, even though it does not provide a specific identification. Μελάνθιος is a pan-Hellenic name: see e.g. *LGPN* i, s.v. (23 exx.) The canal Δράκων, attested only here, might represent a survival of the story apparently told by Apollonius regarding the birth of poisonous animals from the blood of the Gorgon; cf. above, n. 19.

[22] i. 32. 12: ἐκέλευσε δὲ ὁ Ἀλέξανδρος τοῖς φύλαξι τῶν οἴκων σῖτον δοθῆναι· οἱ δὲ λαβόντες ἀλήσαντες καὶ ἀθηροποιησάμενοι τὴν †ἡμέραν τοῖς ἐνοικοῦσι† θάλλον διδόασιν. ὅθεν καὶ μέχρι τοῦ δεῦρο τοῦτον τὸν νόμον φυλάττουσι παρ' Ἀλεξανδρεῦσιν. The survival of the tomb of Alexander, the Σῆμα or Σῶμα (cf. *Ptol. Alex.* ii. 32, n. 79) is similarly described ibid. 34. 6, τότε οὖν ποιεῖ αὐτῶι τάφον Πτολεμαῖος ἐν τῆι Ἀλεξανδρείαι, ὃς μέχρι τοῦ νῦν καλεῖται Ἀλεξάνδρου σῆμα, καὶ ἐκεῖ ἔθαψεν αὐτὸν μεγαλοπρεπῶς. This,

the topographical names and the names of the public buildings that occur in the *Romance*, none of which occurs in Ptolemaic documentary sources or in Strabo.[23] One example of this may serve for many. Alexander is reliably reported to have founded the city in the area of the Egyptian village of Rhakotis, and Rhakotis, which embraced the Hill of the Serapeum, lay in the south of the city close to the canal which linked the city with Schedia in the northern delta, and so eventually with the Nile. In the Ptolemaic period the canal was in full use, and there was a harbour close to the Serapeum, attested by contemporary documents, for transshipment of goods to the main Mediterranean harbour.[24] In the *Romance* the Rhakotis canal and the harbour have disappeared, and their place is taken by 'what is *now* called the street of the Great God Sarapis'.[25] This was the ceremonial dromos that led up to the Serapeum Hill from the south, that is, from the canal, when the Serapeum was monumentalized in the reign of Hadrian. Of course, the description precedes the destruction of the Serapeum by Theophilus and his monks in the eighties of the fourth century.[26]

From these specific elements, which indicate the nature of the material which the author of α either incorporated ready-made into his narrative, unchanged, or else (as is the case with the last item) slightly modified to meet the material conditions of Imperial Alexandria, we may turn to consider two elements which run through the whole narrative.

6. The most noticeable overall feature of the *Romance* is the preponderance of letters. Much of the narrative consists of correspondence between Alexander and Olympias and Alexander and Aristotle. There is not a single major episode, except for the birth and death of Alexander, which is not covered in part or in whole by this elaborate complex of correspondence, which not only deals with the conventional themes of Alexander's claims to divinity, his aims, and so on, but also includes extended records of 'mirabilia' seen, about which he writes to Aristotle (the correspondence has a long history in the east, particularly in Arab writers, and in the west, notably in the *Secreta Secretorum*).[27] Papyri containing parts of collections of

however, does not occur in A but is found in Arm (§ 284), and the *B* version, as well as in various subsidiary texts; these are worked into one text by Kroll in his edition, on the basis of Arm. as iii. 34.

    [23] On this point see already Ausfeld, *Rh.Mus.* 55 (1900), 348 ff., esp. pp. 357 ff.
    [24] See *PRyl.* 576, a papyrus of the last quarter of the 3rd cent. BC, which refers to the unloading of river craft πρὸς τῶι ἐν Ῥακώτει Σαραπιείωι. See *Ptol. Alex.* ii. 78 n. 182.
    [25] i. 31. 4 (in continuation of the passage quoted above, n. 20): . . . ἐπικαλούμενοι Ῥακωτίτης ποταμός, ὃς νῦν δρόμος τοῦ μεγάλου θεοῦ Σαράπιδος τυγχάνει.
    [26] For this epochal event see above, p. 15.
    [27] I cannot give here a full account of this correspondence. See the summary in G. Cary, *The Medieval Alexander* (Cambridge, 1956), 21–3, and M. Plezia, *Aristot. Epist. Fragm.* (Warsaw, 1961), *passim*; the *Secreta Secretorum* has been edited by M. Manzalaoui as vol. 276 of the Early English Texts series (Oxford, 1977). For the Arabic traditions see above, p. 47 n. 1.

similar, or the same, letters date from the first century BC, and others of Imperial date show that interest in such collections was maintained.[28] Merkelbach has argued that the original form of the *Romance* was such a *Briefroman*,[29] and though it is clear that letters, however early we may suppose them to have originated, cannot be the sole nucleus of the work, there is no doubt that they represent a major, detachable element which runs right through the *Romance*, and developed subsequently. Enoch Powell had argued previously, on the basis of the frequent citations of letters in

---

[28] The earliest papyrus is *PHamb.* 129, of the 1st cent. BC, no. XI in Merkelbach's corpus (see next note). L. L. Gunderson, in Ἀρχαία Μακεδονία, i (1970), 356 ff. claims that the letter from Alexander to Aristotle preserved as Ps. Call. iii. 17, in A (immediately following on the inserted text of Palladius, *De Brahmanibus*, for which see below, pp. 223-4) dates to the years 316-308 BC, on the ground that the partially independent Latin version of this, the *Epistola Alexandri ad Aristotelem* (Jul. Val. 216, ll. 2-5, ed. Kuebler; see also the edition by W. W. Boer, *Epistola Alexandri ad codicum fidem* etc., The Hague, 1953 [repr. 1973]) contains an oracular reference to the forthcoming death of Olympias and to the sisters of Alexander as being alive: *Mater tua* (i.e *Alexander*) *turpissimo quandoque exitu insepulta iacebit in via, praeda avium ferarumque. Sorores tuae felices diu erunt ut factae.* The corresponding passage in A is quite different (iii, 17, 41: μετὰ δὲ ὀλίγον χρόνον καὶ ἡ μήτηρ σου καὶ ἡ γυνή σου κακὴν κακῶς ἀπολοῦνται ὑπὸ τῶν ἰδίων καὶ αἱ ἀδελφαί σου ὑπὸ τῶν περὶ σέ, while Julius and Arm. omit the relations altogether. B follows the A-tradition (p. 152, Bergson): μετὰ δὲ ὀλίγον χρόνον καὶ ἡ μήτηρ σου καὶ ἡ γυνή σου κακὴν κακῶς ἀπολοῦνται. In spite of the unanimity of the α-tradition it is possible that the version in the *Epistola* is a stray from one of the early propaganda pamphlets. I may note in this connection the fragmentary block in the Paul Getty Museum, published by S. Bernstein in the *Getty Museum Annual*, 12 (1984), 154 ff. (*SEG* xxxiii. 802; cf. above, p. 12, n. 25), the front face of which shows the central portion of a relief of a horse and chariot, or cart, and unidentifiable figures, belonging to a *Tabula Iliaca*, (cf. *IGUR*, sub 1633) below which is the central portion of four lines of text in which a Darius speaks or writes in the first person (. . . καὶ γὰρ Ξέρξης ὁ τὸ φῶς μοὶ δούς . . .). Bernstein subsequently, in *ZPE* 77 (1989), 275 ff., identified this as part of the same text of correspondence between Alexander and Darius as that preserved in *PHamb.* ii. 129, and this is reinforced by R. Merkelbach, ibid. 277 ff., who prints the identical passage from A and the B-texts (both having δείξας for the stone's δούς). The inscription and the relief are part of one and the same monument, to be dated (I would guess) to the 2nd cent. BC. The back of the relief contains a later inscription consisting of a part of the *Chronicon Romanum* (IG xiv. 1297 = FGrH 252). It is very remarkable that this apocryphal correspondence should have been inscribed on a chance (?) monument. This shows once more how many and various, and in this case inexplicable, are the ways in which the *Romance* tradition was handed down to posterity before it became canonized in the α-text. Another recently published fragment, *POxy* 3823 of the 1st cent. AD, is clearly on the historical side of the dividing line between popular history and rhetorical exposition on the one hand and fable and the *Romance* on the other.

[29] Op. cit. 32 ff., for an analysis of the material. Merkelbach gives a complete collection of such letters, both as given in the *Romance* and in papyri on pp. 195-219 (thirty-eight items). The theory of a collection of letters as an element in the early strata of the *Romance* was already put forward by Erwin Rohde, *Die Griechische Roman* (1876), 183 ff. = 3rd edn. 197 ff.

Plutarch's *Life of Alexander*, that a corpus of such letters was one of his sources.[30]

7. The other general ingredient is verse. A good deal of the narrative is in choliambic verse—scazons, limping iambic trimeters—and more that is not so transmitted can be very easily put into choliambs (for instance, Hephaestus' oracle to Alexander, already mentioned above in connection with the Nectanebos story). A. D. Knox, who did not invent the theory, but certainly gave it wide circulation, maintained that 'It is clear that for large portions this life of Alexander rests on a choliambic basis; and we may hazard a guess that the whole is based on an anthology of Alexander's deeds in which the choliambic verses (as far as they extended) occupied pride of place.'[31] That is a large claim, and no doubt Knox exaggerated, though it is no argument against him to say that there are no choliambs in the *Liber de Morte Alexandri*, for he claimed only that they once held pride of place 'as far as they extended'. Nor were the *Letters* in choliambs; they are in normal epistolary style (the papyrus versions were unknown to Knox). Nevertheless, there are some 250 such verses, and Knox supplied more by minor manipulations.

There are parallels to this mélange of prose and simple verse in two or three very different milieux. First, we may note the fragments assigned to the astrological treatise that passed under the names of the two early astrologers, Nechepso and Petosiris, in which there are a good many iambic senarii, and of which Usener rearranged sections of the prose fragments in iambics.[32] A still more striking parallel occurs in a Christian context, in the versions of the *Life* of St Spyridon, Bishop of Trimithus, on Cyprus, at the time of the Council of Nikaia, the same who is now, and has been for long centuries, the Patron Saint of Kerkyra. Of the *Life* of Spyridon there exist several versions, which bear to each other a relationship not unlike that which we know from the Alexander-*Romance*, two or three different versions that have developed from a lost original that can be seen in different degrees below the various versions. In this case the base-text was an iambic hagiographical biography assigned to Bishop Triphyllius, the pupil of Spyridon, and later Bishop of Ledra or Leukosia, though he did not write it. The fact that the poem, which is largely an account of the miracles of the saint, was written in the later part of the

[30] *JHS* 69 (1939), 229 ff.
[31] See the Loeb *Herodas*, p. 288. It is to be noted that the verses in which Ammon replies to Alexander's enquiry regarding his death (i. 33, 11) contains only a few scazonic endings among some forty iambic lines. The corresponding section of Jul. Val. (i. 31) is wholly in iambic senarii.
[32] The fragments are in *Philol. Suppbd.* 6 (1891–3), 327–94, with notes by Usener; cf. *Ptol. Alex.* ii. 630 f. nn. 489 ff. In a different context, we may compare the *Letters* of Alciphron, based on Attic New Comedy, especially Menander, much of which can be turned back into the 'original' iambic senarii: see the Introduction by Fobes to the Loeb *Alciphron, Aelian* etc.

fourth century, and was thus read in Christian circles (certainly in Cyprus, and probably in Alexandria) at about the same time as the choliambics of the *Romance* were in circulation in pagan circles, makes it of especial interest to us, and justifies a further analysis at this point. Similarly the fact that some of the miracles ascribed to the saint were eventually represented in frescoes, for the benefit of those unable to read the edifying poem provides a valuable parallel between hagiographical literature and the Alexandrian illustrated World-Chronicles and smaller works which are linked to the *Romance*.[33]

There are two main versions of the biography, the full version by Theodore, Bishop of Paphos, written in AD 655, which exists in a number of manuscripts of the tenth and eleventh centuries, and an anonymous, truncated version, preserved in a single Laurentian MS of AD 1021. Of these two versions the latter, so far as it goes, is closer to the iambic original, the rhythms of which can be detected in several places. The language is more 'elevated' and more diffuse than that of Theodore. Theodore, for his part explains that the elevation of the style of the poem, which he did not believe to have been written by Triphyllius, had led him to write his prose version.[34] He also provides the interesting information that when the poem was recited on the occasion of the saint's festival the unlettered faithful were able to appreciate his θαύματα by their depiction in frescoes on the walls of the Church at Trimithous.[35] We are reminded

[33] There is a very full study, with edition of all versions of the *Life*, by P. Van den Ven, *La Légende de S. Spyridon, Évêque de Trimouthe* (Bibl. du Muséon, 33) (Louvain, 1953). The recoverable Iambic portions are there assembled (pp. 115*-120*) by Paul Maas, a less prolific composer of verses than A. D. Knox. Spyridon himself is a figure who occurs in the ecclesiastical historians as a participant at the Council of Nikaia, and Triphyllius as Bishop of Ledra, a highly respected literary figure (see DCB, s.v.), *eloquentissimus*, according to Jerome, *De Viris Illustr.* 92, the supposed author of the poem, was also known to Socrates, Sozomenos and others: see Van den Ven, pp. 1*ff., esp. pp. 44*ff. The *Suda*, T 1032 has Τριφύλλιος, ἐπίσκοπος, μαθητὴς Σπυρίδωνος τοῦ θαυματουργοῦ τοῦ Κυπρίου· ὃς ἔγραψε τὰ θαύματα τοῦ ὁσίου καὶ τερατουργοῦ πατρὸς ἡμῶν Σπυρίδωνος· ὡς γέγραπται ἐν τῶι βίωι αὐτοῦ δι᾽ ἰάμβων· ἃ χρὴ ἐκζητῆσαι ὡς λίαν ὠφέλιμα. The whole tradition of the *Life*, investigated in great detail by Van den Ven, provides a very instructive parallel to the early development of the *Romance*.

[34] p. 77: ταῦτα μὲν οὖν ἐν τῆι βίβλωι τῆι διὰ ἰάμβων ἐκτεθείσηι εὗρον, ἥντινα βίβλον λέγουσιν ὑπὸ τοῦ ἁγίου πατρὸς ἡμῶν Τριφυλλίου τοῦ μαθητοῦ τοῦ αὐτοῦ γενομένου ἐπισκόπου τῆς Καλλινικήσεων πόλεως ἤτοι Λευκῶν Θεῶν ἁγίας τοῦ Θεοῦ ἐκκλησίας ἀναγεγράφθαι. He continues: ἐγὼ δὲ οὐκ οἶμαι τοῦ προρρηθέντος πατρὸς Τριφυλλίου εἶναι τὸ τοιοῦτον σύγγραμμα, ἀλλὰ τινὸς μετασχόντος ὀλίγης τινὸς προπαιδείας ποίημα ὑπολαμβάνω εἶναι, ὅπερ σύγγραμμα εἴτε ἐπὶ ζωῆς εἴτε μετὰ θανάτου ἐκ πολλῆς πρὸς τὸν ἅγιον Τριφύλλιον τὸν ἐπίσκοπον ἀγαπῆς ὁ ποιήσας τόδε τὸ σύγγραμμα ὡς ἐξ αὐτοῦ γενόμενον αὐτῶι ἐπέγραψεν. The anonymous author of the Laurentian version stresses the need for a 'demotic' version for the faithful (p. 104, init., § 1, κοινότερος λόγος).

[35] p. 89, top: at the entrance to the cathedral at Tremithous, ἐπάνω τοῦ | (89) μέσου πυλεῶνος ἤγουν τῆς ἀρχοντικῆς θύρας τοῦ ναοῦ ἔνθα κεῖται τὸ τίμιον λείψανον τοῦ

both of the illuminated cycles of the Alexander-*Romance* and of the illustrated World-Chronicles discussed in the body of this essay. All these productions, Christian or pagan, secular and religious, thus catered for the needs of the illiterate as well as the literate.

A significant earlier example of the same prosaic metrical habit is to be seen in an Alexandrian choliambic epitaph of the second century AD some thirty lines long,[36] which refers in its closing lines to Alexander and his father—Ammon:

οἶδ' αὖ Μακηδὼν ὁ βασιλεὺς Ἀλέξανδρος
ὃν τίκτεν Ἄμμων θέμενος εἰς ὄφιν μορφήν, κ.τ.λ.

This resembles the scazons of the *Romance* in theme and language (in this couplet), and Knox thought that it might have been composed by the author of those scazons. That is no doubt fanciful, but there seems at present at least no reason to assign the verses of the *Romance* to a pre-Imperial date; they represent a metrical tradition of the Alexander-story, verse of a humble order, analogous to the hagiographical iambics, and foreshadowing the Byzantine versions in political verse. Humble though it is, however, it is still literature, and not folk-poetry. It is to be noted that the scrupulous Julius Valerius, when he translated the Greek version of α, a translation which is extremely close to A, retained many, but not all, of these choliambic verses, and indeed preserved a section of some twenty-five lines that are not in A. On the other hand the *B* and *Γ* traditions jettisoned, or lost, them, though a trace of them may survive in a Syriac metrical version which shows affinities with those traditions.[37]

ἁγίου πατρὸς ἡμῶν Σπυρίδωνος, εἰκὼν πᾶσαν τὴν διήγησιν ταύτην γεγραμμένη ἔχουσα μετὰ καὶ ἄλλων τινῶν μὴ γεγραμμένων ἐνταῦθα, κ.τ.λ. . . . (90. 4 ff.): ἐγένετο δὲ μεγάλη χαρὰ πᾶσιν τοῖς τὴν φιλόχριστον πόλιν Τριμουθοῦντα οἰκοῦσιν καὶ πᾶσιν τοῖς συναχθεῖσιν ἐν τῆι μνήμηι τοῦ σεβασμίου πατρός. διηπορούντο γάρ τινες περὶ τούτου τοῦ θαύματος μετὰ τὴν ἀνάγνωσιν εἰ ἄρα ἀληθῆ εἰσιν τὰ εἰρημένα ἐν τῶι βίωι τοῦ ἁγίου τῶι διὰ ἰάμβων συνταχθέντι. ἡνίκα δὲ ἐπέσκεψαν τῆι γραφῆι τῆς εἰκόνος οἱ προειρημένοι φιλόχριστοι ἄνδρες καὶ λοιπὸν ἐγνώσθη ἡ ἱστορία διὰ τῆς τῶν ἀναγνωσθέντων διηγήσεως, πάντες ηὐφράνθησαν καὶ ἐδόξασαν τῶι θεῶι ἐπὶ τούτωι. ἥντινα εἰκόνα καὶ οἱ προειρημένοι ἅγιοι ἀρχιερεῖς θεασάμενοι καὶ ἀκριβῶς τὴν ταύτης γραφὴν καταμαθόντες καὶ πληροφορηθέντες πάνυ ηὐγάσθησαν, κ.τ.λ. On this passage see further Van den Ven, pp. 81*-84*.

[36] *SEG* viii. 372 (*GVI* 1935) = E. Bernand, *Inscript. métr. de l'Égypte*, 71.

[37] For this text, translated by Budge at the back of his Syriac *Alexander* see C. Hunnius, *Das syrische Alexanderlied* (Göttingen, 1904), with the text in *ZDMG* 59 (1906). The fantastic legend embodied in these verses has much in common with the two later Greek traditions, and has no connection with the prose Syriac *Romance* translated by Budge, which derives from the *A*-tradition (see above, p. 48 n. 2; cf. Hunnius, *Alexanderlied*, 17 n. 1. The original date of the legend in the poem derives from the statement that the Hun will invade the *oikoumene* in 826 and 940, and bring about the final downfall of the Roman Empire. These are years of the Seleucid era: 826 = AD 514, and 940 (which lies in the future, and must be close to the date of composition) = AD 628. The peace of AD 638 was evidently not yet signed. The surviving poem is later than the legend.

Finally, when we have considered all these constituent parts of the text, what can we say of the author of α itself? Some indications of this having been given above, with reference to the list of Alexandrias, I may confine myself here to the evidence that has not been referred to earlier in this study. I therefore regard as unnecessary of further demonstration the fact that the author wrote his work in Alexandria, some time before the surviving Alexandrian Annals, the Golenischev papyrus, and the *Paschal Chronicle*, but we may note that internal evidence establishes this date within more precise limits. A passage dealing with Alexander's supposed teachers, missing in A, but given by both the Latin translator, Julius Valerius, and the Armenian version, reads, *Si quid inquirere curiosius voles, sat tibi lector habeto quartum Favorini librum, qui Omnigenae Historiae superscribitur*, and the Armenian version has 'but Paphovranos mentioned these matters in the fourth book of his all-encompassing learned histories'; a clear reference to the fourth book of Favorinus' Παντοδαπὴ Ἱστορία.[38] The passage must have stood in α, since the Armenian version is translated from the Greek, not the Latin. So, whether we regard the passage as a contribution to the narrative by the author himself (as seems most likely), or as part of a block of imported material, the work as a whole must be later than Favorinus, irrelevant though he is to the narrative itself. Consequently the reign of Antoninus Pius, during which Favorinus was active, must furnish a *terminus post quem*. Julius Valerius himself provides a fairly close upper limit. He is probably identical with the homonymous consul of AD 338; his full name is known from the Excipit of bk. i and the *Incipit* of bk. ii of his translation to have been Julius Valerius Alexander, vir clarissimus, Polemius.[39] A date *c.* AD 350, within a few decades, is recommended by this identification alone. If he is also identical with the anonymous author of the *Itinerarium Alexandri Magni Traianique*, the short (and incomplete) work dedicated to Constantius to encourage him on the occasion of his departure to the Persian Wars in AD 340, we reach approximately the same date. The *Itinerarium* has a great deal in common verbally with Julius, and the most likely explanation is that they are the work either of the same man or of two men, both writing in similar Latin, who used the same source. The date fits very well with the known date of Julius' consulship, and his authorship should probably be accepted.[40]

---

[38] The passage relating to Favorinus would have stood at i. 13. 4 in A: see Kroll ad loc. In Julius, i. 7 Kuebler read *Graecum* from the Paris MS Lat. 4880 (see his p. xxiii), but Rosellini has restored *Quartum* from the much earlier Epitome originally published by Zacher (see her note 33 on p. xxvi). The Armenian passage is on p. 33, § 29. For Favorinus see further above, p. 44; it will be recalled that he is quoted by Stephanus of Byzantium s.v. Ἀλεξάνδρεια.

[39] See *RE*, Julius (520); *PLRE* i, s.v. Julius Polemius 3–4.

[40] For the text of this short work which in Cod. Ambr. P. 49 follows the text of Julius (cf. Kuebler, pp. xxii–xxiii, Rosellini, pp. xix ff.), see the recent edition by H. J. Hausmann (Diss. Köln, 1968/70), which has a full apparatus criticus, with

A further point provided by Julius is unfortunately indecisive. To the list given in A,[41] of cities comparable in size to Alexandria, where A gives Rome as '14 miles' (he says 'stades', but he means 'miles'), followed immediately by the dimensions of Alexandria, Julius very precisely adds *nondum adiectis his partibus, quae multum congeminasse maiestatis eius magnificentiam visuntur.*[42] Whether he himself added the unmistakable reference to Aurelian's extension of the Roman Walls between 270 and 275, or whether he found it in α, we cannot tell, because the Armenian version seems to be incomplete at this point; it has a reference to Rome, but it is not very specific, nor is it clear that the translator has reproduced the printed Armenian text in full in his translation. We can only use the reference to Aurelian's rebuilding as a *terminus ante quem* for α if we are satisfied that some comparable phrase has not dropped out of A, and we cannot be certain of that. If α does actually date to before 275 then we must envisage a period of about half a century between it and Julius's translation. In any case a date in the early part of the fourth century places the author of the work in the milieu of the period when history and legend were barely distinguishable, and when the Alexandrian Annals took the shape in which they survive for us in the annalistic works which derive directly from the *Romance*, at least as far as the list of Alexandrias and the associated reference to the cities that were still inhabited and continued to prosper—probably within the frontiers of the Sassanian Kingdom—are concerned.[43] If this date is approximately correct one

prolegomena, but does not deal with the question of authorship. Ch. Müller's edn., op. cit. after his text of Ps. Call., is very incomplete: see the valuable article of Kubitschek, RE, s.v. Itinerarium Alexandri. Merkelbach discusses the work (on the basis of Müller's edition), op. cit. (1st edn. only), 179-82, with further bibliography (see also Rosellini, p. xix n. 21). The early study of Zacher, *Pseudocallisthenes* (Halle, 1867), 49-84, is very full and clear; he accepts a direct derivation from Julius, but does not argue for a single author; so also apparently Hausmann, pp. iv-v. The *Itin.* and Julius agree against A in a small detail which suggests unity of authorship (see Zacher, 54 ff., Merkelbach, 179 ff.). According to A (ii. 8. 1; p. 74. 4 ff.) and Arm. (§ 154) (and the *B*-tradition: ἀποδυσάμενος) Alexander swam in the Cydnus river naked (ἀπεδύσατο) while Jul. (p. 84, 14) and *Itin.* (ch. xxviii) say he was wearing his armour (Jul., *una cum armis*; *Itin. retentans arma*). The historians and their followers do not allow us to determine which course Alexander followed. Arr. ii. 8, says only οἱ δὲ ἐς τὸν Κύδνον ποταμὸν λέγουσι ῥίψαντα νήξασθαι, Diod. xvii. 31. 4-6, omits the swim and refers only to the consequent illness, Plut. *Alex.* 19 has only οἱ δὲ λουσαμένωι ἐν τῶι τοῦ Κύδνου ῥεύματι καταπαγέντι προσπεσεῖν λέγουσι, while CR iii. 5. 2, has *pulvere simul ac sudore perfusum regem invitavit liquor fluminis, ut calidum hac corpus ablueret; itaque veste deposita in conspectu agminis . . . descendit in flumine*, which Val. Max. iii. 8. Ext. 6, resembles: *aestu et itineris fervore in Cilicia percalefactus, Cydno, qui aquae liquore conspicuus Tarson interfluit, corpus suum immersit.* It seems most probable that Julius has reproduced the same version. [See Addenda]

[41] i. 31. 10
[42] i. 26.
[43] See above, pp. 11 ff.

claimant to authorship of the original *Romance* may be excluded. This is the Heracleides whom Plutarch quotes as 'the authority relied on by the Alexandrians' as witness to the legend of Alexander's vision of Proteus at the time of the foundation of the city, which closely resembles the version in the *A*-tradition. This authority, whoever he was, is far too early to have co-ordinated all the strands that make up the *Romance* as we have reconstructed it. The survival of his name as a separate authority for a fictitious legend shows once more that local Alexandrian legends not far removed from the 'Vulgate' historical tradition, sometimes associated with a specific name, circulated from a comparatively early date, and were available to the author of the α-version, but shows no more than that.[44] A tantalizing reference to 'the work in one book which the Alexandrians wrote about the Life of Alexander' which appears in a corrupt Byzantine text unfortunately does not stand up to examination.[45]

I end this analysis with an example of how the mythopoeic element continued and developed even after the α-version of the *Romance* had taken approximately the form we must suppose it to have had when it first circulated. This concerns Alexander's well-known dialogue with the Gymnosophists, to which I have already referred as being one of the detachable elements in the *Romance*. Palladius, the Bishop of Helenopolis,

---

[44] See Plut. *Alex.* 26. 3: εἰ δ', ὅπερ οἱ Ἀλεξανδρεῖς λέγουσιν, Ἡρακλείδηι πιστεύοντες, ἀληθές ἐστιν, οὔκουν ἀργὸς οὐδὲ ἀσύμβολος αὐτῶι συστρατεύειν ἔοικεν Ὅμηρος. λέγουσι γὰρ ὅτι τῆς Αἰγύπτου κρατήσας ἐβούλετο πόλιν μεγάλην καὶ πολυάνθρωπον Ἑλληνίδα συνοικίσας ἐπώνυμον ἑαυτοῦ καταλιπεῖν, καί τινα τόπον γνώμηι τῶν ἀρχιτεκτόνων ὅσον οὐδέπω διεμετρεῖτο καὶ περιέβαλλεν. εἶτα νύκτωρ κοιμώμενος ὄψιν εἶδε θαυμαστήν· ἀνὴρ πολιὸς εὖ μάλα τὴν κόμην καὶ γεραρὸς τὸ εἶδος ἔδοξεν αὐτῶι παραστὰς λέγειν τὰ ἔπη τάδε·

> Νῆσος ἔπειτά τις ἔστι πολυκλύστωι ἐνὶ πόντωι,
> Αἰγύπτου προπάροιθε· Φάρον δέ ἑ κικλήσκουσιν.

[45] Niceph. Call. (*PG* 146, p. 564), refers to a μονόβιβλον ὃ εἰς τὸν Ἀλεξάνδρου βίον ἐπέγραψαν οἱ Ἀλεξανδρεῖς. This reproduces Socr. *HE* iii. 23 fin., a corrupt passage in which Socrates is describing the ease with which oracles prophesied immortality: καίτοι καὶ τοὺς χρησμοὺς καὶ τὸ μονόβιβλον ὁ Ἀδρίας εἰς τὸν Ἀλεξάνδρου βίον ἐπέγραψεν, ἐπιστάμενος, κ.τ.λ. This passage was emended by Valesius in his translation of Socrates as follows: 'singularem librum quem Arrianus de Alexandri vita composuit', but he thought that the true reference was to Lucian's *Life of Alexander of Abunoteichos*: Adnot. in Socr. p. 47: 'certe vox Ἀδρίας tolerari non potest. Neque enim ullus unquam eo nomine est appellatus. Itaque Nicephorus pro ea voce substituit Ἀλεξανδρεῖς pessime. Intelligit porro Socrates hoc loco librum Luciani, qui vulgo Ἀλέξανδρος ἢ Ψευδόμαντις inscribitur. Quo in libro Lucianus fraudem & praestigias Alexandri cujusdam Paphlagonis, qui oraculum callide machinatus fuerat, describit. Quare pro Ἀδρίας vel ἀνδρίας ut in Florentino codice legitur, scribendum est Λουκιανός. Nisi dicamus Socratem memoria lapsum, librum hunc Adriano vel Arriano cuidam adscripsisse.' From this it seems to emerge that a μονόβιβλος was known to Socrates, but it is quite impossible to determine whether it did describe oracles uttered to Alexander the Great or Alexander of Abunoteichos (the context would suit either), though of course numerous oracles relating to the former were known, both in and outside the tradition of the *Romance*.

author of the *Lausiac History* and of the biography, in dialogue-form, of John Chrysostom (I take the identification of the author for granted; it does not very much matter in this context), also wrote a small pamphlet called, in its Latin translation, the *De Gentibus Indiae et Bragmanibus*, which is to be found at the end of some MSS of the *Lausiac History* and is also inserted in the text of A, without indication of separate authorship, after a brief account of Alexander's own meeting with the Brachmans.[46] This little work of only a few pages exists in almost as many variants, excerpts and Latin translations as the *Romance* itself.[47] It is divided into two parts, in the first of which Palladius himself speaks, whereas the second is ascribed by Palladius at the end of the first part to Arrian,[48] who is known to have intended to write on the Brachmans, and the first eleven sections of this second part are included by Jacoby among the dubious fragments of Arrian.[49] The first part of the work describes how Palladius met a grammarian from Thebes when he (Palladius) was on his way to India, at Adulis on the Ethiopic coast; the grammarian then describes to Palladius his experiences in trying to enter Ceylon. Part II follows, with the pseudo-Arrianic version of Alexander's meeting with the Gymnosophists.

It is obvious that this pamphlet, written at about the turn of the fourth and fifth centuries AD, has nothing to do with the *Romance*. We may be certain that it was not in α since it is neither in Valerius nor in the Armenian version. But it is in A, and also (in part only) in *B* and *Γ*, and in later variations. The presence of this little story in the middle of A is, then, a very good illustration both of the need to distinguish between α and A, and of the links between *A, B* and *Γ*. The author of Mandeville's *Travels* also recorded this dialogue. He calls the Gymnosophists 'Gynoscriphe'.

Additional Note: Craterus' Letter to his Mother

A further trace of the literary propaganda between the Diadochi in the years 323–321 BC is, I believe, to be found in the strange fragment of a (fabricated) letter from Craterus to his mother, conceived, it may be hazarded, along the lines of Alexander's letters to his mother in the primary sources. Strabo (702) quotes this disapprovingly with the unfamiliar introductory formula 'A letter from Craterus to his mother Aristopatra has been published which contains a great many marvellous stories (παράδοξα)

---

[46] iii. 5.
[47] Ed. W. Berghoff, Beitr. z. Klass. Philol. 24, 1969.
[48] i. 15.
[49] See Arr. *Anab.* vi. 16. 5; cf. *FGrHist*. 156 F175. The publication of a fragment of the *De Gentibus* in a papyrus dated to the first half of the 2nd cent. AD suggests that Arrian's authorship can hardly be sustained on chronological grounds: see ZPE 74 (1988), 59 ff. (*PGenev.* Inv. 271).

which no other authority confirms, in particular that Alexander advanced
as far as the Ganges. And he says that he himself saw the river and the
monsters in it, and (reports) its approximate (length?) width and depth.'⁵⁰
This requires consideration from two aspects.

First, there can be little doubt that Megasthenes was the first Greek to
give a specific description of the Ganges,⁵¹ and Tarn maintained on that
account that the letter of Craterus must be later than that traveller.⁵²
However, the matter is less cut-and-dried than that. It is difficult to believe
that some knowledge of the Gangetic river-system was not picked up by
Alexander's troops by the time that they reached the Beas. The Vulgate
preserves the tradition that tribesmen, whose ruler was 'Phegeus', offered
to conduct Alexander to the river, a march allegedly of twelve days,⁵³ and
I agree with Brunt that some information about the Ganges and the kingdom centred at Pataliputra was known to Alexander's returning troops.
Nothing more than that was required for the fabrication of the letter.

This brings us to the other aspect of the matter. Craterus, the most
faithful (πιστότατος) of Alexander's closest associates, was ordered back to
Greece by Alexander to take over from Antipater, but did not reach there
before Alexander's death. After the termination of the Lamian War
Craterus joined the coalition against Perdiccas (in whose interest the
passages contained in the *Last Testament* were concocted), but on crossing
into Asia Minor he was killed in battle against Eumenes in 321,⁵⁴ in the
same year that Perdiccas was murdered by his troops in Egypt when
advancing against Ptolemy. What relevance, we may ask, had the letter
to his mother Aristopatra (an 'aristocratic'-sounding Macedonian name of
which no other example exists) after his death? The answer must surely
be 'None', as it is to the recognized pro-Perdiccan items in the *Testament*.
If that it correct, and we bear in mind the chronological coincidence

⁵⁰ Str. 702 = FGrH 342: ἐκδέδοται δέ τις καὶ Κρατεροῦ πρὸς τὴν μητέρα
Ἀριστοπάτραν ἐπιστολή, πολλά τε ἄλλα παράδοξα φράζουσα καὶ οὐχ ὁμολογοῦσα οὐδενί,
καὶ δὴ καὶ τὸ μέχρι τοῦ Γάγγου προελθεῖν τὸν Ἀλέξανδρον· αὐτὸς δέ φησιν ἰδεῖν τὸν
ποταμόν, καὶ κήτη τὰ ἐπ' αὐτῶι καὶ μεγέθους καὶ πλάτους καὶ βάθους πόρρω πίστεως
μᾶλλον ἢ ἐγγύς. The sentence is ungrammatical, and critics have dealt with it in
various ways, as Kramer indicates ad loc. None of the suggested solutions seems
natural (except perhaps to add τά before κήτη). It is possible that, as Kramer,
followed by Meineke and the Loeb editor preferred, μεγέθους should be changed to
μέγεθος, and the two following genitives of width and depth should be regarded as
dependent on it, but the double use of καί is unsatisfactory. The evident corruption
does not affect the general sense.
⁵¹ See Schwanbeck, *Megasthenes*, 30 ff.
⁵² *Alex.* ii. 281, 302. He therefore dismisses Craterus' letter (p. 302) as
'invented out of hand by someone, later than Megasthenes, who was committed to
the support of the legend that Alexander had reached the Ganges.'
⁵³ Diod. xvii. 93; QC ix. 1. 36–2. 4; cf. Brunt, *Arrian*, ii. 464; *contra*, ('pure
myth'), Tarn *Alex.* ii. 275 ff.
⁵⁴ Diod. xix. 25; 29.

between the final careers of the opponent protagonists, Perdiccas and Craterus, the document, or what remains of it, may reasonably be assigned to the war of pamphlets of which the Perdiccan side is evident in the *Testament*. The letter, with its colourful παράδοξα, associated Craterus closely with Alexander in the final and imaginary thrust to the Ganges. The episode could be presented to an uncritical and largely uninformed public as further testimony to the close link between the great captain and Alexander; the more so because Alexander had in fact given Craterus the responsibility of supervising the building of the cities on the Indus, Nikaia and Bucephala.[55]

It seems, then, plausible to suggest that the tiny fragment preserved by Strabo belongs, like the tendentious role assigned to Perdiccas in the *Testament*, to 322 or 321 BC. But we can hardly do more than place it in the context of that opening struggle, which began with the death of Alexander and culminated in the death of the two men two years later. In the *Testament* Craterus' appointment as provisional Governor of Macedonia is clearly stated alongside those of the other Diadochi, including the wholly unhistorical appointment of Perdiccas as 'King of Egypt'. Consequently it should cause no surprise that Craterus, a popular leader, had his supporters no less than the more severe and suspicious Perdikkas. At the least it seems more probable so to regard it than to see it as a fragment divorced from any historical context.

At various points in this book I have called attention to what I believe may be floating fragments of the *Romance* itself, or of its constituent parts. The story of Craterus' letter to his mother shows us more of the struggles of the first years after Alexander's death which did not find their way into the *Testament*. Another specimen occurs in the so-called *Heidelberg-Epitome*,[56] in which Ptolemy after the death of Alexander is said to have married Alexander's sister, Cleopatra (said to be the wife of Perdiccas), which we have already encountered as a feature of the *Will of Alexander*.[57]

---

[55] Arr. v. 20. 1: Κράτερον μὲν δὴ ξὺν μέρει τῆς στρατιᾶς ὑπελείπετο τὰς πόλεις ἄστινας ταύτηι ἔκτιζεν ἀναστήσοντά τε καὶ ἐκτειχιοῦντα. See above, p. 161.

[56] The passage was first published by Reitzenstein, *Poimandres* (Leipzig, 1904), 308–15, who rightly saw it as a part of the earliest stratum of the *Romance*. In republishing the *Epitome* as FGrH 155, (4) Jacoby, ad loc., preferred to regard it as part of the Vulgate tradition, but it is too deeply embedded in the text of the Will for that solution to be acceptable. The passage runs: ὅτι νικήσας, ὡς εἴρηται, ὁ Πτολεμαῖος ἐν Αἰγύπτωι τὸν Περδίκκαν, ἔλαβε τὰ αὐτοῦ στρατεύματα ὅσα ἤθελεν, ἔλαβεν δὲ καὶ τὴν αὐτοῦ γυναῖκα Κλεοπάτραν τὴν ὁμοπάτριον ἀδελφὴν τοῦ μεγάλου Ἀλεξάνδρου καὶ εἶχεν αὐτὴν εἰς γάμου κοινωνίαν σὺν ταῖς ἄλλαις αὐτοῦ γυναιξίν. ἦν δὲ ἡ Κλεοπάτρα αὕτη θυγάτηρ μὲν τοῦ Φιλίππου, ἀλλ' ἐξ ἄλλης γυναικός, Κλεοπάτρας καὶ ἐκείνης γενομένης.

[57] See above, p. 213, n. 16.

APPENDIX 3*
The Chinese Pilgrims

IN this Appendix I try to set in the context of this book the pilgrimage of Hsüan-Tsang (whose name is variously transliterated as Yuan Chwang (Watters); Hiouen Thsang (Julien); Hsuan(g) Tsang or Hwen Thsang (Cunningham), Hiuen Tsiang (Beal), Huan Chwan (Mayers) and Yuen Chwang (Wylie)), the most notable of the Chinese Buddhist pilgrims to Central Asia, whose narrative and life are frequently invoked in the study of the historical geography of Central Asia and the region of the Hindu Kush, and also of a few other of the pilgrim-texts that have been published in a European translation. I am wholly ignorant of Chinese, and I have written this Appendix for my own benefit no less than that of the reader, because I have found that references by Western historians to the narrative of Hsüan-Tsang and the other pilgrims rarely provide a general account of them and their testimony. The narratives of Hsüan-Tsang and of the other Buddhist pilgrims to the West, relating to the area west of the Tarim basin, especially the valleys of the Indus and the Kābul and the other rivers of the Hindu Kush, record pilgrimages to the great Buddhist shrines and sanctuaries in which those regions, as well as the valleys of the Indus and the Ganges, and Ceylon, abounded. The texts are almost all earlier than, or contemporary with, the Arab conquest of Sijistān, Khorāsān and Transoxiana (Tocharistān) between approximately AD 650 and 750.[1] The historical texts of the period of the expansion of the Han dynasty westwards in the second and first centuries BC, which play an important part in piecing together the vicissitudes of the Bactrian Kingdom and the movements of the Yüeh-Chih, though much earlier than the pilgrim texts, provide less geographical information.[2]

* I must express my indebtedness to Professor G. Dudbridge and Mr A. D. S. Roberts for helping me in various ways in a field in which I have had everything to learn. Any errors are naturally my own.

[1] For the conquest of Sijistān and Khorāsān see Caetani, *Annali dell' Islam*, vii. 248 ff., 280–92, and the full account by M. A. Shaban, *The 'Abbāsid Revolution* (Cambridge, 1970; 1979), 16–34. The work of C. E. Bosworth on Sijistān, *Sīstân under the Arabs* (IsMEO 11, 1969), for which see above, p. 126 n. 44, also contains much information up to the establishment of the Ṣaffārid dynasty.

[2] For these texts see the translation and commentary of Pan-Ku, with a valuable introduction, by A. F. P. Hulsewé and M. A. N. Loewe, quoted above, p. 126 n. 43, which removes the need for me to quote the earlier translations and bibliography. The reader will find an interesting general account of the economic and social conditions of Central Asia at the time of the Kushans and later in X. Liu, *Ancient India*

It need not be said that the Chinese evidence does not provide a
tradition of Alexander-foundations, in the way that the Greek, Pehlevi,
and Arabic texts do; the pilgrims are not historians, but simply witnesses
to the world of their own experience. Moreover, it must be emphasized that
the identifications with Greco-Roman or other locations are at best no
more than probable, since the nature of the Chinese language makes any
precise identification, based solely on the morphological resemblance of
names (usually faint), without independent evidence, precarious, and the
forms of geographical expression are usually vague and ambiguous.

The features of these accounts are stereotyped, from the time of the
earliest of them, that of Fa-hsien, written in AD 400, onwards.[3] The
purpose of the pilgrims in pursuing their arduous journeys, often of many
years' duration, was to win for their homeland the texts of the great
Buddhist classics written in the Indian languages. Their mentality has
been admirably described by Chavannes in the following words.

'Ils n'étaient pas cependant, ces intrépides, pareils aux fanatiques
dont la foule se presse, entraînée par un instinct aveugle, vers les lieux
saints d'Islam; ils ne venaient point non plus dans l'espérance de voir se
réaliser pour eux ou pour leurs proches quelque guérison miraculeuse;
leur foi n'était ni si inconsciente, ni si intéressée. Ils se proposaient, regret-
tant de n'avoir pu rencontrer le divin maître lui-même, de visiter les pays
où il s'était trouvé, d'adorer tous les objets qui rappelaient son souvenir;
mais surtout ils voulaient se procurer les livres qui avaient conservé son
enseignement, afin de revenir en Chine répandre la bonne Loi et révéler
les vérités qui délivrent de peine. Ces hommes d'action étaient en même
temps des hommes d'étude qui apprenaient le sanscrit, qui s'initiaient à
une grammaire et à une langue d'un génie tout opposé à celui du chinois,
pour se rendre capables de traduire les livres révérés des Bouddhistes
hindous. Il est rare que de pures idées inspirent de pareils dévouements et
c'est un fait peut-être unique dans l'histoire du monde de voir une religion
se répandre comme une science, grâce aux travaux d'une légion d'érudits.'[4]
From these arduous journeys it is certain that many never returned.[5]

and Ancient China, Trade and Religious Exchanges, AD 1–600 (Delhi, 1988), with, in
particular, a valuable account of the economic role of the Buddhist monasteries.

[3] For the *Fo Kuo Chi* of Fa-hsien see the translation in Beal (see below, n. 7),
Western Records, i, pp. xxiii–lxxxiii. Traditionally the *Fo Kuo Chi* is regarded as the
earliest of the records, and that of Wu-K'ung as the latest (his pilgrimage covered
the years 749–89): for his narrative see below, n. 14. Intermediate between them
lies the narrative of Sung-Yun, who travelled from 518 to 521, but his route did
not take him beyond Udyāna (Swat) in the north and Laghman in the south: see
the summary by Beal, i, pp. xv–xviii, and the translation ibid. pp. lxxxiv–cviii; an
improved translation with a very full commentary was published by Chavannes, in
BEFEO 3 (1903), 380–441.

[4] See Chavannes (op. cit. below, n. 11), pp. xii–xiii.

[5] I-Ching, in Chavannes, ibid., says simply 'it is not known where they are now',

The records focus on the shrines and miracles of the Buddha in the various regions, and of the relics preserved in the stupas and *sangharamas* (convents), and contain innumerable stories of conversion, and other edifying events. They also include descriptions of the inhabitants of the towns and villages passed through, their morals, their devotion (or lack of it) to the Law, their way of life, their produce, social customs, and so on, as well as of the towns themselves, their dimensions, etc. For the student of the historical geography of Central Asia it appears at first sight to be a particularly valuable feature that many of the distances are described and measured from the largest down to the smallest unit, the *li*, approximately one-fifth of an English mile, but these distances are flexible, and several of the routes described were clearly never visited, at least by Hsüan-Tsang. The routes themselves, from Yarkand to Ceylon, from east of the Ganges to west of the Indus, and the countryside traversed, are also frequently described in detailed and colourful terms. Some of the accounts of the great mountain ranges and climatic conditions are particularly memorable, even if it has been maintained that Hsüan-Tsang has sometimes allowed his imagination to run away with him.

The pilgrimage of Hsüan-Tsang, a leading Doctor of the Law, occurred in the years AD 629 to 644, with numerous prolonged stays, sometimes amounting to as much as two years, in one region.[6] The text consists of twelve books, divided according to the countries and regions through which the pilgrim passed, or in some cases of which he had heard, but which he had not himself visited.[7] Further information regarding Hsüan-Tsang's journey is provided by the *Life* of him written by Hui-Li a century

and 'he has not been heard of again'. Beal, in his translation of the *Life* (see below, n. 8), pp. xv–xxxi, describes the lives of some forty of these close successors of Hsüan-Tsang from I-Ching (for whom see below, n. 8). Cf. also A. C. Yu's Introduction to his 4-vol. translation of the notable picaresque novel of the 16 cent., the *Hsi yu Chi*, based on the life of Hsüan-Tsang, *The Journey to the West* (4 vols. London, 1977–83); in i. 1, Yu states that Hsüan-Tsang's pilgrimage was the fifty-fifth in chronological sequence, and that it was followed by some fifty more. Chavannes, loc. cit. 430–41, lists and analyses other texts relative to India published before the T'ang period, the date of Hsüan-Tsang's pilgrimage.

[6] There is a useful chronological table of Hsüan-Tsang's travels in Cunningham, *GAI*, 563 ff.; another, rather fuller and more precise, by V. A. Smith in Watters' translation and commentary (see n. 7), ii. 329 ff.

[7] The old translations of this, the pioneer work of S. Julien, *Les Voyages de Hiouen-Thsang* (2 vols. Paris, 1853), and that of S. Beal, *Buddhist Records of the Western World* (London, 1885; repr. 1906), are superseded by that of T. Watters, *On Yuan Chwang* (2 vols., Orient. Transl. Fund, NS xiv–xv, 1904–5, ed. T. W. Rhys Davids and S. W. Bushell). It was assumed by Julien and Beal that the account of his travels was first edited during his lifetime(?) by Pien Ki, and published after his death, in the early 8th cent., by Chang Yueh, who contributed the surviving flowery introduction and preface. However, this is strenuously denied by Watters, who claimed the work was 'edited' by Hsüan-Tsang himself, and that the two introductory prefaces were the work of two of his contemporaries.

or so later.[8] The names of all places and regions are given in the Chinese form in the transmitted text, though he originally composed the work in Sanskrit, the language of the Buddhist texts that he brought back from the West.[9]

The parts of the narrative with which we are concerned in the context of this book are those dealing with the Hindu Kush area. Hsüan-Tsang's pilgrimage was partly circular over the years, and he visited the region twice, at an interval of fourteen years. The first occasion was on his arrival from China, when he travelled via the Tarim basin and the Yarkand river to Khotan and thence to Samarkand. He then crossed the Oxus, visited Fo-Ho = Balkh, and traversed the Hindu Kush via one of the defiles leading to Fan-yen-na = Bāmiyān, which he describes in some detail, including the Buddha-statues. After a brief stay there he journeyed in a snow storm—it was at the end of April—via the Shībar pass and the valley of the Ghorband river to Kia-Pi-Shi = Kapisa. He describes the 'country' of Kapisa as 4,000 *li* = *c.* 800 miles in circuit, and the city as only ten *li* in circumference. The city is said to be 600 *li* or so from the country of Lan-po = Laghman, that is the area of Jalalabad, and Hi-lo = Haḍḍa (Hiḍḍa), reached, as he rightly says, by skirting the Snowy Mountains, i.e. the Sāfid Koh or Kashmund range of Kafiristān. Hsüan-Tsang tells us a great deal about the city of Kia-Pi-Shi and the adjacent monasteries and stupas, but, as is usual throughout his work, he shows no significant knowledge of the earlier history of the city, other than a story attached to a particular monastery that had connections with Kanishka. Consequently, though the location at the foot of the Ghorband valley and its orientation with reference to the region of Laghman fits very well the site of Begrām, our pilgrim does not clinch the debate for us.[10]

[8] Translated by Julien, *Histoire de la Vie de Hiouen-Thsang et de ses voyages dans l'Inde* (Paris, 1853), and by Beal, *The Life of Hiuen-Tsiang* (London, 1888). A further version is given in Arthur Waley's *The Real Tripitaka and Other Pieces* (London, 1952), 11-130. The *Life* is an essential element in the interpretation of Hsüan-Tsang's own narrative. Julien's translation of the *Life* of Hsüan-Tsang, pp. 353-461, contains a useful alphabetically arranged gazetteer of the places visited by the pilgrim. The analysis of the Afghan section of the narrative by A. Foucher in *Études Asiatiques*, i (1925) (Publications de l'École française de l'Extrême Orient), 257-84, retraces the route of the pilgrim with reference to the archaeological evidence (as then known) and the historical background. See also id. *Vieille Route*, 36 ff., 229-40. For transliterations and equivalents of the Chinese terms for the relevant locations see below, pp. 233 ff.. M. Bretschneider's *Mediaeval Researches from Eastern Asiatic Sources* (2 vols., London, 1888 etc.), esp. ii. 1-136, the commentary on a Chinese map of the 15th cent., contains much useful information on identifications in Central Asia.

[9] For details of how and when the work and its associated prefaces were composed see Watters, i, Introduction, *passim*; cf. above, n. 7.

[10] Beal, *Records*, 53, in translating the brief sentence in which Hsüan-Tsang records his route from Bāmiyān to Kia-Pi-Shi, equates 'the black ridge' with the Shiah Koh: 'Going eastward from this, we enter the defiles of the Snowy Mountains,

On his return journey, more than a decade later, Hsüan-Tsang came from the Indus valley, after a brief stay at Taxila, and crossed into Aghanistan by one of the passes of the Sulimanye range, perhaps by the Khyber Pass. His first *manzil* was at Ho-si-na, usually identified with Ghazna, of which he gives a colourful description of the climate, the flora and the character of the population. From there he passed northwards for 500 *li*, some 60 miles, to the kingdom of Fo-li-shi-sa-t'ang-na, some 400 miles from east to west and 200 from north to south.[11] The capital U-pi-na, identified with (H)Opiān, is four miles round, but its location is not indicated. It is clear, however, that he was still a long way from the main face of the Hindu Kush, for he says that he only reached the mountain pass called Po-lo-si-na, which is evidently on the more easterly face of the mountain, not in the Koh-i-Bābā, that is, in the valley of Bāmiyān, after he passed Kapisa. This seems to indicate that he probably traversed the Khawak pass (cf. above, p. 158 n. 103), and confirmation of this is provided by the fact that he descended from the pass to An-ta-lo-po = Andarāb, and thence to Hwow = Kundūz, and not to the region of the modern Dosht, as he would have done if he had crossed via the Ghorband valley, the Shībar pass and the (almost impassable) Shekari defile. The hardships endured in reaching the pass, if wholly authentic, strongly suggest that Alexander would not, other alternatives being available, have chosen that route to Bactria with an army and baggage-train. This brief account of the routes taken by the pilgrim on his two visits to the area of Turkestan illustrates the natural routes to be taken in both directions: for Balkh and the western reaches of the Oxus the natural route lay by the Bāmiyān valley and the defiles west of the Shībar pass, while for the area of Kundūz it lay over one of the central passes leading down to Andarāb, thence to the upper reaches of the Oxus, not far from Aï Khanūm, and

cross over the black ridge (Siah Koh) and arrive at the country of Kia-pi-shi.' This, however, is the range which lies considerably east of Charikar, and north of the Kābul river in its eastward course, to which the text refers on p. 68, 'skirting the black ridge we enter North India, and crossing the frontier come to the country of Lan-Po (Laghman)'; his own note regarding the site of Kia-Pi-Shi (p. 55 n. 198) indicates that he accepts a location in or near the Ghorband valley; the first 'black ridge' (i.e. not covered in perpetual snow, unlike the peak of Folada to the west, and the peaks of the main range, 'the Snowy Mountains') is the Paghman range that forms the south side of the valley of the Ghorband in the descent from the plateau of Bāmiyān via the Shībar pass, which is nowhere of great height; cf. Smith in Watters, op. cit. ii. 334.

[11] It is to be noted that Hsüan-Tsang does not refer to a kingdom or a city north of Ghazna (if Ghazna is correctly identified) that can be identified with Ortospana. Cunningham, p. 35, took Fo-li-shi-sa-t'ang-na to be that of Ortospana (Sanskrit Urddhasthana, according to him: see above, p. 143 n. 72), with the Bālā Hissar of Kābul as its capital. I have discussed this above, (loc. cit.) and I repeat it here to stress that the intrusion of Ortospana into the topography of the region between Ghazna and Kābul involves violence to the text of Hsüan-Tsang's narrative.

further to Badakshān The determination of this pattern of routes is of particular importance, and it remains valid wherever we may chose to locate Alexandria ad Caucasum, Kapisa and (H)Opiān.

Hsüan-Tsang was not the only pilgrim to traverse the region west of the Indus at the time of the break-up of the Hephthalite kingdom and on the eve and aftermath of the Arab conquest. Also to be noted are I-Ching, who carried out a similar pilgrimage later in the same century, but his travels, recorded by a contemporary, do not seem to have extended west of the Indus beyond Gandhara;[12] Hui-ch'ao, whose pilgrimage lasted from AD 723 to 729;[13] and Wu-K'ung, the latest in date, whose journey seems to have followed roughly the same route as that of Hsüan-Tsang.[14] Of these only Hui-ch'ao adds any significant details to the narrative of Hsüan-Tsang.

Suggested Identifications

For convenience I give here a list of the Chinese locations as given in the translations, and the suggested modern equivalents. In assessing the narrative, and the places mentioned in it, two general considerations have to be borne in mind. The first is that though a *li*, the land-distance regularly used, is conventionally given as one-fifth or one-sixth of an English statute mile, as with other measurements of this type, oriental and western, a time factor closely related to a day's journey is not wholly absent. A *li* over mountain-territory may apparently be not much more than half that on normal terrain.[15] Secondly, Hsüan-Tsang regularly describes a kingdom and its capital city, presumably of a local Hephthalite ruler, by the same place-name, and the value of the larger measurement is usually difficult to assess. For example, of the region of Tashkent (Chi-Shih) and Samarkand(Sa-mo-kan) he says that you enter the 'country of Samarkand, 500 *li* from Tashkent', and 'the country of Samarkand' is said to be '1,600 or 1,700 *li* in extent, and its capital 20 *li* in extent'. Of Kapisa he says 'This country is 4,000 *li* in extent . . . the capital of the country is 10 *li* or so in circuit', and so on.

The identifications themselves within the regions covered by Alexander

---

[12] For I-Ching's pilgrimage see the translation by E. Chavannes, *Les Religieux Éminents* (*Mémoire composé à l'époque de la Grande Dynastie T'ang par I-Tsing*) (Paris, 1894).

[13] For Hui-ch'ao, of whom only a fragment survives, see the translation (with following Chinese text) by W. Fuchs, *SB, Berl. Akad.* 1935, 426–57. The Arab conquests of Turkestan and Transoxiana are more evident in Hui-Ch'ao's narrative than in that of his predecessors, when the conquests were still in progress.

[14] For Wu-K'ung see the translation by Levi and Chavannes, *JA* (1895), 341–84, 'L'Itinéraire d' Ou-K'ong'. On his visit to Kashmir see A. Stein, *SB, Wien. Akad.* 1896 (135)(7).

[15] See esp. Cunningham, *GAI* 571 ff.; Bretschneider, *Mediaeval Researches*, i. 15 n. 10; Smith, in Watters, op. cit. 32 n. 2.

up to his entry into 'India' are in some cases very uncertain, others reasonably certain on either geographical or linguistic grounds or both. In the appended list I follow the sequence of the narrative of Hsüan-Tsang's return journey, that is to say starting from Balkh and moving south-east as far as Jalalabad.[16]

1. Fo-ho-lo = Balkh: Hsüan-Tsang, Beal, i. 43; Watters, i. 108 f., who says it represents not Balkh itself, but Bokhara including Balkh or the region between Kundūz and Balkh ('These transcriptions (Fo-lo-ho and Fo-ko-lo) seem to require an original like Bokhar or Bokhara, the name of the country which included Balkh. The Fo-ho or Balkh of our pilgrim was evidently not very far west from Huo (Kundūz)'; Hui-ch'ao, p. 449 (Fu-ti-Ya); *Life*, pp. 48 f. Bretschneider, *Mediaeval Researches*, ii. 100, cf. ibid. i. 93 n. 241, gives other Chinese names by which Balkh was known: Ban-li, Ban-le-i-ho, Ba-li-ho.

2. Fan-Yen-na = Bāmiyān: Hsüan-Tsang, p. 49; Watters, i. 114-22; Hui-ch'ao, pp. 448-9 (not transliterated); on pp. 115-16 Watters says that Hsüan-Tsang was the first to use this transliteration, and gives other versions (Fan-Yen, Wang), 'each representing a sound like Bam-yan'. On Bretschneider's map, i. 96, Bāmiyān appears as Ba-Mou.

3. Kia-Pi-Shi(h) = Kapisa: Hsüan-Tsang, pp. 54-68; *Life*, pp. 54 ff.; Watters, p. 123, who says 'The country here designated as Ka-Pi-Shih does not seem to have been known to the Chinese generally by that name. We find the Ka-pi-Shih of our author, however, in some later books to denote a country said to be Kipin [see no. 4, below]. In some older books the country is called Ka-pi-Shih.' Similarly, A. V. Williams Jackson in *CHI* i. 332 n. 4 says, 'Capisa is the Kia-pi-shi of Hiuen-Tsiang and the Ki-pin of other Chinese texts.'

4. Ki-pin = Kophen = Kābul; Fa-hsien (*c.* AD 400; cf. Beal, i. p. xi), ibid. p. xxvii and p. c (Sung-Yun, AD 518; cf. p. xv); not in Hsüan-Tsang (cf. Smith, in Watters, ii. 342: 'The city of Kabul, which is 85 miles distant from Ghazni, is never mentioned by the pilgrim, and perhaps was not important in his time'). Cunningham, p. 34, makes the equation Ho-pi-an = Kophen = Kābul. Groot, ii. 86 ff., (Ke-pin), discusses the location and extent of the realm of Ke-pin, assuming that it is identical with Kia-Pi-Shi. Watters, i. 259, says, 'In many Chinese treatises Ka-pin is a geographical term of vague and varying extension, and not the designation of a particular country. It is applied in different works to Kapis, Nagar, Gandhara, Udyāna, and Kashmir.' Bretschneider's map, which is of the fourteenth

---

[16] In referring to Hsüan-Tsang I have given only the references to Beal's translation, as being the most accessible (though not the most accurate), and to that of Watters as containing a full commentary, referring to these authorities simply by name. For the narrative of Hui-ch'ao see above, n. 13.

century, and shows varieties of names from those with which we are dealing, has K'o-Bu-Li where Ki-pin might be expected, and Bretschneider adds (ii. 67) that A. Rémusat, in his *Extension de l'Empire chinois* (1825 ? [*non vidi*]) thought that Ki-pin was Kandahar, which seems too far south to be at all likely. Chavannes, *BEFEO* 3 (1903), 415 n. 8, shows quite clearly that the designation Ki-pin applied at different times to Kapisa, and to Kashmir. In the Han and Sui dynasties it meant Kashmir, and it was not applied to Kapisa until the T'ang dynasty, i.e. the period the beginning of which fell at the time of Hsüan-Tsang's travels. The identity with Kābul can therefore only be accepted if Kapisa-Begrām and Kābul are supposed to have been roughly identified.

5. Lan-po = Laghmān (Lamghan, Skt. Lampaka); Hsüan-Tsang, pp. 90-1; Hui-ch'ao, p. 447.

6. Hi-Lo = Ha(i)ḍḍa; Beal, i. p. xxxiv (Fa-hsien); Hsüan-Tsang, p. 95 (with discussion of term 'Begrām', here used of the mounds of Hiḍḍa).

7. Ho-si-na = Ghazna; Hsüan-Tsang, ii. 283. For Hsüan-Tsang Ho-si-na is the capital of Tsu-ku-Cha (Tsauku-ṭa), which Cunningham (p. 40) takes to be the district of Arachosia. A secondary capital, Ho-sa-la, is mentioned by Hsüan-Tsang ibid., and no location has been associated with it. It could well be the region south of Ghazna dominated by Ḳalāt-i-Ghilzai. Cunningham, ibid., takes the second capital to be 'Guzar or Guzaristan' on the Helmund (the Lo-yo-yin-tu); this is perhaps Uruzghān, in the southern part of the Hazārajat, where two rock-cut Bactrian inscriptions of the Hephthalite period or later have been found (see *Archaeology in Afghanistan*, 243-4, with illustrations; Ball 1221; they seem to belong to the Turki-Shāhi period). Watters, ii. 265, prefers Ho-si-na to be Zābul, near Ghazna.

8. U-pi-na = (H)Opiān; Hsüan-Tsang, ii. 285, where it is the capital of Parsuthana or Vardasthāna, in the region of Charikar. Hsüan-Tsang went from U-pi-na over the Hindu Kush, probably by the Khawak pass: the mountain pass is called Po-lo-se-na, which could be any pass, but since he dropped down to Andarāb (see no. 9), the Khawak, though circuitous (see above, p. 158, n. 103), is the most likely route.

9. An-ta-lo-po = Andarāb; Hsüan-Tsang, ii. 286. The identification is generally accepted.

The reader must assess for himself the value of these identifications. Those in the valley of the Kābul river (5, 6) are more precise than those of the area of the Hindu Kush, for in the former area the identification is rather of individual sites, whereas in the latter regions principalities and capital cities with uncertain boundaries render the locations vague. The uncertainty as to changes in linguistic equations at different periods at all events counsels caution in the use of identifications.

Iran and Central Asia

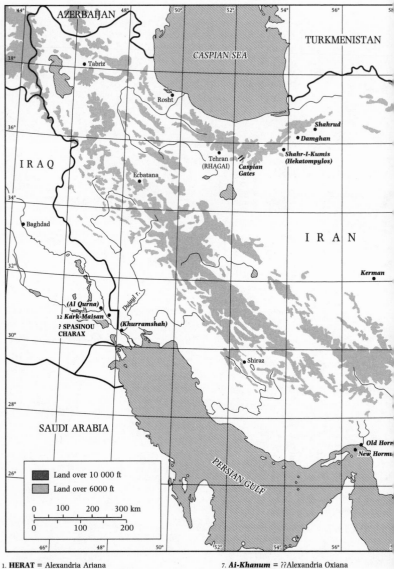

1. **HERAT** = Alexandria Ariana

2. Farah = ?Prophthasia

3. *Zaranj* (area of) = ?Alexandria in Sakastane

4. **KANDAHAR** = Alexandria in Arachosia

5. *Shahr-i-Ghulghula* (area of) = ?Ortospana (34.75N,67.75E)

6. Balkh = Bactra

7. *Ai-Khanum* = ??Alexandria Oxiana

8. **KHOJENDA (LENINABAD)** = Alexandria on the Jaxartes (Alexandreschata) (40.50N,70.75E) (off ▸

9. **BEGRAM** (area of) = Alexandria ad Caucasum

10. **JALAPUR** = ?(Alexandria-) Bucephala (33N,73.5

11. **(LAS) BELA** = ?Alexandria-Rambakia

Iran and Central Asia

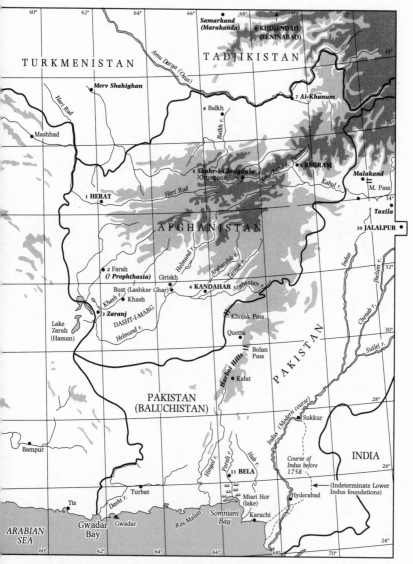

12. **Kark Maisan** (area of) = ?Alexandria-?Spasinou Charax

(Sites 2, 5, and 7, though not the sites of Alexandrias, are included to enable the reader to follow the question of their identification more easily)

Explanation of names on map:
  (1) Alexander-foundations are marked in bold capitals, with their modern name only, preceded by a figure corresponding to that in the list above: 1. **HERAT**
  (2) Other ancient locations discussed in the text and not identified as Alexandrias are printed in bold italics: *Taxila*
  (3) Buddhist, Arab, Persian and other post-antique names are in plain type: Ghazna.

Afghanistan

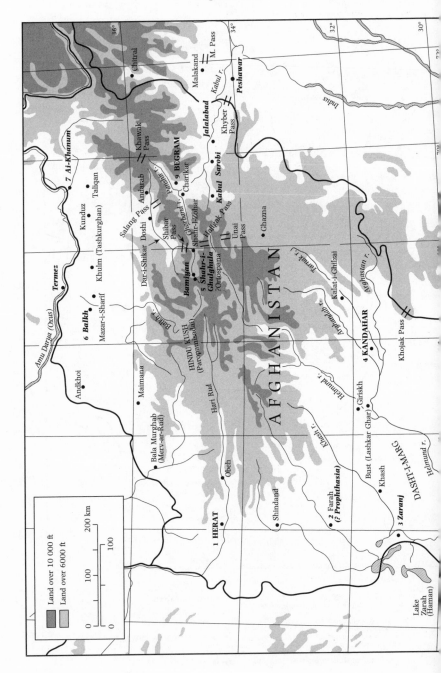

TABLE OF ALEXANDRIAS

Explanation of Symbols and Conventions

• attested in text; each dot represents a separate attestation

(•) not directly attested, but the identity can be assumed with reasonable certainty

[•] attestations suggested as possible candidates for the missing items in the A-list, either because they occur in derived lists or because of arguments developed in Chapter 1.

•(?) uncertain attestations

?(16)• possible identification with number in brackets

•*[48 only] in all cases the text has Ἀλεξάνδρεια ἐπὶ Πώρωι

Notes

1. The numbers in Stephanus' column indicate the ordinal number of the item in his list of Alexandrias.

2. s.v. Yākūt, (1) and (2) refer respectively to the *Mu'jam* and the *Mushtarik*

3. In the 'Iranian Tradition' I have not distinguished between instances in which the name is entered (as by Yākūt s.v. Herāt) in its Arabic or its Greek form.

Name	Hist.						Geogr.				
	Arr.	Diod. xvii	CR	Plut.	Itin. Alex.	Erat Strab.	Isid.	Plin.	Ptol.	Amm. Marc	Steph
[1. A. in Egypt]	•	•	•	•	•	•	•	•	•	•	•(1
2. A. ἐν Ἀρίοις						••	•	••	•	•	•(7
3. A. ἐν Μαργιανῆι								(•)			
4. A. κατὰ Βάκτρα		(•)				(str.) (•)				•	•(1
4a. Ἀ Ὠξιανή										•	
5. A. Ἐσχάτη [Σογδιανή]	::				•			••	••	•	
6. A. ἐν Παροπανισάδαις (=πρὸς τῶι Καυκάσωι)	••	••	••	••				(••)			•(1
7. A. ἐν τῆι Ὠπιανῆι, κατὰ τὴν Ἰνδικήν								(•)			•(5
8. A. Βουκέφαλα	•	•	•								•(6
9. A. ἐν Ὠρείταις (= Ῥαμβακία)	•	•	•						•		•(4
10. A. ἐν Μακαρηνῆι											•(1
11. A. τῆς Καρμανίας								•	•	•	
12. A. Ἀραχωσίας						(•)	::	(••)	•	•	(12 :: (15
12a. A. ἐν Σακαστανῆι						•					
13. A. ἐν Σουσιανῆι (= Σπασίνου Χάραξ)	•							•			
14. A. Assyriae								•			
15. A. κατ' Ἰσσόν						•	•	•	•		(•)
[16. A. ἡ Τρωϊάς]							•	•			•(2
17. A. πρὸς τῶι Λάτμωι											•(1
18. A. ἐν Κύπρωι											•(9
19. A. Θράικης				•							•(3
20. A. κατὰ τὸν Μέλανα κόλπον											•(1
[21. Ἀλεξανδρόπολις]									••	•	
22. A. πρὸς (ἐπὶ) Πέρσας											
23. A. ἐν Σκυθίαι											
24. A. ἐπὶ τοῦ Τίγριδος	(•)								(•)		
25. A. ἐπὶ Βαβυλῶνος											
26. A. ἐν Γρανίκωι											
27. A. εἰς Μασσαγέτας											
28. A. πρὸς Ξάνθον											
29. A. πρὸς Ἅρπας											

Alex.-Romance											Iran. Tradn.								west. Geogr.		
A-text	Arm.	Jul. Val.	Syr.	Eth.	Leo Presb.	Byz.	Exc. Barb.	Chron. Pasch.	B'	Γ''	Yākūt (1)	Yākūt (2)	Qodāma	Tabārī	Dīnawārī	Cap. Eran	Eutych. Annals	Itin. Burd.	Tab. Peut.	Jul. Hon.	Cosmogr.
•	•	•	•	•	•	•	•	•	•	•	•	•			•		•				
											(•)		•	•		•					
														•		•					
											(•)										
•	•	•	•		•	•			•	•		•								•	
		(•)			•					•											
														•							
(•)											•(?)	•(?)									
•	•		•		•	•	(•)	(•)	•	(•)	•	•									
•	•	•			•	•	•	•	•	•											
[•]							•	•	•	•	•										
•				•		•	•	•	•	•											
•	•	•	•		•	•									•						
•	•	•	•(?)		•	•(?)	•	•	•	•	•	•									
•	•	•	•	•	•	•	•	•	•	•	•	•									
[•]	(•)	•	(•)																		
[•]	•	•			•	(•)	•	•	•	•											
[•]	•	•			•																
							•	•	•	•											

Table of Alexander-foundations

Name	Hist.					Geogr.					Steph.
	Arr.	Diod. xvii	CR	Plut.	Itin. Alex.	Erat Strab	Isid.	Plin.	Ptol.	Amm. Marc	
30. A. εἰς Μεσοποταμίαν								?(•)			
31. A. Κυρηναϊκῆς, in Pentapolim											•
32. A. Cabiosa											
33. A. Fortissima (='the Fortified'?)											
34. A. 'of Sehil'											
35. A. of Arabia											
36. A. Barkâ											
37. A. of Karnîkâ											
38. A. of Eutraos											
39. A. of Gebro											
40. A. of Bâbêsdĕyûs											
41. A. of Agmâwĕyân											
42. A. Bardas											
43. A. παρὰ Σωριανοῖς											• (14)(?)
44. A. Ἐπὶ Ταναΐδος					(•)						•(18)
[45. Ortospana]						••		•	••	•	
[46. Prophthasia]				•		••		•	••	•	•
47. Nikaia (1)	•			•							•
48. Nikaia (2)	•	•	•								
49. Rophos (?)											
50. Sod = Samarkand											
51. Kush = Balkh											
52. Margenikos = Merv											
53. A. 'Montuosa'											
54. Alexandri oppidum							•				
55. Alexandropolis Indiae											
56. Alexandri Cindos											
57. Isfahān											

| Alex.-Romance | | | | | | | | | | | Iran. Tradn. | | | | | | | west. Geogr. | | | |
A-text	Arm.	Jul. Val.	Syr.	Eth.	Leo Presb.	Byz.	Exc. Barb.	Chron. Pasch.	B'	Γ'	Yākūt (1)	Yākūt (2)	Qod-āma	Tab-ārī	Dīna-wārī	Cap. Eran	Eutych. Annals	Itin. Burd.	Tab. Peut.	Jul. Hon.	Cos-mogr.
•	•																				
[•]							•	•													
							•	•			•								•		
			•(?)				•		(•)	(•)	•										
				•																	
				•																	
				•																	
				?(16)•																	
				•																	
				?(8)•																	
				?(13)•																	
				?(6)•																	
•*	•*	•*	•*	•*	•*	•*	•*	•*	•*	•*											
				•							(•)	(•)									
				•							•	•	•								
				•							•	•	•	•							
		•																			
																				•	•
																				•	
																					•
													•			•					

ADDENDA

p. 49 n. 6: For aspects of the deeds of Alexander in Sassanian pehlevi texts (other than the *Romance*) see J. Wiesehöfer, *Achaemenid History*, viii, ed. H. Sancisi-Weerdenburg, A, Kuhrt, M. C. Root (Leiden, 1994), 389-97.

p. 80 n. 7: The fullest account of the Persian Royal Road is now that of D. F. Graf, 'The Persian Royal Road System', in *Achaemenid History*, 167-89. For the northern (Armenian) and some southern parts of the road Ronald Syme's posthumous work, *Anatolica*, ed. A. Birley (Oxford, 1995; written largely during the 1939-45 war), ch. 1, should be consulted.

p. 197 n. 5: I owe to Dr. D. M. Bain reference to a passage in the *Cyranides* (?ii AD) (ed. D. Kaimakis, *Beiträge z. Klass. Philol.* 76 (1976) 16. 35 ff. (4 § 6, Mély)). The narrator, one Harpocration, writes to his daughter regarding a journey he had made in Babylonia:

ὁδοιπορίας μοί τινος γενομένης περὶ τὴν Βαβυλωνίαν χώραν, πόλις ἐστίν τις ἐκεῖσε Σελευκεία καλουμένη. Ἱστορίας ἐκεῖθεν ἀπῆρον. Ἡμεῖς δὲ τὰ περὶ τῆς πόλεως ἐκείνης ὡς ἐκεῖνος μακρῶι λόγωι, οὐ χρείαν ἔχομεν ἀναγράφειν, ἵνα μὴ ἀεὶ ἐν τοῖς προοιμίοις ἐνασχολώμεθα· ὅμως ἐπὶ τὸ προκείμενον τοῦ σκοποῦ ἐπανέλθωμεν. Ἔτι δὲ καὶ ἄλλην ἔφη θεάσασθαι πόλιν πρὸ δεκαεπτὰ τῆς Σελευκίας σχοινίων ἣν Ἀλέξανδρος ὁ τῶν Μακεδόνων βασιλεὺς ὑποστρέφων κατέστρεψε καὶ ἔκτισεν ἑτέραν Σελεύκειαν ὑπὸ Περσῶν κειμένην ὡς εἶναι περσογενῆ. καλεῖται δὲ πρώτη Ἀλεξάνδρεια ἡ πρὸς Βαβυλῶνα.

Such delusive and confused statements illustrate once more the virtual impossibility of deciding positively whether or not the Seleucids named cities after Alexander. One can only say that there is as yet no trustworthy evidence that they did so.

p. 222 n. 40: The *Itinerarium Alexandri*. Raffaella Tabacco, *Per una nuova edizione critica dell' Itinerarium Alexandri* (Bologna, 1992), contains a critical introduction, text, translation, bibliography, and notes of chs. 1-11 and 12-23. The editor does not express an opinion about the authorship of the work, or about the passage under discussion in this note.

I   GENERAL INDEX

In this index only significant references to persons and places have been entered, since many occur repeatedly in general narrative contexts and the reader would not be helped by looking up every reference to 'Alexander' or 'Alexandria', 'Stephanus' or 'the *Alexander-Romance*', 'Pliny' or 'Strabo'. In such cases I have chosen a few key discussions, and added 'passim'. Full references to classical and oriental sources are given in Indexes II*a* and *b*.

Names given in the text in Greek are transliterated here in Roman characters and are not repeated in Index IV, the Index of Greek Words. For Muslim personal names I have used the conventional European style, mostly without the article, while for Arabic-Persian place-names I have used the most familiar form.

IIa INDEX OF GREEK AND LATIN AUTHORS

This index contains references to particular passages of the authors listed, except that general discussions of, and passing references to, the authors will be found in Index I, and references to the principal texts comprising the lists of Alexandrias, given in Appendix I (Steph. Byz., s.v. *Ἀλεξάνδρεια*; *Romance*, A-text iii. 35; *Excerpta Latina Barbari*, 34a-34b; *Pasch. Chron.* 321) are not entered individually, since the passages can be found there. Other references from the same works are, however, given.

George, of Cyprus
  i. 824-5: 22

Hecataeus (*FGrH* 1)
  F299: 148 n. 84
Heidelberg Epitome (*FGrH* 155)
  4: 226 n. 57
Herodian
  iii. 4. 3: 20 n. 42
Herodotus
  ii. 6: 76 n. 2; iii. 93: 130 n. 50; v.
    52: 79 n. 7
Heron, *Dioptra* (*op.* iii)
  34-5: 83 n. 13
Homer, *Iliad*
  13. 363: 22 n. 49

Isidore of Charax, *Parthian Stations*
    (*GGM*, i. 244 ff.;*FGrH* 781):
  88 n. 20;
  F1: 90 n. 27; F2, §1: 89 n. 26; F2,
    §§14-19:91-3; F2, §14: 116;
    F2, §15: 114 n. 21, 115 n. 23;
    F2, §16-7: 124 n. 37, 136 n. 64,
    139 n. 66; F2, §18: 136 n. 63,
    137 n. 64, 138-9 & n 66; F2,
    §19: 90 n. 26, 200 n. 1 F*3-4:
    90 n. 26-7; F6-8, 11:
    89 nn. 23-4
Isocrates
  Paneg.
    187: 174 n. 1
  Philip
    103: 174 n. 2; 122: 174 n. 3
Itineraria Romana I (ed. Cuntz 1929)
  i. 146. 3, 580.8: 22. n 49
Itinerarium Alexandri: 221-2 n. 41
  xxxvi: 151 n. 90; xxxviii: 222 n. 41;
    civ: 146 n. 78

John of Epiphaneia (*FHG*, iv. 272 ff.):
  61 n. 37
Josephus, *AJ*
  i. 5. 5 (§121): 88 n. 19
Juba, King of Mauretania (*FGrH* 275)
  F1: 168 n. 120; F28 ff., F47, F54 ff.,
    F62 ff., F70 ff.: 93 n. 32,
    165 n. 115
Julius Honorius (Riese,*GLM*)
  A6: 29 n. 61
Julius Valerius Alexander (Polemius),
    Res Gestae Alex.
  i. 7: 221 n. 39; i. 26: 222 n. 43; ii.

  24: 222 n. 40; iii. 60: 23-4 &
    n. 61
  see also Index I, Julius Valerius
Justin, *Trog. Pomp. Epit.*: xii. 5. 12-3:
  154 n. 95

Kallixeinos (*FGrH* 627)
  33. 205 ff.: 42 n. 84
Liber de Morte Alexandri
  62: 162 n. 111, 212-4
Lucian, *Macrob.*
  218-9 (Isid. F*3-4): 90 n. 26

Malalas
  220: 8 n. 13; 443: 9 n. 16
Marcianus of Heracleia
  Periplus (*GGM* i)
    516: 76 n. 29; 530. 24:
      165 n. 115
  Epit. Menipp.
    565. 2 (*FGrH* 781,T2): 89 n. 25;
      566. 3: 87 n. 17
Marmor Parium, see Index 3a
Martianus Capella
  vi. 598: 81 n. 10; vi. 691: 31 n. 57
Megasthenes (*FGrH* 715)
  F31: 83 n. 13
Menippus (? of Perinthos, *FGrH* 82):
  5 n. 5
Menippus (*FGrH* 541): 5 n. 5
Metrol.Graec.
  i. 181. 3: 77 n. 2; i. 201. 9. 9: 76 n. 2

Nicephorus Callistus (*PG* 146)
  564: 223 n. 45

Onesicritus (*FGrH* 134)
  F28: 165 n. 115

Palladius, *De gentibus Indiae*
  i. 15: 224
  see also Alexander-Romance iii. 5
Paschal Chronicle (*Chronicon Paschale*):
  App. 1(*d*)
  274-5: 12 nn. 27-8; 397: 22 n. 46
Pausanias
  i. 6. 3: 184 n. 18
Periplus Maris Erythr.
  30: 62 nn. 40-1; 35: 169 n. 121,
    180 n. 14; 47: 162 n. 111; 52:
    162 n. 111
Philon, Herennius (*FGrH* 790)
  F15-21: 5 n. 5

IIb INDEX OF ARABIC AND PEHLEVI TEXTS

IIIb INDEX OF GREEK PAPYRI

IV INDEX OF GREEK WORDS

This Index contains references to Greek words discussed in the text and notes. Proper names, geographical and personal, are mostly to be found in Index I.